Adolescents

Guy R. Lefrancois

University of Alberta

Wadsworth Publishing Company, Inc.
Belmont, California

Dedicated to Rita, an adolescent,
and to the enchanted, groping, bubbling,
bemused, happy, impulsive adolescent
in you and me.

Psychology Editor: Kenneth King
Designer: Dare Porter
Editor: Susan Yessne
Cartoonist: Tony Hall

ISBN 0-534-00433-4
L. C. Cat. Card No. 75-36880
Printed in the United States of America
1 2 3 4 5 6 7 8 9 10−80 79 78 77 76

Acknowledgements

Adolescent contributors to this book include the following people.

Art: Francie Binder, Sheelagh Powrie, Sandi Urschel, Brian Campbell, David Bell, Shelley Drinkwater, and Robin Gutierrez.

Poetry: Sam Bellott, Thysselina Dammeyer, Cheryl Sawchuk, Ron Mulligan, Pat Ozuko, Marian Kuchera, Gerrit Rysdak, and Sandra Kordak.

Interviews: James Moulden, Sandy Urschel, Diane Stas, Don Barnhouse, Kelly Kibbs, Karen Kochan, Brian Rud, Annette Flamand, Bob Fletcher, and Delbert Jensen.

Teachers: Roy Sveningsen, Sharon Busby, and Richard Bookham.

Reviewers of this book were Professors Judith Langlois, University of Texas; Cathleen M. White, Boston University; Cindy Gray, California State University at Los Angeles; and Frank Harper, University of Western Ontario.

Contents

Preface

My ancient grandmother, though she has often remarked on the social and natural ills of this planet, strongly maintains that it is a good place to live. True, she has few other planets with which to compare it. But she does have numerous images of what her heaven will be like and of what a better earth might be.

Concerning adolescents, she has a great deal to say. And it is remarkable how closely she agrees with numerous observers of the contemporary scene. She, like a number of allegedly more expert observers, has been guilty of propagating myths, or sometimes half-truths, concerning typical adolescent rebelliousness, delinquency, apathy, and abject and total degeneracy. My grandmother, like most other people, knows and truly loves a large number of adolescents. "But these are clearly the exception," she maintains, "hardly representative of adolescents in general." Radio, television, and newspapers have convinced her that she is quite right in her estimate of the present adolescent population, though she is willing to admit that there are exceptions. I have not yet been able to convince her that those adolescents about whom she hears most frequently in the various media are, in fact, the exception; and that the adolescents that she knows personally are far more representative of today's adolescent population than are those whose behaviors make them eligible for media attention.

This collection of chapters is, in a sense, a rather long letter to my grandmother. I wrote it so that both you and she would understand it and hopefully enjoy it. More important, I have tried valiantly to tell both of you what it is that psychologists know or suspect about adolescents. And although I have dealt with the delinquent, drug-cultist, anti-intellectual, rebellious, and non-conformist adolescents, I have also tried to make clear the extent to which they are exceptions, and the extent to which this behavior should be interpreted as serious.

The book is divided into six major sections that deal in turn with the biological, theoretical, psychological, sociological, and moral aspects of adolescence. Within each section, specific chapters look at such topics as primitive initiation rites; biological changes that occur during adolescence; theoretical explanations for the phenomenon of adolescence; personality, intelligence, and creativity; development, learning, and motivation; the relationships of adolescents with their families, peers, and schools; and the moral aspects of

1

adolescents as reflected in their behavior, in judgments of right and wrong, in delinquency, drug abuse, sexual permissiveness, and rebellion.

Wherever possible, representative studies have been cited to illustrate and support the contentions made. This is not, however, an encyclopedic collection of research data. While some of the research in this area is notably good, a great deal is not. Opinions, speculation, and emotional analyses of the contemporary scene, even when attributed to allegedly expert observers of that scene, are frequently no more valid than my grandmother's wisdom, or yours. I hope that once you have availed yourself of the information in this text, you will understand adolescence better—and perhaps yourself. Your opinions may then be more valid as well.

Special features of the book include a detailed glossary, summaries and main point reviews at the end of each chapter, chapter outlines providing simple overviews, and cartoons and adolescent contributions. Sam and I felt it might be highly revealing to interview adolescents and to include some of their unedited statements in the printed text.

We hope you enjoy and learn,

Guy R. Lefrançois

Sam Dellott

Part 1

2

Introduction

Chapter 1

Adolescence Here and Elsewhere

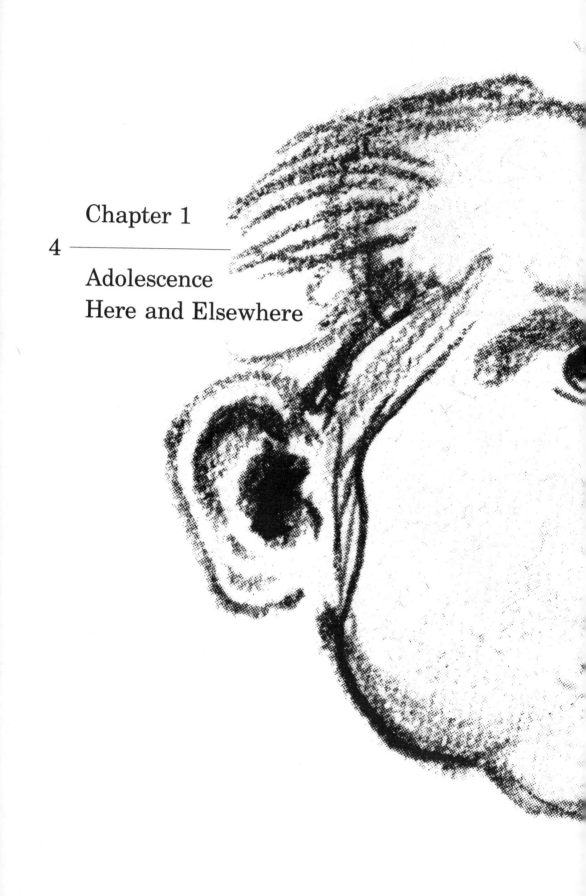

Chapter 1

4 ————————————

Adolescence Here and Elsewhere

Francie Binder, Grade 11

———————————————— 5

6

I had not seen Sam for some time following the episode with the City Police — an episode that did little to relieve his paranoia. Because the entire thing had been largely my fault, I did my best to extricate him from his apparent difficulties. I was sufficiently successful, I might add, to remain in his good graces, although he insists that I am no longer his "sole acquaintance," as I had written elsewhere. And it was, in fact, this other writing that caused Sam's problems on that night.

Some of you may recall that in an earlier book (Lefrancois, 1973) I made reference to Sam, pointing out, among other things, that he is a professor who was denied tenure at this University a few years ago. Since then, he has been living in some abandoned coal mines in the very bowels of what is otherwise a fairly acceptable city — as cities go. His is a lonely existence. And a poor one. But he is not unhappy! And that is the point that I had not made strongly or clearly enough. Some zealous undergraduate student accidentally happened across the text, and having nothing else to do at the time, struggled through several paragraphs, thus becoming slightly acquainted with Sam and his present position. Moved by strong feelings of idealism and goodwill, he immediately wrote a social aid agency in this city, imploring its members to come to Sam's assistance. In a moment of great fervor, he even promised that his father would contribute substantially to Sam's maintenance. Enthusiastic goodwill knows no geographic boundaries, and although this student lives slightly more than thirty-five hundred miles from here, he promised, also, that he would personally visit Sam the following weekend.

This letter was initially read with some amusement, and then ignored. The following week, however, a group of students from a small midwest campus held a love-in designed to raise money for a fund appropriately named Sam's Legal Aid Fund. These well-intentioned students were, of course, convinced that Sam had been denied tenure unjustly and that the University in question should be taken to court. Unfortunately, or perhaps fortunately, love-in's ordinarily don't make a great deal of money. Accordingly, the students sent Sam a long letter expressing their concern and sympathy and describing in some detail the enjoyable time they had had while trying to come to his rescue. Sam enjoyed the letter.

Things would have returned to normal quickly had it not been for the politically minded undergraduate from Florida who appeared unannounced at my office door one cold winter morning. She had come to take Sam away from his "misery, poverty and injustice — an example of totalitarianism disguised as democracy — a blow to the principles of egalitarianism!" "Take me to him at once," she insisted. But of course I couldn't, having long ago promised Sam that I would never allow anyone to disturb his solitude and perhaps jeopardize some of the research programs that he has undertaken with his younger rats. Undaunted, she went alone to search for an entry into the coal mines. Finding none, she approached the city police, who, helpful individuals that they are, brought her back to my office and confronted me with the simple, rather tactless question, "Where is this Sam character? He isn't listed as a missing person."

I played dumb, a posture that Sam assures me I assume with considerable skill. However, I had relatively little success with these minions of the law. Since crime doesn't run too rampant in this city, its minions frequently have pathetically little to do. Determining Sam's whereabouts, of course, afforded them with an excellent opportunity to do something. Besides, policemen are well aware that university professors frequently have things to hide. So they obtained a search warrant and sent one of their more literate members to wade through my files. Bright individual that he was, he eventually discovered a filing cabinet labeled *Correspondence with Sam.* I frequently make use of this imaginative labeling system. He and the politically minded Florida student then read most of this correspondence concluding, rather brilliantly, that there is indeed an individual named Sam Bellott.

You would have been proud of me. I continued to deny any knowledge of Sam, eventually hitting upon the brilliant idea that I had in fact invented him in the course of my writings. I told them that I had filled my correspondence file with letters between us in order to convince myself of his existence so that I could make more realistic use of this character in my books. A highly plausible story, but one that the unimaginative police officer would not believe, even reluctantly.

A full-scale search was then launched for openings into the coal mines that were to have been completely sealed some thirty years earlier — a clever developer had decided that surface land is more valuable than underground coal. I hastened to see Sam and apprised him of what had been transpiring during the past few days. Together we moved his rats deeper into the tortuous shafts. We sealed off the main tunnel that might have led the police to his "home" had they discovered the opening below the rosebushes behind the big hotel.

But they never did, and I will continue to officially deny any knowledge of

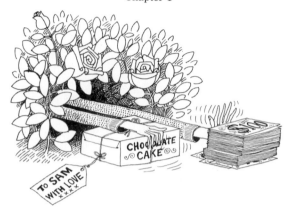

8

Sam Bellott or his whereabouts. And I plead with you not to become concerned over Sam's apparently unpleasant circumstances. I assure you that he is happy. Although he enjoys *most* of your letters, he wishes that you not take it upon yourselves to attempt to change his life-style. Send chocolate cakes, but not money!

Yesterday evening, as I sat with Sam on a discarded crate, we talked of this book that I am writing. Like most of us, he was once an **adolescent,**[*] and he has much to say about **adolescence.** He offered to write an essay for inclusion in this text, and I promised him that, if my editors were willing, it would be included. In addition, Sam will be reading the manuscript as it progresses and has agreed to help me with it.

His first advice was, "Start at the beginning." But there is no beginning. And perhaps no end as well.

Order in Science and in Fact

Psychologists, sociologists, anthropologists, and others who seek order in a world of unordered things are quick to label that order when they find it. Indeed, they occasionally seek to impose order on chaos through the use of language. And to say that a theory or a classification system oversimplifies is to recognize either that there is less order in the external world than our description of it implies, or that we have yet to discover what order does exist.

Psychology is one discipline where **theories,** classifications, and labels often impose a somewhat artificial, overly simple, and sometimes inaccurate order. This order is useful, nevertheless, for it permits us to at least begin to understand things that otherwise would not be understood at all. However, it is wise to bear in mind that few aspects of human behavior, the subject matter of psychology, are as simple as they sometimes appear to be in textbooks. Although the great laws and principles of psychology may be generally true, their validity and usefulness is often limited when interpreted in the context of a single individual's behavior.

The study of **adolescent psychology** is no exception. There is, in fact, no reason to believe that the confusion that exists in our attempts to understand

[*] Boldface terms appear in the glossary.

9

this area is any less than that in any other area; indeed, there is some reason to believe that it is greater. Nevertheless, psychologists and others have given us some general principles of adolescent growth and behavior that are valuable not only in understanding adolescents, but in working and living with them as parents, teachers, counselors, policemen, or friends. These principles are the subject matter of this text. Principles, laws, observations, and theories that we have no reason to believe incorrect or inappropriate are presented as fact; the majority, however, are presented as speculative but logical extrapolations, perhaps generally correct, but not always precisely and without exception correct. I have made my own affirmations on the basis of the data that I present in this text, trusting that, at least in some cases, they are the most logical affirmations that can be made on the basis of the information available. You can accept these, arrive at your own, or simply conclude that we really don't know. The truth may be served in any case.

Adolescence

We all know what adolescence is. In fact, if this text had continued without pausing to define its subject, most of you would not have noticed. The title has already informed you that the subject is adolescence; you yourself have, at some time in the past, been an adolescent; therefore you know what adolescence is.

Or do you?

Is adolescence the period of development that begins at the age of thirteen and ends at age nineteen—the period of the "teen years"? Or are the age boundaries really as clear and definite as these?

Is adolescence then that developmental period that begins with the onset of sexual maturity—labeled **puberty**—and terminates with adulthood? If it is, then adolescence begins around the age of twelve for girls and fourteen for boys. But that is simply on the average. It is known that sexual maturity can occur as early as age ten in girls and twelve in boys—or as late as ages sixteen and eighteen, respectively. Furthermore, the age of sexual maturity varies in different countries, at least for girls. Smart and Smart (1967) review a number of studies that indicate that the average age for girls' first menstrual period (termed **menarche**) is 12.75 in the United States, 13.2 in southern

England, and 13.9 in Jerusalem. Tanner (1955) found, as well, that menarche has been occurring as much as one-half to one-third of a year earlier per decade since 1850. At that rate, by the year 2070, seven-year-old girls and nine-year-old boys will be adolescents. It appears, however, that this trend is now stopped or at least slowing down, although the evidence is not yet conclusive. Poppleton and Brown (1966) and Frisch and Revelle (1970), among others, provide evidence indicating that there has been little change in age of menarche in very recent years.

If adolescence begins with sexual maturity and ends with adulthood, when does adulthood begin? And how do we know when sexual maturity begins? Is menarche, the first menstrual period, a valid indicator in girls? And the capacity to ejaculate semen, a valid indicator in boys? Yes and no. Most girls continue to be incapable of reproducing for approximately one year following their first menstrual period. Boys, on the other hand, are usually capable of fathering a child when they are capable of ejaculating semen.

Is adolescence the period of development that begins with those changes that precede sexual maturity — changes that are collectively labeled **pubescence?** These include changes in voice, in breast development, and a number of other events discussed later. Pubescence generally begins a year or more prior to puberty (sexual maturity defined in terms of menarche and the capacity to ejaculate semen? or sexual maturity defined in terms of the ability to reproduce?)

Or, as Friedenberg (1960) contends, is adolescence primarily a social rather than a physical process, better defined in terms of a search for clear and stable **self-identification** than in terms of sexual maturation? If it is, then it is probably still generally true* that adolescence begins with the dawning awareness of sexual maturity, but that it may not terminate as early as we usually assume it does. Indeed, it would then be true that many individuals whose ages would lead us to believe them adult are, in fact, still very much in their adolescence.

Clarifying the preceding passages requires an arbitrary decision. While

---

* Truth is, of course, relative. In considering definitions of this nature, keep in mind that utility, convenience, clarity, and logical consistency are the determining criteria — not truth. In short, "adolescence" is what it is because it is defined as such; and it is defined as such not because that is necessarily what it is, but because it is convenient, useful, and hence logical to define it in that manner.

it is true that adolescence does encompass all definitions given above, it is perhaps important to define it more clearly in order to make it amenable to scientific study. Hence for purposes of this text, adolescence is defined as that period of life beginning around the ages of eleven or twelve and terminating somewhere just before or after the age of twenty. It is important to keep in mind that girls are adolescents at a younger age than boys and that they cease to be adolescents also at a younger age. It is also important to keep in mind that there are wide variations in the ages at which it is appropriate to label a specific individual "adolescent." The arbitrary age boundaries are given simply as convenient guidelines.

Adolescent Psychology

Psychology is that branch of the social sciences concerned primarily with the study of human behavior and experience. As such, it encompasses studies of how humans think, learn, remember, feel, and act; of normal, abnormal, and subnormal ways of thinking, learning, remembering, feeling, and acting; and of the ways in which thinking, remembering, feeling, and acting change from infancy to adulthood—indeed, from birth to death. Psychologists are concerned with describing, explaining, and, in some cases, controlling human behavior; the latter function is particularly important in schools and in psychiatric practice.

Adolescent psychology, as a branch of general psychology, is concerned with the developmental period encompassed by our definition of adolescence. And to bring about a more complete understanding of the adolescent, it is not limited simply to this period, but deals with others as well. It is easier to understand what an adolescent is when one also understands what a child is, what an adult is, and how these two differ from the adolescent.

More precisely, adolescent psychology is concerned with the developmental forces that lead to adolescence; with the physical, behavioral, psychological, and moral aspects of adolescence; with the effects of family, school, and society on the adolescent; and with theories that have addressed themselves to problems of adolescent development and behavior. In addition, it typically deals with problems of delinquency, drugs, sex, rebellion, and alternative lifestyles as well.

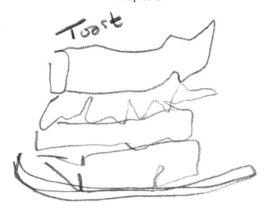

12

Methods of Studying Adolescents

The basis of most information in adolescent psychology is observation, as it is in most areas of human knowledge. In scientific research, however, observation is seldom incidental; rather, it frequently involves deliberate and systematic effort on the part of the investigators. Rosenzweig (1949) identifies three methods of observing, all of which are employed in the study of adolescents: **objective, subjective,** and **projective.**

Objective observation is employed when the investigators observe and interpret adolescent behavior directly. This occurs, for example, in naturalistic situations where the experimenters attempt to record adolescent behavior in a nonobtrusive manner without affecting that behavior. Dunphy (1963), for example, examined the structure and predominant activities of adolescent groups in natural situations; the experimenter attempted to become privy to group activities so that he could observe them without altering them (see Chapter 9).

Objective observation sometimes makes use of tests so that the behavior being observed is of a specific nature. Investigations of the interests, attitudes, and intellectual abilities of adolescents often involve the use of measuring instruments designed to assess these variables. Investigators can usually arrive at a more valid indication of a specific individual's intellectual abilities by observing the individual's behavior on a test designed to measure these abilities than they can by simply observing the adolescent's behavior at random.

Subjective observation involves the subject's own interpretation of his or her behavior rather than the investigators' interpretation. Various questionnaires designed to measure such qualities as attitudes and interests frequently require subjects to report their own feelings and activities directly. In this way, subjective observation frees the investigators from the time-consuming task of attempting to observe that behavior. In many situations, it is clearly impossible for the investigators to observe the behaviors they wish to examine. Studies of adolescent sexual behavior, for example (Luckey and Nass, 1969), could not be accomplished easily by attempting to observe the behavior in question.

Projective observation requires that the subjects respond in their own way to a structured situation or problem. The investigators then interpret responses in terms of their possible relevance as indicators of the subjects' pre-occupations, interests, attitudes, or other personality characteristics. Unlike the subjective approach, the projective technique does not require subjects to interpret or report their own behavior. And unlike the objective approach, the experimenters do not obtain a direct sample of the behavior in question.

Projective techniques are based on the assumption that individuals tend to *project* major preoccupations or feelings when responding to relatively nebulous situations. Among the best known of the projective techniques is the Rorschach inkblot test where subjects are simply asked to describe a figure highly reminiscent of a complicated inkblot. The Thematic Appercep-tion Test (TAT), which requires the subjects to describe various photographs, is another widely used projective test. Interpretation of these tests requires considerable training and practice, and their use is accordingly somewhat less common than the use of the simpler objective and subjective techniques.

Interpretations to which observations — whether subjective, objective, or projective — are subjected depend largely on the purposes for which the ob-servations are gathered. Psychological research based on observation is fre-quently categorized as being experimental or nonexperimental. These broad classifications reflect both a particular method of handling data (observational information) and, frequently, different objectives on the part of the investi-gators.

Nonexperimental Methods

When the intent is simply to describe behavior that is typical of adoles-cents or of a particular subgroup of adolescents, or to compare that behavior with behavior that might be expected of other groups of individuals, the investigators often use nonexperimental methods. For example, determining the average age at which adolescent girls experience their first menstrual period does not require experimentation but rather the simple averaging of observations gathered through subjective reports or objective clinical exam-ination. Comparing the average age of the first menstrual period in different countries (see, for example, Tanner, 1962) requires only simple mathematical (statistical) comparisons.

Comparative studies are frequently described as **longitudinal** or **cross-**

sectional. Comparing average age of first menstrual period among different countries typically involves cross-sectional research. Different groups are examined at the same time and compared directly.

In longitudinal studies, the same group of subjects is observed at different times, and observations gathered at one time are compared with observations gathered for the same subjects at another time. For example, investigations of the sequence of physical changes that precede sexual maturity necessitate longitudinal studies. That is, it would be difficult to determine whether facial hair appears before pubic hair if different age groups were examined at the same time and compared. **Early** and **late maturers** would confuse the results. Examining the same individuals at different ages would, in this case, provide the observations required.

Experimental Methods

In an **experiment,** the investigators manipulate some aspects of a situation in order to observe the effects of the manipulation. The thing manipulated is called the **independent variable.** The effect looked for is the **dependent variable.** If, for example, investigators suspect that social class is related to delinquency, they might use a nonexperimental method and simply observe the relative incidence of **delinquency** among different social classes. Alternately, the investigators might approach the problem experimentally by attempting to alter the experiences (independent variables) of a group of subjects. In this case, they would try to counteract whatever effects they think social class might have on the incidence of delinquency. They might, for example, arrange for a group of lower-class subjects to be transferred to foster homes in middle-class neighborhoods. This group of subjects would then become an **experimental group,** that is, the subjects whose independent variable (social class) has been manipulated. Subsequently this experimental group might be compared to a second group of subjects who were initially similar to the experimental group, but whose lives were not affected by the experiment. They serve as the **control group.** Comparisons of delinquency (the dependent variable) between these two groups can now serve as evidence supporting or contradicting the investigators' initial suspicions — suspicions that they would label **hypotheses** in keeping with scientific terminology. The

15

function of the control group is to ensure that the conclusions reached are not simply a function of other factors common to all subjects. Profound social changes resulting from inflation, recession, a major war, or the bubonic plague could conceivably account for changes in delinquency rates and patterns. The effect of these might not be detected without a comparison (control) group.

This experimental model (design) is only one of many, though it is the simplest and most common. All experiments manipulate one or more **variables** in order to investigate the effects on other variables. And all are subject to certain pitfalls, shortcomings, and misinterpretations that can do much to invalidate the conclusions.

Evaluating Psychological Research

The usefulness of the many conclusions derived from psychological research depends to a large extent on the **validity** of the conclusions. Bear in mind, however, that validity (accuracy or truthfulness) is a relative term, particularly in the social sciences. Results that are perfectly valid for a specific group under investigation may not be valid for other groups. Furthermore, these same results may be valid only because of some unidentified peculiarity of the situation in which relevant observations were made; they may cease to be valid under different circumstances. Hence one of the important considerations in psychological research is the **generalizability** of conclusions. And generalizability may be severely affected by sampling.

Sampling Researchers try to obtain as representative a **sample** as they can. In other words, if results are to be generalized to a particular population (group of subjects from which the sample is drawn), the subjects employed in the study must be representative of that sample. Generalizations made about the American adolescent, or even about the adolescent in general, are suspect when a small, highly selective sample is employed. A *Psychology Today* survey (*Involvement in Developmental Psychology,* 1971) of the sexual attitudes and behaviors of men and women revealed that 80 percent of college males and 78 percent of college females had engaged in premarital **intercourse.** An earlier study (Luckey and Nass, 1969) had found that only 58 percent of the men and 43 percent of the women had had intercourse. Would it be accurate to conclude that there was a tremendous increase in premarital sexual activity between 1969 and 1971? Perhaps. In fact, however, the Luckey and Nass sample were randomly selected from large college populations. The *Psychology Today* sample were also selected primarily from very large college populations, but the questionnaires were included in the magazine *Psychology Today.* Hence the sample was not only restricted to the individuals who subscribe to the magazine, but was further restricted to those who chose to fill it out and return it. Should we now conclude that the Luckey and Nass study is a more valid indicator of sexual practices and beliefs? Again, perhaps. But there are other problems involved.

Subject Honesty Questionnaire, interview, and to some extent direct testing procedures must all rely on the honesty of the respondents. This is one of the major weaknesses of most subjective techniques. Because sexual exploits have long been reinforced among males, there is the possibility that the nature and frequency of these exploits is often exaggerated by the individuals concerned. Alternately, there is a possibility that females would be more reluctant to admit to premarital sexual activity. In any case, the validity of results obtained from studies such as these is a very direct function of the honesty of the individuals concerned.

Memory Distortion Related to this is the problem of remembering accurately over a number of years. Studies of the incidence of menarche (first menstrual period) over generations have frequently relied on mothers remembering when they experienced their first menstrual period. The accuracy with which they can do so is open to question, and thus we have a problem of **reliability.**

Experimenter Bias Experimenter bias is not necessarily a conscious prejudging of alleged facts, but more often an unconscious expectation based on the experimenter's awareness of what the results of his or her experimental observation should be. Rosenthal and Fode (1963) report an experiment where psychology students were given **rats** to train. Some students were told that their rats were of the **maze-bright** variety; others were told that their rats were **maze-dull.** Actually, all rats were randomly chosen and were, in all probability, highly similar. The students who had been told that they had bright rats reported considerably more success in training these rats than did those who thought they had dull rats. While it is unlikely that these students deliberately falsified their reports, it is probable that their expectations colored both their behavior and their observations. Consider an investigator who is convinced by colleagues' research that more lower-class boys are delinquent than middle-class boys. Won't this investigator have some tendency, however slight, to verify the initial conviction?

One method frequently employed to ensure against experimenter bias is called the **double blind procedure.** Essentially, it involves ensuring that neither the investigators nor the subjects know what the experimental results should be. In medical research, for example, **placebos** (harmless, nonmedicinal pills) are often administered to a control group whereas the real subjects receive the experimental medication. If neither the subjects nor the people who assess the effects of the medication are aware of which subjects received the placebo and which received the actual medication, the possibility of experimenter bias is effectively eliminated.

Interpretation A common error in interpreting experimental results is known as the "correlational fallacy." Events (variables) are **correlated** when one changes predictably as the other changes. Thus, a variable that increases (or decreases) as another increases (or decreases) is correlated to the first. The assumption that changes in one of these variables *cause* changes in the other is not warranted, however. This assumption is, in fact, the correlational fallacy. It has been established, for example, that adolescents who score high on tests of need for **achievement** also tend to do better in school than those who don't score as highly. On the surface, it might appear logical to conclude that need for achievement causes high achievement and conversely, that low need for achievement causes low achievement. However, the only conclusion that is fully warranted by this observation is that measured need for achievement and actual achievement are related for logical reasons; these reasons do not imply causality. It may be, for example, that measured high need for achievement reflects measured intelligence. Because actual achievement is also correlated to intelligence, the relationship between need for achievement and school achievement may be "caused" by intelligence. If, however, mea-

18

sured intelligence and measured need for achievement were, in fact, highly correlated, this would not prove that high intelligence causes either high achievement or high need for achievement. Perhaps other important factors, related to all three of these variables, are involved either singly or in combination. Consider, for example, the observation that the number of prisons increases in newly settled areas as the number of churches increases. It is clear that there is a high positive correlation between number of churches and number of prisons. Can this be interpreted to mean that churches in some strange way cause prisons?

Conceptualization One of the problems inherent in a great deal of psychological research is that of definition. Very few psychological characteristics of human beings are sufficiently obvious that they lend themselves to unequivocal definition. Thus, what one psychologist understands by words such as **learning, development, masculinity, femininity,** or adolescence may be quite different from what another psychologist understands. For example, such statements as "masculinity and femininity are established during adolescence" can lead to a great deal of misinterpretation and controversy if the terms in question are not defined and qualified. And, as noted earlier, the criteria of a good definition when dealing with abstract psychological concepts are its usefulness, clarity, and logical consistency. Because these qualities are seldom universally agreed upon, it becomes extremely important to understand a particular author's definitions before attempting to interpret the results of his or her research and to compare it to related research.

The Universality of Adolescence

There has been considerable discussion in academic circles concerning the universality of the adolescent phenomenon. It would appear, quite simply, that if adolescence were solely or principally a biological event, its manifestations would be highly similar in different cultures. If, however, it were primarily a cultural phenomenon, its manifestations would vary across cultures. Current evidence suggests that, in fact, it is both a biological and a sociocultural happening. Hence the usefulness of examining adolescence in cultures other than our own. It is particularly useful to examine cultures sometimes described as **discontinuous** because they have clearer demarcations between developmental stages than we have.

Continuous and Discontinuous Cultures

The knife trembled slightly in the hands of the old man. But he had done it a thousand times before. Maybe more. And so Oran told himself that he should not be afraid, but he could not still the shivering of his body, or be rid of the dryness in his mouth. He *was* afraid.

It was an old knife; easily as old as the man who stood before him, his aged face hidden behind the grotesque mask. The mask of the crocodile. Oran could not keep his eyes from the blade. He saw the many nicks and marks on its worn surface. The little pocks where tiny specks of rust lay imprisoned, impervious to even the most vigorous honing. And he imagined that he saw blood on the blade, though he knew that there could be none for he was to be the first as befit his position as son of the chief. And as son of the chief, he would make no noise when the knife descended on him. He would try to smile, and his father would be proud.

The chanting grew louder as the circle of men closed in on Oran and the old man. These were the songs of the people; songs that had been sung at every Coming since the beginning of time. Oran had always heard them from outside the circle, and he had been moved by them, for he was of the people. But now, as he heard the songs from the center of the circle, knowing that they were being sung for him, he was less moved. Or perhaps it is more accurate to say that he was moved even more, but in a different direction.

Now the voice of the old man rose above those of the chanters. Oran tensed, and prepared to smile, as he had told himself he would. During the last four months, he had thought of little else in the small hut to which he had been driven when it was decided that he should become a man.

The knife rose, poised momentarily above Oran, and came down, viciously it seemed, on his most private parts. The old man picked up the foreskin, shrieked jubilantly, and danced away in a mad frenzy. Oran was now a man.

Oran was, one day, a child. He had none of the responsibilities of adulthood, knew that he had none of these responsibilities, and behaved, indeed, in the carefree manner of most children in contemporary cultures. He was not, in this sense, very different from children in our own culture.

The next day, however, he was an adult with all the responsibilities of adulthood placed irrevocably upon his shoulders. Of this he had no doubt whatsoever. Nor did he have any doubts concerning the behavior that would now be appropriate for him—indeed, that would be expected of him. In this sense, he was quite different from most children/young adults in our society.

Oran's culture is discontinuous. It is a culture that, by definition, clearly marks passage from one state to the next—a culture where there is no ambiguity concerning the social position occupied by the individual and the behavior that is expected of that individual. It is a culture where, in short, there is no adolescence as described earlier in this chapter.

Our culture, on the other hand, is referred to as a **continuous culture.** It does not differentiate clearly between childhood and adulthood—not even between infancy and childhood for that matter. The elders do not gather around the young adolescents and tell them that yesterday they were children but today and for all tomorrows they will be adults. In a continuous culture, all children must discover for themselves when they have passed from childhood to adulthood. The transition, however, does not ordinarily occur in one day. In fact it requires several years. These are the adolescent years—the years with which this text is concerned.

Primitive Rites

Many **"primitive" societies** characterized by discontinuous cultures mark the transition from childhood to adulthood with various ceremonies that have been collectively labeled **rites de passage.**

Initiation rites have been held for centuries among a large number of primitive tribes; they are still held among a small number of societies that have resisted both Christianity and industrialization. Characteristically, these rites are common to an entire tribe or culture, although within a given culture they are usually different for the two sexes. Indeed, quite frequently there are ceremonies for only one of the sexes. A description of the main features of these rites follows.

Separation Almost all initiation rites (also sometimes called *puberty rites* or *rites de passage*) involve separation, usually from adult women and sometimes from adult men (Webster, 1932). Frequently the separation occurs dur-

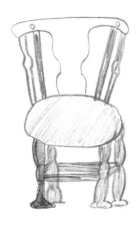

21

ing the first stage of puberty (ages eight to ten or even earlier) (Cohen, 1964). The separation usually lasts until the initiation rites of the second stage of puberty (between ages twelve and fifteen). During this period, the child often lives with distant relatives, or, as is the case among Pueblo and Navaho Indians and Eskimos, may live in buildings established especially for this purpose (Lowie, 1941).

One of the most common **taboos** during the period of separation is that of brother-sister contact. This varies from cultures where no contact is permitted to those where limited forms of contact are allowed. Among the Gros Ventres Indian tribe, for example, girls were removed from their own families while still very young. Not only were they not allowed to speak with their brothers, but if it could be avoided, they were strongly encouraged not to look at them directly. Any communication between the two would take place through a third person (Eggan, 1950).

More extreme is the situation of the Kurtatchi, a Melanesian tribe. At the age of eight or nine, the Kurtatchi boy was removed from his parents' home and went to live in a hut. At about the same time, he began to wear a particular form of headgear (called *upi*) to indicate that he was no longer a child, but also that he had not yet been initiated into manhood. From this moment until his final initiation, the Kurtatchi boy was expressly forbidden to enter any home in which there lived a woman (including that of his own mother). Although his food would be prepared for him by his mother or some other female relative, it would be passed to him through the door. In earlier times, any boy daring to enter a woman's hut, or inadvertently doing so, would have been killed and eaten by the older men of the village. More recently, the medicine men of the tribe would simply evoke such magic as they felt would be sufficient to have him die and to have his mother and father die along with him (Blackwood, 1935).

A less extreme form of separation is exemplified by the Bantu of western Kenya, where children of both sexes have their lower incisors knocked out at the age of five or six; from that time on they sleep with a widowed grandparent or in the girls' or boys' hut, respectively. During this time the children continue to live and eat at home during the daytime (Wagner, 1949).

Scarification Self-mutilation or mutilation by others occurs prior to or during initiation ceremonies in several primitive tribes, particularly in Africa,

22

though it is not as common now as it was several decades ago. The African Bagesu women (Roscoe, 1915) begin the process of scarification during adolescence and continue it throughout life. They carry the instrument of their self-torture much as contemporary women sometimes carry makeup with them. In the case of the Bagesu, the makeup consists of a single instrument: a crescent-shaped metal hook, approximately four inches long and one-quarter inch thick, beaten to a needle-sharp point at one end. Proper use of this instrument requires simply that the woman take a relatively thick roll of her own flesh between her thumb and forefinger, and that she pierce this roll with her hook. Several such self-inflicted wounds are made at one time. Ashes are then rubbed into them, not only to stop the bleeding, but primarily to ensure that the resulting scars will be raised. The object of the process, repeated frequently through the years, is to adorn the body, from the breasts down to the pit of the stomach, with rows of small, almond-shaped scars. The Bagesu women also create similar scars on each other's foreheads.

Young Nuer boys (an African tribe) endure a particularly painful, and sometimes fatal, form of scarification during their initiation rites. At puberty, a shallow depression is hollowed out in the ground to hold the boy during the operation. While he is held flat on his back in this hollow, an older man of the tribe takes a sharp knife and draws it from the center of the forehead, just above the eyebrow, in a curved line down toward the center of the ear. The incision is made right to the bone. Five additional cuts are made above this initial incision, parallel to it and approximately one centimeter apart. The boy is then removed to a hut where he must lie motionless for several days to promote healing and prevent further bleeding that might lead to his death.

Bloch and Niederhoffer (1958) report numerous other forms of mutilation during initiation rites. Frequent among them is the removal, chipping, or filing of teeth.

Circumcision Among males **circumcision** has been a common feature of initiation rites. Among females, various forms of subincisions, excisions, and amplification have been a less frequent counterpart.

Bantu boys of western Kenya go through an elaborate initiation ceremony that culminates in a group circumcision. At that point boys stand with their fathers next to them while the operator wields his knife. The father's function is to admonish both his son and the operator, the son to be brave, and the operator to be careful. The entire operation takes place in public view of women and children, though they maintain a discreet distance. After the operation the boy is allowed to run after the operator if he remains sufficiently strong. Should the operator be caught, he is beaten with a stick, his headdress is torn off, and he must give the newly initiated boy three chickens (Wagner, 1949).

Once Bena boys have had a nocturnal emission, they are given "medicine" to eat by the tribal doctor and are then driven to a river and beaten with sticks (Culwick and Culwick, 1935). That is the extent of their initiation. Bena girls, on the other hand, have the *labia minora* cut off, in the belief that if they are not removed they will grow and block entrance to the vagina.

Why Initiation Rites? Numerous explanations have been advanced for the widespread existence of puberty rites among primitive tribes. It is widely accepted, for example, that ceremonies are one way in which a culture imparts a sense of adult responsibility to its children. Clearly, in most such cultures, the behavior that is expected of children after the initiation ceremonies is sometimes dramatically different from that expected before the ceremonies. Hence there is usually little ambiguity concerning the roles that individuals must play.

Initiation rites also help develop a sense of identification among newly initiated members. In effect, initiation ceremonies serve to admit the child into adult society. In a sense, the child is being given an identity as a member of the group.

Initiation ceremonies also serve to reinforce certain almost universal incest taboos. Brother-sister separation and, in some cases, separation of the boy from his mother, illustrates dramatically one such incest taboo.

Bloch and Niederhoffer (1958) describe several other functions served by initiation rites. The extrusion of the child from the immediate family group, together with the pain that is inflicted at the time of the initiation ceremony, help sever the close emotional bonds that ordinarily exist between members of the immediate nuclear family. It is as though the child is being told to look to the remainder of the tribe for kinship. The mutual ordeals that all young initiates have suffered serve to form a strong bond among them, ensuring the survival of the tribe and its customs as well as the psychological well-being of its individual members.

24

A second function of initiation ceremonies discussed by Bloch and Nieder-hoffer (1958) is related to nothing more complicated than the cultural stand-ards of beauty and sexual desirability peculiar to the tribe. Thus those forms of scarification, circumcision, incision, tattooing, and so on that are common to a given tribe are often viewed as being cosmetic in nature. Nuer boys are not considered fit to marry unless their foreheads bear the six parallel scars of their initiation ceremonies. Bagesu women are beautiful to the extent that they have succeeded in adorning their bodies with scars.

Modern Rites

Although there are no universal *rites de passage* in contemporary western societies, parallels have often been drawn between the behaviors of certain contemporary adolescent groups and that of primitive societies.* Bloch and Niederhoffer (1958) maintain, for example, that many contemporary adoles-cent gangs have developed informal rituals very similar to those of initiation rites in primitive societies — rituals that have been developed in order to provide "psychologically supportive devices to assist the maturing male to weather the crisis of adolescence" (p. 29). They go on to state that adolescents who are denied adult responsibilities (marital, economic, and civic) are apt to take on the superficial aspects of adult privilege. Thus they explain ado-lescent drinking, sexual escapades, and violence.

The parallels between primitive initiation rites and the rituals of contem-porary groups are somewhat tenuous. True, membership in some gangs in-volves rituals that seem to have their counterpart in primitive initiation rites. Thus the bodily self-adornment that takes place in some puberty rites — tattoo-ing, scarification, circumcision, or painting the body or face — may seem to have its parallel in the dress of some teenagers — dress designed to accentuate sexual properties of the body; in the tattoos that mark membership in some teenage gangs; in the use of various cosmetics thought to render the individual more desirable; and in the battle- or skirmish-earned scars proudly worn by

---

* Although some anthropologists have suggested that wedding ceremonies and the accompany-ing honeymoon are a *rite de passage* to adulthood, these are not nearly as universal as "primitive" rites. Furthermore, they are not restricted to a particular age group and do not differ significantly for the sexes as do most of the rites described here.

some members of adolescent gangs. Similarly, the separation of children from their parents and the separation of brothers and sisters in primitive societies may appear to have some parallel in adolescents' increasing desire to associate with age and sex peers and the consequent disassociation with their parents. It is clear, however, that these parallels in contemporary culture do not constitute anything like most primitive initiation ceremonies. Not only are they much less severe and much less clear-cut, they are by no means universal even within small segments of our society, unlike puberty rites, which tend to be common to an entire culture or at least to an entire tribe.

An argument has been advanced that if our culture were discontinuous — that is, if we clearly marked passage from childhood to adulthood though not necessarily through the use of initiation rites — much of the turmoil now associated with adolescence would cease to exist. Children would know clearly when they have become adults and, consequently, what behavior is permitted and expected. However, the problem is by no means as clear or as simple as this would suggest. It is inaccurate to contend that adolescence is necessarily, or even generally, a period of turmoil and rebellion. The differences between our society and the primitive societies where puberty rites have been (and still are being) employed go far beyond the simple observation that one appears to be discontinuous and the other continuous. Ours is a complex technological society where the skills required of an individual for effective commerce in adult society cannot easily be imparted to children in their prepubertal years. In fact, it is necessary for most of our children to spend a considerable amount of time in learning institutions to obtain sufficient knowledge and skills to assume the responsibilities of adulthood. The fundamental difference between this society and "primitive" ones is not that we don't recognize puberty. It is, rather, that the complexity of our society makes it impossible for children who are sexually mature and hence ready to assume sexual independence to also assume economic and social responsibility as adults. The increasing complexity of our society requires that we prolong the period during which children learn that which is necessary in order to adapt as adults. Hence we have prolonged the period of adolescence. And perhaps the problems associated with adolescence would be improved if we could shorten this period. This can be done, obviously, by simplifying the society or by increasing the age at which children achieve sexual maturity. Because we are now incapable of doing either, we are faced with an adolescence that is not only longer and more difficult to understand than that of simpler societies, but that is also somewhat artificial in the sense that its duration is socially and culturally rather than simply biologically determined.

Adolescent Profiles

While writing this text, I talked to a great many adolescents: most well adjusted and reasonably happy; some unhappy and rebellious; a number, convicted juvenile delinquents in detention. Initially, my conversations with them were haphazard and largely unplanned; I wished only to familiarize myself with their interests, their preoccupations, their predominant activities, their sources of joy, and their sources of sorrow. But I found that so much of what they said was pertinent to what I wished to say that I recorded several dozen conversations from which I painfully extracted small bits to sprinkle wherever appropriate throughout the manuscript. While these conversations are not part of the academic substance of this text, they lend much to its flavor. Hopefully, they will make the substance more immediate and more real for you.

Following are brief profiles of the adolescents whose conversations found their way into these pages. Some of the information was obtained directly from the people involved; some came from school records, teachers, counselors, probation officers, and parents. To ensure the anonymity of those who participated, the names used are fictitious.* In reading the conversations, it might be wise to return to the profiles occasionally in order to understand better what it is that the adolescent is saying and why he or she might be saying it.

Dan, Age 14

An only child who lives with his mother occasionally. Highly verbal and cooperative. Believes that his father is in a rather exotic foreign land, although

---

* To make things simpler, the names of all "delinquents" interviewed in a detention center begin with the letter D.

his counselor was reluctant to accept this as fact. A relatively long history of minor trouble with law enforcement officers. Presently serving an 18-month sentence in a detention center following conviction on a theft charge. Allegedly stole and pawned an object that he claims was his. His mother reported him to the police and apparently asked that he be "taken care of" since she wasn't able to "handle him." Claims to have tried most available drugs, including heroin and morphine, and to "turn on" with marijuana or hashish as frequently as possible. Was previously arrested for trafficking. Major preoccupations when "outside": girls, drugs, fighting, and motorcycles. Overriding ambition: to join a specific motorcycle gang well known for its members' aggressive physical and sexual exploits.

Donalda, Age 14

An apathetic, listless girl, who lived with both parents until her present detention following conviction in juvenile court on a breaking and entering charge. According to her counselor, she has serious family problems. By her own admission, she feels left out of family activities. She is the third oldest girl in a family of six girls and two boys. None of her siblings have been in similar difficulties. At the time that she was apprehended, she had been running away from home with some friends. They had run out of food and money and had broken into a house in order to obtain "supplies." Her father is perennially unemployed and has been ever since she can remember. Money and food have always been relatively serious problems. Sees no hope for the future and expects to have to live "off the street" when released from detention. Does not want to return home.

Dominique, Age 15

An unhappy boy living with father who divorced his mother and remarried. Has one brother and one sister living with his mother, and one stepbrother and one stepsister living with his father and himself. Home situation unhappy. Has been chronically truant from school since primary grades, and thinks he might have the equivalent of fifth grade. Relatively nonverbal; highly reluctant to be interviewed. Noncommunicative with teachers and counselors presently in charge of him at detention center. Has been in previous trouble. Latest detention sentence resulted from a large number of possession and trafficking charges involving "speed." Has been in detention for two and a half years. Sees no hope of ever getting a job; has an extremely negative attitude toward school and teachers; and fully expects to be returned to a detention center once he is released. Expects to be in and out of jails later, until all drugs become legal, because the police are constantly watching him. Describes the effect of mainlining speed as being equivalent to an orgasm. Looks forward to nothing except drugs.

Darcy, Age 14

A bored, cynical boy, living with both mother and father. Father is an "old age pensioner," but not retired since he never worked. Has four older brothers and sisters. One of the brothers is currently in jail; all others have been at least once. Darcy is presently in detention following conviction on a charge of car theft. Has been stealing cars since the age of nine, and has been in court more than thirty times. Also serving concurrent sentences on several breaking and entering charges. Like most hard-core delinquents I interviewed, he has given up hope of leading a law-abiding life. Is not certain he would want to, but is convinced that he couldn't even if he wanted to. Thinks no one would give him a job, and that he will never obtain a driver's license since he has been involved in nine accidents with stolen cars. His most frequent expression: "What else is there to do?"

George, Age 18

A mature and handsome student, living at home with both parents and one older sister. Father is self-employed, and George plans to get into his father's business. Despite having been expelled from school on two occasions, each for the balance of a school year, he has university ambitions and readily concedes that the most important factor for his future success is education. Frequents bars, as apparently do the majority of the students in his school. Legal drink-

ing age is eighteen, but most enter bars relatively freely from sixteen on. Has taken drugs, but says he is no longer interested in taking any, because he simply fell asleep most of the time. "It's a waste of time and money." Believes that use of drugs is declining among his schoolmates.

Jean, Age 18

A very attractive eighteen-year-old, not overly involved in social activities and not interested in taking drugs—especially chemicals. Father is a professional. She has lived in Europe and would like to return. Has two younger brothers. Gets along well at home, and thinks she and her parents are highly similar in terms of values and interests. Is interested in solitary activities, and has considerable artistic talent. Described by her teacher as withdrawn but not particularly shy.

Tracy, Age 17

A highly verbal, very mature young woman, with an outstanding academic record. Plans to be the first of her family to attend college. She claims her parents came from poor backgrounds and were therefore not able to obtain college degrees. Some conflict with parents concerning dating and clothes, but considerably more harmony than conflict. There is one younger sister in the family. Tracy thinks drugs are unintelligent. "You can have real mental highs without something artificial."

Joe, Age 16

An only child living with his mother who has recently separated from his father. Is trying to work and go to school at the same time, and is finding it very difficult to do both. His mother disapproves of his working. Joe thinks it is primarily for this reason that he and his mother do not get along well. Most of his friends are from work. Sees little in common with his school peers, particularly with respect to drugs, which he thinks are a "turnoff." His mother is

30 ————————————————————————————————

frequently ill and depressed, and Joe finds comfort and purpose in his work. He goes to school because he thinks it is important in order to get a better job.

Kris, Age 16

A pert, vivacious girl. Has two older sisters and two younger brothers. Lives at home with both parents. Another of the many adolescents I talked to who claims she does not take drugs. Has tried marijuana only once. Does not think there is a lot of pressure on people to take drugs, but does think there is more pressure to engage in premarital sex. Believes it is important to be a virgin until marriage, but expects that approximately 85 percent of her girlfriends are not. Feels that she is stronger than they are, that she has more will power.

Summary

This chapter began with a note about Sam and a promise that he would write portions of this text. It then attempted to describe and define adolescence, examining, as well, methods of obtaining information about adolescence. For a number of pages, it lost itself in an examination of adolescence in primitive cultures where there frequently is no adolescence as we know it. It appears that adolescence is therefore both a biological and a cultural phenomenon. Finally, the chapter presented descriptive profiles of adolescents, portions of whose conversations are included in this text.

Main Points

1. Send Sam chocolate cake—not money, sympathy, or advice.

2. There is no single, accepted body of facts that comprises adolescent psychology. While there are numerous facts, some relevant and some less so, there is also considerable speculation, a fair amount of opinion, some controversy, and many misconceptions. Separating these is not simple.

3. Adolescence has been defined in various ways. Most generally, it includes that developmental period beginning with pubescence (physical changes preceding sexual maturity) and terminating with adulthood. For purposes of simplicity and clarity, the ages associated with adolescence are considered to be eleven or twelve to twenty.

4. Adolescence begins approximately two years earlier for girls than for boys.

5. Adolescent psychology is concerned with changes that occur during adolescence — specifically with the physical, behavioral, and psychological aspects of adolescents.

6. The basis of most information in psychology is observation. Objective observation occurs when the investigators observe and interpret the subjects' behavior; subjective observation requires that the subjects observe and report on their own behavior; projective observation requires the subjects to respond to some relatively nebulous stimulus and assumes that their responses constitute projections of themselves.

7. Nonexperimental research is frequently employed for descriptive or comparative studies. These are frequently cross-sectional, where different samples are examined and compared at the same time; or longitudinal, where a single sample is observed at different times and compared with itself.

8. In an experiment, the investigators manipulate some aspect of the situation (independent variable) in order to observe its effects on some other aspect of the situation (dependent variable). Experiments frequently involve the use of control or comparison groups.

9. The nature of the sample employed in psychological investigations may affect the generalizability and the validity of conclusions.

10. One of the serious limitations of a great deal of research in the social sciences is that the investigators must rely on the honesty of their subjects. In addition, the investigators must rely on the accuracy of the subjects' memories when they are being asked to recall past events.

11. Experimenter bias sometimes affects experimental results, presumably without the experimenter being aware of it. When experimenters know what the results of their experiments should be, the probability that they will observe these expected results is increased.

32

12. The correlation fallacy, assuming that two events are causally related if they are statistically correlated, is a common interpretative error in experimentation.

13. Conceptualization problems, most evident in disagreements concerning the meanings of abstract terms, plague interpretation of psychological research and writing.

14. A discontinuous culture clearly marks passage from one state to another. The initiation rites of many primitive societies are indicative of discontinuous cultures that identify passage from childhood to adulthood.

15. Contemporary Western cultures are primarily continuous in that they do not clearly mark passage between important developmental states.

16. *Rites de passage* (initiation rites) are frequently characterized by separation, scarification, circumcision, or combinations of all three.

17. One of the principal functions of an initiation rite is to impart a sense of adult responsibility unto the children of that culture. In addition, it fosters a sense of identification among initiates and, to some extent, ensures the propagation of the culture.

18. Contemporary societies do not ordinarily have anything resembling primitive initiation rites. The argument is sometimes advanced that adolescence is a cultural phenomenon aggravated by society's failure to provide children with clear information concerning their status. That is, they are not told or shown the difference between childhood and adulthood, but must discover it for themselves.

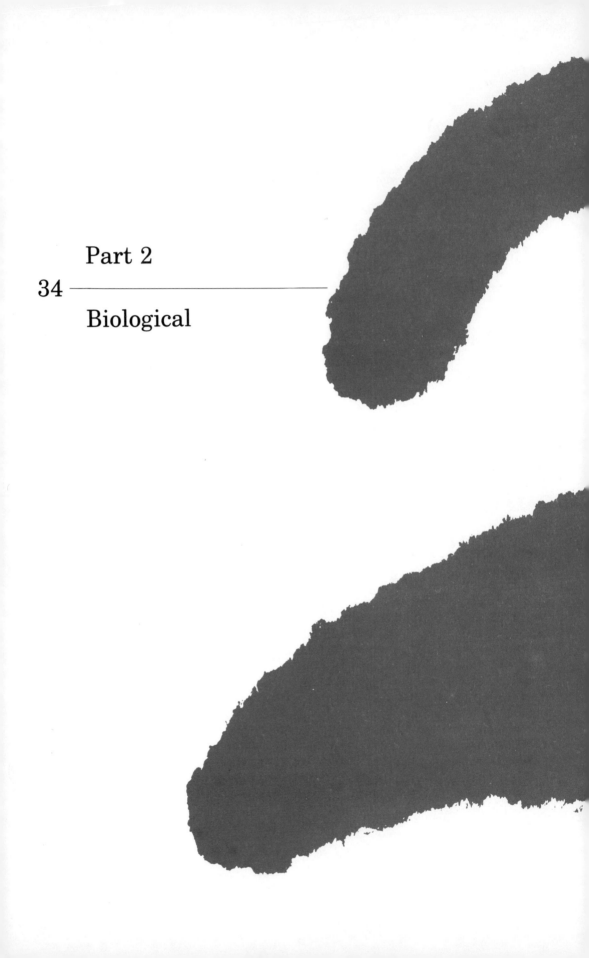

Part 2

34

Biological

Chapter 2

**The Immense Journey:
Biological Changes**

Chapter 3

Adolescent Verse and Art

Chapter 2

36

The Immense Journey:
Biological Changes

Francie Binder, Grade 11

Loren Eiseley, in his book *The Immense Journey* (1957), traces the evolution of life through its myriad forms over the distant ages of geologic time. It is not a clear and obvious journey, for we are looking back into a dim region where the only records are those that nature accidently provided. And these are records that not all can read; nor can those who claim to read them do so with perfect clarity and consistency. So it is that when Eiseley tells us of the **Snout,** that remarkable product of **evolution** who many millions of years ago found itself living in the oxygen poor environment of drying mud flats, we know from the outset that the Snout is at least in part a product of Eiseley's imagination. But this product of his imagination conforms to the facts, as they are alleged to exist, at least as well as the product of anybody else's imagination.

The Snout, Eiseley tells us, was a generalized rather than a specialized creature, though we would probably not have thought so had we been there to observe its miserable existence in the slimy waters of past ages. But that it was generalized becomes evident later when it is observed that the Snout possessed an air sac—a primitive lung that could obtain oxygen directly from the air. Unlike its fellow creatures, the Snout did not have to be restricted to the muddy waters. It could rear its head above that of its fellows and gaze upon a different world. And when food became too scarce, it could ooze from the slime and drag itself painfully into the terrestrial vegetation. More important, it could obtain sufficient oxygen to feed its evolving brain.

We are one of the contemporary products of the Snout. It is not a very flattering beginning; indeed, it is not even a beginning. Life, according to evolutionary theory (though not according to other theories), had begun long before then. Nor are we necessarily the final product of evolution. Although we tend to look forever backwards in our attempts to understand evolution, there may also be a future. And perhaps we, like the now extinct Snout, are merely a short stage in the course of earthly evolution. It *has* been an immense journey, but we still don't know where we are going or how far we have yet to go.

From a biological point of view, humans are interesting for a number of reasons. The human animal is the only mammal more at ease walking on two legs than on four, though a number of other mammals such as the kangaroo can hop quite impressively on their hind legs. In addition, of course, humans are remarkable in the development and use of their brain, in the use of their hands and juxtaposed thumb, and in the development of languages. But perhaps

MODERN
SNOUT →
(FULLY EVOLVED)

ORIGINAL
SNOUT
↓

39

most interesting of all, and most relevant for the study of developmental psychology, is the observation that no other species remains immature for as long a period of time. Some of the fishes, such as the sturgeon, and some mammals, such as the elephant, are sexually immature for even longer; but, these species do not undergo nearly as long a period of dependency upon parents. Indeed, among subhuman species, it is not at all unusual for offspring to be completely independent of their parents immediately upon their first appearance. Human children are not only physically dependent upon their parents (or some other adult), but remain dependent both physically and emotionally throughout much of their childhood.

The transformation of the Snout into the human was, indeed, an immense journey, though only part of a much longer trek. The transformation of a child into an adult is also an immense journey; but it too is only part of a larger journey. This chapter is concerned with one small part of this journey: the biological changes that intervene between childhood and adulthood—the changes of adolescence.

A Changing Statistic

The number of adolescents has increased dramatically in the past few decades. The U.S. Bureau of the Census (1971a) indicates that the number of persons between fourteen and seventeen increased by 5 million between 1960 and 1971. It had increased by 2.7 million between 1950 and 1960. Thus the proportion of adolescents to adults has increased in spite of the fact that life expectancy has also increased. In the 1971 census, adolescents aged fourteen to seventeen comprised 7.7 percent of the population compared with 5.6 percent in 1950 (Gordon, 1972). The median age in the United States has dropped from slightly over thirty in the late 1940s to slightly under twenty-eight in 1971.

The proportion of males to females among white adolescents is approximately 103 males for every 100 females. On the average, there are 104 males born for every 100 females, but more males succumb to childhood diseases (Gordon, 1972). Among blacks, the proportion of males to females between the ages of fourteen and seventeen is 97 to 100. It is not certain whether more die in infancy, whether it is more difficult for census takers to find black male adolescents, or both.

40

Coleman (1974) suggests that a more valid indication of the impact of the youth population in the United States can be arrived at by looking at the proportion of adolescents to those who are primarily responsible for the socialization of youth and, not insignificantly, for the payment of taxes. Accordingly he looks at those aged fourteen to twenty-four relative to those aged twenty-five to sixty-four. The ratio of youth (defined as those between fourteen and twenty-four) declined from .556 in 1890 to .322 in 1960, but increased more sharply in the 1960s than it had during any other decade of this century. By 1970 the ratio was up to .449. This increase was probably related to the activism and rebellion characteristic of adolescents in the 1960s.

With present decreasing population growth the ratio of adolescents to the middle-aged population is now declining. Relatively accurate projections can be arrived at for the next fourteen years because all children who will be fourteen or more at that time have now been born. These projections indicate that, barring some major catastrophe or unrestricted immigration or emigration, the proportion of adolescents will continue to decline (U.S. Bureau of the Census, 1971b).

Among the implications of this decline is the possibility that social problems associated with this age group will also decline in occurrence and in severity. Coleman (1974) suggests two additional possibilities. During this "moratorium" in adolescent population growth, society may avail itself of "the opportunity for reformation without the apprehension of being numerically engulfed" (p. 6). He suggests, in addition, that work opportunities for young people will become increasingly available as the average population age increases and as the number of younger people declines relative to the number of older people.

These population statistics are of considerable relevance to an understanding of contemporary adolescents. They may also be of relevance to an understanding of adolescence in the future. It will be interesting to look back in 1984 and try to determine to what extent predicted demographic changes have affected this society and its adolescents. For the present, however, the sheer weight of adolescent numbers makes adolescents an impressive social force, a force that can hardly be ignored. It has now become vastly more important for governments, schools, and parents to reach a deeper understanding of adolescents' needs and desires as well as values and beliefs.

Biological Changes

We all begin life as microscopic specks in the **uteri** of our mothers. It's a prosaic beginning for individuals as special as you and I are, not that a more poetic beginning would necessarily alter the final product.

True, there is a somewhat less prosaic beginning some time before our existence as microscopic specks. A beginning that involves the interaction of two relatively mature human beings of different sexes. But, as I have pointed out in an earlier "work" (the term is a euphemism; or is it an overstatement?), that beginning is not sufficiently prosaic, nor indeed of sufficient academic interest, to be a suitable subject for inclusion in a book that poses as a college textbook (Lefrancois, 1973). Suffice it to say that there is a beginning before the beginning. And perhaps that there was a beginning even before then. Or was there?

Our microscopic existence at the dawn of our personal beginnings is described in some detail — both scientific and speculative as neither excludes the other — as follows.

Origins

Every mature, healthy, and normal (at least in this respect) female of our species releases an **ovum** approximately once every twenty-eight days. In this imprecise world, even this statement is partly inexact. Some women release more than one mature ovum at one time; some women release their ova at irregular intervals, and a large number cleverly tamper with Mother Nature through chemical means and release ova only at will. Most often, their will is to not release any ova.

Ovum is a sophisticated Latin term for egg.

The egg cell released by the female is, under certain circumstances, assaulted by one or more male sex cells called **sperm.**

Sperm is a sophisticated Latin term for sperm.

The union of the ovum and the sperm results in a fertilized egg called a **zygote.** The zygote is, in effect, the microscopic beginning to which I referred earlier.

Every cell in your body (your *soma* in Latin; hence your somatoplasm) consists of twenty-three pairs of **chromosomes,** chromosomes being the carriers of hereditary information. Each sex cell (germ plasm), however, contains only half this number: twenty-three rather than twenty-three pairs. That is, both the egg and the sperm, at maturity, possess half the normal number of chromosomes for human beings. Body cells reproduce through **mitosis** — the splitting of a single cell into two identical cells. Sex cells reproduce through **meiosis** — the splitting of a single cell into two different cells.

Each chromosome contains some forty to sixty thousand **genes.** And it is these genes that are allegedly responsible for inherited human characteristics. But to make the matter even more complex, at least mathematically, each gene is made up of **DNA (deoxyribonucleic acid)** molecules — molecules whose complexity must have boggled even Mother Nature's clever mind. DNA is a long chainlike molecule consisting of four chemical subunits that can be arranged in enough different combinations to code fifty times more information than there is in the *Encyclopaedia Britannica* (Munsinger, 1971).

The peculiar arrangement of DNA molecules in your originating zygote was largely responsible for what you have become. In addition, the cultural, physical, and nutritive environment have had some effect on the eventual product of that zygote.

Average Growth

The average American environment, coupled with the average American zygote (in your average American uterus, to be sure) dictates some of the following great American averages:

The average American male child weighs $7\frac{1}{2}$ pounds at birth. At the age of two he weighs $27\frac{3}{4}$ pounds.

The average American female child weighs just slightly under $7\frac{1}{2}$ pounds at birth. At two she weighs 27 pounds.

At the age of ten, average American males and females weigh 72 and $70\frac{1}{4}$ pounds respectively. At twelve they weigh $84\frac{1}{2}$ and $87\frac{1}{2}$ pounds. But at eighteen the average American male weighs 139 pounds compared with 120 for the average American female.

The substance of these averages is summarized in Figure 2.1; the import of these averages is summarized in the following paragraphs.

Figure 2.1   Height in inches, weight in pounds, and age in years at the fiftieth percentile for American males and females aged six to eighteen. (Adapted by the Health Department, Milwaukee, Wisconsin; based on data by H. C. Stuart and H. V. Meredith, prepared for use in Children's Medical Center, Boston. Reprinted by permission of the Milwaukee Health Department.)

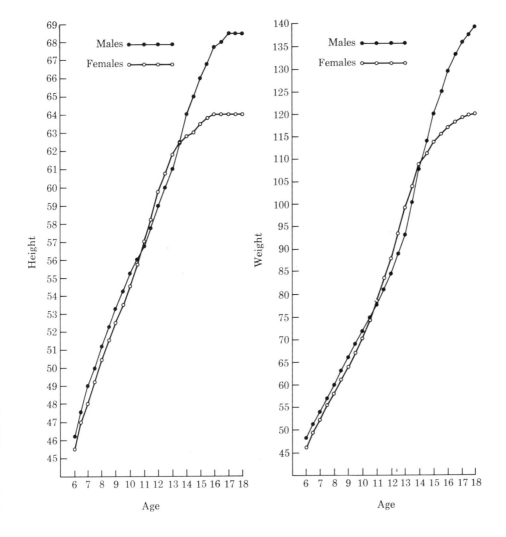

44 ──

The Growth Spurt

The biological **growth** timetables contained in average American zygotes dictate that, given adequate environmental conditions, boys will be both heavier and taller than girls throughout most of their childhood. At the age of ten and one-half or eleven, girls will suddenly spurt, both in height and weight, and surpass the average American boy. This superiority in height and weight will disappear between the ages of fourteen and fourteen and one-half. From then on, the average American male will be both taller and heavier than the average American female, an advantage that will continue uninterrupted until death renders both equally short and light.

The growth spurt that accounts for the temporary disruption of the relatively parallel growth curves of boys and girls begins at around the age of eleven for girls and thirteen for boys (Tanner, 1972), although it can begin as early as seven and one-half or as late as eleven and one-half for girls, and ten and one-half or sixteen for boys. This growth spurt is of both biological and psychological importance.

The growth spurt is biologically important as it relates closely to other pubertal changes. Pubescence is defined as the conglomerate of biological changes that occur in late childhood or early adolescence, culminating in sexual maturity.

The growth spurt is psychologically important as it relates to the adolescent's changing bodily image, the congruence between this new image and the "ideal" image, and the consequent adjustment to the rapidly changing self. More is said about this later in this chapter. At this moment, like a clever magician, I am directing my words back to the biological concomitants of the growth spurt and to a discussion of biological adolescence. 'Tis a sleight of thought as opposed to a sleight of hand trick.

Pubescence

Prepubertal changes are spurred by changes in the endocrine glands—the ductless glands whose products, **hormones,** are emptied directly into the bloodstream rather than via a specialized duct into a specialized organ in a specialized sense for a specialized function. Among the most important of these are the thyroid, which produces a hormone important for growth (thyroxine), and the pituitary, which also produces a hormone important for growth (somatotrophin) and in stimulating other endocrine glands in the production of their own hormones. Two additional hormones are of primary importance for sexual maturation: **estrogens** in girls and **androgens** in boys. These are known as the sex hormones and are responsible for the initiation and development of "masculine" and "feminine" sexual characteristics in the biological domain. They are produced by the gonads located in the **testes** in boys and in the ovaries in girls (see Figures 2.2 and 2.3). The psychological significance of the presence of these hormones in mature males and females is evident in that injections of **testosterone** (an androgen) given to men can bring about sexual arousal. Indeed, there was a theory extant at one point (relatively recently) that individuals identified as homosexuals suffered from an imbalance of these sex hormones. It is known that both males and females produce estrogen and testosterone, but that the former is ordinarily more plentiful in girls and the latter more plentiful in boys. The theory simply maintained that homosexual males had too much estrogen; homosexual females, too much testosterone. In view of conflicting evidence, the theory is generally discounted. More is said about sexuality in Chapter 12.*

The growth spurt is a systematic though nonuniform phenomenon in the average American adolescent. Height and weight are not simply added proportionally to all parts of the body. The head, the hands, and the feet are the first to reach adult size. And adult size is no longer the same as it was several generations ago. Shoe salesmen know this. Or at least they suspect it. The average adult male wears a size 9 to 10 shoe (Muuss, 1970). That is important if you sell shoes. The average American shoe salesman a mere two generations ago knew that the average American male wore a size 7 shoe.

Medieval armor, made for the average medieval knight, who might well have been taller than the average medieval gentleman, was made to fit a man slightly under five feet, and weighing little more than ninety pounds.

Seats in old opera houses were approximately 25 percent narrower than seats in contemporary theatres.

We don't have many opera houses nowadays.

---

* If you have just now returned to this chapter from Chapter 12, you are not the only one. Blame your sex hormones. Or your originating zygote.

Figure 2.2 Human male reproductive organs depicted in cross-section.

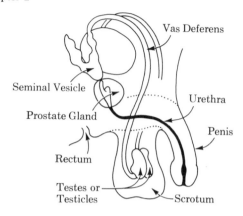

Vas Deferens

Seminal Vesicle

Urethra

Prostate Gland

Penis

Rectum

Testes or Testicles

Scrotum

46

We now have wider asses.

And we are taller, and heavier, and our feet are bigger. "Experts" lay it on nutrition. Some of these "experts" have predicted that in a dozen or so centuries the average American male, if the beast is not yet extinct, may be eleven feet tall. His feet would be quite large too.

The same observations and predictions apply to the age of menarche, as was pointed out four days ago in Chapter 1. By the year 2500, the average American three-year-old kindergarten girl could experience menarche.

Other "experts" claim that the trend toward accelerated growth (called the secular trend) will reach a ceiling; that, in fact, it has already begun to decelerate (Frisch and Revelle, 1970).

Arm and leg length reach adult size following the head, hands, and feet. Finally the **trunk** widens. Muscles develop rapidly along with increasing height, especially in boys. The accumulation of fatty tissue does not take place nearly as rapidly. Strength increases as well. Especially in boys. Cratty (1970) did a series of studies investigating the relative strength and agility of boys and girls. He found that boys were typically stronger and better coordinated than girls throughout childhood—that they excelled on almost all tasks save for a few rhythmic exercises involving such activities as hopscotch (see Lefrancois, 1973).

The many biological changes that take place during pubescence follow a relatively definite though not invariable timetable in both boys and girls. In boys the first sign of impending sexual maturation is the enlargement of the testes and their container, the **scrotum.** This is followed by the appearance of the first pigmented **pubic** hair. Shortly thereafter the **penis** begins to lengthen, the boy commences his growth spurt in height, he grows **axillary** hair (armpit hair), and facial hair. One of the final noticeable changes is in his voice.

Visible signs of pubescence in girls include the development of **breasts.** Breast development is followed by or occurs at the same time as the appearance of pigmented pubic hair. Uterine, vaginal, labial, and clitoral enlargement all take place at approximately the same time. Relatively late in this sequence is the occurrence of the first menstrual period (menarche).

Pubescence includes all of these changes that culminate in sexual maturity. Sexual maturity itself is denoted as puberty. Although it has generally been accepted that puberty is reached when a boy is capable of ejaculating **semen**

Figure 2.3 The process of fertilization and implantation. At 1 sperm cells have entered the vagina and are finding their way into the uterus. At 2 some of these spermatozoa are moving up the fallopian tube (there is a similar tube on the other side) toward the ovum. At 3, fertilization occurs. The fertilized ovum drifts down the current, dividing and forming new cells as it goes, until it implants itself in the wall of the uterus 4 by the seventh or eighth day after fertilization.

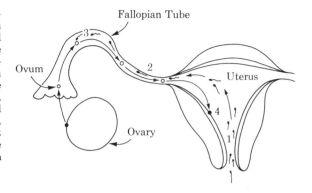

and the girl has had her first menstrual period, these indicators are by no means exact. While it is true that most males can produce sperm capable of reproducing life shortly after their first ejaculation of sperm, it is also true that females are ordinarily incapable of conceiving for a period of one, two, or even three years following their first menstrual period (Tanner, 1962).*

Advancement of bone formation (ossification) as detected through X rays is one of the better indicators of the relative stage of an individual's maturity. This is particularly true in children. However, the ordinary individual, elsewhere referred to as the average American, tends to judge maturity in terms of physical appearance. Thus a boy's maturity is determined in terms of his voice and the presence or absence of hair on his face. A girl's maturity tends to be judged in terms of her figure.

Early and Late Maturing

Because maturity tends to be judged in terms of physical appearance, the changes that take place during pubescence are of paramount importance to the adolescent. And the time at which they take place is also important. Although we speak of the average male or female, there is no such animal. The average person does not exist. The average person has been invented by scientists — and sometimes by grandmothers — to facilitate discussion and comparison. Some people mature early; some late.

In general, early-maturing boys suffer fewer psychological problems associated with physical changes of puberty than do those who mature later. The boy whose voice has gone deeper and whose head has reached closer to the sky than the voices and heads of his age mates tends to be looked up to by them. Contrary to the often-held belief that adolescents go through a period of awkwardness and clumsiness, it is more generally true that they become stronger and better coordinated. Thus the early-maturing boy finds himself considerably stronger than his friends. He may well develop an image of himself as a leader among men, because this is the behavior that is likely to be expected of him and that he is likely to expect of himself. And he may become a leader.

* But don't count on it!

AN EARLY
PUBIC HAIR WAITS
ANXIOUSLY FOR
HIS FRIENDS
TO EMERGE

48

A number of detailed longitudinal studies have been conducted on early- and late-maturing boys and girls by a group of researchers at the University of California (Ames, 1957; Jones, 1957, 1965; Mussen and Jones, 1957; and Jones and Mussen, 1958). Some of these studies have involved the same original sample over a number of years. For example, Jones (1965) studied a group of forty-year-old men who had been identified as early or late maturers in a 1938 study.

Findings concerning the implications of early and late maturation for boys are clear and consistent. The early-maturing male appears to have a definite advantage in terms of psychological adjustment, positive **self-concept,** and peer acceptance throughout adolescence. Peer ratings of early and late maturers describe late maturers as talkative, restless, attention seeking, and lacking in confidence. In contrast, early maturers are rated as more popular, more confident, more aggressive, more outgoing, and more successful in heterosexual relationships.

A subsequent follow-up study mentioned above (Jones, 1965) indicates that some of these advantages may be carried into adulthood. All subjects were administered the California Personality Inventory. Early maturers continued to be more confident, more poised, more mature, more responsible, and engaged in more social activities. On the other hand, later maturers showed evidence of "compensatory adaptations." They were now more independent and more outgoing and exploring.

Mussen and Jones (1957) suggest that "in our culture, a boy whose physical development is retarded is exposed to a sociopsychological environment which may have adverse effects on his personality development" (p. 252). Conversely, it appears that early maturers are exposed to an environment that has positive effects on their development. As indicated earlier, society tends to judge maturity in terms of physique, facial hair, and voice. Independence, aggressiveness, leadership, and other qualities that are probably related to adjustment and "success" in societies such as ours are likely to be expected and encouraged in the early maturer at a time when his like-aged but slow-maturing peers are still being treated as children. It is not entirely surprising that late maturers often develop feelings of inadequacy and inferiority. Because they are physically inferior in terms of strength and size, they develop a consistent self-concept. Unfortunately, it may not be consistent with their image of their ideal self.

The picture is much less clear for early- and late-maturing girls. Researchers have noted that at maturity, early-maturing girls tend to be stockier than those who mature later, a finding that appears to hold true for boys as well, with late-maturing boys generally being more slender (more ectomorphic, see Chapter 7) than early maturers. Because contemporary American culture tends to place a premium on slenderness among girls, and because girls who mature early find themselves considerably ahead of their age peers, early maturation is probably not as advantageous for girls as for boys. Consider the fact, for example, that girls are typically two years ahead of boys in age of puberty. It follows that an early-maturing girl may be five or more years ahead of like-aged boys. Such seemingly trivial problems as finding boys tall enough to date or to dance with may become highly significant for the girl concerned.

Studies investigating the effects of age of maturation in girls have produced contradictory results. Jones (1949) found that early maturers were at a disadvantage, a finding directly contradictory to that consistently reported for boys. Douglas and Ross (1964) and Poppleton (1968), on the other hand, found early-maturing girls to be superior to late-maturing girls. However, none of these studies found differences as large as those evident in comparisons of early- and late-maturing boys. Indeed, it appears that the effects of accelerated development among girls is highly dependent upon the girl's age. Faust (1960) correlated peer ratings with grade level and degree of maturation. He found that while early maturation appeared to be a disadvantage in the early grades (grade six in this case), it became more of an advantage in subsequent grades. In other words, early-maturing girls whose peers have not yet begun to show signs of sexual maturity are accorded less prestige than girls who are developmentally average. Subsequently, however, when a majority of the girls have entered pubescence, the more advanced girls are accorded greater prestige. At the same time, late-maturing girls are now accorded less prestige. Indications are, however, that the effects of early and late maturing among girls are not manifested following adolescence as they appear to be among boys.

While the effects of early and late maturation are relatively clear and consistent for boys, there are individual exceptions. The advantages that are generally characteristic of the early maturer are by no means characteristic of *all* early maturers. Nor are the disadvantages of late maturation evident

50

in all late maturers. With respect to girls, exceptions are evidently even more frequent. This accounts, at least in part, for contradictions among research conclusions. It is nevertheless useful for parents, teachers, and others to know what some of the possible effects of accelerated or retarded development are.

Anxiety

Adolescents frequently suffer from anxiety related to the events that occur during puberty. The late-maturing boy is frequently anxious about being small. He may fear that the gods have decreed that he will forever be a puny individual unable to rub shoulders with the **average American** man. Perhaps a few of the early-maturing boys fear that they will become tall skinny freaks.

Some early-maturing girls fear that they will be too tall. Late-maturing girls sometimes fear that they will never develop breasts, or that if they do, their's will never be as big as the average American woman's.

Adolescents sometimes suffer anxiety over just simply being different or over the possibility of being different (Clifford, 1971). Being different is not highly rewarded in contemporary society; being different is lonely; being different is not average. Many of us think that because the average is normal, not being average must be abnormal. Many of us are wrong.

Male adolescents are sometimes anxious about **nocturnal emissions** (less politely called wet dreams). Others are anxious about masturbation. The anxiety is sometimes due to religious factors. In addition, there are probably some parents or others who still lead children to believe that **masturbation** may lead to **impotence,** feeble-mindedness, or insanity; or that, in the end, the entire organ will turn black and fall off as some form of primitive punishment. Most girls don't masturbate as frequently; consequently the average adolescent female is less anxious about masturbation. (See Chapter 12. Not now. Later.)

What else is there for an adolescent to suffer anxiety over? **Acne,** bad teeth, bad breath, and a variety of existential dilemmas.

Overview

This all started with a discussion of the zygote. A beginning. This zygote, in a highly protective and nurturant uterus, becomes a small human in

approximately 266 days. That, of course, is for the average American woman; some take considerably longer. Some don't take as long.

These little humans, in interaction with the environment, progress through the neonatal period (approximately two weeks), losing some weight and then regaining it. They learn little during these first several weeks, but they do exercise relatively simple behaviors of which they were capable at birth. Sucking, reaching, grasping, coughing, hiccuping, and sneezing behaviors are perfected, or at least improved upon.

In time the **neonates** become infants, learn to move of their own accord, and begin to develop some understanding of the concrete realities that comprise their environment. They also begin to acquire some proficiency in the use and understanding of the most powerful of symbol systems invented by humans: language.

Infants become children. They continue to learn and to adapt to an ever-demanding and ever-complex environment. They develop certain notions about who they are, a sense of identity — a self-concept, as the psychologists would put it.

Finally, children become adolescents. And the single most important thing that happens to adolescents is sexual maturity. As Jersild (1963) put it, before this time they were children; now they can have children.

Concomitant with this sudden (or gradual) advent of sexual maturity, the adolescent's body undergoes significant changes. Not only does it stretch upwards and sideways, but its proportions change, and its muscle-to-fat ratio changes. There is now hair where there had previously been no hair. She has breasts where there were no breasts before. His voice sounds different inside his own head. And the adolescent body begins to respond differently to sexual stimuli.

Partly for reasons related to the adolescent's newfound sexual maturity, and partly for a variety of other reasons, adolescence can be a period of intense turmoil. It has been discussed in these terms by many writers.

It can also be a period of peace and happiness. It has been discussed in these terms as well.

Summary

This chapter began with a look at the Immense Journey from the Snout to humans, and then moved to the journey between childhood and adulthood.

It was noted that proportionally more individuals were involved in that journey in recent years than had been some decades earlier, but that the number of adolescents relative to adults is now decreasing and may be expected to continue doing so. The chapter then looked at human biological origins, progressing to a discussion of the major physical changes that occur during adolescence—the changes of pubescence that precede sexual maturity (puberty). The effects of early and late maturation were examined, and a brief discussion of possible sources of anxiety for developing adolescents were provided. In the end, the chapter turned backward on itself and recapitulated its content in simple form.

Main Points

1. The number of adolescents relative to the number of adults has increased dramatically in the past few decades despite decreasing birth rates and increasing life expectancies. It is likely, however, that their number will again decrease proportionally as fewer children are born and as numbers increase in higher age brackets.

2. The unique combination of genetic information in the form of DNA molecules in sperm and egg cells accounts for the individual's biologically determined characteristics. Human development results as a function of the interaction between these biological forces and environmental forces.

3. At the age of ten and one-half or eleven, girls show a remarkable spurt in physical growth. This spurt occurs approximately two years later for boys. It heralds the beginning of those changes that lead to sexual maturity and, in a sense, defines the onset of adolescence.

4. Pubescence includes changes that lead to sexual maturity. These include changes of a genital nature; changes in secondary sexual characteristics such as breasts, voice, and body hair; and changes in body proportion and hormonal balances.

5. Puberty is defined as sexual maturity and is frequently considered to occur when the girl has had her first menstrual period (menarche) and when the boy is capable of ejaculating semen.

6. A girl ordinarily remains infertile for one or more years following her first menstrual period.

7. Early or late maturing is sometimes associated with problems of adjustment in the adolescent. These tend to be more severe for the late-maturing boy. Research concerning early and late maturation in girls has not produced firm conclusions.

8. There are a number of causes of anxiety among adolescents, many of which are related directly to the biological changes of adolescence.

Chapter 3

Adolescent Verse and Art

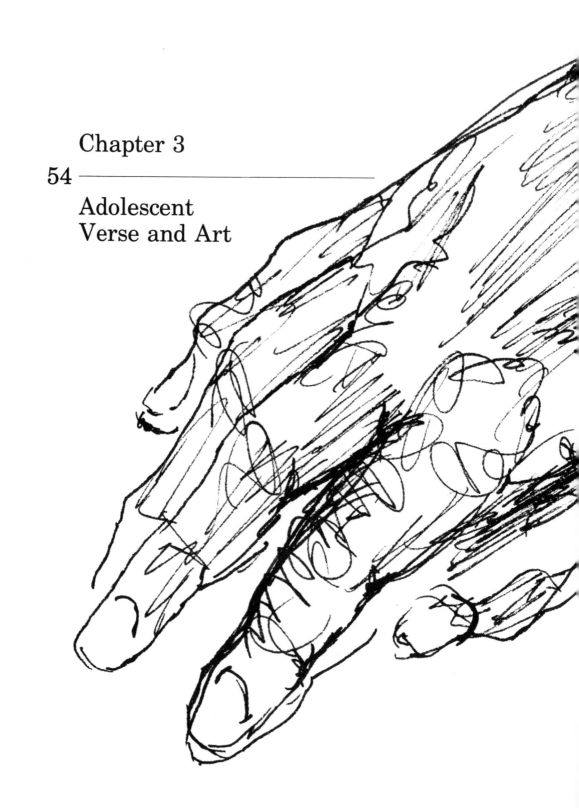

Francie Binder, Grade 11

The Beast
The Sacrifice
You're Rarely Really There
Illusions
A Search for Meaning
A Reflection
Misery
Cry with Me
Thoughts
Afterthoughts
Nora
Lyrics for an Unpopular Song
Swan Song: A Sonnet
Birth
Birth
Birth
Sex to Birth
Hands
Freedom
Death Is the End of Your Life
Horse

56

This chapter is not an academic chapter in the ordinary sense. It does not lead you logically, conclusion to conclusion, through the often tortuous and uncertain paths of research and good sense; it does not present you with items of information with which you can impress your professor, nor with pearls of wisdom that you can flaunt in the face of the world. In this sense it has little for the amazement of the people or the erudition of the scholars.

But perhaps it has more than all this, for there is some virtue in the scholar's efforts to be detached from the objective trappings of science in order to be closer to its subject. Make no mistake; the trappings of a science can indeed trap those scientists who become so concerned with the minutiae of their research that they lose sight of their subject.

For a number of reasons, it was not possible to include a real adolescent in the pages of this book, although I would have liked to have done so. It seems to me that scientists who study reptiles may well be better scientists if they can occasionally look up from their notes or microscope and peer into the eyes of a reptile, or reach out and touch it. You might have been a better student of adolescence had you been able to look into the eyes of an adolescent as you rested between paragraphs and pages in this text—or if you had been able to reach out and touch one.

57

In lieu of a real adolescent, I have included in this chapter something of the hearts and minds of a number of adolescents. In their poetry (the age of each poet is included after the title) and their art, adolescents reveal much of themselves—of their preoccupations, their interests, their joys, and their sorrows. Elsewhere in these pages, I have also included brief excerpts of actual, unedited conversations that I have had with them. These are not meant to be studied as an academic subject might be studied. Feel them; think about them; enjoy them. In the end adolescents may be more immediate, more real, and more meaningful than they would otherwise have been.

The Beast (Age 18)

I would like to find a man
who could say "stop"
and it would stop
at once
and turn
and eat.

I would like to find that man.

First it would eat its tail;
hungrier now, its legs,
its belly,
its arms,
its chest,
its neck.
And what of its head?

Still, I would like to find that man.

58 ―――――――――――――――――――――――――――

The Sacrifice (Age 16)

He went away—
He went to fight—
He went for the glories of war—
But he was a sacrifice

He fought—
He combatted the enemy—
He struggled and won—
But he was a sacrifice.

He returned—
He was alive—
He was in one piece—
But he was a sacrifice

He had been expendable—
He was a sacrifice . . .

60 ──

**You're Rarely
Really There** (Age 17)

You're rarely really there
Now and again
I see you
    for a moment
  Tantalising
    But forbidden
        Like Eve's apple.
Choke not on the wrath of human grapes
    But what are words?
Can you survive the driving torrents
    That undermine me
      Sometimes
            when all seems lost?
    Aha! I found the question
    Typographed in my mind
  Descending
Descending
Descending
      I don't even know what I'm writing.

Illusions (Age 18)

I float
  I float over the clouds
    With my mind
      While my body remains behind

I know
  I know it is but a dream
    A fantasy of splendor
      I never will surrender

Turn on
  Turn onward world of strife and misery
    I have my illusion
      My escape from the confusion

A Search for Meaning (Age 18)

A human being
   A body?
   A mind?
   A soul?
      maybe

A human being
   A thought?
   A look?
   An action?
      maybe

62

A Reflection (Age 19)

A reflection
   in murky water
a puddle of hang-ups
   insecurities
     doubts
   and unfulfilled love
society has left its mark
on all of us
   even the few
     who think they have escaped
morning glory
   sunshine and rain
     a black blade of grass
      blowing in the wind

I want to wander
   across the fields
     over and under
      the mounds of dirt that are

A human being
   Love?
   Power?
   Justice?
     maybe

A human being
   Hate?
   Confusion?
   Pain?
     maybe
      And maybe not.

63

look and try
    to understand how i am
    underneath
    the involuntary ellipses
    which aren't really me

i feel only love
    yet show only hatred
      unmeaningfully
caught a whirl
   of bewilderment
     not knowing what to do

we must all go to the fair
    but i don't have to
      because life is just a chocolate cake

Cry with Me (Age 18)

Silver slaps on outstretched palms of rich men
     fat feet planted uncaring on thighs and groins and hollow
     bellies of empty paupers
Cry with me

Silver slurps of greedy tongues anoint corrupt politicians
     in obsequious zeal to taste small morsels of power and fame
Cry with me

64

Silver streaks of howling death
       tear through black jungles searching green boys in green clothes
Cry with me

Silver slivers of moonlight pass among the trees
       faintly edging leafy moon-shadows where I stand alone
Cry with me
Cry with me
Cry with me

65

Misery (Age 19)

My soul is sick with sores of misery,
Vile and leprous menace to my sanity.
Sadness dulls my usual blade-edged wit
And makes my verse both ponderous and thick.
Here on the eve of my maturity
When all in me should bode fertility
And cause conception of vast happiness,
I stand a failure, dull and fruitless.
Outcast by those who once did give me love,
Without beguiling art of fawning tongue,
Spurned because I shun conformity,
Outraged by blows of cruel fatality!
Oh God!! I'll quench with death this mortal flame
And cast all pain far out this tortured brain!
I'll do, I'll kill, I'll leave this maddened earth
Away my soul, my body back to dirt!
Away my soul, but where, oh God, but where?
To that horrid, sulphurous, ever-burning lair?
To ever-lasting Satan's cruel, painful hell,
To suffer through a thousand bitter deaths?
Oh God, then were it not the better choice
To live on earth, and wait thy calling voice?

66

Thoughts (Age 19)

3. Will there be room for me when I am six hundred years old?

7. When the oil is all gone, the wood all used, the coal all burned, will the sun still shine? And will there still be gold?

32. If God is dead, why did He take Nora?

33. If God is alive, why did He take Nora?

34. We seek no supernatural explanations for the presence of a nice steak on our plates; nor any for the absence of a fine steer in the pasture. And why should we seek supernatural explanations for Nora's absence?

42. Society with its customary far-sighted intelligence sanctions the poisoning of human bodies with certain types of drugs, but not with others. The nature of the drug and the seriousness of its effects seems far less important than its social history.

47. The human race is, in fact, the beast that is eating itself. But what of its head?

53. Fat people tend to have fat problems.

56. My problems are not rendered insignificant by the cosmic nature of the great events that surround me.

Afterthoughts (Age 19)

2. I should have. And if I say that too often, I'll spend the rest of my life regretting.

3. I shouldn't have. That too can lead to memories that are all regrets.

4. I should. But in fact I should nothing. I should do what feels good when it feels good.

7. Now is the only reality. And so I drink to the nows of all tomorrows. But I need someone with whom to drink.

8. Tomorrow needs today.

14. If I tell myself that I can often enough, it is probably because I know that I really can't. If I tell myself that I can't often enough, it is probably because I don't want to.

68

Nora (Age 18)

Love is such a hollow word for what happens to me when I think of the
way your hair frames your hazel eyes flowing around your face and
curling below your chin which slides softly down your neck into that long,
graceful young woman's body that I imagine in all my waking dreams
wrapped in my arms and smiling fondly to observe that I am still the
suave and debonair connoisseur, the daring rescuer, the idolized
performer, the famous, world renown, but humble me that you love so
desperately even as I love you, but I wish there were some way you
could see inside my waking dreams to know how worthy I am of your love
even if you don't remember my name.

69

Lyrics for an Unpopular Song (Age 16)

Chorus: I am the hero of my dreams
          I win all I ever play
          No matter what you might have seen
          I am the hero of my dreams

          When I was still a baby boy
          A bouncin' on the floor
          I didn't need not any toy
          In my head was all my joy

70

(Chorus)
>In time I went to a country school
>to learn to read and write
>It turned out I was just a fool
>I couldn't get it right
>No matter

(Chorus)
>And now that I've become a man
>I live on welfare cheques
>But I don't really give a damn
>'Cause I'm the hero of my dreams

(Chorus)

Swan Song: A Sonnet (Age 17)

I die. So soon are drawn the shades of life.
As a feathered smoke dispersed on air, now gone,
So now doth wisp away my prime-spent light.
Tonight I breathe my last, soft plaintive song.
How short this frame doth feed on earthly joys;
Twixt first and last, how numbered are our breaths.
A youth, scarce fledged, I straightway am no more;
Much begun, not done, and now, forever, rest.
But God, it hurts to leave all this behind!
Oh 'tis not the cut that hurts as does the thought
How quick, once dead in flesh, I'll die in minds;
Despite both pen and stone, how soon forgot.
But soft weak flesh, and fragile human brain;
Is not your God, to this, a greater gain?

72

The next four poems on birth were written by students of below average intelligence who are at least two years behind in regular schooling and who are presently attending a school whose programs are designed to prepare them for vocational training. They are between twelve and sixteen years of age. The poems were written during a unit on childbirth.

Birth

Male meet Female
Have Intercourse
Egg meet Sperm
Egg turns to Embryo
Embryo turns to Human
Life is born

Birth

Where does it all come from
There's nothing but darkness,
The cells are together
And the fetus is floating
Where does it all go to.

Birth

Birth is caused by both Male and Female to have intercourse
Birth is the cause of overpopulation and inflation
Thanks to the thousands of girls who forgot to take there birth control
  pill we are stuck with thousands of unwanted babies

Kiss Me

Sex to Birth

The lights were out
  We were all alone
We crawled into bed.
  I touched her soft body
  We made sex
A month went by
She told me he kicked
  Our baby
Went to the hospital
  Paced all night
Life was born
  Our baby
I'm a father

74 _____

The following four short poems were written by students described by their teachers as "problem adolescents of below average intelligence or who are underachieving significantly."

Freedom (Age 14)

Freedom is turning
On all the sane people and
Letting the whole world mouth off

Hands (Age 14)

I'm reaching out for you
I feel warmth in the air
I feel you're not far away
Come to me I love you

Horse (Age 15)

all alone

modern needle

seeing things

cops

two hits worth

work

help

busted

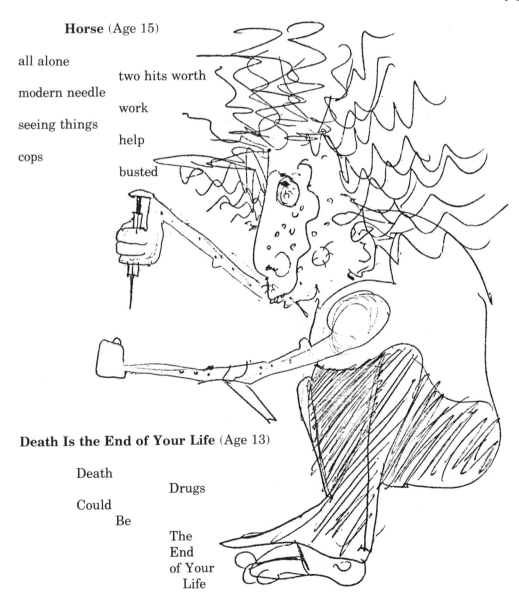

Death Is the End of Your Life (Age 13)

Death

Could
    Be

Drugs

The
End
of Your
Life

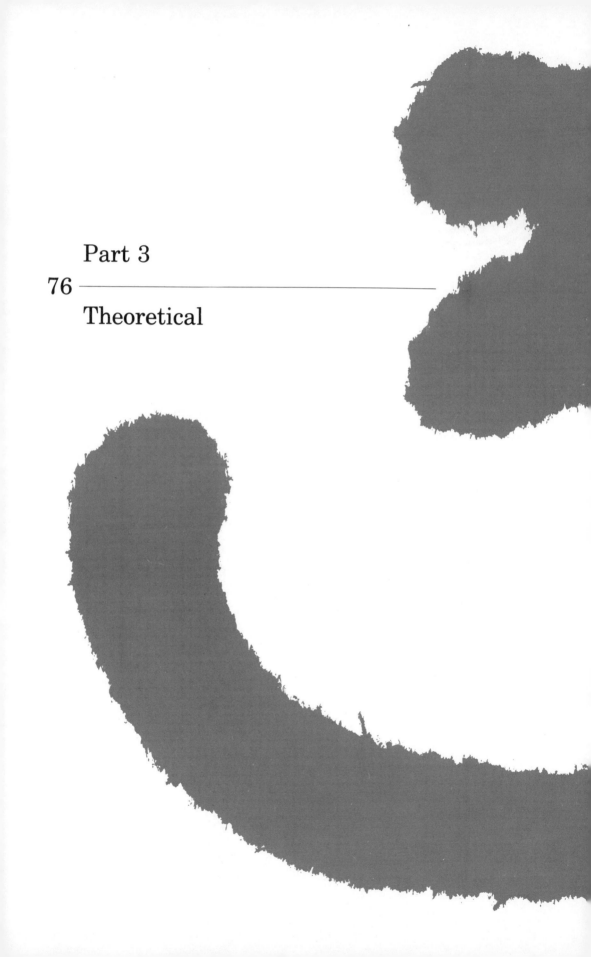

Part 3

76

Theoretical

Chapter 4

**Development, Learning,
and Motivation**

Chapter 5

**Fact and Opinion: Theories of
Adolescent Development**

Chapter 4

Development, Learning, and Motivation

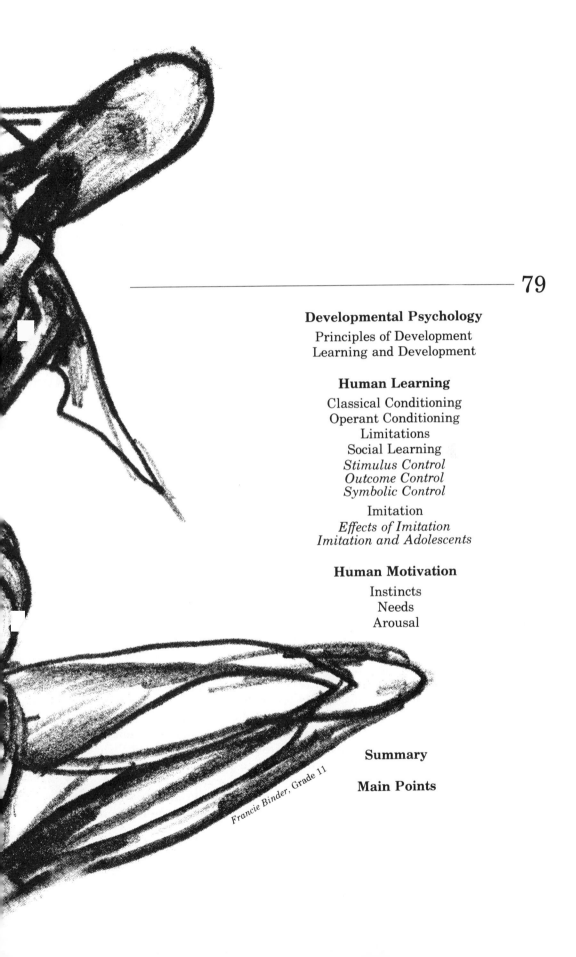

Francie Binder, Grade 11

Throughout history humans have been concerned with increasing their understanding of their environment and with inventing or discovering better ways of adapting to it. They were ingenious and clever and quickly able to note regularities in some of the great cosmic events that they observed. Thus they learned to divide their existence into temporal periods according to the movements of their planet in relation to the other great and less great spheres in the known universe. They invented Time, and, in time, they invented the wheel. There are no wheels in nature; no animal is born with them.

In the early years of their existence, humans were probably much less concerned about understanding their own functioning than with understanding the environment. It would clearly be more important for an isolated group of nomad hunters to understand and to predict the behavior of the animals upon which they preyed for food than it would be for them to understand the behavior of other humans. And from a simple survival point of view, understanding the behavior of animals that were likely to prey upon human animals would be of some considerable importance as well.

Eventually, however, humans mastered most of their environment. They tamed those animals that would be useful if tamed; they eradicated most of the really dangerous ones or drove them into areas of the planet in which they were not particularly interested.

In addition, they discovered better ways of producing and storing food and invented all manner of machines to help do this. Throughout this period the task of physical survival continued to become easier, until human numbers had reached such heights that they were once again in danger of dying from starvation. What humans will do about this problem remains to be seen.

In more recent times humans, having learned most of what they thought they needed to know about their world, began to examine themselves, began to study human behavior in a deliberate and systematic manner. That study is, in effect, psychology. And though a great deal concerning human behavior remains unknown or is known only very imprecisely, there are a number of general principles based on relatively well substantiated findings that are of central importance in any study of psychology. This chapter discusses some of these principles in three major areas of study: development, learning, and motivation. Much of this material serves as background information for more detailed discussions of adolescent psychology in later chapters.

Developmental Psychology

Developmental psychology is concerned with describing and explaining the **adaptation** of humans from birth to adulthood. There are several approaches to the area, but one of the most fruitful has been the approach adopted by such researchers as Jean Piaget (1969, 1952; Piaget and Inhelder, 1941). In effect, Piaget is concerned with questions very similar to those implicit in the work of biologists. Not surprisingly, Piaget's own formal academic training was in biology.

Biologists are concerned with classifying species. That is, they ask what it is that differentiates one animal from another, thereby arriving at a classification of animals according to the complexity of their structures as well as according to the complexity of their functions (behaviors). In addition, they are concerned with discovering the mechanisms that contribute to the adaptation of specific animals. Thus they can occasionally arrive at some reasonable explanation for the fact that some animals have survived and continue to do so easily while others have become extinct.

The same general questions can be applied to a study of human development. In this case they apply to the development of single individuals within a species (termed **ontogenetic development**), as opposed to the development of entire species (termed **phylogenetic development**). Piaget, the biologically oriented developmental psychologist, therefore asks two basic questions about human beings: What is it that allows **children** to adapt as they change from **infants** into adults? How can the behaviors and abilities of children be classified at different stages of development? Answers to these two questions comprise the substance of contemporary developmental psychology. The following principles merely outline that substance.

Principles of Development

1. Development is influenced by both heredity and environment. Whatever it is that a child becomes is a combined function of genetic endowment and interaction with the environment. Although this principle is widely accepted as being valid, one of the oldest controversies in psychology, and one that is by no means completely over, is concerned precisely with the ways in which **heredity** and environment are responsible for the behavioral and psychological characteristics of individuals. This is the ancient **nature-nurture controversy.** At its historical extremes, one camp maintained that nurture is primarily responsible for whatever an individual becomes. This point of view was expressed most strongly by John Watson (1914, 1930) whose famous line "Give me a dozen healthy infants and I shall make of them what I will" has been quoted and paraphrased (as it is here) hundreds of times. Watson firmly believed that the environment was solely responsible for the **attitudes,** interests, personality characteristics, and intelligence of all humans—that whatever we are is solely a function of the environments in which we found ourselves at crucial stages in our development.

One of the strong early advocates of the opposing view, the nature as opposed to nurture position, was Galton (1869). He maintained that most of what we are is a function of our genetic background rather than of our environment, and became a strong advocate of what he termed **eugenics,** the selective breeding of individuals. Because we can breed animals for ferocity, tenderness, **intelligence,** stupidity, physical size, muscle to fat ratio, milk or egg production, and so on, it would seem reasonable that we could also breed people in the same way. Not that there would be any great rush to breed people for milk or egg production. But there was, in fact, some urgency associated with Hitler's attempt to breed his German supermen. Hitler reasoned that if he mated his tallest and strongest soldiers with robust peasant girls, the result would be a truly admirable specimen, well fit to conquer the remainder of the human race. His short-lived experiment suffered from his inability to control the mating activities of his strong soldiers and robust peasant girls.

Alfred Noyes, founder of a type of nineteenth-century hippie commune in Oneida, New York, attempted much the same thing, but with different objectives (Noyes, 1937). His goal was to produce truly intelligent human beings by selecting those of his flock who would mate in order to have children (Holbrook, 1957). His experiment apparently flourished for almost two generations before coming to an abrupt halt when the federal government in the United States began prosecuting **polygamy** among the Mormons. In the process they wiped out Noyes's "free love" society. Some years later Noyes (1937) reported having tested a number of the progeny from his community and having found that they had significantly higher intelligence test scores

Table 4.1 Correlations between intelligence test scores for persons with varying degrees of genetic similarity

Subject	Correlation Coefficient
Identical twins	.90
Fraternal twins	.65
Siblings	.50
Parents and their children	.50
Cousins	.25
Grandparent-grandchild	.15
Unrelated children	.00

than the population average. Given the crudeness of the measures then in use and the uncontrolled nature of the experiment, these results are not accorded a great deal of scientific credence.

Early attempts to resolve the nature-nurture controversy made considerable use of twins (Wingfield, 1928; Newman, Freeman, and Holzinger, 1937). Because **identical twins** are genetically alike, all characteristics that are solely determined by heredity should be identical in such pairs of twins. On the other hand, **fraternal twins** are no more alike genetically than are ordinary siblings (brothers and sisters), but their environments are much more similar than those of most siblings (twins are the same ages at the same time in usually very similar environments). As a result, any greater similarity among twins than among other siblings should be due to the effect of the environment rather than to genetics. Table 4.1 summarizes a number of correlations* for intelligence test scores of twin paris and other individuals (based on data provided by Hunt, 1961, p. 18).

The results are interesting because they provide rather strong evidence for both sides of the question. The correlation is considerably higher for identical twins than it is for fraternal twins largely because they are genetically identical. Lower correlation coefficients as relatedness decreases suggest that heredity is important to intelligence.

At the same time, however, the fact that fraternal twins have higher correlations than siblings, although they are no more alike genetically, can only be explained in terms of the greater similarity of their environments (including prenatal environment). Recently Jensen (1968) reported research that has led to a revival of the controversy. His research led him to the hypothesis (note: not conclusion, but merely hypothesis) that heredity is of more importance in determining intelligence than the environment.

In essence, Jensen summarized most of the important research that relates to intelligence, heredity, and environment; he then reported major findings

* A correlation coefficient is a mathematical expression of relationship between two variables (scores, for example). This type of correlation coefficient ranges from -1.00 to $+1.00$. In Table 4.1, a high correlation coefficient (.90 for example) simply indicates that if one member of a pair of twins has a high score, the corresponding member will also be likely to have a high score. A high negative correlation would indicate the opposite. If one had a high score, then the other would be likely to have a low score. A correlation of .00 simply indicates that there is no systematic relationship among the variables in question.

from his summary in a 123-page article. His most salient conclusion was: "The preponderance of the evidence is, in my opinion, less consistent with a strictly environmental hypothesis than with a genetic hypothesis, which, of course, does not exclude the influence of environment or its interaction with genetic factors" (Jensen, 1969, p. 82). In other words, heredity may be more potent in determining measured intelligence than the environment. The most popular explanation of individual differences among intelligence test scores has traditionally been an environmental one. Consequently the observation that blacks *on the average* do less well than whites on measures of intelligence is more often explained in terms of environmental factors (socioeconomic background, education opportunity, early stimulation, and a host of related variables). Genetic explanations for these differences (such as that hypothesized by Jensen) have sometimes been interpreted as racist because they imply genetic inferiority.

The immediate reaction to Jensen's hypothesis was highly negative. Because his research came at a time of considerable social unrest related to the black-white problem, it inevitably created controversy. Numerous methodological, theoretical, and ethical objections to Jensen's work were published shortly after the appearance of his initial article. (See *Harvard Educational Review*, Reprint Series No. 2, 1969, for eight critical reviews of Jensen's article and for the article itself.) Demonstrations, student protests, and public statements issued by various professional and lay groups denounced Jensen, his work, the implication of his work, or all three. A partial account of this controversy is presented by Jensen (1972).

The relative contributions of heredity and environment to adolescence are reflected in the roles of physiological growth and **culture** in adolescence. Growth is ordinarily defined in terms of such quantitative changes as increase in height and weight, changes in bodily proportions, as well as other predictable physical changes that correspond closely with chronological age. These events are largely dependent upon "biological clocks" (Brown, 1959) — innate growth timetables that all individuals are born with. Biological clocks are somehow related to the age at which teeth first appear, the age at which the deciduous teeth fall out, and, more important for our study, the age at which the growth spurt and other events related to pubescence occur. There is, in fact, a high correlation among the ages at which all these events take place. Early-maturing infants are more likely to be early-maturing adolescents than average- or late-maturing infants. Children who are already tall (for their chronological age) prior to their growth spurt are more likely to be tall as adults (even if they should happen to be late maturers). Hence many of the significant events associated with adolescence are determined by genetic factors.

But adolescence is also a function of culture; and culture is environmental rather than hereditary in the genetic sense. Indeed the nature of adolescence in some primitive cultures is markedly different from that in contemporary Western cultures. Clearly the primary tasks of achieving independence, a sense of identity, and sexual as well as vocational employment are very different in a culture where adolescents are expected to behave as adults (and permitted to do so) once they have reached puberty, compared with a culture that prolongs this period over a long number of years. Indeed, adolescence as we know it is largely a cultural phenomenon that is precipitated by genetically determined changes in individuals at a certain stage in their development.

2. Development takes place at different rates for different parts of the organism. This principle appears to be valid for both physical and psychological development. From a psychological point of view, certain personality characteristics appear to develop at different rates. Bloom (1964), in reviewing the literature on aggression and intelligence, found that each has its own characteristic growth curve. Half of a male's aggressiveness is thought to be established by age three; two-thirds of a person's intellectual capacity has already been developed by the age of six. This should not be interpreted to mean that two-thirds or one-half of some fixed amount of aggression and intelligence are already manifest at these ages. Psychological measurement is not nearly precise enough to measure these qualities in terms of any absolute amount; it must, instead, content itself with relative comparisons. Thus a specific individual's performance on an intelligence test may be compared to the average performance of other individuals, but cannot be expressed in precise quantitative terms. It is, in fact, variation from average performance (*variance* in statistical terminology) that gives an intelligence test score its meaning. Bloom's conclusions regarding individual growth curves in intelligence and aggression are based on his observation that individual variations from the age group mean becomes less pronounced with advancing age, thus implying that a certain proportion of tendency to perform above or below that mean is established relatively early in life.

Differential growth curves are even more striking for physical development. Half of a child's adult height has been reached by the age of two and one-half, although by this time a much smaller fraction of the adult weight will have been reached.

Patterns of differential growth curves continue in adolescence, with various parts of the organism reaching adult size at different times. As has been noted, the head, hands, and feet are the first to reach adult size, followed by arm and leg length, and finally by trunk width (Tanner, 1962). Barring unfortunate accidents, pants will last longer than jackets among adolescent boys, a fact that is not true among adults.

3. Variations in environment have greatest quantitative effect on a characteristic at its period of most rapid change, and least effect on a characteristic at its period of least rapid change (Bloom, 1964, p. VIII). Illustrations of this principle can be found both for intellectual and for physical development. A large number of studies demonstrate that it is possible to increase the intellectual potential and/or the scholastic achievement of groups of children by modifying their environments; this is done by providing them with optimally stimulating environments at crucial stages of their developments. Among the better known of these studies is that reported by Lee (1951). Lee did a study involving comparisons among groups of black children. One group had been born and raised in Philadelphia. A second group had been born in the South and moved to Philadelphia in their fourth grade. The third group had also been born in the South, but did not move to Philadelphia until ninth grade. Subjects were administered intelligence tests in first, fourth, and ninth grades. Results are summarized in Figure 4.1.

Lee's assumption, probably a valid one, was that the intellectual stimulation offered black children in the South at that time was significantly inferior to that available to them in Philadelphia, and that any increases in measured intelligence after they had moved to Philadelphia would then likely be due to increased environmental stimulation. Two aspects of the findings are especially noteworthy. The first is the disparity in test scores between children born and raised in Philadelphia and those who moved there later; the second is the increase in measured intelligence that occurred among the black groups after they had moved to Philadelphia. Especially pertinent here is the observation that those children who moved later in their lives tended to do less well

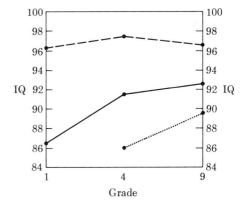

Figure 4.1 Changes in intelligence test scores on measures obtained in first, fourth, and ninth grades for black students born and raised in Philadelphia (dashed line), those born in the South and moving to Philadelphia in fourth grade (solid line), and those who did not move to Philadelphia until ninth grade (dotted line). (Adapted from Lee, *American Sociological Review 1951*, p. 231. Copyright 1951 by The American Sociological Association. Used by permission of the American Sociological Association and the author.)

on these measures than those who had lived in Philadelphia longer. This observation supports the contention that the environment had a greater effect on measured intelligence earlier in life — in short, during that period when intelligence was developing at a more rapid rate.

The effects of such crucial environmental factors as nutrition on the physical development of children also support the notion that these effects will be most pronounced during the period of most rapid growth. Clearly, starving adults is not likely to stunt their growth appreciably since they have already reached maximum growth. Starving children, on the other hand, can have very different results. The observation that each succeeding generation tends to be slightly taller than the preceding generation, or that menarche has been occurring earlier, have been attributed largely to nutrition. Indeed, in noting these facts, Tanner (1962) has observed that the single factor that correlates most highly with age of **maturation** appears to be socioeconomic. Children from low socioeconomic backgrounds tend to mature later than those from more privileged backgrounds. Their ultimate heights and weights also tend to be lower. It is very likely that nutrition is a significant factor in determining these events.

Other factors that can significantly affect rate of maturation in adolescents (as well as in children) include illness and various other forms of stress. Landauer and Whiting (1964) compared eventual adult height in five societies where children were systematically inoculated prior to the age of two, with average adult height in societies where children were not inoculated before two. In the first five societies, the average adult male height was 66.8 inches compared with 63 inches in the other societies. Another study within the United States compared some Ohio and California boys who were inoculated early with some who weren't; this study yielded similar results (Landauer and Whiting, 1964).

4. Development follows an orderly sequence. The biological clocks to which we referred earlier do indeed seem to be geared toward orderly sequential development. While it is true that there is a considerable amount of variation among individuals with respect to the ages at which certain developmental phenomena occur, the sequence itself appears to be relatively invariant. Again, this is true both for physical and intellectual development. Researchers have observed, for example, that there is a relatively fixed progression of sequential abilities underlying the acquisition of all sorts of simple motor abilities. Infants do not learn to walk until they have learned to sit, to stand, and to creep (Shirley, 1933).

Intellectual development can also be described in terms of a relatively fixed sequence of stages. A number of developmental theories, most notably Piaget's, deal largely with a description of these stages. Piaget informs us that children initially understand their world only in terms of their actual sensation of it, and in terms of those concrete acts they can perform with respect to real objects and people. Thus objects are present only when they can be seen, touched, heard, felt, tasted, or smelled; and their meanings are implicit in these behaviors. Milk is to drink; a ball is to roll; a bed is to sleep. Piaget labels this first stage as the period of **sensorimotor** development. From there children progress to a more symbolic though often illogical understanding of the objective world – the period of **preoperational** thought. This stage lasts from approximately two to seven years of age. It is followed by the period of **concrete operations** (till approximately age eleven or twelve) and finally by the period of **formal operations.** (Each of these stages is described in some detail in Chapter 6.) The important point is, again, that although the ages at which the abilities and characteristics that define each of these major stages varies from one child to another, the sequence in which they appear seems to be invariant.

Within each of the major stages, Piaget describes a wide variety of substages for specific abilities and understandings (i.e., the development of notions of time, space, causality, morality, play behavior, and so on). In general, substages within each of these areas also exhibit the same sequential progression that is characteristic of all development.

5. Development is continuous rather than discrete. Although development can be described in terms of separate, sequential stages in physical, motor, and intellectual development, the stages form a relatively smooth, continuous progression. There are few obvious breaks between stages, although there are occasional spurts or slow downs. There is very little genital development throughout most of childhood, for example; but adolescence is heralded by a remarkable acceleration of development in this area. However, the developmental phenomena are sufficiently gradual that they often go unnoticed by parents.

6. There is a great deal of variability among individuals. The sheer obviousness of this principle makes it no less important. There is often a tendency when discussing human behavior in general to assume unthinkingly that the rules, principles, conclusions, and **norms** derived from the study of a group of individuals must also apply to each individual in the group. Suspecting, for example, that the average age for menarche in this country is eleven and one-half, many mothers would be inclined to think that their daughter is slow if she has not yet experienced menarche by the age of thirteen. Yet, among the group who furnished the data leading to the average of eleven and one-half, perhaps only a few experienced menarche at exactly eleven and one-half. Some would be much younger, others much older. An average, or a norm, is, in fact, an indication of normal expected developments. On the other hand, not being at the average is not, by any means, a sure indication that the individual in question is abnormal in the sense that the term is used by most grandmothers.

In any study of psychology, it is extremely important to keep in mind that there is, in fact, no average, normal human being; that is, there is no single individual who is exactly average in all respects. As stated above, there is a great deal of variability among individuals.

7. Any breaks in the continuity of development will generally be due to environmental factors. Given an adequate environment, development will ordinarily take place in a relatively predictable way. Infants will grow physically as do most other children in the culture: they will learn to creep before they walk; by the age of two they will have a rough working knowledge of the language that surrounds them; and toward the end of childhood they will experience rapid physical changes culminating in sexual maturity and adult physical size and proportion. Under certain conditions, however, either physical, motor, or intellectual development may be impeded. This is most obvious in cases of severe childhood diseases or as a result of certain maternal diseases while the child is still in embryo. Various forms of mental retardation can result from the mother having rubella (German measles), syphilis, gonorrhea, or poliomyelitis. Blindness or deafness can also result from these maternal conditions. Similarly a thyroid malfunction in the mother can lead to **cretinism,** and other endocrine imbalances may result in mongolism.

In much the same way, diet, drugs, and illness can affect children directly

90

at various stages of their development—may serve to stunt both physical and intellectual growth. And, according to a principle already stated, the effects of these conditions will be most pronounced during the period of most rapid growth.

8. Correlation and not compensation is the rule in development. It has often been assumed by grandmothers that nature makes up for deficiencies in some areas by compensating for them in others. Thus children who develop with frail and uncoordinated bodies, will most likely be given exceptional minds to make up for it. Only rarely will nature give the same individual both a superior body and a superior mind.

There is yet another form of compensation in which a lot of grandmothers believe. Children who are short until they begin the adolescent growth spurt will be blessed or otherwise favored so that in the end they will reach a height more in keeping with their age and sex. Similarly, those who are already tall at the beginning of the spurt will grow more slowly and for a shorter period of time. Mother Nature compensates in other ways. People who might otherwise be miserable because they are overly obese are given remarkably sunny dispositions, charm, a sense of humor, and various other subtle gifts that will enable them to make many friends. People who are stupid are created strong and athletic. And vice versa?

In reality, Mother Nature is probably not responsible for the events described above. And even if she is, they are not quite as described. Striking incidents of compensation that can be gleaned from personal experience or anecdotal evidence are probably most often the result of considerable, directed effort on the part of the individuals concerned. Because all individuals have a need for acceptance by others and by themselves, as well as a variety of other needs that are discussed later in this chapter, it follows that if the needs cannot be met in one area, effort will be directed toward having them met in another. Children who are unsuited for the competitive aggressive sports of their peers because they are significantly smaller may naturally become more interested in intellectual or other matters. The point is that the compensation is not a natural (a la Mother Nature) phenomenon, but results instead from the individual's activities motivated by whatever needs are predominant at the time.

That correlation rather than compensation is the rule is supported by evidence from a number of studies of gifted children. Most well known are studies by Terman and Oden (1947), who found that children gifted in one area were more likely to be gifted in all other areas than were children not gifted in one area. In other words, intelligent people tend to be better athletes than those who are less intelligent (or is it vice versa, again?) Similarly, children who are taller than average prior to the growth spurt will probably be taller than average following the spurt. Clearly, however, there are many exceptions to this general observation, exceptions that illustrate once again that there is a great deal of variability among individuals.

9. Development usually proceeds at the rate at which it started. Children who learn to walk and talk at an early age are likely to be advanced in all areas of development throughout their childhood. This does not mean, of course, that they will be more intelligent and better developed physically than children who mature more slowly. Although their biological clocks may be faster, they are not necessarily programmed for more superior development. As pointed out earlier, children who grow teeth at an earlier than average age will probably begin the growth spurt at an earlier age as well. Children who do not get six-year-old molars until the age of eight will probably not begin the growth spurt until most of their peers are well into theirs (Tanner, 1972). In the end, however, their relative heights and weights will be a function of their genetic backgrounds and their environments (nutrition among other factors), rather than of the rate at which they matured.

Learning and Development

Although a great deal of effort has been devoted to the attempt to understand the processes by which individuals progress from conception to adulthood, there is much that remains unknown. It is considerably easier to describe the characteristic abilities and inabilities of children at various stages in their development and to arrive at some understanding of normal behavior at each of these stages than it is to explain what it is that enables infants to progress in their attempts to make sense out of the physical environment. Very few other species on this planet have a period of immaturity that is as long as the humans'; no other species has an environment as artificially com-

92

plex. Young baboons have merely to learn about the natural environment; about substances that are edible and those that are not; about animals that are predators and those that are not; about locations that are safe and those that are not; and about those social behaviors that are appropriate and those that are not. Young human infants must also learn about the edible, the poisonous; the enemy, the friend; the safe place and the unsafe; and the behaviors that are appropriate to their social position. True, learning some of these things is probably less crucial for humans than for baboons. There is little danger that little humans will eat a poisonous **toadstool** simply because toadstools don't grow well in most cribs; there is also little danger of attack by a leopard or a cheetah since most suburbs have few of these. Their chances of physical survival are probably higher than those of most young baboons.

But human infants must learn much more than all this. They must learn the incredibly complex patterns of vocal utterances by which humans symbolize their concrete and abstract environments and by which they communicate at a level far beyond that reached by even the most intelligent of nonhuman earth creatures.* And the incredible rapidity and expertness with which human infants master this **language** remains largely unexplained.

In addition, before becoming adults children will have developed a large number of abstract and complex notions regarding space, time, causality, movement, and so on. They will have learned an elaborate set of implicit rules governing social behavior; will have mastered a considerable body of knowledge, some of which is useful for commerce in the adult world and some of which is somewhat less than useful; and will have progressed some distance toward an understanding of the most complex of all systems, the human **nervous system.** That is, they will know something about their own behavior, thoughts, and feelings; and they will know something about behaving, thinking, and feeling as it occurs in other humans. We have little reason to suppose that baboons, or any other animal, have as much to learn.

What adolescents are is a function of many factors, including the particular culture, sex, social climate of the time, and what each has become as a com-

---

* There is a possibility, though remote, that the dolphin may have an intellectual and verbal environment that approaches the human's (at some distance, nevertheless). The dolphin is one of the few animals whose brain-to-body weight ratio equals (actually slightly surpasses) a human's, and the complexity of the sounds emitted have led some to speculate that they are a form of language.

bined function of heredity and environment throughout the early years. Hence the importance of understanding some of the principles of human development in order to arrive at a more thorough understanding of adolescence. Hence, also, the importance of understanding some principles of human learning, principles that are treated in the following section.

Human Learning

Learning is frequently defined by psychologists as "the modification of behavior as a function of experience." (Lefrancois, 1972). A simpler definition, most frequently found in ordinary dictionaries, is that learning involves the acquisition of information. This is often the case, but there are a number of situations in which individuals *learn* without acquiring any new information. This is obvious in the development of certain motor skills where practice rather than information leads to gradual modifications in behavior. In addition, **affective** learning (learning involving **emotional** behavior) does not necessarily involve the acquisition of information as it is ordinarily defined.

Learning, defined as a behavior change due to experience, includes all affective, motor, and **cognitive** (intellectual) changes that do not result from other causes. For example, behavior can change as a result of fatigue, drugs, or maturation; but these changes are of a transient nature, result from genetic forces, or are induced artificially; they are not considered to involve learning.

Among the earliest preoccupations in psychology was the quest to explain the processes by which individuals learn. Classical, historical explanations centered around the formation of bonds between stimuli (conditions that lead to behavior) and responses, or between pairs of **stimuli** or **responses.** Early learning theorists, particularly Watson (1913, 1930), Guthrie (1952), Thorndike (1932, 1935), and Skinner (1951, 1953), used the term **conditioning** for this learning phenomenon; they attempted valiantly to explain all human learning using as simple a model as was logically possible. None of the models advanced (for example, **classical conditioning, instrumental conditioning, operant conditioning**) was entirely adequate to explain all facets of human learning; nor was any entirely inaccurate. The conditioning models outlined in the following pages of this section are an attempt to synthesize the contribu-

Figure 4.2 Classical conditioning. In 1. the UCS (food) elicits the UCR (salivation) in a dog, but in 2. a buzzer (CS) elicits only a general orienting reaction (OR). In 3. the UCS and the CS are paired (presented simultaneously) a number of times. The dog responds by salivating as a result of the UCS. In 4. the UCS and the CS have been paired sufficiently often that the CS (buzzer) alone now elicits the CR (salivation).

tion of these early theorists together with those of more recent researchers in order to arrive at a relatively clear picture of what is known or suspected about human learning. Bear in mind that a clear picture of what is known or suspected is not necessarily a clear picture of the beast itself.

Classical Conditioning

Pavlov, a Russian physiologist, was embarked on a series of experiments involving dogs in the late nineteenth century. In the course of these experiments, he noticed that some of the older, more experienced dogs behaved somewhat differently from the newer dogs. Whenever their keeper appeared, they began to **salivate,** apparently in anticipation of being fed. Because this behavior was not apparent in the newer dogs, Pavlov concluded that it must have been learned as a function of their experiences in the laboratory. His explanation of this learning, together with the experiments that he subsequently used to clarify the explanation, have now become basic in a study of human learning.

Pavlov's explanation, later elaborated by Watson (1930), is known as the model of classical conditioning. Very simply it says: A stimulus that readily and reliably elicits a response is paired (presented simultaneously or nearly simultaneously) with another stimulus that does not elicit the same response. If this is repeated often enough, the second stimulus will eventually come to elicit the response originally associated only with the first stimulus. At that point there will have been a change in behavior that can be interpreted as an example of learning. Consider, for example, Pavlov's dogs. Initially the dogs would not salivate at the sight of their keeper, but they would when presented with food. Because the keeper and the food are always presented together, eventually the sight of the keeper, even in the absence of food, is sufficient to elicit the response of salivation.

In his classical experiments Pavlov repeatedly demonstrated this phenomenon by pairing the presentation of food (actually the injection of food powder directly into the dog's mouth) with some neutral stimulus such as a bell or buzzer. After a number of pairings the bell or buzzer alone would elicit salivation. In psychological terminology, the dog was conditioned to salivate in response to a tone.

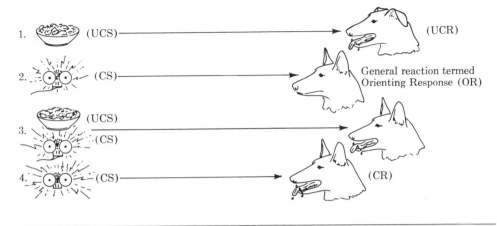

The psychological jargon employed in the model of classical conditioning is as follows:

The stimulus that readily and reliably elicits a response prior to any actual learning is termed an **unconditioned stimulus** (UCS).

A response that occurs in response to an unconditioned stimulus is referred to as an **unconditioned response** (UCR).

The initially neutral stimulus is termed a **conditioned** or **conditioning stimulus** (CS).

A response that initially occurs in response to a conditioned stimulus is termed an **orienting response** (OR).

The response that is eventually elicited by the conditioned stimulus is termed a **conditioned response** (CR).

The model of classical conditioning is presented graphically in Figure 4.2, with reference to the Pavlov experiments.

Watson demonstrated the applicability of this model for explaining the acquisition of simple emotional reactions in humans. In one experiment (Jones, 1924) he employed a young boy, Little Albert, and a white rat or, in some variations, a white rabbit. Little Albert initially loved the rat, but came to fear it desperately as a result of classical conditioning. Over a number of trials, Watson presented Little Albert with the rat, but at the same time made a loud noise. The noise served as an unconditioned stimulus bringing about fear reactions (an unconditioned response) in Little Albert. Just as Pavlov's dogs had salivated, the rat alone was sufficient to bring about intense fear reactions in Little Albert after the rat and the loud noise had been paired often enough.

This experiment and others like it can be generalized to a wide variety of situations in life where individuals react emotionally for no apparent reason. Young children who dislike school may do so because of associations that have been formed between stimuli present in the school and other stimuli that have been linked with negative emotions in the past. The teacher's physical appearance may be similar to that of other individuals with whom a child has had bad experiences (a doctor, for example); the smell of chalkdust may be reminiscent of odors in a barn where a child was stepped on by a horse; the windows may resemble those in a grandmother's basement where a child was sent for punishment. At the same time, however, positive emotions can also be classically conditioned. Children who like school may do so at least

96

in part because of associations that have been formed between other pleasant situations and school related stimuli.

It is important to bear in mind that what is learned can also be unlearned, that life is a continuous process of learning. Hence reactions to particular situations are not irrevocably fixed by prior situations where classical conditioning took place. Jones illustrated this dramatically by curing a boy, Peter, of his fear of rats (Jones, 1924), a fear that had been conditioned as in Little Albert's case. The cure was also effected through classical conditioning. In this case the rat, which had now become a stimulus that reliably elicited a fear reaction, was paired with another stimulus that equally reliably elicited positive emotions. Peter was fed a dish of ice cream while the rat was brought to where he could see it at a distance. Over successive trials, the rat was brought closer, but always kept far enough away that the boy would not be frightened. Eventually, Peter could happily eat ice cream with the rat right next to him. Peter was no longer afraid of rats.

There is much evidence to suggest that the behavior of adolescents and adults is also under the influence of classical conditioning, a learning process that generally occurs unconsciously. But human behavior is too complex to be easily explained by a model as simple as this. Therefore, while classical conditioning is a useful model for some types of simple learning, it is not sufficient to explain more complex forms of human behavior. Attempts by early **behavioristic theorists** (so-called because they were concerned only with the observable aspects of behavior) to explain all human behavior employing models of classical conditioning or variations thereof have not been successful. Other theories have had to be introduced.

Operant Conditioning

One such model was developed by B. F. Skinner (1938, 1951, 1953, 1961). It states, in effect, that behavior is controlled by its outcome. If the outcome of a response is pleasant, the behavior will tend to be repeated under similar circumstances; if it is not pleasant, the behavior will tend to be avoided.

The model of operant conditioning can be illustrated most easily by reference to some of Skinner's early experiments with rats. In a typical experiment,

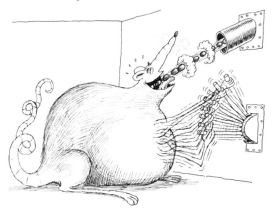

a hungry rat would be placed in a cage (called a **Skinner box**) where it would be fed for performing certain behaviors. Initially the rat would not know specifically what behaviors were required of it; or, indeed, that any behavior was required of it. But it would naturally emit a wide range of responses while in the Skinner box. These responses are labeled operants as opposed to respondents. A **respondent** is a response elicited by an obvious stimulus. An **operant** is a response that is simply emitted by the organism rather than elicited by the environment.

In the most often replicated experiments, the rat would be required to depress a lever. This would activate a food-releasing mechanism, resulting in a food pellet dropping into a tray where the rat could get to it. Over a period of time the bar-pressing behavior would become associated with food, and the rat would unhesitatingly depress the lever whenever it was placed in the Skinner box. At this point learning had taken place. Unlike classical conditioning, however, the learning does not involve the formation of an association between two stimuli, but rather the formation of an association between a behavior and its outcome.

In the course of a large number of experiments, Skinner discovered that the nature, frequency, and strength of a specific response could be controlled in a highly predictable way by manipulating the outcome. This is termed **reinforcement,** which is defined as a condition that increases the probability of response recurring. Reinforcement can be given to an animal—human or subhuman—in a variety of ways, referred to as **schedules.** In a **continuous schedule** of reinforcement, every correct response is reinforced. In this case, the rat is fed every time it depresses the lever. In **intermittent schedules of reinforcement,** the rat's bar-pressing behavior leads to reinforcement only part of the time. Intermittent schedules can be based on time intervals (called **interval schedules**) or on a proportion of responses (called **ratio schedules**). For example, a rat might receive a food pellet once every two minutes (interval schedule) or once for every five correct responses (ratio schedule). Both interval and ratio schedules of reinforcement can be **fixed** or **variable.** That is, the reinforcement can occur at fixed intervals of time or after a fixed number of trials; or it can occur **randomly** during time intervals or series of correct responses. In each case the animal's typical behavior will be different in a predictable way. For example, under a continuous reinforcement schedule

Figure 4.3 An approximate representation of bar-pressing behavior under two different schedules of reinforcement with reinforcement occurring at Z.

the animal will tend to respond at a relatively high, uniform rate initially until it is satiated (no longer hungry); then its responses will decline abruptly in frequency. Following withdrawal of reinforcement, **extinction** (ceasing of behavior) will occur rapidly and easily (see Figure 4.3).

Under intermittent schedules of reinforcement, extinction will take a significantly longer period of time. Patterns of responses will also vary, depending on the type of schedule employed. Under variable schedules, where the animal is unable to predict when the next reinforcement will occur, responses will tend to be maintained at a high rate. Under fixed schedules, particularly fixed interval schedules, behavior will increase and decrease in frequency in a systematic way. If, for example, a rat is being reinforced once every two minutes following a correct response, it will eventually cease to respond entirely following a reinforcement and will begin to depress the bar again, in a rather frantic fashion, immediately prior to the next two-minute mark.

There is considerable evidence that a great deal of human behavior also comes under the control of reinforcement (or its absence). Indeed, it appears axiomatic that people behave in order to achieve desirable outcomes and to avoid undesirable outcomes. This fundamental principle of human behavior, known as the pain-pleasure principle (also known as the **hedonistic principle**) is discussed in more detail in the following section on human motivation. It is of crucial importance to an understanding of adolescent behavior.

In order to understand the implications of operant theory for human behavior, it is necessary to understand what it is that is reinforcing for people. Food, for example, is reinforcing both for animals and for humans because it satisfies a fundamental biological need — as do drink, physical comfort, and sex. But human existence goes far beyond the satisfaction of these unlearned **needs** — it includes as well a host of what are termed psychological needs: the need to be loved, to be accepted, to accomplish something worthwhile, and so on. A great deal of human behavior can therefore be interpreted, explained, and even predicted in terms of the extent to which it relates to the satisfaction of psychological needs. This is no less true in a study of adolescent behavior than it is in any other area of psychology. In fact, during adolescence, there is a fundamental change in the individual's needs. Consequently much of the behavior that is interpreted as being typically adolescent can be understood in terms of adolescent needs.

High | | | | | |
Rate of Responding

Low

Z Z Z

Fixed
Interval

High
Rate of Responding

Low

Z ZZ Z Z Z

Random
Ratio

Limitations

There is a great deal of human learning that does not appear to involve anything as simple as observable stimuli or clearly defined reinforcement. Furthermore, certain situations that appear to be reinforcing for one individual can be punishment for others. To say that some individuals drive cars at high speeds because they find doing so reinforcing whereas others drive very slowly because they do not find speed reinforcing, does not reveal a great deal about human learning and motivation. At best, the explanation is rather tautological: reinforcement is defined as that which increases the probability of a response recurring. In fact, however, in most situations it is impossible to predict beforehand whether a particular outcome will have a reinforcing effect or not. A reinforcer increases the probability of a certain behavior. How do we know it is reinforcement? Because it increases the probability of a response occurring? Why does it do so? Because it is a reinforcement? How do we know it is reinforcement? Because . . . That, in short, is what is meant by a tautological definition. And this is, in fact, one of the most serious limitations of operant theory as a tool for understanding and explaining human behavior. True, it is sometimes possible to predict how individuals will behave in certain situations, given knowledge of the outcome and of the individuals. Money is a powerful reinforcer. Hence one can predict that most individuals will do a wide variety of things for money. But there are certain things that some won't do and others will. Psychologists' predictions are general. Perhaps they apply most of the time, but the predictions are forever plagued by the individual exception.

Other attempts to explain human learning have moved away from the behavioristic positions (concern with objective, measurable events such as stimuli and responses) toward the **neo-behavioristic** and cognitive positions. The neo-behavioristic positions are concerned with unobserved events that mediate between stimuli and responses—in short, with mediating events. The link between a stimulus and its corresponding response is rarely simple and immediate. Only in the case of unlearned reflex activity does the response occur immediately with little need or opportunity for rational activity. For example, if I hold a candle to your finger while you are blindfolded, you will withdraw your hand before you realize what has happened. If, however, I give you the verbal instruction, "In approximately two minutes, I want you

to close your eyes and count to ten before you open them again," the response is anything but immediate and unmediated. Instead it is deliberately delayed. That is, there is presumably some intellectual activity that intervenes between the presentation of the stimulus and the appearance of the response. This activity, which takes up a great deal of an individual's waking time, is essentially ignored by the simple conditioning theories. The neo-behavioristic theories, on the other hand, attempt to explain and describe it in terms of hypothetical constructs—that is, in terms of mechanisms that could explain intellectual activities. Most of this theorizing, even where it attempts to involve what is known about neurological activity in humans, remains at the speculative, hypothetical level.

Some attempts to explain "higher learning" have taken the form of **cognitive** theories—theories that are concerned primarily with understanding, knowing, perceiving, decision-making, and related topics. Typically, such theories are minimally concerned with stimuli and responses, but more concerned with the processes by which individuals come to organize their knowledge of the world and their strategies for dealing effectively with it. Prime examples of cognitive learning theories are those of Bruner (1957(a), 1957(b), 1968) and Ausubel (1963, 1968). Classical examples of neo-behavioristic theories are those of Osgood (1957) and Hebb (1949, 1966). For a detailed treatment of them, see Lefrancois (1975).

Social Learning

There have been numerous attempts to integrate various learning theories in order to arrive at a clearer understanding of how people learn. These integrations have frequently taken the form of hierarchical models where simple stimulus response explanations are employed at the lowest level of the hierarchy, and progressively more complex explanations are resorted to at higher levels (for example, Gagne, 1965, 1970; Melton, 1964).

Notable among recent integrations of learning theories is that advanced by Bandura (1969) and Bandura and Walters (1963). Although the theory discussed by these psychologists is primarily concerned with an explanation of **social learning** by reference to the effects of **imitation** (sometimes called

observational learning), Bandura (1969) describes a number of *behavior control systems* that are substantially similar to some of the fundamentals of conditioning theory.

Stimulus Control There are a great number of human behaviors that appear to be under direct control of external stimulus events. Such **reflexive** acts as sneezing, flinching, and blinking are clearly under the control of external stimuli. In addition, a great many other human behaviors that are not originally under external stimulus control become controlled as a function of conditioning. Little Albert's reaction to the white rat following conditioning is a case in point.

Outcome Control A second, large class of human behaviors are under the control of their outcomes rather than under direct stimulus control. Such behaviors would include the host of responses that are acquired through operant conditioning. Thus, if it is true that people work in order to achieve fame, fortune, and friendship, it can be said that these outcomes do, to some extent, control their behavior.

Symbolic Control Perhaps even more important for human behavior is a consideration of those situations where the behavior is controlled neither by external stimuli nor by its outcomes. Such behaviors, according to Bandura (1969), may be under symbolic control in one of several ways. Behavior may be directed by the verbalization of intended behavior or of behavior's outcomes. In addition, it may be directed by imagined anticipation of its eventual outcomes. Thus a great many behaviors that we engage in daily have no roots in conditioned habit and no immediate reinforcement, but do have the possibility of some long-term gain of one kind of another. It is our ability to foresee these possible gains that accounts for goal and purpose in a great deal of our activities.

Bandura is careful to note that no single aspect of human behavior need be solely under the control of only one of these three systems. Indeed, it is reasonable to suppose that much of our behavior is controlled symbolically, by external stimuli, and by its consequences.

Imitation

Some of the shortcomings of traditional explanations of learning have been noted earlier. Perhaps most obvious is that these explanations are inadequate for many specific behaviors. Bandura and Walters (1963), among others, have postulated that an examination of **imitation** may be useful in our attempt to understand human learning and behavior. Clearly, acquiring the complex skills necessary to driving a car would be difficult at best employing classical conditioning or some combination of **trial and error** with operant conditioning. It is likely that individuals attempting to do the learning would either kill themselves or give up before the appropriate authorities saw fit to grant them driving permits. How much simpler it is to take individuals, place them in the driver's seat, and *tell* them what to do while allowing them to practice the instructions given them. Do they learn through classical conditioning? Probably to some extent because their reactions to changes in the feel of the wheel, car movement, acceleration, deceleration, and cornering will all eventually become unconscious. Do they learn through operant conditioning? Again, probably, because there is clearly some reinforcement associated with being able to drive a car for oneself. In addition there is frequently direct reinforcement provided by the instructors. Perhaps most significant, however, is that they are learning through imitation, even though they may not at the time be directly imitating other drivers.

Imitation is ordinarily defined as the copying of a **model.** It is important to note, however, that a model is not necessarily other individuals engaging in the behavior that is being learned, although it may be. More often in advanced societies such as ours, imitation involves the use of symbolic models: books, written or spoken instructions, television, and so on. Indeed, anything that provides some sort of pattern for behavior may be considered a model. In learning to drive a car, therefore, the instructions provided by the instructors, other written instructions, as well as memories of other drivers whom they have observed may all serve as models. The efficiency and power of models in determining human behavior is considerable.

Effects of Imitation Bandura and Walters (1963) describe three distinct manifestations of learning through imitation. The most obvious situation is

one where the learner acquires some novel behavior as a function of observing a model. This is labeled the **modeling effect.**

In a second situation, the learner suppresses some previously acquired deviant behavior after seeing a model punished for similar behavior. Conversely, a learner may cease to suppress deviant behavior after observing a model being rewarded for that behavior. This **inhibitory or disinhibitory effect** is frequently employed by teachers who, consciously or unconsciously, assume that punishment of the most obvious troublemakers will serve as models to inhibit similar behaviors in other potential wrongdoers. Similarly, the contemporary practice of incarcerating or otherwise punishing lawbreakers is frequently assumed to act as a deterrent for other lawbreakers. Statistics on **recidivism** (the repetition of an offense by a lawbreaker who has already been apprehended and sentenced) indicate that although this type of punishment may serve as a deterrent for other potential lawbreakers, it does not appear to be particularly effective with respect to the individual who was initially punished. In fact, it is extremely difficult to obtain evidence regarding the effectiveness of this form of punishment in inhibiting similar behavior in others.

A third manifestation of the effects of imitation occurs when learners do not imitate the model precisely, but engage instead in some related behavior, frequently intended to lead to the same sort of reinforcement. Thus individuals who are obviously successful in a material sense may serve as models for any number of other individuals who do not engage in the same behaviors, but who engage in other behaviors also intended to lead them to material success. This third type of imitation is labeled the **eliciting effect.**

Imitation and Adolescents Evidence of imitation among adolescents, as among most other age groups, is relatively obvious. Much of the learning engaged in by adolescents is of a social nature; and because imitation now appears to present one of the better explanations of social learning, it is of particular relevance to an examination of adolescent learning. Consider, for example, the fact that many adolescents are highly concerned with not being different from the groups to which they belong or wish to belong (see Chapter 9). It is unlikely that the high similarity among them in terms of dress, speech, and grooming happens accidently. The modeling and eliciting effects are manifest here. Related to this is the observation that some members of juvenile gangs serve as models for others in matters relating to the types of antisocial behavior that are not only tolerated, but expected and reinforced by the gang (Bloch and Niederhoffer, 1958). This is a striking example of the disinhibitory effect; more is said about this in the section on juvenile delinquency in Chapter 11.

Human Motivation

While it is sometimes discouraging to contemplate all that is not known about human behavior, it must always be kept in mind that a great deal is known. The gaps in our knowledge should not blind us to the usefulness of that which we know or suspect with a high degree of certainty. This applies equally to developmental psychology, the psychology of human learning, and **motivation** theory.

Instincts

Early attempts to explain the cause of specific human behaviors were based largely on what was then known or suspected about animal behavior, and that knowledge involved little more than instincts. An **instinct** is an unlearned, complex, species specific, relatively unmodifiable tendency to behave in given ways in specific situations (Thorpe, 1963). The animal world is filled with examples of instincts. Birds nesting in the spring, bears hibernating, geese migrating, salmon going up rivers to spawn; all these behaviors are examples of unlearned behaviors, as are reflexes. Unlike reflexes, however, they are complex behavior patterns that persist over a long period of time. They are species specific in that they are general across an entire species, but do not apply to other species who have their own repertoire of instincts. They are relatively unmodifiable in that the environment has little effect on them. Various experimental attempts to tamper with nesting or migrating instincts have demonstrated that it is extremely difficult to alter these intense compulsions to behave in very specific ways.

Early motivation theorists assumed that because much of the significant

behavior observed in the nonhuman animal world was explainable in terms of instincts, the same should be true of humans (McDougall, 1908; Bernard, 1924). It seemed reasonable to suppose that mothers were possessed of a maternal instinct that would account for their childbearing and rearing behavior; that fathers and mothers mated as a function of a mating instinct; that humans were sociable because of a gregarious instinct and that they were aggressive because of an aggression instinct. However, there was great difficulty in determining which instincts were human because many individuals behave in ways that indicate a lack of one or more of the instincts thought to be peculiarly human. Not all humans mate and rear children; not all are aggressive; not all are gregarious. Demonstrating the unequivocal existence of a species specific instinct among humans—that is, of an instinct that is peculiar to the entire species—has proven impossible. Hence the study of instinct has not been particularly useful in humanity's attempt to understand itself.

There is yet another reason why the study of human instincts is not particularly fruitful. Most definitions advanced for specific instincts are tautological. Why do humans mate? Because they have a mating instinct? How do we know they have a mating instinct? Because they mate. Why do they mate? Because they have a mating instinct? And so on. The existence of the instinct is proven by the existence of a behavior that in turn is dependent upon the existence of an instinct.

Needs

The relationship between needs and behavior is most obvious in the subhuman animal world. Most of the behavior of adult animals is directed toward survival—obtaining food, avoiding enemies, and resting. It is generally assumed that the need for survival is the strongest of all needs, and that such subsidiary needs as the need for food, drink, and physical comfort are clearly related to the need for survival. Hence lower animal behavior can be interpreted directly and simply in terms of these basic needs.

Humans also have a similar need for survival that expresses itself in related needs for food, drink, temperature regulation, and sex. The first three of these needs obviously relate to immediate survival; the last, sex, relates to the need for survival in an evolutionary sense. Not surprisingly, the reproductive drive seems to be extremely powerful in virtually all animal forms.

Humans, however, lead an existence considerably more complex than that of most subhuman animal forms. They engage in a great deal of behavior that doesn't appear to be related to these needs, or that is related to them only very remotely. Indeed, because basic human needs are often met with relatively little effort on their part and with considerably less expenditure of waking hours than is the case among most other animals, a consideration of basic needs in attempting to explain human behavior is of somewhat less value than in the explanation of more primitive behavior. Consider, for example, the host of human behaviors that are directed toward obtaining recognition, accumulating money, gaining prestige, achieving social or political power, maintaining independence, and so on. Most of these behaviors are not strictly essential to the satisfaction of basic unlearned needs. Humans would survive, at least physically, without engaging in them. Why do they then spend so much time in such activities?

In an attempt to answer this question — a question that is of central importance to an understanding of human as opposed to subhuman motivation — psychologists have postulated the existence of a second set of human needs. These are referred to variously as psychological needs, learned needs, or secondary needs. The need for food, drink, sex, regulation of body temperature, are referred to as biological, unlearned, or basic needs.

A large number of complementary and conflicting lists of psychological needs have been postulated by various theorists. Mouly (1968), for example, lists six such needs: affection, belonging, achievement, independence, social recognition, and self-esteem. Raths and Burrell (1963) present a longer list that includes the need to belong, to achieve, to acquire economic security, to avoid fear, to love and be affectionate, to be free from feelings of guilt, to achieve self-respect, and to understand. Murray (1938) lists 28 psychological needs among which are the need to avoid humiliation, the need for autonomy, for deference, for dominance, for exhibition, for achievement, for abasement, and so on.

A perusal of lists of psychological needs such as these leads again to the observation that they are not of any great value in explaining or predicting human behavior. The fundamental logical problem in this area is the inability of researchers to isolate a need and demonstrate its existence without refer-

Figure 4.4 Maslow's hierarchy of human needs. The needs at the lowest level of the hierarchy must be satisfied first. Once these are satisfied, higher-level needs can be tended to.

ence to the specific behavior of given individuals. In other words, it becomes apparent that humans have a need to belong only when one observes a number of individuals behaving in ways that are designed to ensure their belonging. Unfortunately for a study of human behavior, however, it is also apparent that many individuals sometimes behave in ways that would tend to contradict the existence of needs that have been described by theorists. Not all individuals always act as though they needed to belong, to love, to achieve, or to gain or maintain self-respect.

Maslow (1954) has proposed a hierarchical classification of need systems that differs in some significant respects from older conceptualizations of human needs (Figure 4.4) and that has some important implications for understanding human behavior in general and adolescent behavior in particular. These needs are assumed to be hierarchical in the sense that they vary in terms of their importance to the individual and in the extent to which the individual will exert effort in order to satisfy them. At the lowest level of the hierarchy are the physiological needs. These include the basic biological needs described earlier, the need for food, water, and temperature regulation. Because these are the basic survival needs, they will be the needs to which individuals will attend before anything else. Only when these fundamental basic needs are satisfied will individuals be motivated to tend to the second level of needs, the safety needs. Maslow describes these needs as those related to individuals' desires to maintain a safe, predictable, and orderly environment, an environment that they understand and that they can therefore cope with. At a slightly higher level are the love and belongingness needs manifested in attempts to establish relationships of mutual affection and love and to belong to accepting social groups. If these needs, as well as the safety and physiological needs, are satisfied, individuals are then motivated by the self-esteem need system. They behave in such ways as to maintain high opinions of themselves, and in such ways as to have others also hold high opinions of them. It is not difficult to imagine that starving people would feel no great guilt at stealing or cheating in order to obtain food. These same people would, however, be much less likely to steal or cheat if they had no need to do so in order to obtain food. And because to do so under these circumstances would result in a lowering of self-esteem, one could predict with a fairly high degree of certainty that most individuals whose basic needs are well satisfied will neither lie nor cheat.

108

And yet some people who are well fed, socially secure, and well loved do indeed lie and cheat. This, however, does not necessarily invalidate Maslow's contentions. In a society of thieves, clever thieves are more likely to satisfy their love and belongingness needs than less clever thieves, and their self-esteem may rise accordingly. Indeed, clever thieves, in a society of thieves to be sure, may well be among the most self-actualized of individuals. And self-actualization is at the highest level in Maslow's hierarchy. Quite simply, **self-actualization** is the process of becoming what one is suited for, the process of actualizing (making actual or real) one's potential; of developing one's identify; of fulfilling oneself.

In his treatment of youth, Erikson (1968) discusses in considerable detail and length the significance of the identity crisis through which individuals pass before reaching adulthood—not that the crisis is necessarily and irrevocably resolved at that time. During adolescence individuals become most aware of the necessity of solidifying their self—of developing personal identities—and of the difficulties inherent therein. In Maslow's terminology, it is during adolescence that individuals become most conscious of the need for self-actualization. Accordingly, they must not only determine how they can best actualize potential, but they must also determine *who* it is that they are and what the nature of their potential is. The problem is compounded by the fact that there is no real, concrete, immediate, and everlasting solution for these problems. The process of self-actualization is an ongoing one; it is never complete. As numerous humanistic psychologists and philosophers have pointed out, the process of becoming is never completely realized; and the term self-realization is, at best, paradoxical. It is a process that continues till death provides the final solution. But perhaps the crisis can be resolved before death. Perhaps it can even be resolved in adolescence.

Arousal

Arousal is both a physiological and psychological term. As a physiological term it denotes those changes that take place in the human body between deep sleep (or coma) and panic (or hysterical behavior). The former represents the lowest level of arousal short of death; the latter represents the highest level of arousal short of epileptic seizures and other forms of neural convul-

sions. Normally an individual's arousal varies from a resting state characterized by such physiological activity as slow respiration and heart rate,
reduced galvanic skin response (GSR, conductivity of the skin to electricity),
and electrical activity in the brain described as Alpha (or sometimes Delta
or Theta in states of extremely low arousal). With increasing arousal, respiration and heart rate increase, GSR increases, and brain wave activity changes
from Alpha to Beta. **Alpha waves** are typically regular, deeply undulating
waves of relatively slow frequency. **Beta waves** are more irregular, shallower,
and of higher frequency.

Psychologically, arousal denotes a state of relative alertness, ranging,
again, from very low arousal (low alertness) such as is characteristic of individuals who are asleep or almost asleep, to very high arousal (high vigilance)
such as is characteristic of individuals concentrating intensely on difficult
or exciting (arousing) tasks.

A number of motivation theorists (for example, Hebb, 1955; Heron, 1957;
Fowler, 1965; and French, 1957) have built their theories around the notion
that individuals behave in order to maintain arousal at an optimal level. The
relationship between behavior and arousal is expressed in Figure 4.5. With
very low states of arousal, behavior is typically least effective. With increasing
levels of arousal, behavior increases in appropriateness and effectiveness until
an optimal level of arousal is reached. Following this, further increases in
arousal lead to a decrease in the effectiveness and appropriateness of behavior.
Consider, for example, the case of persons just awoken from deep sleep. They
are typically unable to respond correctly to questions of only moderate difficulty. As they become more awake—more alert and vigilant and therefore
more aroused—the appropriateness of their responses increases. If arousal
continues to increase, however, as might be the case of persons awoken by a
fire, they might respond by panicking, in which case behavior might be highly
inappropriate.

Arousal level appears to be a direct function of external sensory stimulation,
where it is not so much the amount as the variety of stimulation that serves to
increase arousal. Thus with continued unchanging sensory stimulation,
arousal level will tend to decrease. The psychological effect of this condition
will be boredom. In order to alleviate boredom, individuals will then seek to
increase their arousal. Or perhaps, in order to increase arousal, individuals
will seek to alleviate boredom. In any case, it can be predicted that when

Figure 4.5 The relationship of level of arousal to effective behavior. With increasing arousal, behavior becomes more appropriate until an optimal level is reached. Beyond this point, further increases in arousal result in decreased effectiveness.

arousal levels are too low, people will engage in activity designed to raise arousal; they will seek out stimulation. This stimulation can be external or internal. That is, not only does external stimulation serve to increase arousal, but so does internal stimulation. One of the great benefits of daydreaming is simply that it serves to increase arousal level.

Similarly, if arousal level is too high, people will engage in those behaviors that they expect will serve to lower arousal. Thus individuals in a situation that might lead to panic will either attempt to change the situation or to escape from it. Such activities as are involved in risk taking, problem solving, and various intellectual pursuits (termed epistemic curiosity by Berlyne [1966]) also serve to increase arousal level. Solving a difficult problem or living through mild risk (skydiving; ski jumping; tightrope walking) may serve to reduce arousal and, according to some motivation theorists (Berlyne, 1966), result in a pleasing or reinforcing state of affairs.

Summary

This chapter began with a brief discussion of humanity's early beginnings, noting, in particular, that it was not until humans had mastered the essentials of physical survival that they began a systematic study of themselves. This study, psychology, dates back a hundred years with most theories and discoveries being considerably younger than that. The chapter then moved to a presentation of basic background information in three of psychology's most important areas: development, learning, and motivation. Principles relevant to an understanding of each of these areas were detailed in the remainder of the chapter. Care was taken to point out that psychology does not, in fact, know all that there is to know about humans. Much is known, but much remains to be discovered.

Main Points

1. Developmental psychology attempts to describe and explain the processes by which infants change into children, into adolescents, and finally into adults — those that do.

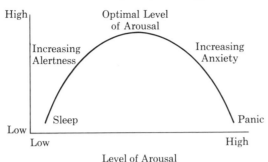

Development, Learning, and Motivation

2. Although a great deal has been written about human development, it is possible to summarize what is known or suspected in the form of a number of principles. These are summarized in points 3 to 11 below.

3. Development is influenced both by heredity and by environment. Studies of twins have frequently been used in attempts to prove the importance of one or the other of these factors. It has now become relatively clear that the extent to which each contributes to specific facets of development is not known and may never be known. Nor is there any assurance that the effects of each are the same for every individual.

4. Different parts of the organism develop at different rates. It appears, for example, that growth curves for almost all areas of development are not linear. In other words, increments are not uniform over all periods of development. This is especially evident in areas of physical growth where it can easily be shown that height increases much more rapidly initially than it does later and that 50 percent of adult height is reached considerably before 50 percent of adult weight is reached. This principle also applies to development in other less easily measured areas such as in the development of personality characteristics.

5. Changes in childhood environment have a more pronounced effect on development if they occur during periods of rapid growth. For example, changes in nutrition have the greatest effect during periods of most rapid physical growth. The same is assumed to be true for social and emotional development.

6. Most researchers in the area of child development premise their work on the assumption that development follows some sort of orderly sequence. Accordingly, they view their task as consisting primarily of discovering that orderly sequence and identifying the factors that are responsible for it.

7. Despite the postulation of various stages in attempts to describe development, it is generally recognized that the entire process is continuous rather than discrete. That is, there are no clear breaks in the continuity of development. Although development may occasionally slow down in various areas or accelerate in others (as is notably true during the early adolescent growth spurt), it is true that changes are continuous.

8. It might appear platitudinous to make a point of the fact that there is a great deal of variability among individuals. It is, but there is. It is not altogether uncommon for academicians to overlook this fact in their search for simple explanations for their observations. For us it would be considerably simpler if there weren't quite so much variability among humans.

9. The environment rather than genetic factors will usually account for any observed breaks in the continuity of development whether they involve physical or psychological development.

10. It is not generally true that individuals who are poorly endowed in one or more areas tend to be exceptionally endowed in others. The poor scholar is less likely to be a good athlete than is the good scholar.

11. Development, if it begins rapidly, generally continues at the same rate. The converse is also true. In other words, infants who develop more rapidly than their peers do not usually stop somewhere along the way and wait for others to catch up. They stay ahead.

12. Learning is usually defined as changes in behavior that result from experience. Among the earliest and simplest explanations of human learning were those based on the principles of conditioning.

13. Classical conditioning, also referred to as learning through stimulus substitution, involves the acquisition of a response as a function of repeated associations between responses, stimuli, or stimuli and responses. Pavlov's work with salivating dogs is most often cited as an example of classical conditioning.

14. Operant conditioning explanations of learning are based on a consideration of the effects of the outcomes of behavior on learning. An operant is a response that is emitted by an organism rather than one that is elicited by a stimulus. If that response is followed by reinforcement, it will tend to be repeated again under similar circumstances. This change in behavior is defined as operant conditioning.

15. Reinforcement employed in operant conditioning may be administered in a variety of ways referred to as schedules. These appear to be important not only in determining whether or not learning will take place, but also how rapidly it will occur and how durable it will be once it has occurred. In addition, responses that have been learned through operant conditioning tend to be regulated by the expectations that the organism appears to have concerning reinforcement, not that a true behaviorist would employ the term *expectations*.

16. Explanations of human learning based solely on models of conditioning are inadequate to explain a great deal of human behavior. Alternative explanations rely on hypothetical mediating events and on such other cognitive structures as they have seen fit to invent. In addition, social learning theory premised on a consideration of the effects of imitation is of particular relevance to an understanding of adolescent behavior.

17. Motivation theory attempts to explain why humans behave as they do.

18. Instincts have generally been discarded as useful explanations for human behavior.

19. It appears correct that some human behavior is governed by such basic unlearned, biological needs as the need for food, for air, for water, and for temperature regulation — in other words, by the need to survive.

20. A large number of significant human behaviors are not directly affected by these needs, but appear instead to be under the influence of other needs sometimes called learned or secondary needs. These more psychological needs (as opposed to biological needs) include the need for affection, for belonging, for self-esteem, and so on.

21. Maslow has posited the existence of a hierarchy of human needs. At the lowest level are the biological needs; at the highest is the need for self-actualization. The primary assumption is that higher-level needs will not be attended to until lower-level needs are satisfied.

22. Some motivation theories are based on the notion that humans behave in order to maintain an optimal level of arousal where arousal is defined in terms of alertness or attentiveness. It can be measured through physiological changes that occur as a person becomes more or less alert. These changes appear to be correlated with the effectiveness of behavior.

23. Not everything is known about human development, learning, and motivation. Nor are we completely ignorant. But then, neither is a reasonably intelligent grandmother.

Chapter 5

Fact and Opinion:
Theories of Adolescent Development

Sheelagh Powrie, Grade 11

116

I stopped by to see Sam on the way to my office tonight. He didn't really expect me, considering the weather. Today was one of those days when I start thinking of going to California—a gray, blustery, snow-filled day; not the fluffy, 20° above flakes of romantic literature, nor the dazzling powder of popular ski slopes; instead, the icy frozen blasts of wind-driven crystals nurtured in 25° below temperatures. Car oil and human blood both congealed, neither left with any spirit or inspiration. And so I stopped to see Sam who is always an inspiration.

"Theories!" he grumbled as I pulled off my mitts and accepted a cup of scalding tea. "There are no valid theories dealing specifically with adolescent psychology. You should know that!"

I began to protest, for the sake of form if nothing else, but Sam interrupted me as soon as he had settled his mouth around another chunk of chocolate cake. "Listen," he said, "I've just finished reading a whole series of textbooks in biology. I should know."

Politely, as is my custom, I enquired as to what it is that he should know. Sam was busy feeding Samuel at the time, so I continued my line of questioning in what seemed to me to be a most logical fashion. "And what, precisely, does biology have to do with theories of adolescent development?"

He looked at me, then, with that look that he reserves for such moments, a look that the intelligent bestow upon the less intelligent who have just revealed their peculiar lack of logical reasoning ability. I silenced myself with a piece of cake while he continued.

"Biology," Sam explained patiently, as to a child, "is a natural as opposed to a social science. Natural sciences deal with events, phenomena, and properties of objects that are not subject to the same kind of erratic and unpredictable variations as is human behavior. Hence it is a fact that truth in the natural sciences has an objective quality seldom found in social sciences. Apples fall. They always fall. And if they didn't fall, the scientist could tell you why."

Sam stopped here, as though his point had been made, and well made at that. I tried to look as though I understood. But Sam, shrewd observer that he is, detected at once that I still didn't know precisely what it was that he was trying to say.

"The point," Sam continued, "is that there are very few phenomena in human behavior about which the same observation can be made. At best, predic-

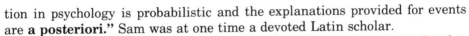

tion in psychology is probabilistic and the explanations provided for events are **a posteriori.**" Sam was at one time a devoted Latin scholar.

"Now what I observed in these biology texts," Sam informed me, "is that they make extremely little use of references. In fact, a great many of these texts make no references whatever to other learned texts, journal articles, or to the opinions of currently eminent men. We are told that apples fall, even as we are told that the earth is five billion years old. We are told what happens when potassium nitrate is mixed with activated charcoal and various other ingredients, and it is totally unnecessary for the author to support his statement by references to some other source. Do you know why that is?"

Before I could venture an answer, Sam continued. "It's because biology deals with facts! And do you know why it is that there are so many references in the most widely accepted textbooks in psychology and other social sciences? It is because they are not based on facts. There is no doubt in my mind that there is an inverse relationship between the truthfulness of a science and the extent to which expressions of that science are documented by reference to so-called authorities. The less sure a science is of itself, the more it attempts to convince by weight of referencing. The irony is that frequently the references cited are authorities that are themselves substantiated by reference to other authorities that were themselves initially substantiated in the same manner. Because research is so difficult in the social sciences, and because its results are so frequently contradictory, it is always possible to find references that will support almost any point of view. And this has often been demonstrated in psychology."

Sam continued at some length, elaborating on this initial point and making one additional observation that appears to be relevant. He strongly maintains that the conviction with which social scientists adhere to their opinions and seek to impose them on others is inversely related to the amount of evidence that exists in support of these opinions. He says, for example, that the passionate convictions that psychologists have had concerning the principal characteristics of adolescence are explainable in terms of the fact that there is usually very little evidence to support these convictions. In the natural sciences, on the other hand, where there is considerable evidence to support currently popular opinions, the conviction with which these opinions are espoused is correspondingly less. Natural scientists have no fear of being tentative; they are quite willing to admit that further evidence might re-

118

quire that they change their opinions. Social scientists refuse to be tentative; whatever they believe, they believe adamantly.

Theory

In lay terminology, a theory is what is resorted to when the facts are unknown. When a grandmother says, in her wisdom, "I have a theory about this," or "about that" as the case may be, you can be fairly certain it is because she is unable to say "I know about this" or "about that." Frequently, grandmothers' theories are no less interesting than theories propounded by the various experts in fields much narrower than those in which grandmothers are accustomed to thinking. But a scientific theory does profess to be different from the lay theory. It is, to begin with, allegedly based on observation rather than on speculation. Indeed, the speculation is more often accepted as an integral part of the theory than as a basis for it.

A scientific theory is a set of related statements that attempts to make some sort of logical sense of observed phenomena. At a simple level, it is nothing more than an attempt to provide a clear, concise, and accurate description or explanation of observations. Its usefulness, however, often goes considerably beyond its explanatory value, including, as well, its predictive value. That is, a theory's greatest value often lies in the possibilities it offers for predicting future states of affairs given certain conditions. This is clearly obvious in the natural sciences, but no less true in such social sciences as psychology. Being able to predict the probable outcome of specific child-rearing techniques on adolescent personality and behavior may, in many cases, be more important than simply being able to explain these observed outcomes after the fact.

The usefulness of a theory can also be assessed in at least one other way, particularly in those sciences that are still in a developmental stage — as is notably true of psychology. A useful theory is one that allows researchers to derive testable hypotheses, hypotheses that can be tested in order to provide supporting or contradictory evidence for the validity of the theory. If the theory that parental affection is important for the development of stable and positive self-concepts in children is valid, one can hypothesize that those children whose parents are highly affectionate will differ significantly with respect to self-concept from children whose parents are cold and rejecting. Providing that it is possible to identify affectionate and nonaffectionate parents, and providing it is also possible to evaluate the nature of children's self-concepts, this hypothesis is in fact testable. Thus a theory that is initially based on facts can be of crucial importance in leading to the discovery of hitherto unknown facts—assuming, of course, that there is some law and order governing human development and behavior.

This chapter examines a number of theories of adolescence, some historical as well as some contemporary attempts to make sense out of various observed characteristics of adolescent behavior. There are also some attempts to explain the origin of this behavior. For convenience and conceptual simplicity, these theories have been characterized as biological, sociological, psychoanalytical, and cognitive. It is clear, however, that these divisions are to some extent artificial. There is considerable overlap and some degree of redundancy among the theories, much of which has been omitted in this abbreviated treatment of them.

Biological Theory

The biological theories of adolescent development attempt to explain adolescence in terms of biologically determined changes. Accordingly one of their chief distinguishing characteristics is a strong belief in the central importance of genetically determined maturational processes. In other words, the characteristics of the adolescent period are assumed to result more from hereditary forces than from environmental conditions.

G. Stanley Hall

The first of the major biological theories of adolescence was formulated by G. Stanley Hall (1904, 1905). Hall was heavily influenced by the work of Darwin and sought to apply the principles of evolution to an understanding of human development. His most fundamental belief, derived directly from evolutionary theory, is expressed simply in the phrase: "ontogeny recapitulates phylogeny." Ontogeny refers to the changes that individuals within a

George *Age 18* **On the State of the World**

Me: *What would you change about the world if you had the power?*

George: *Nothing. I suppose I like the way things are right now.*

George *Age 18* **On Idealism and Materialism**

George is asked to react to the proposition that adolescents are not now as idealistic as they were once thought to be; that they have become either apathetic or materialistic; that the nature of their concerns is directed toward the likelihood that they will obtain the benefits of society for themselves.

George: *Well that's the way I feel. I'm quite satisfied with the way the world is going, except maybe the war, but I think that's slowing down a bit. Other than that I can't think of anything else that's really horrible about it. I for one want a hell of a lot of money and want nice cars and stuff like that.*

120

species undergo from conception to maturity. Phylogeny refers to the series of changes through which species passed as they evolved from primitive life forms to those forms presently known. Hall's contention was, then, that in the course of their development (ontogeny), children would progress through a series of stages similar to those through which the race had progressed in its evolutionary history (phylogeny). Some of the evidence for this belief has been derived from the observation that the fetuses of many animals, including humans, are highly similar at various stages of their early development, and that those of higher-order animals such as the primates resemble the fetuses of much more primitive animals. The human embryo has gill-like structures, for example, in the early stages of embryonic development — structures that some believe to be related to a distant time when the ancestors of humans dwelt in the ocean.

Additional evidence for Hall's theory of recapitulation is derived from his observation that the interests and preoccupations of young children appear to progress through a series of stages that roughly parallel the early preoccupations and habits of primitive humans. Crawling infants recapitulate that period in evolutionary history when humans walked on all fours. Childhood, with its preoccupation with climbing, digging holes, exploring caves, and playing hide-and-seek, recapitulates human cave-dwelling or tree-dwelling as well as hunting and fishing. The period that Hall called "youth," from ages 8 to 12, recapitulates what he terms a "life of savagery." Finally, adolescent behavior is a recapitulation of the beginning of modern civilization.

This belief in recapitulation theory was one of the fundamental tenets of Hall's developmental theory. A second fundamental belief was that the course of development was largely genetically predetermined. Accordingly he strongly advised parents and teachers not to be overly concerned at what they interpreted to be unruly or inappropriate behavior because that particular stage of recapitualtion would inevitably pass in any case. Indeed, it would come and go regardless of the child's environment, because the course of development is determined by genetics alone. Subsequent evidence, particularly of an anthropological nature, demonstrating that children do indeed behave very differently in different cultures, and demonstrating as well that the environment does have a significant effect on a child's development, has largely invalidated this aspect of the theory.

MR. STURM AND MR. DRANG LOOKING
FOR AN UNSUSPECTING TEENAGER

Hall's description of adolescence is of considerable interest both for contemporary and historical reasons. He described it as a period of **"sturm und drang,"** an expression borrowed from a predominant literary movement of the time. This movement is exemplified in the early writings of such men as Goethe and Schiller. Translated directly, it means "storm and stress"; not surprisingly, it has come to be known as the storm and stress hypothesis. The literary movement that gave rise to the expression was characterized by excessive idealism, commitment to avant-garde goals, rebelliousness against established order, and a preoccupation with the expression of such intense personal feelings as love, despair, exuberance, and agony. Hall saw a parallel between adolescent turbulence and turmoil and this literary movement. He described adolescence as a period of contradictions among intense emotions: between the burning desire to love and be loved among a company of peers and the desire for solitude and seclusion; between idealistic commitments to grandiose goals and the pragmatic pursuit of immediate material comfort; between strong beliefs in moral purity and an aching desire to succumb to temptation; between childish selfishness and selfless altruism.

The storm and stress hypothesis has found some support among more contemporary writers, though not all have ascribed to it the same degree of intensity and seriousness as did Hall. Jung (1960) pictures adolescence as being a period of stress, a period during which adolescents become less of a problem to others than they were as children, but more of a problem to themselves. Menninger (1968), Hurlock (1968), and Erikson (1956, 1968) also describe adolescence as a period of stress, though both Menninger and Hurlock explain the stress as being more a problem of adjusting to a specific society than a simple maturational problem. Erikson, about whom more is said later in this chapter, believes that adolescent stress stems largely from problems associated with developing a sense of ego identity.

While few writers deny that adolescent development is frequently characterized by stressful emotional changes, many do not see the stress as being particularly difficult or even undesirable. Anna Freud (1958), for example, believed that stress is not only normal but probably necessary as a motivating force for the resolution of such important personal problems as the development of an appropriate life-style, a stable self-concept, and a viable and proper set of moral values.

Gesell

Like Hall, Gesell (1940; 1946; Gesell, Ilg, and Ames, 1956) based his developmental theories on the belief that biological factors were largely responsible for the personality characteristics of children at various stages in their development. Unlike Hall, however, he gave the environment an important role in accounting for variations among individuals. These differences, he felt, would be due first to genetic factors that determine not only the sequence of maturation but also the "constitution" of the individual; second, they would be due to "environmental factors ranging from home and school to the total cultural setting" (Gesell, Ilg, and Ames, 1956, p. 22).

Gesell's theory has been described as a **maturational theory** primarily because of his strong belief that various capabilities as well as personality characteristics result from the genetically determined unfolding of a maturational sequence. It is as though every individual is born with a growth timetable (earlier referred to as a biological clock) that determines not only the order in which certain changes will occur, but also the time at which they will occur. No amount of training will affect such maturationally determined abilities as walking, climbing stairs, and so on. The accuracy of this contention is still open to question, however. Attempts to accelerate development in various areas have sometimes been successful, sometimes not. In almost all cases, however, children who are not accelerated eventually learn the activity or skill later in any case; and, they are usually at least as successful at it. (See Lefrancois, 1973, for a more detailed discussion of some of this research.)

Gesell's own term for the maturational processes at work during development is **morphogenesis.** This term denotes changes in the forms or patterns of behavior. Patterns of behavior undergo morphogenesis—change—as a function of what Gesell described as a spiral forward and backward movement—progression followed by regression. He noted that children progress until they learn some new pattern of behavior. Then, for a period of time, they appear to regress to an earlier point where they were unable to accomplish the behavior in question. This regression is, according to Gesell, nature's way of providing children with time to consolidate the gains they have made. Following this temporary regression, they again progess, but this time to a point beyond that at which they had originally stopped. Thus through this continual process of progression followed by regression and then followed

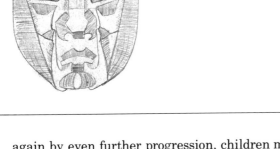

again by even further progression, children move from infancy to adolescence and finally to adulthood. Throughout this process, maturational forces in interaction with certain environmental forces combine to determine the outcome of the developmental process.

Age Profiles Much of Gesell's work was concerned with describing the behavior of children at specific ages. Although he was well aware of the many weaknesses of this approach, he has nevertheless provided mothers and educators with detailed age profiles against which they can compare their children in order to arrive at some judgment regarding their accomplishments and characteristics relative to other children of the same age. Short summaries of these descriptions as they apply to children between the ages of ten and sixteen are presented here (based on Gesell, Ilg, and Ames, 1956).

Ten-Year-Olds. The age of ten is a culmination of childhood. It is a period characterized by remarkable stability, almost total absence of "storm and stress," and general contentment. The ten-year-olds are well adjusted, highly sensitive to fairness, and not at all interested in the opposite sex. They are pleased with their homes, obedient, confident, and, in short, model children.

Eleven-Year-Olds. A year later children have crossed the threshold of adolescence. They now begin to evidence the symptoms of "sturm und drang" described by Hall. They are moody, rebellious, restless, given to long periods of sullen silence, and quarrelsome. Frequently, their relationships with their parents become strained. And parents are at a loss to understand what has happened to their model ten-year-olds.

Twelve-Year-Olds. Progression follows regression follows progression; succeeding ages are contradictions of those that went before. And thus it is with twelve-year-olds. The formerly impossible eleven-year-olds now become sensible, tolerant, and cooperative twelve-year-olds; they are much more predisposed to being optimists than pessimists, believers than cynics, lovers than haters. And they do, finally, become interested in the opposite sex. Coupled with this is a new-found enthusiasm and self-directed initiative. Parents now relax, thinking that the worst is over.

Thirteen-Year-Olds. But it isn't. By the age of thirteen, the pleasant, agreeable twelve-year-olds become sullen and withdrawn. They are tense, critical, and highly self-conscious. The major changes of pubescence present them with problems of adjustment that are reflected in their reactions to people around

them. They have fewer friends than they had a year ago, and they tend to be highly critical of their parents. And because they are withdrawn rather than openly argumentative, parents are again at a loss to understand what has happened to their children.

Fourteen-Year-Olds. Until they become fourteen. Now they suddenly become extroverts, confident, outgoing persons of the world. Their major preoccupations, according to Gesell, are with the subjects of amateur "applied psychology." They spend hours discussing personalities and characters with their friends; and they discover themselves on a thousand movie screens and in a hundred books. The center of their world has shifted dramatically from home to peers. And their parents watch, not quite understanding, but relatively powerless in any case.

Fifteen-Year-Olds. The fifteen-year-olds are boisterous, rebellious, and unpredictable. They are prone to delinquent acts, disrespectful of authority, and generally hostile. But there are considerable individual differences during this period, with many fifteen-year-olds simply manifesting an increasing degree of independence with only occasional confrontations with various authorities; and with others, of course, encountering virtually no confrontations, having already achieved their emancipation, or perhaps not desiring it yet.

Sixteen-Year-Olds. The sixteen-year-olds are future-oriented, characterized by stable emotional adjustment, relatively little rebelliousness, and an outgoing and friendly attitude.

There are several major weaknesses of age profiles such as these. To begin with, girls are typically two years ahead of boys in terms of biological changes at the onset of adolescence. Hence, if there were, in fact, a profile applicable to the twelve-year-old as opposed to the ten-year-old, it should presumably be different for girls and boys. Second, chronological age is a notoriously bad index of social, emotional, and physical development during adolescence. As Tanner (1962) points out, skeletal age is a better predictor of impending biological changes than is actual age. Changes that occur during adolescence, while highly correlated one to the other both in terms of sequence and rate of appearance, are not nearly as highly correlated with chronological age.

Finally, the point should be made here, as it is elsewhere (see Chapter 7), that relatively consistent sex differences in terms of interests, values, and activities serve largely to invalidate relatively naive descriptions of what typical adolescents are like at a given age. In short, these profiles do not take into consideration early and late maturers; sex differences; the various effects of home, school, peer groups; and other environmental factors that are of considerable importance in determining the nature of individual adolescents. Their greatest value is perhaps that they serve to point out dramatically the great variability in adolescent behavior over time. These profiles, in a sense, provide additional evidence that adolescents are, in fact, in the process of discovering who they are. They also show that adolescents have not, during the course of these years, succeeded in developing a strong sense of ego identity. Each adolescent is many different individuals seeking which of these individuals to be, a point that is made again in the discussion of Erikson's work later in this chapter.

Sociological Theory

Whereas the biological theories are concerned primarily with the role of genetic and evolutionary factors in development, the sociological theories are concerned with the role of society and culture. Sociological theories generally maintain that adolescence varies from culture to culture and is not due primarily to genetic factors. Chief among sociological approaches is that advanced by Havighurst.

Havighurst

Havighurst describes development in terms of the mastery of a series of tasks. These tasks are, in effect, the goals or criteria by which particular societies judge the relative maturity of their children. Quite simply, children do not have to understand the ethical implications of abstract moral decisions, but adults probably should; infants do not need to be able to establish stable emotional relationships with opposite-sexed, like-aged peers, but older adolescents should. These are **developmental tasks** that must be mastered as children progress toward adulthood.

At every stage of development there are a sequential series of tasks identified by Havighurst. These are sequential not only in the sense that progression in development is ordinarily continuous, but also in the sense that one task is frequently a requisite for the mastery of subsequent tasks. Nor is mastery of each task solely a function of maturational factors. In addition, it is a function of personal efforts, as well as of the expectations that the immediate social environment communicates to the children. One additional aspect of Havighurst's conception of developmental tasks is noteworthy. He believes that there is frequently a **critical period** during which the task can be mastered most easily, and that failure to do so at that time may lead to considerable difficulties in mastering the task later. Specifically, he points out that if young children have not begun to learn to speak by the age of two, they will probably find it very difficult if not impossible to do so later. Similarly, it might be argued that adolescents who do not learn to establish the sorts of emotional relationships that are expected of them during adolescence may experience considerable difficulty in establishing those relationships when they are older.

Developmental Tasks Among the developmental tasks that Havighurst (1951) lists for adolescents are the following:

Accepting One's Physique. Because adolescence is a time of very rapid physical changes, and because these changes are not always completely expected nor perfectly ideal for the individual concerned, there is frequently considerable adjustment required. The need for adjustment and its difficulty will, of course, vary from individual to individual. The adjustment involves, in part, learning the nature and limitations of the changing body. It also involves reconciling the former image of the physical self with the new physical self. The occasional difficulty of this adjustment is sometimes illustrated by overly obese adults who are successful in losing a great deal of weight from their physical selves, but not always from their images of themselves, and who subsequently spend a great deal of time looking at a skinny stranger looking back at them from the other side of a mirror. Some of these individuals continue to act as though their physical selves had not changed.

Accepting an Appropriate Masculine or Feminine Role. Although society has become somewhat more tolerant of deviations from "normal" sexual patterns with respect to masculinity and femininity, it is still largely true that certain behaviors, attitudes, and values—rightly or wrongly—are ex-

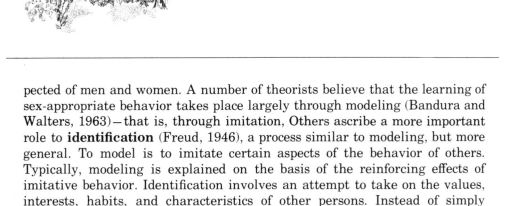

pected of men and women. A number of theorists believe that the learning of sex-appropriate behavior takes place largely through modeling (Bandura and Walters, 1963)—that is, through imitation, Others ascribe a more important role to **identification** (Freud, 1946), a process similar to modeling, but more general. To model is to imitate certain aspects of the behavior of others. Typically, modeling is explained on the basis of the reinforcing effects of imitative behavior. Identification involves an attempt to take on the values, interests, habits, and characteristics of other persons. Instead of simply attempting to imitate specific behaviors that they see others engaging in, individuals behave as though they were trying to be someone else.

Although the physical manifestations of sexual differences are genetically determined to a large extent, such is not the case for the behavioral manifestation of masculinity-femininity. Nor can the characteristics of masculinity and femininity be defined objectively except within specific cultural contexts. The aggressiveness, assertiveness, competitiveness, and relative lack of emotionality that have traditionally been associated with masculinity in Western cultures are perhaps not inherently masculine; in the same way, the tenderness, emotionality, and submissiveness that have sometimes been associated with femininity are perhaps not inherently feminine. True, a good argument can be made for the contention that those traits generally associated with masculinity and femininity were most likely to develop given the physical differences in musculature and strength, for example, between men and women; also supporting the argument are the fundamentally different biological roles genetically assigned men and women with respect to childbearing. At the same time, a good argument can be made for the belief that masculinity and femininity as we know them are to a large degree a function of cultural and social pressures; and this may be considerably more obvious within a few decades as both men and women work toward their liberation from culturally defined, restrictive, and sometimes unfair sex roles.

Mead (1935) reports some anthropological research that dramatically illustrates how masculine and feminine traits are culture-bound. Her work involved observations of three New Guinea tribes: the Arapesh, the Mundugumor, and the Tchambuli. The Arapesh are described as a people where both sexes are "placid and contented, unaggressive and non-initiatory, noncompetitive and responsive, warm, docile, and trusting" (Mead, 1935, p. 39).

Put more simply, among the Arapesh, both men and women exhibit personality characteristics that contemporary Western cultures would describe as being feminine.

The Mundugumor are described as "ruthless, aggressive, positively sexed individuals, with the maternal cherishing aspects of personality at a minimum" (p. 190). In contrast, then, among the Mundugumor, both men and women display overwhelmingly masculine traits.

Finally, the Tchambuli evidenced a "genuine reversal of the sex attitudes of our own culture" (p. 190). In this primarily agricultural and artistic tribe, women spent most of their time gathering food whereas men spent their time devising new dances, fixing their hair, experimenting with new cosmetics, and engaging in various forms of art work.

It is interesting to note that these three tribes had life-styles all differing dramatically from our own as well as one from the other. These life-styles differ not only in terms of the predominant personality characteristics expected of men and women, but in terms of the major activities they engage in for their livelihood. The Arapesh, where both sexes are predominantly feminine by our standards, live in an inhospitable and relatively infertile region some distance from the coast. It is perhaps because food-gathering activities are a major preoccupation, that both men and women engage in them; it is also perhaps because of the ever present danger of starvation that they have developed into a peaceful, cooperative "feminine" culture. In contrast, the Mundugumor, where both sexes are predominantly masculine by our standards, live on the banks of a fast flowing jungle river, the Sepik. Far from being an agricultural people, they are a tribe of cannibals whose food-gathering expeditions involve not a walk to the fields or jungles, but a ride down the Sepik to a neighboring village where fresh victuals walk about. It is not surprising that here both men and women should be aggressive, competitive, and dominating—in short, masculine.

Contemporary adolescents are faced with considerable ambiguity concerning sex roles. Numerous writers have noted a remarkable change among adolescents toward greater uniformity and similarity among sexes, most notably in the area of dress and hair styles; there are also less obvious changes involving dating, sexual behavior, vocational choice, and general interests and values. Perhaps the ambiguity lies solely in the minds of those adults who still remember clearly how these things were when they were adolescents;

perhaps it doesn't present any serious problem for adolescents in their quest to find themselves.

Achieving Emotional and Economic Independence from Parents and Other Adults. Throughout their growing years, children are usually emotionally, financially, and physically dependent upon their immediate families; as adults they will ordinarily become relatively independent from them in all these areas. The transition from dependence to independence is frequently difficult not only for the adolescents, but for parents as well. It imposes new demands on the adolescents—demands that require a dramatic change in their image of their capabilities and needs; demands that, as well, require that they be able to form emotional relationships outside the sphere of the immediate family. On the part of parents, it requires that they accept a rupturing of bonds that have held for more than a decade. The alleged **generation gap,** rebelliousness, hostility, and turmoil of the family, when they occur, may result in part from the adolescents' attempts to achieve these developmental tasks (see Chapter 8).

Selecting and Preparing for a Vocation. Traditionally the selection of a vocation and preparation for it has been a relatively easy task for adolescents, particularly in those primitive cultures where the choice of occupations is either limited or nonexistent, and where appropriate training for that occupation has been achieved through informal teaching and imitation from early childhood. In contemporary, technological societies, choice of vocation is large; and formal education has not, during childhood, been geared for any specific vocation.

Developing Intellectual Skills and Concepts Necessary for Civic Competence. Lip service has long been paid to the notion that honest, hard-working people who are dedicated to a way of life that is nationally recognized as the best of all possible lives make good and worthy politicians. Similarly, "good" citizens are those who recognize this way of life as a "good" way of life; who are also honest and hard working; and who are driven by the Puritan Ethic and willing to fight to the death for Flag, Country, God, Freedom, and Apple Pie.

In recent years there has been some disenchantment with the confessed and suspected behavior of politicians in high places—and politicians in lower places as well. Conflict of interest, greed, corruption, and an unshakable dedication to the service of self have become the hallmark of politics. Perhaps the adolescent suffers some confusion in this area as well. Growing adolescents in this cultural context are faced with the task of developing the attitudes and skills that will make them "good citizens," or, at least, of making some decisions concerning the types of citizens they wish to become. For the more socially and politically conscious adolescent, the choice may not be simple.

Desiring and Achieving Socially Responsible Behavior and Preparing for Marriage and Family Life. Sweeping changes in life-styles, particularly as they are related to marriage and the family, have obscured the clarity of these developmental tasks. Society now provides numerous models of apparently "responsible" social lives involving cohabitation, communal living, and other varieties of hetero- and homosexual behavior. Nevertheless, it does remain true that for the majority of adolescents, responsible social behavior and preparation for marriage are socially expected and hence socially desirable behaviors (even if for no other reason).

Achieving New Relations with Age Mates of Both Sexes. Freud labels the developmental period immediately preceding adolescence *latency*. It is a relatively long period during which children have little interest in members of the opposite sex. However, with the advent of puberty and the sexual awakening of children in a biological sense, there come profound changes in their relationships not only to members of the opposite sex, but also to like-sexed peers. Normal adult relationships require that these changes take place. These are discussed in some detail in Chapter 9.

Acquiring a Set of Values That Are in Harmony with the Social Environment. One of the fundamental differences between preadolescence and adolescence concerns cognitive (intellectual) abilities. Piaget (1952) describes preadolescence in terms of what he labels *the period of concrete operations.* From ages seven or eight to eleven or twelve, children develop their abilities to deal logically with a variety of situations, but their thinking remains tied to the concrete. In other words, they find it impossible to go beyond that which is actual or at least capable of being imagined in relatively concrete terms. With the onset of the next developmental period, *formal operations,* children acquire the ability to deal with the hypothetical as well as with the actual. They can now reason about states of affairs that do not exist; they can go from the actual to the merely possible, and from the hypothetical to the real. Thus they can now imagine states of affairs that could replace the present ones. They are now capable of becoming idealistic, of recognizing that many of the world's problems are more than merely accidental, that what humans have created could

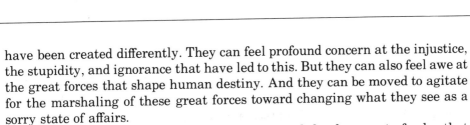

have been created differently. They can feel profound concern at the injustice, the stupidity, and ignorance that have led to this. But they can also feel awe at the great forces that shape human destiny. And they can be moved to agitate for the marshaling of these great forces toward changing what they see as a sorry state of affairs.

It is during this period that the **conscience,** defined as a set of rules that govern behavior, undergoes profound changes. The most significant of these involves a reexamination of rules that have been accepted either because they come from some external authority or because they have made some sort of social sense in interaction with peers. And as these rules are reexamined, evaluated, discarded, modified, or accepted, they become internalized; and, as Kohlberg (1964) put it, they become "individualized" rules of behavior. Chapter 11 of this text is devoted to an examination of adolescent **morality.**

Psychoanalytical Theory

One of the most influential of psychological theories, particularly in personality theory, clinical psychology, and developmental psychology, is that advanced by Freud — **psychoanalytic** theory. Although it is perhaps more pertinent to an understanding of abnormal personality development than of normal development, it nevertheless provides valuable insights into human functioning.

Freud

Freud's account of human development encompasses two parallel aspects (Brill, 1938; Brown, 1961). On the one hand he describes a series of **psychosexual** stages through which all individuals normally progress; on the other, he describes cognitive, personality, and moral characteristics of individuals at each of these stages.

Basic Ideas There are two great fundamental urges that account for the direction of human behavior. All individuals are born with an overwhelming urge to survive and an equally overwhelming desire to procreate. Because

Figure 5.1 The Freudian conception of the three levels of human personality in order of development.

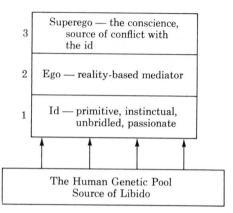

132

the urge to survive is frequently not impeded by external reality, it receives relatively little attention in Freud's writings. The urge to procreate, however, is frequently thwarted by the childhood environment and is consequently of central importance in understanding both normal and abnormal behavior. Manifestations of the urge to procreate, however, are not limited solely to those actions leading directly to propagation; they also include all sorts of other behaviors that are simply manifestations of sexuality beginning in infancy and not ceasing, presumably, until death. The collective term for these urges is **libido** or libidinal urges. Freud later divided libido into two separate instinctive urges: **Eros** and **Thanatos.** Eros refers to the life or love urges; Thanatos refers to the much discussed Freudian death wish, a concept that is not of central importance in most of his writings.

Human Personality Freud describes three structures of human personality that appear in the course of development. Initially human children have simple, undeveloped personalities characterized by "seething, unbridled" instincts. Their sole preoccupation at this stage is to satisfy the instinctual urges to which they are heir, their libidinal urges. They have no concept of external reality; no realization of what is possible or impossible with respect to these urges. If they are hungry, they *must* eat. Now. And if their bowels must move, they must. Quite apart from the fact that they have not yet achieved any muscular control over their body, they have yet to achieve any control over the urge to gratify their impulses. They are, as Freud put it, all **id** (see Figure 5.1). Id is the level of personality that encompasses all of the primitive urges of humans and all of the energy for their behavior.

As infants develop, their instinctual urges clash more and more frequently with reality. They discover that they cannot always eat when they want to; that wanting to drink does not necessarily produce something to drink; and that various behaviors are likely to be met with some degree of resistance. In short, they begin to develop some notion of reality as it relates to their basic urges. This sense of reality is labelled the **ego.** That is, the ego is not the external reality itself, but the notions that individuals develop regarding reality. Ego is, in a sense, a mediator between individuals' primitive impulses and an external world. Like the id, the ego tends toward the satisfaction of the children's wishes, but within constraints imposed by reality. The ego is an outgrowth of conflict between the id and the external world.

BABY SUCK

TEENAGE SUCK

ADULT SUCK

133

The third personality structure is the **superego;** it is concerned more with social than with physical reality. The superego is, in a sense, the individual's conscience. It incorporates rules concerning right and wrong, moral goodness and evil. The superego is created as a function of identification with the like-sexed parent following resolution of the Oedipus or Electra complex (which will be explained later). Parts of it may be derived from religious teachings, school, family, and peers. According to Freud, it does not become manifest until early childhood. By its very nature, the superego sets itself up in opposition to the id and the ego. Whereas both the id and the ego are concerned with satisfying individuals' basic urges subject only to the constraints of physical reality, the superego imposes additional social and moral constraints, particularly in the area of sexual behavior. It is little wonder that Freud saw this conflict as one of the basic sources of personality disturbances.

Psychosexual Stages Freud describes a series of sequential stages through which individuals progress in the course of normal development. Each of these stages is labeled in terms of the primary source of sexual gratification during that period (see Table 5.1).

Oral Stage. From birth to the age of approximately eight months, infants' primary source of sexual gratification is through the mouth—the **oral stage.** Thus eating, sucking, biting, chewing, and playing with the lips are predominant infantile activities. At this stage children are pure id. That is, they are still bundles of passions seeking to satisfy themselves by whatever means are available; and they express their frustration as best they can when these urges are not satisfied.

Anal Stage. Following this first stage, children's sources of pleasure gradually shift from the oral to the anal region—the **anal stage.** Such activities as elimination or even retention of feces become gratifying. At the same time, children are beginning to develop some notion of external reality, particular with regard to the likelihood of being fed in response to certain behaviors. They also acquire some degree of control over their bowels and some reality-based notions regarding the advisability of expelling or withholding feces. Their personalities are beginning to develop as a function of interaction with the environment.

Phallic Stage. From the ages of approximately eighteen months to six years, children are in the **phallic stage,** a stage during which they become pre-

Table 5.1   Freud's Stages of Psychosexual Development

Stage	Approximate Age	Characteristics
Oral	0–8 months	Sources of pleasure include sucking, biting, swallowing, playing with lips.
		Preoccupation with immediate gratification of impulses.
		Id is dominant.
Anal	8–18 months	Sources of sexual gratification include expelling feces and urination, as well as retaining feces.
		Id and ego.

134

occupied with their genitals, and where their major source of gratification is masturbation. It is also during this period that the male child goes through the troubled period of the **Oedipus complex.** His increasing awareness of the sexual significance of his genitals leads him to desire his mother (unconsciously, to be sure) and to become jealous of his father. Thus he is torn between his love for his father and hatred stemming from his jealousy. At the same time, he may be tormented by the castration complex: fear that his father will retaliate, defend his position as lover of the woman desired by the boy, and ensure his victory by castrating the boy or cutting off his penis. Solution of the conflict presumably involves simply renouncing all claims to the mother's sexual attentions and identifying with the father. Identification, as was pointed out earlier, involves unconscious efforts to become the person being identified with. Accordingly, the boy, in assuming some of his father's values and beliefs, develops his superego as a function of resolving his Oedipus complex. The phallic stage girl suffers through a similar complex termed **Electra,** stemming from her initial assumption that all people have or should have penises and her eventual discovery that she has been deprived of that instrument. The resulting penis envy is thought to disappear as she enters the next stage of psychosexual development.

It should be noted, however, that Freud paid little attention to the problem of how girls came to identify with their mothers and consequently develop superegos, despite the fact that most of his patients were women. Indeed, he believed that because the Electra complex was not nearly as powerful in girls as the Oedipus complex in boys, their superegos would be correspondingly weaker, and they would therefore be less moral than boys. Evidence suggests that this supposition is clearly wrong. In fact, studies of cheating among adolescents typically reveal that more boys than girls cheat (Chapter 10). Similarly, more identified juvenile delinquents are male than female (Chapter 11).

Latency Stage. During the **latency stage,** from ages six to eleven, children lose interest in sexual gratification and identify strongly with the like-sexed parent. During this period boys tend to play with boys in what they consider to be primarily masculine games. Similarly, girls play with girls. The superego that has begun to develop during the phallic stage continues to become more differentiated from the ego and more powerful in determining children's behavior.

Stage	Approximate Age	Characteristics
Phallic	18 months to 6 years	Children become concerned with their genitals. Source of sexual pleasure involves manipulating genitals. Period of Oedipus or Electra complex.
		Id, ego, and superego.
Latency	6–11 years	Loss of interest in sexual gratification. Identification with like-sexed parent.
		Id, ego, and superego.
Genital	11–18 years	Concern with adult modes of sexual pleasure, barring fixations or regressions.

135

Genital Stage. The final stage of psychosexual development, from ages eleven to eighteen, is the **genital stage.** It is marked by a concern with adult modes of sexual gratification. With the biological changes of adolescence comes a recapitulation of the phallic stage complete with a return to infantile modes of sexual gratification — particularly masturbation — and a reenactment of the classical oedipal conflict. Resolution of this conflict does not, in this case, involve identification with the father, but with peers. Thus the eventual outcome of the resolution is the establishment of heterosexual relations with peers rather than with the mother. At the same time, the superego that has initially been highly intolerant and highly rigid becomes more flexible as adolescents begin to examine rules of behavior and to individualize them.

Abnormal Development In the course of normal psychosexual development, according to Freud, all children progress through the stages described above. There are, however, at least two alternatives to normal progression through the stages, both of which may be associated with personality abnormalities. The first is **fixation;** the second, **regression.** Fixation occurs when individuals fail to progress beyond one of the early psychosexual stages. It is as though the amount of sexual gratification that they receive during this stage is sufficient to motivate them not to progress further; or, progression to the next stage is impeded by **trauma** (anxiety) sometimes resulting from over- or understimulation. Regression occurs when children have passed successfully through a stage, but then revert to it from a later stage, perhaps because they obtain too little sexual gratification at the more advanced stage and are exposed to stress with which they have difficulty coping.

The characteristics of individuals fixated (totally or in part) at an early stage or who have regressed to that stage tend to correspond to the predominant forms of sexual gratification peculiar to that stage. Adults partially fixated at the oral stage, for example, are described simply as having oral characters. They may chew their nails, smoke, suck their lips or their thumbs, drink a great deal, and talk a lot. In other words, they will engage in activities that involve their oral region. Similarly, phallic characters display an inadequate superego development. They may develop an overriding preoccupation with satisfying their sexual urges regardless of the object of their satisfaction. They are the rapists, **sadists, masochists,** alcoholics, or **psychopaths.**

Table 5.2   Some Freudian Defense Mechanisms

Mechanism	One Possible Manifestation
Displacement. The appearance of a suppressed behavior in a more acceptable form.	A potential murderer hunts subhuman Primates.
Reaction Formation. Behavior that is the opposite of what the individual would like it to be.	A woman loves an unobtainable man and behaves as though she dislikes him.
Intellectualization. Behavior is stripped of its emotional concomitants.	A grown man who loves his mother too dearly treats her with extreme consideration, kindness, and devotion but convinces himself that he is motivated by duty and not by love.

136

Defense Mechanisms Understanding some simple **defense mechanisms** is important in understanding Freud's theorizing; it is also important in understanding adolescent behavior.

Defense mechanisms are ways that individuals compensate for their inability to satisfy the demands of their id, and ways to overcome the anxiety accompanying the constant struggles between the superego and the id. In one sense, they are tools employed by the ego to minimize the anxiety that arises from these conflicts. Chief among these defense mechanisms are **displacement, reaction formation, intellectualization, projection, denial, and repression.** Each of these is defined briefly and illustrated in Table 5.2.

Erikson

Erikson's theory of adolescence draws heavily upon the work of Freud. These psychoanalytic theories view sexuality as a part of infancy and childhood and not simply a new discovery during adolescence. Accordingly, individuals' histories become of crucial importance to understanding adolescent behavior.

Although Erikson refers to Freud continually throughout his writings and is at pains to point out that his is not an original theory but merely an extension and elaboration of Freudian theory, he does introduce a number of significantly different emphases. For example, he replaces the classical mother-father-child triangle of the oedipal conflict of the phallic stage with a sociocultural complex. Development and the resolution of conflicts take place not solely or even primarily within the mother-father-child triangle, but rather within this context in relation to the wider social and cultural groups of which they are part.

A second deviation from classical Freudian theory introduced by Erikson is his emphasis on the role of the ego rather than the superego. This becomes particularly evident in his discussion of adolescence, where the primary task facing children is the development of a stable and integrated sense of self: the development of ego identity. Accordingly, Erikson's writings focus on the process of socialization rather than on conflicts between unconscious id-motivated desires and the ego.

A third and highly significant deviation from Freudian theory is Erikson's

Mechanism	One Possible Manifestation
Projection. Persons come to believe that their own undesirable feelings or inclinations are more descriptive of others than of themselves.	A claustrophobic individual who unconsciously avoids closed spaces is amazed at the number of persons who suffer from claustrophobia.
Denial. The distortion of reality to make it conform to the individual's wishes.	A heavy smoker is unable to give up the habit and decides that there is no substantial evidence linking nicotine with human diseases.
Repression. Unpleasant experiences are stored deep in the subconscious mind and become inaccessible to waking memory.	A soldier comes very close to death, but remembers no details of the event.

137

preoccupation with describing the development of healthy individuals. Freud has often been interpreted as being more concerned with describing and explaining the development of various pathologies.

Developmental Phases Erikson's (1950, 1959, 1968) description of human development is conceptually simple, though highly complex in detail. He describes the course of development as involving progression through eight distinct phases, the first five of which span infancy, childhood, and adolescence. The final three phases correspond to the adult years. Each of these eight phases is labeled in terms of a conflict that is to be resolved during a particular developmental phase. In other words, every developmental phase involves a crisis that can be resolved by the achievement of "a sense of" some particular competence as opposed to "a sense of" the corresponding incompetence. Erikson employed the word *versus* to indicate the struggles that he assumed would take place at each developmental phase. The first five of these developmental phases correspond closely to Freud's psychosexual stages. They are described briefly here, and summarized in Table 5.3.

Trust versus Mistrust. The central theme during the first phase of development, a phase corresponding to Freud's oral stage, is that of achieving a sense of trust. Because children contact the world largely through their oral regions initially—that is, through sucking, swallowing, chewing, and so on—it is necessary for them to achieve the trust required for them to explore unfamiliar objects with their mouths. This sense of trust involves feelings of comfort and security, and increases as a function of the positive experiences that children have. At the same time, however, a sense of mistrust remains in conflict with this basic sense of trust, and increases with unsatisfactory experiences. The major developmental achievement of this period will be a relatively unquestioning trust of the environment as children are exposed to it by the significant adults in their life—a sense of trust that will extend to people as well as to the physical environment.

Autonomy versus Shame and Doubt. Once children have achieved basic trust in their activities and in those objects and people that surround them, they make the interesting and important discovery that they are, in fact, authors of their own activities. While it is true that in the early stages of infant development children remain relatively incapable of action as opposed to reaction, this is no longer the case when they reach the second phase. That

Table 5.3   Erikson's Worksheet of Developmental Phases

	A Psychosocial Crises	B Radius of Significant Relations	C Related Elements of Social Order	D Psychosocial Modalities	E Psychosexual Stages
1	Trust versus mistrust	Maternal person	Cosmic order	To get To give in return	Oral-respiratory, sensory-kinesthetic (incorporative modes)
2	Autonomy versus shame, doubt	Parental persons	"Law and order"	To hold (on) To let (go)	Anal-urethral, muscular (retentive-eliminative)
3	Initiative versus guilt	Basic family	Ideal prototypes	To make (= going after) To "make like" (= playing)	Infantile-genital, locomotor (intrusive, inclusive)
4	Industry versus inferiority	"Neighborhood," school	Technological elements	To make things (= completing) To make things together	"Latency"

is, young infants tend to react reflexively and without control in the face of environmental or internal stimulation. Sucking happens not when children *intend* to suck, but when the corners of their mouths, their lips, or their tongues are stimulated in the appropriate manner. The discovery that they can, at last, control their own actions leads them toward the acquisition of a sense of autonomy. In conflict with this, however, is a competing tendency to abdicate responsibility for their own actions; to revert to the comfort and trust that resulted from not having to assert themselves. They find themselves engaged in a struggle between wanting to experiment with newly discovered, autonomous physical powers and a sense of doubt concerning these powers. They also experience doubt concerning their abdication of their previous

A Psychosocial Crises	B Radius of Significant Relations	C Related Elements of Social Order	D Psychosocial Modalities	E Psychosexual Stages
5 Identity and repudiation versus identity diffusion	Peer groups and outgroups; models of leadership	Ideological perspectives	To be oneself (or not to be) To share being oneself	Puberty
6 Intimacy and solidarity versus isolation	Partners in friendship, sex, competition, cooperation	Patterns of cooperation and competition	To lose and find oneself in another	Genitality
7 Generativity versus self-absorption	Divided labor and shared household	Currents of education and tradition	To make be To take care of	
8 Integrity versus despair	"Mankind" "My Kind"	Wisdom	To be, through having been To face not being	

Reprinted from "Identity and the Life Cycle" by Erik H. Erikson. From *Psychological Issues*, Vol. 1, No. 1. By permission of W. W. Norton & Company, Inc., and the author. Copyright © 1959 by International Universities Press, Inc.

dependency and trust (Erikson, 1961). But experiment they must if they are to learn that behavior is not sufficient in and of itself—as it perhaps is during early infancy—but that it can be employed as a means to an end. Indeed, it becomes essential that they learn this if they are to develop normally because most of the physical activities of this period of approximately eighteen months to four years—walking, climbing, jumping, and so on—are means to various ends.

Initiative versus Guilt. With increasing mastery over their actions and the complete realization of their autonomy over these actions, children almost naturally develop a sense of initiative, particularly in relation to the mastery of new tasks. Indeed, their whole social environment demands not only that they actively explore their physical capabilities, but that they accept the initiative for this exploration. The development of a sense of initiative, however, requires that children at the same time overcome the feelings of guilt and doubt that arise from the occasional frustration of their efforts by the activities of their peers (and parents as well at times), and from a sense of loss that they experience at leaving the comfort associated with earlier developmental phases. Here, as in all developmental phases described by Erikson, a specific crisis is met; and here, again as in all other developmental phases, the crisis is resolved by the achievement of a sense of competence. In this case, the competence involves the realization of initiative in spite of whatever guilt or doubt might accompany it. One major dimension that has been added to their lives and their understanding of it in relation to their social milieu is their use of language. They now employ language much as they might have employed physical activity during an earlier developmental phase; as a means of exploring and understanding themselves and their activities. It is during this period, as well, that children are subjected to the complexes of the phallic stage: the Oedipus and the Electra complexes that, according to Erikson, are worked out partly through solitary play (daydreaming for example) and partly through interaction with peers, frequently also in play situations.

Industry versus Inferiority. The fourth phase, corresponding to Freud's period of latency, is marked by children's increasing need to be accepted by their peers. It becomes crucially important for them to discover that they are someone of importance among others like themselves—that their egos, their selves, are not inferior. Thus they avail themselves of all opportunities to learn those things that appear to be of importance in their culture; they develop their skills to the extent that they can, hoping that by so doing they will become *someone*. Hence they acquire a sense of industry while at the same time minimizing, if they are successful, those feelings of inferiority with which they are initially plagued. Erikson points out clearly that the only way in which children are "latent" during this period—which does in fact correspond to Freud's latency stage—is with respect to the formation of heterosexual attachments. In all other areas, they are actively concerned with learning and doing. And they are most intensely concerned with establishing secure and mutually accepting relationships with like-sexed peers.

Identity versus Role Diffusion. The fifth phase is of more critical importance

for our purposes because it deals expressly with the period of early adolescence, a period to which Erikson devoted a considerable amount of his writing (1968). The central theme during the adolescent period is the development of a sense of identity. And if any single crisis is more obvious and more crucial than any other in his description of development, the crisis involving conflicts between the establishment of identity and the diffusion of concepts of self is perhaps the most important.

The term *identity* is never defined very simply and clearly in Erikson's writings. In the work that deals most specifically with the identity crisis and youth, he begins by noting that the terms *identity* and *identity crisis* have always been subject to changing meanings (Erikson, 1968, p. 15):

> [These terms] alternately circumscribe something so large and so seemingly self-evident that to demand a definition would almost seem petty, while at other times they designate something made so narrow for purposes of measurement that the over-all meaning is lost, and it could just as well be called something else.

His subsequent attempts to define the term as he uses it make considerable use of anecdotal and historical evidence. He becomes specific, but still rather unclear, when he presents the following definition (Erikson, 1968, p. 22):

> [I]n psychological terms, identity formation employs a process of simultaneous reflection and observation, a process taking place on all levels of mental functioning, by which the individual judges himself in the light of what he perceives to be the way in which others judge him in comparison to themselves and to a typology significant to them; while he judges their way of judging him in the light of how he perceives himself in comparison to them and to types that have become relevant to him. This process is, luckily, and necessarily, for the most part unconscious except where inner conditions and outer circumstances combine to aggravate a painful, or elated, "identity-consciousness."

At a simpler level, the formation of an identity involves arriving at a notion not so much of what one is, but rather of what one *can* be. That is, adolescents are not faced with the task of discovering a self that already exists, but rather of developing one of several selves that are potential. The crisis stems in part from having to develop a stable and clear identity and in part from the varied

142

choices of identities that present themselves to each adolescent. In the end, it is a sense of identity that permits adolescents to make those decisions that will be required of them as adults. These decisions include choice of vocation, marriage partner, or alternative life-style. The predominant conflict of this developmental phase, as it is described by Erikson, is one between accepting, discovering, or choosing an identity, and the diffusion of the adolescent's energies resulting from conflict and doubt regarding choice of identities. One possible solution to this dilemma is to become delinquent, an act which by its very nature implies assuming an identity that runs directly counter to that which would be accepted by society. This type of identity formation is labeled **negative identity.**

One of the primary sociocultural functions of adolescence is to serve as a delay of adulthood, as a psychological safety device. During this period of time, when adolescents are neither clearly children nor clearly adults, they are, to some extent, permitted to experiment with a variety of roles, some of which may involve negative identities; that is, identities that would not be conducive to normal adjustment as adults. But because they are not yet adults, adolescents can, even as they are experimenting with negative identities, re-affirm their ego strength and move in the direction of more positive identities (Erikson, 1956). The important point is that the period of adolescence provides them with time to arrive at some clear and positive identities. Note that Erikson's conception of the usefulness of this period differs dramatically from theorists who have speculated that much of the turmoil associated with adolescence in contemporary cultures would not exist if these cultures clearly marked passage between childhood and adulthood.

Identity and Crises Various dimensions of the crises that can (but do not necessarily) beset adolescents have been discussed by Erikson (1954, 1959) and summarized briefly by Maier (1965). These, like other developmental phases described by Erikson, are expressed as bipolar tendencies. The resolution of these tendencies requires the development of a specific competence, attitude, or manner of behaving and the rejection of opposing tendencies. They are summarized here (based on Maier, 1965, pp. 58–60):

Time Perspective versus Time Diffusion. In order to develop a stable concept of identity, adolescents must also develop stable concepts of time as it relates to their changing self and their eventual position in adult society. Erikson labels excessive difficulty in establishing an identity or reluctance to do so for one reason or another as *time diffusion,* an inexact and confused notion of time. Some adolescents react to this crisis by doing nothing. In a sense, it is as though they have not yet developed a proper perspective of time; they hope that time will either stand still, thus not exposing them to anticipated problems; or they hope that time, in and of itself, will resolve all problems.

Self-certainty versus Apathy. The development of confidence with regard to who they are or who they can be is of central importance to the emergence of a strong sense of ego identity. Lacking this confidence, some adolescents react as though they were unconcerned; they react with apathy. Resolution of this crisis requires that the image that youths have of themselves agree with the way they think others see them.

Role Experimentation versus Negative Identity. In their quest to discover who they *can* be as opposed to who they are, adolescents may find it easier and considerably more comfortable to assume one of several negative identities rather than to experiment with a variety of more positive identities. That is, they may adopt a form of behavior rejecting those values and expectations that society sanctions; they may become delinquent in any of a variety of ways. Frequently the adolescent moratorium is sufficiently long to permit them to take their place in society as adults. But there are adult delinquents who have never progressed beyond adolescence psychologically.

Anticipation of Achievement versus Work Paralysis. Adjustment to adult society, particularly to those societies where the Puritan Ethic is still dominant, requires the focusing of energies toward productive ends and a rejection of inactivity, or at least of unfocused activity. The resolution of this crisis is of particular importance to future adjustment to vocational choice.

Sexual Identity versus Bisexual Diffusion. Resolving the sexual identity crisis involves identifying with an appropriate sex role (masculine or feminine) and rejecting bisexual tendencies. Erikson (1968) notes elements of a negative identity in the contemporary tendency of adolescents to mock the behavior and dress of the opposite sex. He says, "Sexual identity confusion? Yes, indeed; sometimes when we see them walking down the street it is impossible for us to tell, without indelicate scrutiny, who is a boy and who is a girl" (Erikson, 1968, p. 26).

Leadership Polarization versus Authority Diffusion. With the advent of adolescence comes the awareness that it is possible to lead; it is possible, as well, to be led. It becomes important for adolescents to develop some clear notion of their leadership potential, and, at the same time, to develop a willingness to lead when leadership is required or expected. Their appraisal of their own leadership qualities must somehow coincide with that of society.

Ideological Polarization versus Diffusion of Ideals. In an ideologically simple culture, it is relatively easy for adolescents to adopt a set of values and interests that conform to their sociocultural milieu. More important, it is easy for such adolescents to accept these values as valid and socially useful. In a diffuse and contradictory social milieu, however, adolescents are presented with a variety of ideological positions, many in conflict with traditional values. An important and difficult question, and one not easily resolved by many intelligent and apparently well adjusted adults, concerns whether these alternative ideological positions are in any absolute or relative sense inferior to those that appear to be predominant in the culture. Thus the crisis peculiar to the development of values and ideological beliefs is compounded by the ambiguity of the surrounding culture. Perhaps it is little wonder that the crises that surround adolescence sometimes appear to be more severe in contemporary, technological, nontotalitarian societies than they have been historically in simpler or more cohesive societies.

During the adolescent years children are presented with a relatively long period of time during which they are expected to resolve these various crises. Ideally, the end result of successful adjustment during this period would be adolescents who have little doubt concerning their ideological position; who are confident; who know clearly which sex they belong to and which behavior is acceptable for that sex; who are work-oriented, or at least fully prepared to be so; who have a clear and stable notion of time and its relationship to their position in society. In short, it would result in individuals who have developed clear, strong, and positive notions of who they will be, if not of who they are. And that, in a very real sense, may be considered to be the major developmental task of all life.

Erikson describes three additional stages that are relevant to the adult years: intimacy versus isolation (young adulthood); generativity versus stagnation (adulthood), and ego integrity versus disgust, despair (maturity). Because a discussion of these would contribute relatively little to an understanding of the central subject of this book, the adolescent, they are not commented upon here. Besides, Sam has promised to write a book on the psychology of

145

postadolescence. "It will once and for all firmly establish the position of the grandmother and the grandfather in our social context," he claims. I await with unbated breath.

Cognitive Theory

Biological developmental theories (Hall and Gesell) rely heavily on genetic and evolutionary facts; sociological theories attempt to explain development in terms of social and cultural forces and their effects on individuals; psychoanalytic theories place greater emphasis on unconscious motivational forces in interaction with environmental forces and draw heavily on the work of Freud; cognitive developmental theories are concerned primarily with describing and explaining the processes by which individuals progress in their intellectual (cognitive) understanding of the world.

Piaget

The best known and by far the most influential of all contemporary cognitive theories is that advanced by Piaget and elaborated by a great variety of his followers, most notable among whom is Inhelder. An outline of the basic theory is presented in the remainder of this chapter. More detailed discussions of his stage theory, particularly as it applies to adolescence, are left to the following chapter, which deals specifically with cognitive development, intelligence, and creativity in the adolescent.

In one sense Piaget's is also a biological theory, although the description of development that he provides goes considerably beyond most biological theories in both detail and emphasis. One of the models underlying Piaget's description of children, particularly in infancy, is drawn directly from biology.

The biologists' primary concerns have traditionally been with classifying species in phylogenetic order and with accounting for the fact that certain species have survived while others have not. The first concern of the biologist, that of classifying species, is reflected in Piaget's description of the characteristics of development. This description classifies forms of behavior from simple to most complex very much as a biologist classifies species from simplest to most complex. The second concern is solved by some discussion of adaptation, a concept that Piaget applied directly to his discussion of children at various stages of their development.

The single great force that has been predominant in discussions of evolution, adaptation, is also predominant in Piaget's discussion of his basic developmental model. Newborn children are obviously incapable of immediate independent adaptation to their world. Indeed, during early infancy they are capable of only a limited number of extremely simple, though adaptive, behaviors. They respond reflexively to a variety of external or internal situations, either by sucking, swallowing, sneezing, hiccuping, defecating, turning their heads, grasping, or regurgitating. They remain incapable of controlled, conscious activity, reacting to the world rather than acting upon it. Effective adaptation requires that they progressively modify their reactions in order to cope with increasingly demanding situations. This they accomplish through two related processes, **assimilation** and **accommodation.** Assimilation involves using aspects of the environment or responding to them in terms of already learned behaviors. Thus, when children suck in response to the presence of a nipple in their mouth, they can be said to be assimilating the nipple to the activity of sucking, or, more precisely, to their collection of "things to suck on." Assimilation, as such, requires no new learning and hence no real adaptation. If, however, some change, however slight, is required of children's behavior in order to respond to the stimulation, they must then accommodate to it. If, for example, objects placed in children's mouths require a slightly different placement of the lips and tongue, and perhaps a slightly different movement of these sucking components, these changes define accommodation. Piaget maintains that all activity involves both assimilation and accommodation, although one may predominate over the other. Because the function of assimilating or of accommodating does not change from birth to adulthood, these activities are referred to as *invariants;* and because it is only by means of these activities that children can function with respect to their environment, they are also labeled **functional.** Hence assimilation and accommodation are the **functional invariants** of adaptation.

Intimately related with the processes of adaptation are certain structures assumed to be present in children's minds at birth. These structures, initially called **schemes** (or sometimes schema or schemata) correspond to the overt physical reactions of which children are capable. Thus there is a sucking

A SUCKING SCHEMA MEETS A GRASPING SCHEMA

schema corresponding to the activity of sucking; a grasping schema corresponding to the activity of grasping; and a reaching schema corresponding to the activity of reaching. It is important to note, however, that the schema is more than the simple overt behavior that names it; it also includes certain neurological or **structural** connotations. That is, for every behavior of which children are capable, there must be a corresponding "something" in their neurological systems (Flavell, 1963).

Piaget's description of development is premised on the notion that through the continual interaction of assimilation and accommodation in the face of environmental demands, children's intellectual structures (schemata) are modified. Thus a description of development is in effect a description of cognitive structures at various stages of elaboration beginning with the very primitive reflexive repertoire of the newborn infant and culminating in the relatively sophisticated intellectual functioning of the normal adult. Piaget's four major developmental stages, the last of which corresponds to the period of adolescence, are described in detail in Chapter 6. Piaget's notions concerning intelligence are also discussed in that chapter.

Summary

This chapter began with a brief visit with Sam. Sam has very definite opinions concerning the opinions of social scientists relative to those of natural scientists. It then moved on to a consideration of psychological theories particularly as they apply to an understanding of adolescence. Four major approaches to theorizing in this area were identified: the biological, the sociological, the psychoanalytical, and the cognitive. The recapitulation theory of G. Stanley Hall was discussed as an example of a biological theory. Gesell's more recent formulations, together with a resume of some of his age profiles, were presented as a second example of the biological approach. Moving to sociological positions, the chapter looked at Havighurst's work, paying particular attention to his concept of developmental tasks: tasks that must be mastered by the children of a culture. Freud's work was then introduced in a section on psychoanalytical theory, as was Erikson's. Psychosexual stages and developmental periods were described. Finally the chapter stopped briefly before Piaget's monumental cognitive theory, promising to describe it in detail in Chapter 6.

Main Points

1. Sam expounds on the extent to which social sciences rely on documentation to support their opinions and on the relationship between strength of convictions and empirical evidence.

2. Theories are attempts to provide clear, concise, and accurate explanations and descriptions of observed phenomena. Their value lies both in explanation and in prediction. They can also be valuable in suggesting ways of gathering new information.

3. Biological theories of adolescent development are premised on the notion that the phenomenon of adolescence is primarily genetically based.

4. Hall's biological theory of development describes adolescence as a period of storm and stress ("sturm und drang"). He believed that ontogeny recapitulates phylogeny, that every child in the course of development goes through a series of stages that parallel the stages that humans went through during their evolution.

5. Gesell's biological theory is somewhat less genetically deterministic than is Hall's. He admitted that variations in individual characteristics would sometimes be caused by environmental factors. Much of his work consisted of providing descriptive profiles of children at different ages.

6. One of the most notable characteristics of Gesell's profiles for the adolescent years is that succeeding years are always a contradiction of those that precede them. Conflict and calm recur in cyclical patterns.

7. Sociological theories of adolescence interpret this period as being primarily a cultural phenomenon. Evidence that this is so is derived chiefly from the observation that adolescence varies across cultures.

8. Havighurst's sociological theory of adolescence describes this period in terms of a number of tasks that individuals must master if they are to attain adulthood within their culture. That is, there are a number of competences that are expected of children at different ages. In the same manner, there are competences expected of adults but not of children. These constitute learning tasks for adolescents.

9. Chief among the adolescent's developmental tasks described by Havighurst are the following: accepting one's physique; developing appropriate sex roles; achieving economic and emotional independence from parents; achieving appropriate relationships with peers; and preparing for an adult life-style and a vocation.

10. Psychoanalytic theory is derived from the work of Freud.

11. Among the most basic ideas advanced by Freud was the notion that all energy for human behavior is derived from basic instinctual urges collectively called *libidinal urges*. These are expressed as survival/pleasure urges (Eros) manifested in sexually related activities and, to a less important extent, in the Freudian death wish (Thanatos).

12. Human personality, according to Freud, is divided into three structures that develop progressively. The most basic stage is the id; it is characteristic of infants and consists of unlearned instincts. The ego arises as children become aware of environmental restrictions and therefore represents the reality-based level of personality. The superego is an embodiment of social and moral constraints imposed on behavior either by society, by religion, or by both.

13. Freud's description of development is a description of psychosexual stages: stages that derive their labels from the activities that serve as the major sources of sexual gratification during that period.

14. The psychosexual stages described by Freud are, in order: oral, anal, phallic, latent, and genital.

15. Abnormal personality development is sometimes thought to involve arrested development at one of these stages (fixation) or a reversion to the modes of sexual gratification most common during an earlier developmental stage (regression).

16. Conflicts between basic impulses (id impulses) and moral and social constraints (the superego) are frequently resolved through mediation of the ego, which utilizes various defense mechanisms.

17. In essence, defense mechanisms serve to distort individuals' perceptions of reality, of their motives, or of their desires. The main defense mechanisms

are displacement, reaction formation, intellectualization, projection, denial, and repression.

18. Erikson has also advanced a psychoanalytical theory of adolescent development based in part on Freud's writings. It differs from Freud's theory in its emphasis on will (ego), on the process of socialization, and in terms of its concern with healthy development.

19. Erikson describes human development as involving progression through eight distinct phases. Each of these stages is characterized by the resolution of a conflict. The resolution is considered to involve the development of a sense of some competence in the face of opposing feelings of incompetence.

20. Erikson's first five phases are, in sequence: trust versus mistrust; autonomy versus shame and doubt; initiative versus guilt; industry versus inferiority; and identity versus role diffusion.

21. In addition, Erikson outlines a number of crises that are specific to adolescence. The most significant of these involves the development of a sense of identity. This involves a selection of who the individual can be from among a number of competing identities, some of which are negative rather than positive.

22. Cognitive theories of adolescent development are concerned primarily with describing the intellectual changes that occur during adolescence.

23. Piaget is the foremost contemporary cognitive theorist. He describes development in terms of progression through stages that reflect increasing intellectual organization. Children's progressive adaptation to their world is assumed to require that they develop certain cognitive skills in interaction with their environment.

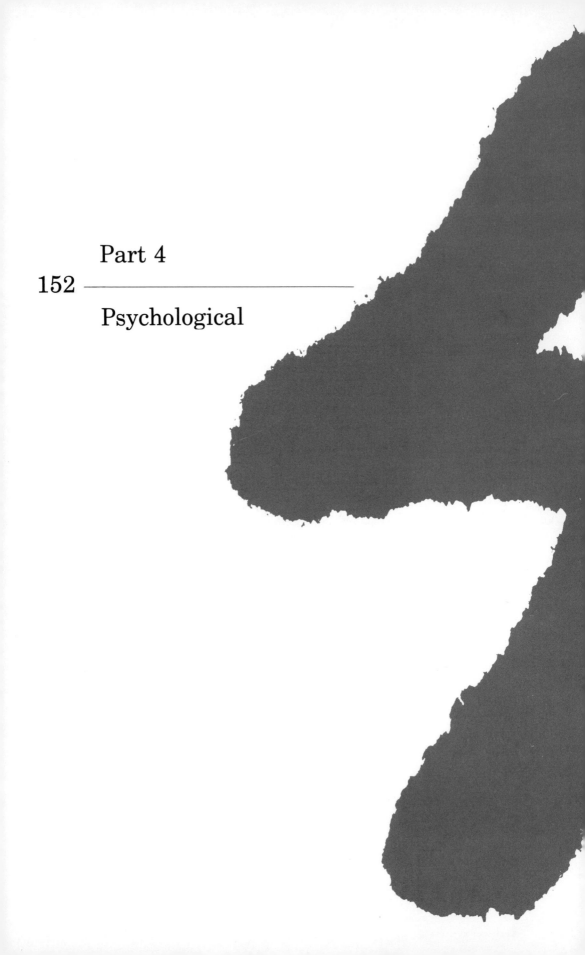

Part 4

152

Psychological

Chapter 6

**Samuel the First:
Intellectual Development
and Creativity**

Chapter 7

**A Proposal of Marriage:
Personality and the Self**

Chapter 6

Samuel the First: Intellectual Development and Creativity

Shelley Drinkwater, Grade 11

156

* If there is one thing more important than any other in my essay on adolescence, it must surely be the account that I have given of the many reasons why children today find it difficult to adjust to the demands of their teachers, their parents, and other well-intentioned but frequently misguided authorities. It is small wonder that the drug culture proliferates, that delinquency and rebellion have become a way of life, and that young girls get pregnant out of spite.

Yes, out of spite, for the act has become so mechanical and so matter of fact that there can surely be no other reason why a young girl would allow herself to engage in activities leading to pregnancy. Besides it is well known that girls don't enjoy sex much more than do rats. And I know from experience that rats don't enjoy it very much at all.

Things were indeed different when I was an adolescent. Not that I always had an easy time of it. But in general life was pleasant and we had not yet discovered ways of expanding, shrinking, deforming, reforming, or otherwise altering our minds. Except alcohol, of course, but that was always on rare occasions, because adults would seldom buy it for us even when we had enough money.

But I did get into some difficulty with one of my teachers. Well, perhaps with both of them. There were only two in the high school I attended. One was the principal; the other, the vice-principal.

In those days I had a peculiar penchant for writing poetry and for doing scientific research. My acne was then too severe to allow me to participate confidently in most of the social activities of my peers. In any case, I had little time left over for them. I had begun breeding a colony of rats with a view to determining the principal causes of intelligence in these creatures. It seemed to me reasonable to suppose that whatever causes intelligence in rats also causes intelligence, or the lack thereof, in humans. Accordingly I had devised various experimental programs in an attempt to increase manifestations of intelligence among my rats. One group was on a specially prepared diet of spinach and various other mineral rich foods. A second group was being fed nothing but organ meats with selected chemical additives. For a third group I had purchased a large variety of toys. A fourth group was in isolation and deprivation. The fifth group caused me the greatest difficulty. These were the rats that I brought to school with me. It seemed possible, though admittedly improbable, that some

---

* This excerpt from Sam's essay on adolescence is reprinted with his permission.

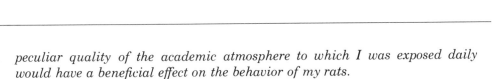

peculiar quality of the academic atmosphere to which I was exposed daily would have a beneficial effect on the behavior of my rats.

The principal objected rather strenuously to my efforts on behalf of science and insisted that I remove the two cages that I had brought with me. I felt it wise to cooperate at the time, and removed the cages. Ingenious as I then was, I devised a new experimental program for all of these rats save one. This last rat I simply inserted in my pocket so that I could bring him to school undetected.

That was how Samuel's great-great-grandfather went to school. He spent most of his days curled up quietly inside my pocket, only occasionally raising his head to peer about curiously. He seemed little impressed by esoteric academic proceedings.

My research would have continued quite uneventfully had it not been for what happened on the second last day of school that year. I had worn an old brown sweater to school that day and had tucked Samuel the First in my pocket. It happened, much to my embarrassment, that there was a small hole in one corner of that pocket, and when I was asked to go to the board in order to demonstrate my scholarship for the other peasants in the classroom, Samuel the First's tail protruded unashamedly from this hole. Some intelligent young damsel noticed this unusual appendage and laughed in a somewhat hysterical and silly manner thereby calling the attention of my classmates, and of my teacher I might add, away from my scholarship to my anatomy. I attempted desperately to make my explanation sufficiently lucid that all concerned would grasp as clearly as I did the tremendous potential significance of the research that I had undertaken. In particular, I demonstrated for them how Samuel the First responded clearly and directly when his name was called, a phenomenon that I have since been able to replicate with very few of my rats. Smiling ingratiatingly, I suggested to the teacher that this was probably a direct reflection of the academic atmosphere of his classroom.

He disputed neither this final contention nor the potential significance of my research, but simply, though in a rather uncontrolled manner, informed me that I was forthwith suspended from school pending an investigation, report, and other quasi-legal procedures that would be invoked to determine my desirability and my eligibility as a student of that particular school.

Intelligence, dear reader, and creativity, are not easily tolerated by those who have been charged with developing these qualities, but who possess them to a limited degree. As Oscar Wilde once said in The Decay of Lying, *"Everybody*

Table 6.1 Piaget's Stages of Cognitive Development

Stage	Approximate Age	Some Major Characteristics
Sensorimotor	0–2 years	Motoric intelligence. World of the here and now. No language, no thought in early stages. No notion of objective reality.
Preoperational Preconceptual Intuitive	2–7 years 2–4 years 4–7 years	Egocentric thought. Reason dominated by perception. Intuitive rather than logical solutions. Inability to conserve.

158

who is incapable of learning has taken to teaching." More prosaic minds have since paraphrased this statement to "Those who can, do; those who can't, teach."
It is an abject shame, considering . . .

Piaget's Theory of Development

Piaget's theory of human development is among the most comprehensive and far reaching of all developmental theories. It touches not only on the central problem of the development of intelligence, but explores as well the development of specific knowledge, capabilities, and understanding in such diverse areas as time, space, causality, morality, number, language, and so on. A brief review of Piaget's description of the major characteristics of children at each of the four developmental stages is provided here before going to a more detailed description of adolescent thinking (see also Table 6.1). It is important to keep in mind that the ages assigned to each of these stages is merely an approximation. While there is considerable variation in the ages at which different children attain each of these stages, their order appears to be relatively invariant.

Sensorimotor (Birth to Two Years)

The labels assigned to each of Piaget's stages are generally indicative of the major characteristics of children's thinking during the stage. Thus **sensorimotor** children can be described in terms of a sensory and a motoric type of intelligence. They understand their world only in terms of their sensations of it and in terms of their activities toward it. And it is precisely for this reason that the world of infants is a world of the "here and now," for it is impossible for infants to sense an object or to react to it when it is not physically present. One of the major developmental achievements of this period is, in fact, the eventual realization that objects continue to exist even when they are not immediately being sensed. This realization, sometimes referred to as the development of the **object concept,** is made possible by children's internalization of aspects of their environment. By this is meant simply that children are eventually able to represent real objects or activities mentally, an ac-

Stage	Approximate Age	Some Major Characteristics
Concrete operations	7–11 or 12 years	Ability to conserve. Logic of classes and relations. Understanding of number. Thinking bound to concrete. Development of reversibility in thought.
Formal operations	11 or 12– 14 or 15 years	Complete generality of thought. Propositional thinking. Ability to deal with the hypothetical. Development of strong idealism.

complishment of tremendous significance for future intellectual development. Internal representation (imagination in one sense) makes thought possible. It also contributes significantly to the development of language because a word is, in a very real sense, an internalized representation of an object or activity. Toward the end of the sensorimotor period, as a function of continued interaction with their environment, children's initially primitive intellectual structures have been elaborated to the point where they have developed some reasonably accurate notions concerning the objective world and its existence apart from them, and where they have begun to use language in their interaction with and interpretation of this world.

Preoperational Thought
(Two to Seven Years)

The predominant characteristics of children in the period of preoperational thought are again defined by this stage's label, **preoperational.** An operation is a mental activity or a thought that is subject to certain rules of logic, the most important of which is labeled **reversibility.** A thought (also called an internalized action by Piaget) is reversible when it is capable of being "un-thought": that is, when the action it represents is capable of being reversed and the logical implications of doing so are understood. Consider, for example, the following problem. Two identical balls of plasticene are presented to a young child. She admits that they both have the same amount of plasticene in them since they are identical in appearance. One of the balls is then flattened, lengthened, or otherwise deformed. The child now thinks that the deformed ball no longer has the same amount of plasticene in it because its appearance has changed drastically. She may, for example, believe that a lengthened ball has more plasticene in it because it is so much longer. Alternately, she may think that it has less because it is thinner. What she does not yet realize is that the operation of deforming the ball can be reversed both in fact and mentally. That is, the deformed ball can be made identical to what it was before. It follows, then, that it must still have the same amount of plasticene as it had previously. Because preoperational children cannot yet deal with

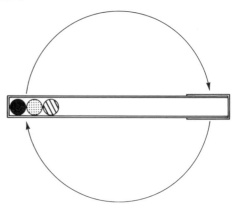

Figure 6.1 An experiment that demonstrates the intuitive nature of children's thought. Three different-colored beads are inserted into the tube, the ends are closed, and the tube is slowly rotated a small number of turns or half turns. The child must decide what the order of the beads in the tube is after each rotation.

160

operations, they are typically incapable of answering correctly when faced with a problem of this nature. In other words, their thought processes are still irreversible.

Several other characteristics of preoperational children's thinking processes are revealed in this **conservation** of mass problem. Children's thought is dominated largely by their **perceptions.** And where there is an apparent conflict between perception and thought, unlike an adult, they will rely on what they perceive rather than on what they think. In addition, their solutions for many problems continue to be **intuitive** rather than logical. A clear illustration of this is provided by an experiment involving three colored beads that are placed on a rod and inserted into a cardboard tube. The beads are of different colors, and the child is asked to note what order they are in—for example, red, then yellow, then green (see Figure 6.1). Once the beads are inserted in the tube, the child can no longer see the beads. The tube is then rotated through a half turn, a whole turn, or a number of turns; and the child is asked in what order the beads will be now. The preoperational child is capable of answering correctly as long as the number of turns is small enough that he can continue to *imagine* the positions of the beads. That is, he can arrive at a correct answer through an intuitive imagination of the problem. More significant, however, he cannot arrive at a rule concerning the position of the beads following odd or even numbers of turns.

Preoperational thought, then, is not yet completely logical; it is dominated by perception and by intuition. In addition, it is described as being **transductive** rather than deductive or inductive. That is, children do not reason from the general to the particular (deductively), or from an array of specifics to a general rule (inductively), but reason instead from particular to particular (transductively). Transductive reasoning can, in some instances, provide children with a correct conclusion; at other times it can be quite faulty. The observation, for example, that A flies and B flies may lead to the correct conclusion that both A and B are birds—if indeed they *are* birds. It may also lead to the incorrect conclusion that B is an A where A is a bird and B is a plane. Children who call all furry animals "dogs" are probably reasoning transductively. Dogs have hair; that thing there has hair; therefore that thing is a dog. In point of fact, however, that thing is frequently a cat, a horse, a cow, or any number of other animals.

DOGGY!!

Concrete Operations
(Seven to Eleven or Twelve Years)

One of the major intellectual achievements of the period of concrete operations is the attainment of the ability to conserve. Conservation is defined as the realization that certain quantitative attributes of objects such as mass, length, distance, weight, and volume can remain unchanged despite a series of spatial displacements or changes in form (see Figure 6.2). The conservation of mass problem described earlier, for example, seldom presents any difficulty for children who have reached concrete operations. In fact the problem has become so simple for them that they are sometimes embarrassed at being required to answer it and will, on occasion, look desperately for some trick. Several years ago when a group of elementary school children were presented with similar problems, a number of the children answered incorrectly even though they clearly understood conservation of mass. It seemed that they doubted the honesty of psychologists and believed that I would probably surreptitiously take some material from the deformed ball, or add some.

The realization of conservation is important because it provides evidence of several logical rules that now govern children's thinking. The most important of these, reversibility, has already been described. In addition, children now understand **identity** and **compensation,** both of which can be illustrated by reference to any of several problems of conservation. In a typical conservation of liquids problem, for example, the subject is presented with two identical beakers filled to the same level with water. She admits that they both contain the same quantities of water. One of the beakers is then taken and its contents poured into a tall, narrow container where its resulting height will be much greater. A preoperational child will most likely think that the tall, thin container contains more water because it is higher, or that it contains less because it is thinner. A child at the stage of concrete operations, however, will realize that the new container has the same amount of water in it as the original container. If she is asked to justify her response, she may reason in one of three ways: 1. The water could be poured back into its original container, and it would look the same as it did then: it must therefore still have the same amount of water (reversibility). 2. The new container is taller, but it is also thinner. Its increase in height is compensated for by the decrease in width

Figure 6.2 Some simple tests for conservation with approximate ages of attainment.

1. Conservation of Substance (6-7)

A

The experimenter presents two identical plasticene balls. The subject admits that they have equal amounts of plasticene.

B

One of the balls is deformed. The subject is asked whether they still contain equal amounts.

2. Conservation of Length (6-7)

A

Two sticks are aligned in front of the subject. He admits their equality.

B

One of the sticks is moved to the right. The subject is asked whether they are still the same length.

3. Conservation of Number (6-7)

A

Two rows of counters are placed in one-to-one correspondence. Subject admits their equality.

B

One of the rows is elongated (or contracted). Subject is asked whether each row still has the same number.

4. Conservation of Liquids (6-7)

A

Two beakers are filled to the same level with water. The subject sees that they are equal.

B

The liquid of one container is poured into a tall tube (or a flat dish). The subject is asked whether each contains the same amount.

5. Conservation of Area (9-10)

A

The subject and the experimenter each have identical sheets of cardboard. Wooden blocks are placed on these in identical positions. The subject is asked whether each cardboard has the same amount of space remaining.

B

The experimenter scatters the blocks on one of the cardboards. The subject is asked the same question.

Figure 6.3 A test of a child's understanding of seriation. The series are presented in random order to a child who is asked to arrange them in correspondence so that the tallest doll has the longest cane and so on.

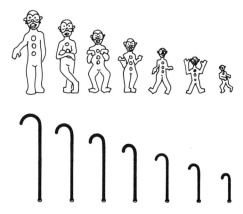

(compensation). 3. Nothing has been added to or taken away from the original amount and it has therefore remained unchanged (identity).

In addition to their ability to apply these rules of logic to problems of conservation, concrete operations children have acquired new capabilities with respect to classes, seriation, and numbers. They can now deal with classes as subsets of larger classes. A simple Piagetian problem illustrates this clearly. A child is presented with a bouquet of flowers, a few of which are roses; the majority are daffodils. The child is asked whether there are more daffodils or more flowers. A preconcrete operations child will typically answer that there are indeed more daffodils, failing to realize that because daffodils is a subset of the larger class, flowers, there must be fewer of them. It is as though the larger class, flowers, were destroyed when it is broken down into its subclasses. Of course, children at the period of concrete operations do not make this error.

Coupled with this ability to deal with classes, children can now deal with series. That is, they can order objects serially in terms of some changing dimension, and they can set up correspondences among several series. When Piaget asked children to arrange dolls from shortest to longest, and to place a series of canes that also ranged from long to short, in an order corresponding to that of the dolls, children at the preoperational stage were typically unable to respond correctly whereas children in concrete operations experienced no difficulty (see Figure 6.3).

Because an understanding of classification and seriation is essential to a complete understanding of the cardinal (class) and ordinal (series) properties of number, children also gain an understanding of number with the development of these two abilities.

One of the major characteristics of the thinking of children at the stage of concrete operations, and one that is particularly important because it reveals a striking contrast to the thinking of adolescents, is that thought at this stage is still bound to the concrete; hence the label "concrete operations." Children's thinking remains tied to the real or to the potentially real. They have no difficulty, for example, in ordering real series of concrete objects or events, but when faced with an identical verbal problem, they often find themselves at a loss. Consider, for example, the problem of determining which of three children is the heaviest when all three children are standing in front of the subject and when differences in weight are readily apparent. The problem poses little difficulty. If, however, the child is presented with the same problem verbally, it becomes considerably more difficult: "Betty is heavier than Sam, but lighter than Joe. Who is the heaviest and who is the lightest?"

Formal Operations (Eleven or Twelve to Fourteen or Fifteen Years)

Adolescence is marked by some highly significant changes in children's intellectual operations. Perhaps the most striking and the most important of these is children's newfound ability to deal with the hypothetical. Adolescents' thought processes are no longer tied to the concrete; they can now deal with that which can merely be imagined, and they can deal with it at a level of logical sophistication as advanced as that of any adult (potentially at least, because not all adolescents are capable of advanced logical thought. Nor, of course, are all adults).

The thinking of adolescents is described as **propositional** rather than as concrete. A proposition is simply a statement that can be either right or wrong. It can be tied to the probable or improbable hypothetical, or it can be tied to some objective reality. Regardless, it will be dealt with in terms of an implicit set of logical rules that govern all thinking.

Adolescent thought has also been described as **hypothetico-deductive** because it permits the deduction of conclusions derived from hypothetical propositions. It has also been described as involving **combinatorial analysis,** a logical procedure where all possible alternatives are systematically examined, discarded, or accepted. The model employed by Piaget to serve as an explanatory and descriptive analogy for adolescent thought processes is a mathematical-logical model borrowed from Boolean logic and from the Bourbaki school of mathematics. Its sophistication and complexity place it somewhat beyond the scope of this text.

Representative Experiments The nature of adolescent thought as it is revealed by Inhelder and Piaget (1958) is best illustrated by direct reference to their experiments.

In the pendulum experiment, the adolescent is presented with strings of different lengths and a variety of weights. He is asked to determine what

Table 6.2   The Pendulum Problem as Seen by the Adolescent

	Length	Weight	Force of Push	Observation
1	long	heavy	strong	slow
2	long	light	strong	slow
3	short	heavy	strong	fast
4	short	light	strong	fast
5	long	heavy	weak	slow
6	long	light	weak	slow
7	short	heavy	weak	fast
8	short	light	weak	fast

factors will cause a pendulum to oscillate more rapidly or less rapidly. In order to solve the problem, he is allowed to arrange the weights and strings in whatever combinations he wishes. He is also allowed to push the pendulum as hard or as softly as he wishes.

When this problem is presented to a preoperational child, he will typically experiment with one or more combinations of the elements involved. Not infrequently, he will conclude that the force with which he pushes the pendulum is a significant factor in determining the speed of the oscillation – a clearly incorrect solution based largely on the child's expectations rather than on his observations. A child at the stage of concrete operations will not make the same mistake. Tied to the concrete world, he is relatively unlikely to make a mistake regarding concrete observations. What he will not do, however, is systematically arrange all factors in all possible combinations. Thus he may arrive at a correct solution of the problem; namely, that the length of the string is a crucial factor in determining the frequency of oscillations. At the same time, however, he is likely to conclude that the weight of the pendulum is important as well. The adolescent, however, will systematically vary weights and length in all possible manners as depicted in Table 6.2. Having arranged the experimental situation in this manner, he makes his observations, and generally arrives at the correct solution (or solutions). While the problem and its solution may appear trivial, note that the preadolescent could not solve it systematically as did the adolescent. His was, in a sense, a failure to arrive at all relevant testable hypotheses (long, heavy; long, light; and so on), as well as a failure to carry on the experiment and make observations that would be free from bias.

A second experiment that dramatically illustrates differences between adolescent and preadolescent thought processes is one involving liquids in five separate test tubes. A specific combination of these liquids will result in a yellow liquid. This fact is demonstrated to the child by the experimenter who pours a small quantity of liquid from one test tube (potassium iodide) into another. The potassium iodide is kept apart so that the child knows beforehand that it is necessary. She is simply asked to discover what combination or combinations of the remaining four test tubes together with the one that has been kept apart, will yield the yellow liquid.

Not surprisingly, the preadolescent begins her experimentation in an unsystematic and haphazard fashion, combining liquids almost at random by

Figure 6.4 All possible combinations of the four test tubes to which the fifth can be added. The experiment requires the subject to discover the combination(s) that yield a yellow liquid when potassium iodide is added. The correct solutions are circled.

twos, perhaps by threes, but seldom in a fashion that will allow her to exhaust all possible combinations. Thus, if she does arrive at a correct solution, she is likely to stop. If asked whether there are any other possible solutions, she will have to begin her experimentation again, frequently repeating combinations that she has already tested.

The adolescent, on the other hand, will combine all liquids in all possible ways (depicted in Figure 6.4). Thus not only will she discover a correct solution, but she will discover two. Moreover, she will know beyond any reasonable doubt that there are two, and only two, correct solutions.

In summary, these experiments illustrate several of the important differences between children's thought and adolescents' thought. Children's hypotheses are actual combinations translated into action. That is, they do not envision the range of possible solutions, but instead attempt directly to verify the first solution that presents itself, then the next, the next, and so on. Adolescents, on the other hand, begin by envisioning all possibilities before translating them into those actions that will serve as direct (or indirect) tests of their hypotheses. This is the fundamental distinction between concrete thinking and hypothetico-deductive thought.

The experiments also illustrate the combinatorial nature of adolescents' thought. Because they do not consider each hypothesis as separate from all others, they are able to eliminate a number of them without overlooking any. Preadolescents view each hypothesis as an unrelated test, and because they arrive at them haphazardly to begin with, they are likely to overlook a number. Their solutions are exhaustive only by accident. Frequently they are not exhaustive, and that too perhaps only by accident.

The Piagetian Adolescent

Adolescents do not spend most of their time engaged in problems of the type just described. Indeed, they are likely to encounter these problems relatively infrequently in schools, and even less frequently in out-of-school life. They serve more as illustrations of the power of their thinking than as descriptions of it as it is manifested in everyday life.

Yet the same intellectual powers that are illustrated so forcefully in Piagetian problems are also brought to bear when adolescents consider their

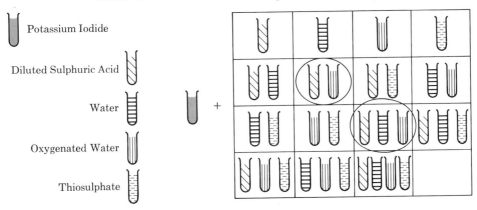

Potassium Iodide

Diluted Sulphuric Acid

Water

Oxygenated Water

Thiosulphate

world and their society. And for the first time in the history of their development, these intellectual powers are no longer restricted to concrete objects
and events. They go far beyond, into the realm of worlds that don't exist,
states of affairs that are not actual. Because adolescents are capable of handling these states of affairs in a logical manner, they are now capable of an
idealism of which they were quite incapable during an earlier period. They can
envision the world as they think it should be rather than as it is. And they can
be profoundly distressed at the space that separates their utopia from actuality. The idealism of adolescence is not merely a social accident; rather, it is
made possible by intellectual abilities now being exercised for the first time.
As Inhelder and Piaget (1958) noted, children live very much in the present,
but adolescents live very much in the hypothetical future. Their world is a
world of theories and plans concerning both themselves and their society. And
the adaptive significance of this dramatic change is inherent in the fact that
adolescents are in the process of preparing themselves to assume adult roles
(Flavell, 1963). Piaget suggests, as well, that with the advent of formal operations, there is also a reaffirmation of an egocentricism that was earlier
apparent in the infant's self-centered view of the physical world. This more
advanced egocentricism centers around an abstract world; and it manifests
itself in a "kind of naive idealism, bent on intemperate proposals for reforming
and reshaping reality and—here the 'omnipotence of thought' characteristic
of all egocentrism—with an immoderate belief in the efficacy of its thought
coupled with a cavalier disregard for the practical obstacles which may face
its proposals" (Flavell, 1963, p. 224). Adolescents firmly believe in the possibility of transforming the world through ideas. It is worth noting that most
adults no longer adhere to the same belief. And perhaps the feelings of powerlessness and alienation that are descriptive of contemporary existentialism
result from the clash of brutal reality with untempered idealism; and eventually they result in adult as opposed to adolescent ideals.

Intelligence

Among the most nebulous, but the most highly prized, of all human characteristics is **intelligence.** Not that intelligence is necessarily a human as
opposed to a subhuman quality. There are stupid dogs and intelligent yaks

Dominique *Age 15* **On Being Concerned**

Me: *Do you see any difference between you and kids who are on the outside?*
Dominique: *My group, no. But some. Guys who go to school every day and church and everything. Yeah, they're different.*
Me: *Do you feel sorry for them? (Pause) How do you feel about the way they're different from you?*

Dominique: *I don't really care.*
Me: *Is there anything you really care about?*
Dominique: *Nope.*
Me: *Do you follow the news? Are you concerned at all about what is happening in the world.*
Dominique: *Nope.*

168

even as there are stupid people and intelligent people. But the manifestation of intelligence in subhuman species takes a different form from that in humans. And humans have long prided themselves on being the most intelligent of all creatures. Judging from their ability to manipulate the environment and from the complexity of the worlds that they have built, perhaps the pride is justifiable.

We have long assumed that intelligence is directly related to the brain. More particularly, it is related to those portions of the brain concerned with such higher functions as abstract reasoning and numerical and verbal ability in contrast to those portions of the brain concerned with physiological functions such as respiration and heartrate. Physically, the human brain is quite impressive. In the average human male, the brain weighs approximately three and one-quarter pounds; in the female, slightly less than three pounds. The average adult female weighs considerably less than the average adult male and therefore the brain-to-body weight ratio for adult males and females is virtually identical in the human species. And it is probably brain-to-body weight ratio that is most closely related to intelligence among species. Consider, for example, that elephants and whales sometimes develop massive brains; their brains may weigh close to twenty pounds. Given the sheer bulk of these animals, however, their brain-to-body weight ratios are very low (much lower than a human's one-to-fifty ratio), and most of the brain mass must then be given over to the regulation of physiological functions.

There is, however, one animal that has a better brain-to-body weight ratio than humans. The dolphin has a brain that, at maturity, weighs three and three-quarter pounds; an average adult dolphin weighs approximately the same as an average adult human male. And the dolphin's brain is as complex in structure and in convolutions (patterning of wrinkles on the brain's surface). A number of investigators have suggested the possibility that the dolphin is potentially as intelligent as humans. No one yet knows for certain. And though we can point to our material achievements — our cities, our transportation systems, our heating and lighting systems — as evidence of our superior intelligence, is it not true that the dolphin has no use for any of these?

Definition

There is no single, accurate definition of intelligence. There cannot be, because intelligence is not a fixed quantity or even a clearly recognizable

quality. It is, in fact, simply a hypothetical construct, a fiction for which the word *intelligence* has been invented. Unfortunately, we have the tendency to believe that for every noun in our language, there is a corresponding reality that, at the very least, the person who invented the word could point to and say, "Here is an example of a such-and-such." No one can point to an intelligence.

There are, nevertheless, useful definitions of intelligence. They are not definitions that allow anyone to point to anything and say, with reasonable assurance of being correct, "Here is an example of intelligence." But they are definitions that allow one to point to some form of behavior or to some object and say, "Here, perhaps, is an example of one possible manifestation of what is often referred to by some as intelligence, maybe."

Among the earliest of hundreds of different definitions of intelligence is one advanced by Boring (1923): "Intelligence is what the tests test" (p. 35). The definition is not entirely facetious because intelligence can never be measured directly, as can height or weight, for example; it must always be inferred from samples of behavior. Tests that are designed to allow individuals to display their behavior in situations presumably requiring some degree of intelligence can provide an operational definition of intelligence.

A second, often quoted definition is one provided by Wechsler (1958), originator of two of the better known individual intelligence tests: the WISC (Wechsler Intelligence Scale for Children) and the WAIS (Wechsler Adult Intelligence Scale). He defined intelligence as "the global and aggregate capacity of an individual to think rationally, to act purposefully, and to deal effectively with his environment."

Other theorists and researchers have defined intelligence as the ability to adapt to the environment or the ability to profit from experience. Defined in these terms, it becomes clear that intelligence is indeed not peculiarly human, but that many animals provide evidence of high relative intelligence in their adaptive behaviors. This definition is perhaps the most useful for students of psychology. It provides some feeling for the meaning of the term without an exposure to a variety of historical controversies regarding intelligence — controversies concerning whether intelligence is a single quality or quantity, or whether it is a collection of separate abilities; whether intelligence, if it could be measured accurately, would be shown to be a fixed and unchanging quality, or whether it is subject to individual fluctuation; whether intelligence is a function solely of hereditary factors, solely of environment, or of both; or whether intelligence is best defined in terms of potential or in terms of performance. Not that these controversies are irrelevant to a complete understanding of psychological research, theory, and speculation in this area, but simply that these questions are of little concern here.

Intelligence and Memory

That there is some relationship between intelligence and **memory** is obvious. Indeed, performance on any of the multitude of tasks that typically comprise intelligence test batteries requires that individuals have retained something from their former experiences. Even as it is extremely difficult, if not impossible, to assess the intelligence of newborn infants whose experiences are limited to those they might have had while in their mothers' uteri, it is extremely difficult to assess intelligence in those individuals who have not profited from experience sufficiently to learn at least the rudiments of the language that surrounds them.

But intelligence is clearly much more than simple remembering, if it is to be judged in terms of intelligence tests. Typically such tests require that the subjects make use of previously acquired abilities and information in order to solve new problems. They require abstract reasoning, for example, in any or all of a variety of areas including numerical, spatial, and verbal. It is clearly not accurate, therefore, to assume that measuring intelligence is the same as measuring memory, although memory functions are involved. Hence the significance of the following point.

Human grandmothers, and others less wise and perhaps less gifted, have often assumed that young children have better memories than older children and adolescents, and certainly much better memories than adults. They are led to this conclusion by the observation that children can, in a very short period of time, acquire an incredible variety of information and skills, not the least of which is the acquisition of language. Research, however, has demonstrated this venerable belief to be inaccurate.

Cole and Hall (1970) summarize a number of studies that indicate clearly that adolescents have better memories than children. Some of these same studies also indicate that adults have better memories than adolescents. In a typical study subjects were asked to memorize lines of poetry (Stroud and

Maul, 1933). Adolescents successfully remembered twice as many lines as did children when both were allowed the same amount of time for memorization.

As additional evidence that memory improves with age, consider that the average performance on intelligence tests where memory items are employed increases dramatically with age. On the Digit Span subtest of the Stanford-Binet, for example, subjects have a sequence of digits read aloud to them and are asked to recall them in their proper order. The average three-year-old recalls three digits; the average seven-year-old, five; and the average adult, eight.

Testing Intelligence

If intelligence is defined as the ability to profit from experience, then perhaps the best way of measuring it is to provide identical experiences to a group of subjects and to find some way of determining what profit they have gleaned from that experience. Obviously, the resultant measurement will be relative. That is, it will still be impossible to say that a specific individual possesses X amount of intelligence, and that another individual possesses Y. But under these circumstances, it would be possible to say that one individual demonstrates more intelligence than another. Following this, averages can be arrived at, indicating how much intelligence is typically manifested by the average seven-year-old or seventeen-year-old. And it would then also be possible to say that specific seven-year-olds behave as though they had the intelligence of average nine-year-olds whereas others behave as though they had the intelligence of average five-year-olds.

In fact, most attempts to measure intelligence are based directly upon this type of reasoning, with the exception that identical experiences are not provided for each of the subjects in order to determine how they profit from them. Instead, it is assumed that the experiences that a group of five-year-olds bring with them into a testing situation are relatively similar, particularly if they come from similar homes in identical or highly similar cultures. And this assumption is, in fact, one of the very serious limitations of most attempts to assess intelligence. There is no easy way of verifying the assumption that children who appear to have had similar backgrounds have in fact undergone

Figure 6.5 A normal curve depicting the theoretical distribution of IQ scores among humans. Note, for example, that the average score is 100, and that 68.26 percent of the population score between 85 and 115. Only 2.28 percent score above 130 or below 70.

identical, or even similar, experiences. Hence the tests, in whole or in part, are frequently unfair for a number of subjects. They can be unfair in one of two ways: they can provide an overestimate of intelligence if the subject's experiential background was particularly favorable for the items that are included in the test; conversely, they can provide gross underestimates if the experiential background differed significantly from that assumed by the test.

A second problem inherent in intelligence testing concerns the difficulty of standardizing a test; that is, of arriving at a relatively accurate notion concerning what the typical performance of a seven-year-old, for example, should be. For this reason, attempts to standardize tests generally involve very wide sampling across a variety of subcultures (different socioeconomic levels, occupational and genetic backgrounds, and so on).

Once average scores for different age groups have been satisfactorily established, it is then possible to refer to these scores in terms of mental ages. If, for example, the average score for nine-year-olds on a specific test is 72, and the average score for ten-year-olds is 81, it is then meaningful to say that anyone (from the particular experiential background for which the test is intended) who scores 72 has a mental age of nine, and anyone who scores 81 has a mental age of ten. A nine-year-old who has a score of 81, hence a mental age of ten, would be deemed to be more intelligent than a ten-year-old who had a score of 72, hence a mental age of nine.

The **Intelligence Quotient (IQ)** is not a mystical something of which the fortunate few possess a great deal and the ordinary masses only an average amount. It is simply a mathematical function that originally expressed a relationship between real age (chronological age) and mental age. Specifically, an IQ was derived by dividing mental age by chronological age and multiplying by 100 in order to eliminate the resulting decimals that might confuse psychologists. Thus a nine-year-old whose score on an intelligence test corresponds to a mental age of nine has an IQ of $9/9 \times 100 = 100$. A more intelligent nine-year-old would have a higher mental age and the intelligence quotient would be correspondingly higher.

In contemporary psychological measurement IQ is seldom expressed as a function of mental and chronological age, but is arrived at simply by converting raw scores on an intelligence test to what is labeled a "deviation IQ." This IQ, like the old IQ, has an arbitrary mean (average) of 100 and a distribu-

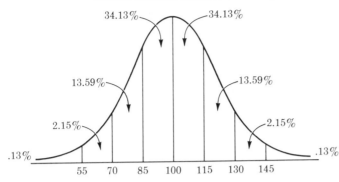

tion that can be interpreted in terms of a mathematical function known as a normal curve.

A normal curve is a bell-shaped distribution where the majority of observations cluster around the average, with progressively fewer observations as one progresses away from the average in either direction. The normal distribution for intelligence test scores is shown in Figure 6.5.

Verbal labels for various IQ ranges have proven useful in working with exceptionally gifted or retarded children, although the vast majority, as in all things, are somewhere around the Great Average. Some of these descriptive labels are given in Table 6.3.

Considerably less work has been done on the measurement of adolescent and adult intelligence than on the measurement of intelligence in younger children because it is more difficult to arrive at good items for older individuals. Not only must the items be difficult enough that not all individuals will answer them correctly if they are to discriminate among the haves and the have nots, but they must not be so highly specific as to be too difficult for the majority. Despite this difficulty, there are a number of tests that are appropriate for adolescents, and even for adults. Notable among these is the Stanford-Binet (Terman and Merrill, 1960). Studies with this and other tests have led to additional speculation and controversy regarding the nature of the intelligence these tests are designed to measure.

Growth Curves

There has long been considerable disagreement concerning the growth pattern of intelligence. Alternative points of view have maintained that intelligence is a fixed quality that does not change with age; that intelligence increases rapidly in early childhood, but ceases to increase equally rapidly in adolescence or early adulthood when the peak of intellectual performance has been reached; or that intelligence decreases slowly or increases slowly throughout childhood and perhaps up into adulthood.

First, the capabilities associated with intelligence do in fact increase, but this does not necessarily mean that measured intelligence will also increase. Twelve-year-olds can memorize more words than can five-year-olds. If they

Table 6.3 Descriptive Labels Sometimes Associated with IQ Ranges

Classification	IQ Range	Percent of Population
Very superior	140–169	1.3
Superior	120–139	11.3
High average	110–119	18.1
Normal	90–109	46.5
Low average	80–89	14.5
Borderline defective	70–79	5.6
Mentally defective	30–69	2.6

From L. M. Terman and M. A. Merrill, *Stanford-Binet Intelligence Scale* (Boston: Houghton Mifflin, 1960). Reprinted by permission of Houghton Mifflin Company, publisher of the Stanford-Binet.

174

couldn't, they wouldn't have the same intelligence quotient as the five-year-olds, but one that would be considerably lower.

Various studies of the growth curve of intelligence (for example, Bayley, 1955) indicate that intelligence does in fact increase from birth onward, but that the rate of increase tends to decline in early adolescence or late childhood. A large number of studies support the contention that intelligence continues to increase significantly, particularly among men, well into middle age and even beyond (Gurvitz, 1951; Jones, 1954; Green, 1969; Kangas and Bradway, 1971). This is most notably true of men who were initially superior in intelligence, more highly educated, and engaged in occupations that made continuing demands upon their intellectual resources. Garai and Scheinfeld (1968) speculate that the reason why men's measured IQs continue to increase long after most women's have ceased to do so is related to men's greater aggressiveness. And, in fact, there are some notable differences between the sexes on measures of intelligence throughout life.

Sex Differences

Maccoby (1963) notes that girls generally have a more rapid and earlier intellectual start than do boys. Not only is their verbal development more rapid, but so is their ability to count. Consequently they experience fewer reading problems, tend to do better on measures of achievement that are directly related to reading, and do at least as well in mathematical achievement. But the middle school years reveal differences between male and female intellectual functioning. Although general intelligence scores for the two sexes tend to be approximately equal, the pattern of abilities that contribute to these scores are noticeably different. Terman and Tyler (1954), Angrist, (1969), and many others found that girls tend to do better in languages, but that boys perform better in mathematics and in the sciences. And during adolescence, boys' verbal skills, on the average, catch up to those of girls and frequently surpass them (Bradway and Thompson, 1962). In their twenty-five year follow-up study of men and women who had been given the Stanford-Binet when they were children, Bradway and Thompson (1962) found that mean increases in measured intelligence were greater for men than for women. As has been noted earlier, they also found that gains in measured

Tracy *Age 18* **On Sex Differences in Achievement**

Me: *Do you think more boys or girls cheat?*
Tracy: *More girls. I think girls . . . girls are a lot more sneaky. Sure. I mean, I don't know, but I think a lot of guys are stupid . . . really dumb (laughter). Cause they rely so much on their physical being, on physical things. Like, this is not to say that all of them are like that, cause you can't stereotype them, but I know a lot of guys that I know are really stupid . . . or they appear stupid. They might not be inside, cause they've never tried—on the outside they're dolts.*

Me: *How do boys on the average make out, compared to girls. Say in this school?*
Tracy: *Make out in what way?*
Me: *In school. In terms of marks?*
Tracy: *Oh. I think, well the boys who do do well in class do superior.*
Me: *Better than the superior girls?*
Tracy: *Yeah. It seems that in the beginning when the school starts they have . . . they're slower verbally and things like that but by the end of grade twelve they're way higher above. The girls kinda get into this . . . trap of beauty.*

175

intelligence were highly related to the amount of formal education the subjects had been exposed to in their adolescence and early adulthood and to the quality of the experiences to which they had subsequently been exposed.

Sex differences in measured intelligence have most reasonably been explained in terms of interests that are largely culturally determined rather than in terms of any innate genetic differences regarding intellectual potential. It is interesting to note that a number of studies have found that girls who are superior in intellectual achievement, and particularly those who do well in the sciences and in mathematics, are more aggressive and more masculine than those who remain closer to the average (Maccoby and Rau, 1962; Kohlberg, 1966). It appears probable that cultural emphases favor less attention to intellectual achievement among girls, particularly in the sciences, and perhaps more attention to the nonaggressive acquiescence sometimes associated with a woman's traditional role as wife and mother. Horner (1969) compared the achievement orientation of groups of men and women in college by analyzing essays written by each subject beginning with the statement: "After first-term finals, John/Anne finds himself/herself at the top of his/her medical school class." Essays written by female subjects consistently showed a much lower achievement orientation than did those written by the men. The author concludes that men view achievement as more socially desirable than do women. Women on the other hand expressed a sometimes explicit fear of social rejection as a result of success and some feelings of guilt and anxiety associated with their apparent belief that success of this nature is not particularly feminine. Horner notes that women find many more social forces that inhibit their movements toward achievement than do men.

Hoffman (1972) investigated differences in achievement orientation of men and women and noted that women were consistently lower in measured need for achievement but exhibited significantly higher affiliative needs. Affiliative needs are manifested primarily in the individual's attempts to establish relationships with others. She notes, also, that women's orientations toward achievement appear to be predicated on different motives. Whereas boys are motivated by a desire to achieve mastery, girls tend to be motivated by affiliative needs. Not surprisingly, boys attempt more difficult tasks whereas girls are more likely to attempt tasks on which they will probably be successful (Veroff, 1969).

What is probably the best summary to date of research on sex differences in

*Like they have to adorn themselves all
the time and look just perfect while the
guys don't even worry about that. They're
just worrying about getting through
school.*
Me: *Do you think there is more pressure
on guys to do well in school than there is
on girls?*
Tracy: *Yes. I think there's a lot of pressure
on them. Like if they want to be doctors,
they have to take physics and chemistry
and biology.*

176

intelligence is provided by Maccoby and Jacklin (1974) in a book length review
of this topic. These authors identify four distinct areas in which there is sub-
stantial agreement concerning sex differences (pp. 351–52): females have
greater verbal ability than males; males excel in spatial-visual ability; males
excel in mathematical ability; males are more aggressive. They note, in
particular, that it is not correct that females lack in achievement motivation.
They do point out, however, that females do as well as males on measures of
achievement motivation only in neutral situations; males typically excel
when tested in competitive situations. Because achievement in contemporary society frequently involves competition, it is not surprising that males
appear to be more achievement oriented.

There are a number of highly plausible culturally based explanations for
these observed sex differences. Parents typically provide their daughters with
considerably less reinforcement for manifestations of independence. At
the same time, they are more protective towards daughters than sons. Hoffman
(1972) suggests that it is partly for these reasons that girls develop neither
the skills nor the confidence that is characteristic of boys when faced with
problem situations. The girl is considerably more likely to seek help and to
attempt to please significant people around her. Evidence that corroborates
these observations is provided by a study of mothers' expectations for their
children. Collard (1964) asked mothers at what age they would permit or
encourage their children to play independently, to go outside the home, to
cut with scissors, and so on. Not surprisingly, mothers of girls generally gave
higher ages than mothers of boys, indicating that boys are given opportunity
for the development of independence at earlier ages than are girls. It appears
that sex-role training begins very early in life.

Cross-cultural studies of sex differences in abilities have not always yielded
the same types of results as have been evident in other research, thereby
indirectly providing additional evidence that many of these differences are
culturally influenced. MacArthur (1973, 1974) administered a battery of
thirty-five tests to 177 Central Eskimos, 176 Greenland Eskimos, 192 Nsenga
Africans, and 206 Alberta Whites. Comparisons of results obtained by different groups led to the conclusion that there were almost no sex differences in
any of the tests. Greenland Eskimo males were only slightly superior in
inductive reasoning tests and on measures of spatial-field-independence (an
ability measured by such tasks as constructing designs with blocks); Central

Eskimo and Alberta White female adolescents showed a slight superiority in verbal-educational tasks. MacArthur notes, in particular, that there were no differences between male and female Nsenga Africans despite his expectations to the contrary and explains this finding in terms of the absence of differences between the sexes with respect to measures of need achievement, occupational plans, and parental aspirations for children. It is notable that in our culture these variables typically reflect major sex differences. These differences may be partly responsible for other differences observed in measures of intellectual ability. Given currently changing social conditions where sex-role stereotypes are being increasingly questioned and modified, it may well be that many sex differences will become less evident in the future.

Usefulness of Intelligence Tests

Despite the fact that intelligence tests are not perfectly valid (do not always measure what they claim to measure) or reliable (do not always measure accurately whatever it is that they do measure), they can be of considerable value for those who work with adolescents, particularly in the area of curricular or vocational guidance.

Because intelligence is to some degree related to the successful performance of school related tasks, very difficult courses will frequently require a higher general level of intelligence than less difficult courses. Knowledge of students' measured intelligence can be useful to counselors who advise students concerning their future educational possibilities. Unfortunately, however, too much emphasis is frequently placed on measured IQ. Not only is it true that an IQ measurement can fluctuate significantly from one situation to another, but it can also vary a great deal depending on the particular measuring instrument employed. Furthermore, it appears that intelligence as measured by tests is perhaps not the most significant variable to be considered. Motivation, interest, persistence, and various other personality attributes can be equally, or in some cases more, important in determining eventual success.

Cohen (1972) examined the relationship between poverty and low intelligence, and between higher intelligence and success in American society. He found, among other things, that poverty and low intelligence are not as highly correlated as one might expect. Even more striking, he found that measured intelligence is not as good a predictor of success (judged materially) as is education. He concluded that American society is not a meritocracy based on intelligence, but is instead a "schoolocracy." Indeed, it appears true that success on school related tasks correlates more highly with success in college than does measured intelligence. This may well be because success in school is dependent not only on intelligence, but also on such personality variables as industriousness, interest, motivation, and so on—factors that tend to be minimized in measurements of intelligence. In short, then, measures of intelligence are most useful when considered in combination with all additional evidence of potential for success.

Creativity

Although success in school is relatively highly correlated with measured intelligence, it appears to be somewhat less highly related to **creativity.** Yet creativity is highly prized in contemporary society, particularly because the solution of many of the critical problems that now confront advanced societies will require considerable creativity.

Definition

There is perhaps even less agreement concerning an acceptable definition of creativity than there is concerning intelligence. A wide variety of definitions have been offered by various researchers (Guilford, 1959; Mednick, 1962), most of them focussing on the nature of the creative process or on the nature of a creative product. Because apparently creative products can result from relatively mundane, noncreative, or perhaps even accidental (serendipitous) acts, and because apparently creative processes frequently fail to result in creative products, none of these definitions has been entirely satisfactory. It has also been suggested (Lefrancois, 1972) that a third dimension needs to be considered: that of the creative person. It is quite possible to consider the creative person, the creative product, and the creative process separately because one does not necessarily lead to the other.

In general, creativity appears to involve novelty or innovation and perhaps

can be defined best in terms of an individual's capacity for innovating—for discovering new ways of doing things or for producing things that are new. The principal intellectual factors that appear to be involved in creativity are listed by Guilford (1950, 1959, 1962, 1967) as fluency, flexibility, and originality. Guilford draws an important distinction between intellectual activity that is ordinarily associated with measured intelligence and that which is associated with creativity. The first type of activity is referred to as **convergent** and is defined as the type of intellectual operation that leads to the discovery of a single, correct solution. It is the type of process that is involved, for example, in the solution of a simple problem in numerical addition. **Divergent thinking** is associated with the production of a variety of solutions for problems that do not necessarily have a single correct solution. Arriving at a list of ideas in attempting to determine the best way of promoting a new product is an example of divergent thinking. Divergent thinking processes, which are often defined as being synonymous with creative thinking, are characterized by the three factors mentioned above: fluency, flexibility, and originality. Each of these can be measured and, in combination, yield a rough index of creativity.

Measuring Creativity

A typical creativity test (for example Yamamoto, 1964; Torrance, 1966) presents subjects with tasks for which there are no single correct solutions. Thus the subjects are forced to emit a variety of answers. Fluency is determined simply by counting the number of responses emitted; flexibility is determined by the number of different categories of responses; and originality, by the uniqueness of the answers—that is, by their frequency or infrequency with the least frequent responses being considered the most original. Table 6.4 presents an item similar to many often seen on tests of creativity, along with an illustration of how a response might be scored in terms of fluency, flexibility, and originality.

There are no widely accepted norms for creativity tests, unlike those provided for intelligence tests. Because most of the work in this area is still at a relatively primitive stage of experimentation, norms are ordinarily arrived at within a single testing group. That is, on the basis of tests administered to

Table 6.4 Sample Answers and Scoring Procedure for One Item from a Test of Creativity

Item: How many uses can you think of for a nylon stocking?

Answers:	*	wear on feet
	@#*	wear over face
	*	wear on hands when it's cold
	#*	make rugs
	*	make clothes
	@#*	make upholstery
	#*	hang flower pots
	*	hang mobiles
	@#*	make Christmas decorations
	#*	use as a sling
	#*	tie up robbers
	@#*	cover broken window panes
	@#*	use as ballast in a dirigible
	#*	make a fishing net

Scoring:	*	Fluency:	14 (total number of different responses)
	#	Flexibility:	10 (number of shifts from one class to another)
	@	Originality:	5 (number of unusual responses—responses that occurred less than 5 percent of the time in the entire sample)

one or more groups, the investigator can decide who the most or least creative individuals in these groups are. These norms are not generalizable to other groups.

There are other, simpler, ways of assessing creativity in individuals. The traditional method has been simply to label individuals creative if they provide tangible evidence of their creativity. Typically, that evidence has taken the form of productivity in the arts or in writing. Unfortunately, many potentially creative people cannot be identified in the schools using productivity as a criterion. In addition, evaluating creative products in terms of their merit is an extremely difficult undertaking as is evidenced by the many controversies surrounding well-known "creative" works.

Having teachers rate students in terms of their apparent creativity has not proven very successful either. Gallagher (1960) reports that teachers typically miss approximately 20 percent of the most highly creative students (as identified by tests of creativity). And if they were identified on a basis of intelligence alone, 70 percent of the most highly creative students would be eliminated from consideration (Torrance, 1962).

Relationship to Intelligence

Psychologists have had some difficulty agreeing about the relationship between creativity and intelligence. Getzels and Jackson (1962) compared two groups of students selected from a private Chicago high school: those high in intelligence but not in the top 20 percent in creativity; and those high in creativity but not in the top 20 percent in intelligence. They found that the high creative students achieved as well in school as did the high intelligence students, but that they were not as well liked by teachers. It must be noted, however, that the sample they employed was highly biased in terms of measured intelligence. The mean IQ score for the entire school was a mere 132. Consequently, the mean IQ for those who were judged to be high on creativity but lower in intelligence (comparatively) was 127. It is not surprising that this group also did well in school.

Wallach and Kogan (1965) investigated the personality characteristics of groups of children identified as high creative-low intelligence, high creative-high intelligence, low creative-low intelligence, and low creative-high intelligence. Although they found that individuals high in intelligence would not necessarily be high in creativity (and vice versa), they also concluded that there is a high relationship between intelligence and creativity. Cropley (1965, 1967) and Dellas and Gaier (1970) also conclude that creativity and intelligence are highly related. It appears that only at the very high ranges of intellectual performance does measured creativity cease to be related to measured intelligence. In other words, a minimum of intelligence is required for creative functioning; beyond that minimum, other variables such as personality factors become most important.

Creativity and Adolescence

The Wallach and Kogan study mentioned above provides some interesting information concerning the predominant personality characteristics of

Table 6.5 Characteristics of adolescents identified as high and low on measures of intelligence and of creativity. (Based on studied reported by Wallach and Kogan, 1965.)

| | | Measured Intelligence | |
		High	Low
Creativity (Divergent Thinking)	High	High control over their own behavior; capable of adultlike and childlike behavior.	High internal conflict; frustration with school; feelings of inadequacy; can perform well in stress-free environment.
	Low	Addicted to school; strive desperately for academic success; well-liked by teachers.	Somewhat bewildered by environment; defense mechanisms include intensive social or athletic activity; occasional maladjustment.

adolescents identified as high or low with respect to creativity and intelligence. These findings are summarized in Table 6.5. It is useful to note that individuals who were high on both creativity and intelligence appear to be the most well adjusted, and that individuals judged to be highly creative but low in intelligence were most frustrated with their schools and with themselves.

Dellas and Gaier (1970) found that adolescents who were highly creative relative to their peers tended also to be more dominant, more independent, more nonconforming, and to have a wider range of interests. Holland's (1961) work provides corroboration of these findings. In addition he found that parents of creative adolescents tended to encourage criticism, evaluation, and nonconformity. In short, they don't bring up their children to conform to traditional teacher expectations of obedient, controlled, nonexploratory, nonquestioning behavior. Small wonder that Getzels and Jackson (1962) should find that highly creative individuals are less well liked by teachers, even if they perform as well in school.

There is nothing mystical about creativity. Like intelligence, it is a quality that is possessed to some degree by all individuals. True, some have so little of either that they cannot function effectively in society. But it is also true that both intelligence and creativity can be encouraged and fostered both in the home and in the school. It is also true that teachers are, in general but with some notable exceptions, more likely to encourage conformist intelligent behavior than nonconformist creative behavior. Let me hasten to add, however, that creativity does not necessarily imply nonconformity. But because it does imply a questioning, exploratory, independent attitude, it is likely to be associated with behaviors that are not as socially acceptable, particularly in schools that foster docile acceptance of the status quo. Despite the fact that we pay considerable lip service to the value of creativity in individuals, it still remains true that noncreative individuals are frequently more comfortable to live with.

Summary

This chapter began with an excerpt from Sam's essay on adolescence, progressing from a consideration of Samuel the First to Piaget. Piaget's descriptions of intellectual development from infancy through adolescence were summarized with particular emphasis on the intellectual changes that accompany adolescence. It was specifically noted that adolescents' thinking is freed from the concrete and that much of their idealism is made possible by the fact that they can now consider hypothetical states of affairs — states that are frequently much more desirable than those that exist. From there the chapter paused to discuss intelligence as it has been defined and measured by psychologists and then moved on to a consideration of creativity.

Main Points

1. Samuel the First is not the last.

2. Piaget's theory is among the most comprehensive of all child development theories. It is often described as a stage theory of intellectual development.

3. The sensorimotor stage, lasting from birth to approximately age two, is characterized by children's sensory and motoric understanding of the world. Initially objects exist only when they can actually be sensed or acted upon. Their meaning is limited to the child's activities upon them.

4. One of the major achievements of the sensorimotor period is the eventual realization that objects have a permanence and an objectivity that are independent of the child's perception of them.

5. The period of preoperational thought (ages two to seven approximately) is characterized by numerous errors of logic. During this stage children's thinking is described as intuitive, egocentric, and perception dominated. Most striking among children's reasoning errors are those evident in their inability to understand simple conservations.

6. During the period of concrete operations (ages seven to eleven or twelve) children acquire the ability to conserve and to deal more logically with classes, serial order, and number. Their thinking continues to be tied to the real and concrete.

7. The period of formal operations corresponds to adolescence (ages eleven or twelve to fifteen or sixteen). One of the major accomplishments of this period is a freeing of thought from the concrete. Children can now deal with the hypothetical—with the merely possible as well as with the actual. Piaget describes adolescent thinking as being potentially highly idealistic because it can now deal with ideal states of affairs and compare them with that which is real.

8. Intelligence has been defined in a variety of ways ranging from "that which the tests test" to such sophisticated statements as "the global and aggregate capacity of an individual to think rationally, to act purposefully, and to deal effectively with his environment." In essence, the term appears to refer to the adaptive qualities of the organism.

9. The ability to remember is clearly implicated in manifestations of intelligence. Research indicates that adolescents have better memories than younger children. It appears also that adults may have better memories than adolescents.

10. Various tests, given individually or in groups, may be employed to assess intelligence. Most of these are based on the assumption that there is an average level of performance that can be expected of various age groups and that intelligence can be inferred by the extent to which specific individuals perform below or above the expected performance for their age. Performance is sometimes translated into a mental age equivalent (the age at which the score obtained is average). The intelligence quotient (IQ) may be arrived at by multiplying the ratio of mental age to chronological age by 100. Frequently, tables are provided that may be employed to convert raw scores to IQ equivalents without any computation.

11. It appears that intelligence increases as children age. No definitive studies exist to demonstrate that there is necessarily an age at which intelligence ceases to increase. In fact, some studies have shown that it can increase indefinitely depending largely upon the occupation and preoccupations of the individual concerned.

12. Although there do not appear to be any real differences in measured intelligence between boys and girls, it appears that girls develop their verbal skills more rapidly than boys. There do appear to be some differences in

patterns of abilities that comprise measured abilities. In general boys tend to have less uniform profiles; that is, they exhibit more extremes.

13. Creativity is perhaps as nebulous a term as is intelligence. It may be defined in terms of a person, a product, or a process. Most often it refers to the capacity of individuals to innovate.

14. Instruments that purport to measure creativity typically make use of questions that have no unique correct solution. Instead they require the subject to generate a large variety of solutions for every problem presented.

15. Although it is true that some individuals may appear to be highly intelligent without being highly creative (or highly creative without being highly intelligent), the correlation between intelligence and creativity is generally high.

16. Creative adolescents appear to be more dominant, more independent, and more nonconforming than those who are less creative. Their parents also appear to be more encouraging of criticism and evaluation.

Chapter 7

A Proposal of Marriage:
Personality and the Self

Personality and Self

Self-Concept

Importance in Adolescence
Factors Affecting Self-Concept
Sex
Expectations
Race
Names and Clothes
Self-Actualization

Personality

Approaches to Personality
Assessing Personality
Adolescent Personality

Summary

Main Points

ncie Binder, Grade 11

188

I dropped in to see Sam this morning. A letter had come for him from some woman at Gustavus Adolphus College. He is always delighted whenever someone writes to him, an event that occurs rather infrequently. This morning he was doubly delighted because I also brought him a two-layer chocolate cake with the fudge frosting that he particularly enjoys. He generously agreed to share the letter with me and the cake with Samuel. The letter is reproduced here (with the kind permission of Ms. Eatonia).

Dear Sam,

I have just read most of Lefrancois' *Of children* which is a required text for our child development course here. I won't say too much about the book because I haven't thought about it very much yet. Our final examination isn't until next Friday.

I've been wondering what kind of person you really are, Sam. I hope you don't mind me calling you by your first name. I don't know your last name, but I suppose I should really say Professor Sam even if you didn't get tenure. To me you'll always be a professor, and from what I gathered from the book, a very good, and kind, and generous, and lovable one. I'm one of those who don't think you're insane just because you choose to live alone where you do. I've been living in a hollow log this last semester, by myself I might add, and I quite enjoy it. I've never had much to do with other people, and even less now. We're alike, you and I, I'm sure of it.

I like you very much from what I know about you Sam, and I think you'd like me too once you got to know me. I'm enclosing a picture of myself, although I'm sure you'll agree with me that physical appearances are unimportant. It's the real person that's inside

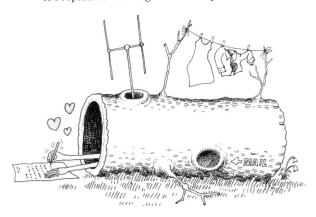

Sam was quite overwhelmed. He is, I'm afraid, seriously considering Mary Lou's proposal. "What a team we might make!" he exclaimed. "Our combined research could well overwhelm the scientific world. And she does seem to be an extremely sensitive and highly perceptive young woman. She's right. Appearances don't really matter. Personality is just the exterior; it's the interior, the real self, that's important."

that counts. I'll admit that my personality is probably not the kind that most people would like immediately unless they were really sensitive and intelligent which I'm sure you must be and which, I assure you, very few people around here are. You must have run into the same sorts of problems when you were denied tenure at your university. I'm running into it here where there is some talk of expelling me from college. I plan to continue my research just as you have. I'm presently doing some very exciting work with memory and flatworms. I started this research when I was in high school and have continued it since.

Sam, I'm going to propose to you because I think people like us have a great deal to offer each other. Besides your research on intelligence and mine on memory could perhaps be combined in the interests of science. Please write and tell me that you'll marry me and I will join you as soon as this semester is finished.

With much love,
Mary Lou

P.S. Say hello to Samuel for me. My brightest flatworm is called Mary Ann.

Sam then went into a long discourse on the extent to which people are deceived by external appearances, referring repeatedly to the precious pearl of wisdom: "Clothes don't make the man," a point that is particularly apropos in his case. I finally left Sam so that I might join you in this discussion of personality and the self.

Personality and Self

For purposes of convenience, simplicity, and clarity, psychologists seldom deal with entire individuals as you and I know them. They are separated instead into various parts and layers, different aspects of their behavior are organized around separate labels, and behavioral phenomena are discussed as though they occurred in isolation one from the other. In the end we are left with bits and pieces: emotions on the one hand, reason on the other; mind here, body there; the self relative to the person; physical growth, mental growth; learning, motivation. It becomes difficult for students of psychology to arrive at a reasonably clear picture of their entire subject, humans.

But then humans are not simple in the sense that an automobile is simple. Their constituent parts cannot be identified so easily; their functioning is not nearly as predictable nor can it be explained as easily. And although we know a fair amount about repairing them in the case of organic breakdowns, we still know very little about repairing their nonorganic malfunctions. And if we are eventually to understand them at all well, it is necessary at this stage to consider their functions and characteristics in relative isolation. But it should always be kept in mind that humans are much more than the fragmented images that one gets of them in textbooks of psychology. They are dynamic, living, *entire* things of incredible complexity; nevertheless, they are whole. And if there is one division in psychology that comes closest to considering the whole being, it must be the study of **personality.**

There is an interesting and useful distinction to be made between personality and self. One is, in effect, a view from the outside; the other, a view from the inside. Personality is not something that people have, but something that they appear to be (or perhaps that they are) when viewed from the outside by others. Self, on the other hand, is what individuals appear to be (or

are) when viewed from the inside by the individuals themselves. In short, *my personality is me as others see me; my self is me as I see myself.*

An interesting and important question develops: Is there just one self and one personality for each person? This would seem to be logically true. But, personality and self are the result of a conglomeration of behaviors reflecting emotions, thoughts, ideals, predispositions, customary ways of doing things, and so on. And because each of these behaviors can change, both personality and self can also change. That is, personality and self are not static properties, but are potentially changeable. Each is treated separately in this chapter, but the relationships between them should be kept in mind.

Self-Concept

Mead (1934), among others, defines the self as a conscious *awareness of being* that develops apart from the physiological organism. It is not a material entity in the sense that the body is material; rather, it is a self-consciousness that arises from the interactions of this organism with the environment (particularly with the social environment). As a result of interacting with others and of observing their reactions to our behavior, we each develop some notion of what we are. This notion, or these sets of notions, define our *self;* and our **self-concept** is nothing more than the opinion that we have of our self. Hence the self is an abstraction; a form, but not a substance. Like any concept, it exists in thought, but not in concrete reality. But its significance for our behavior is incredible.

To simplify the preceding passage, consider the following. Individuals are capable of acting and of reacting in social situations. More than this, they are capable of getting outside of themselves (in thought) and of observing how others react to their actions and reactions. As a result of observing the reactions of others, they develop self-concepts, notions of who and what they are like. If they find that others laugh a great deal as a result of their actions, they develop the notion that they are funny, comical, or humorous (the three not necessarily being synonymous). This notion is incorporated into their self-concepts if it is repeated frequently enough. It follows, then, that if sufficient people think you are brave, you may incorporate this belief into your self-concept, behave as though you were brave, and eventually actually become brave (human characteristics being defined primarily in terms of action and in terms of beliefs that we have about ourselves). Similarly, if people react to you as though you are stupid, you will probably conclude that you are stupid, that your *self* is stupid.

An intriguing series of studies concerning the effects of **expectations** on behavior bears indirectly on this point. Rosenthal and Jacobson (1968a, 1968b) administered a battery of intelligence tests to a group of students in the spring of the year. Teachers were told that they were participating in an experiment designed to validate a new test, a test that was designed to identify academic "bloomers." The hypothesis was simply that some students who are progressing poorly or at a point near the average sometimes show remarkable gains in intelligence and achievement. The investigators told the teachers that they had isolated some of the factors that contribute to this sudden academic spurt (blooming), and that they could now identify these students prior to the onset of the spurt. This, of course, was part of the experimental treatment because the investigators were not concerned with academic blooming, but with the effects of teacher expectations on student performance. The only other experimental treatment involved giving the teachers, the following fall, a list of students who had been identified as potential bloomers. Teachers were given this information in an offhand manner. Students on the list had been carefully matched with those not on the list; the only difference between the two groups would be that the teachers would have reason to expect relatively superior academic performance during the coming year for those on the list. And their expectations were, in fact, confirmed. Not only did these students do better on teacher-made achievement tests, but they did better on tests of intelligence. The most dramatic improvement occurred for students in first grade who presumably had more room to show improvement.

The results of the Rosenthal and Jacobsen studies have since been severely criticized both on methodological and interpretive grounds. Barber and Silver (1969a, 1969b) critically examined conclusions from thirty-one supportive studies cited by Rosenthal and Jacobsen and concluded that the majority of these studies do not illustrate the "experimenter effect." They cite frequent examples of what they allege to be instances of misjudging, misrecording, and misrepresentation. Rosenthal's (1969) reply to these criticisms maintains that some relevant details had been omitted from the studies

Kris *Age 16* **On the Self**

Me: *I'm trying to find out who you are . . . what you're like. I'm going to ask you a question I haven't asked other people. Who are you?*
Kris: *You mean mentally. Like, who am I?*
Me: *Just give me the kind of information you would give a stranger if you wanted them to know what you're really like.*
Kris: *Well mentally, I think I'm really . . . well I guess I'm a straight kid. I like to go out and have fun. Get a little rowdy now and then. That's about all I can say.*

Me: *Okay. I'll take it from t kind of things make you happ*
Kris: *Feeling wanted by peo having a boyfriend that reall, me. Just having a lot of friends.*

193

criticized by Barber and Silver, and that the original conclusions are still valid. A second rejoinder by Barber and Silver (1969b) reaffirms their original criticisms.

It would, at this stage, be unwise to maintain that teacher expectations undeniably and consistently affect student performance; it might be equally unwise to discard this proposition out of hand. It remains a real possibility. While it is difficult to explain why it is that teacher expectations could affect the behavior of students, the implications of this are obvious. In the same way as expectation of superior performance might be related to actual superior performance, expectation of inferior performance could have a similar, though negative, effect. Rosenthal and Jacobson (1968b) suggest that this might frequently be the case with respect to children from minority groups, children who by the very nature of their socioeconomic backgrounds are not expected to do as well in school as are children from more advantaged backgrounds. It may be that their subsequent poorer performance is in part due to the expectations of their teachers. And it may also be that these effects are not the result of anything the teacher does deliberately; rather they might result from the self-concepts that these children develop as a result of their interpretations of a teacher's reactions to them, however subtle these reactions may be.

Importance in Adolescence

"From ten thousand miles away I saw it as a blinding light: the importance, the necessity of a Self!" (Horney, 1949). These lines, written by an adult in psychotherapy, express dramatically the importance not so much of having a self, but of having a self-concept. And it is perhaps during adolescence that problems of developing a self-concept are most crucial.

The term that most closely resembles self-concept in Freud's writings is ego, the conscious link with external reality, impelled simultaneously by the competing urges of the id and superego. It is in the ego that the self resides; and Erikson's contention that the major crisis facing the adolescent is that of developing ego identity can be interpreted as another way of saying that it is important for adolescents to arrive at some notions of who they are, of what their self is.

The most profound biological changes associated with adolescence, those leading to puberty or sexual maturity, are intimately linked with children's developing self-concept. These biological changes together with the emotions and the desires they give rise to force a reexamination of self. In addition the eventual necessity of having to make a choice among a variety of life-styles and occupations requires that adolescents develop some relatively clear notions of what they are as well as what they can be. And it must be noted that it is particularly difficult for adolescents to maintain a consistent notion of self at a time when their biological appearances are changing rapidly and when, consequently, the behavior and attitudes that they observe in others with regard to their persons also change.

The importance of the development of self-concept is also related to the expectations that adolescents have of themselves and that others have for them. If they see themselves as leaders, as financially successful, as influential, it is important that this concept of self be consonant with the view that others have of them. Perhaps even more significant for their psychological well-being, it is important that the results of their behavior confirm the image that they have of themselves. Festinger (1957) and Brehm and Cohen (1962) have advanced a theory of attitudes and attitude change that is of direct relevance to an understanding of the importance of congruity between self-concept, ideal self, and self as it is manifested in behavior. An individual's ideal self, as opposed to the real self, is the way that individual would be if he or she were everything that he or she wanted to be.

Festinger's theory, labeled the theory of **cognitive dissonance,** maintains that whenever there is a conflict between beliefs, between behavior and beliefs, or between what is expected and what is observed, individuals are subjected to cognitive dissonance; that is, they are subjected to a state of affairs in which there is conflict (specifically, conflict between cognitions where cognitions are items of information or knowledge). Cognitive dissonance is a motivating state that leads to behavior designed to reduce the dissonance. The theory maintains that the principal behaviors engaged in as a result of cognitive dissonance involve changes in attitude, and that changes will be greatest where there is the highest degree of conflict. Several experiments have been conducted in order to investigate cognitive dissonance, one of which is reviewed briefly below.

Festinger and Carlsmith (1959) asked a group of college students to participate in a test of motor performance. For an hour subjects were engaged in the most boring and seemingly pointless tasks that the experimenters could design. They spent thirty minutes placing twelve spools on a tray using only one hand, removing each of these twelve spools, placing them back on the tray, removing them, and so on. After thirty minutes they moved to a pegboard containing forty-eight pegs. Subjects had to turn each of these pegs a quarter turn, in order, then begin again, turning each peg another quarter turn. This continued, uninterrupted and unchanged until the hour was up. Following this experience, two-thirds of the subjects were then interviewed separately and asked whether they would do the experimenters a small favor. They were led to believe that other subjects coming after them would be engaged in the same tasks, and that the results of the experiment might be more valid if these new subjects were told by the outgoing subjects that the experiment was an interesting and exciting one. A small lie to be told in the interests of science and in the interests of financial reward: a number of the subjects were paid twenty dollars for telling this lie; those in a second group were paid a dollar. All of these subjects agreed to tell the lie, and proceeded to do so. In a final interview following the telling of the lie, experimenters attempted to discover what the subjects really thought of the hour-long experimental session. The students who had not been paid or asked to tell a lie (the control group) admitted that the experiment was indeed boring and somewhat less than enjoyable. The subjects who were paid twenty dollars also admitted that the experiment was boring. But the group who had been paid a single dollar for their lies now thought the experiment had been quite enjoyable and not very boring at all.

These results can be explained easily in terms of dissonance theory. Telling a lie gives rise to conflict between the individual's behavior and his or her notions of what that behavior ideally should be—hence dissonance. The less the justification for the lie, the greater the conflict. Therefore, those subjects who had been paid a single dollar would be expected to suffer from greater dissonance than those who had been paid twenty dollars, because they would have considerably less justification for telling the lie. The control group who had not been paid and who had not told a lie would feel little dissonance. Accordingly, neither the control group nor the twenty-dollar group changed their attitudes toward the experiment, both admitting that it was indeed boring. The one-dollar group, on the other hand, would seek to reduce dis-

Figure 7.1 Subjects' responses to the question "How enjoyable were the tasks?" in the Festinger and Carlsmith (1959) study. (From the *Journal of Abnormal and Social Psychology*, 1959, 58, pp. 203–210. Copyright 1959 by the American Psychological Association. Used by permission of the American Psychological Association and the author.)

sonance. And the simplest way of doing so would be to actually believe that the experiment was not boring and therefore that they had not really told a lie. In short, they would change their attitudes in order to eliminate, or at least reduce, any dissonance that they might feel. Results of the experiment are summarized in Figure 7.1.

The theory of cognitive dissonance is directly related to an understanding of the importance of congruity between self-concept and the observed results of behavior. Conflict or dissonance can arise in any number of situations. An adolescent sees himself as a Don Juan, and derives considerable satisfaction from the supposed envy and admiration of his peers. Following a publicly unsuccessful attempt to overwhelm a young damsel with his charms, he is faced with the realization that his self-concept is perhaps inaccurate, that what he thought his self was is perhaps not what his self really is. A young woman who has been convinced by her grandmother and her parents that she is of above average intelligence receives considerable confirming evidence from a sympathetic teacher. But she fails her college entrance examinations. Again, a significant aspect of her apparently real self is not as she thought her self was and certainly not as she would like her self to be.

In situations such as these, a number of alternatives are open to the individual, all of which are designed to reduce dissonance. One possibility is simply to change one's behavior. The Don Juan can attempt to behave more like a Don Juan. If he is successful, all or most of his dissonance may disappear. Similarly, an individual who feels dissonance over her smoking, realizing that there is a conflict between her desire to live a long and healthy life and the evidence that various individuals and agencies have placed at her disposal concerning the harmful effects of nicotine, can easily reduce the dissonance by ceasing to smoke (easy in theory if not in practice).

A second alternative, and one that is perhaps more frequent, is to change attitudes in relevant ways. This change implies some modification of self-concept because attitudes are part of the self-concept. The experiment involving the spools and pegs illustrates clearly how individuals can be moved to modify their attitudes as a result of dissonance. Similarly, the girl who thought herself intelligent but who discovered that she was in fact somewhat less than extraordinarily brilliant, can change her attitudes about herself, deciding that she is, in fact, not overly gifted intellectually. She might also use a third method for reducing dissonance, a method sometimes called

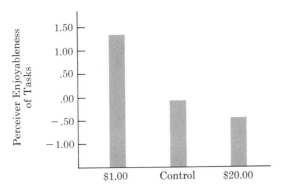

denial. To do this, she would convince herself that it was not particularly important to be intelligent, that she was never really that way, or at least never really wanted to be. Denial has been compared to the sour-grapes phenomenon: if I can't have it, I didn't really want it in the first place.

Perceptual distortion, or the distortion of information, is another defensive reaction to cognitive dissonance. It involves ignoring information that produces dissonance and bolstering or exaggerating information that is consonant with one's beliefs. In the example of the girl who discovers she is not as intelligent as she would like to be, perceptual distortion can take the form of a refusal to admit that her failure on college entrance examinations is evidence of her lack of superior intellectual ability. At the same time, she might choose to exaggerate other evidence of superior ability that she has previously received. Frequently perceptual distortion is a highly unconscious process. Studies have shown, for example, that in reading newspapers in a casual manner, individuals are more likely to remember having read those items of information that they already knew or with which they agreed. Frequently they have no recollection of items of information that are at variance with their beliefs or wishes. Smokers tend not to see items dealing with relationships between cancer and smoking; pessimists tend not to see optimistic news items; optimists tend to overlook pessimistic reports. And in addition, whatever is remembered tends to be distorted in the direction of previously established beliefs or wishes.

In general, however, because individuals' self-concepts are derived largely from what Mead (1934) refers to as the "generalized other"—that is, from the reactions of others to individuals' behavior—they tend to be relatively consonant with individuals' observations of the effects of their behavior. Frequently, however, there is some discrepancy between individuals' self-concepts and their ideal selves. This discrepancy may give rise to cognitive dissonance that can then be reduced in any of the ways mentioned above.

The importance of individuals' self-concepts is related as well to the type of individuals that they will become. Super (1957) points out that the self-concept is instrumental in determining interests, values, life-styles, and habits of individuals. It is interesting to note that the self-concepts of adolescents who have been identified as delinquents are typically more negative than those of well-adjusted adolescents (Ahlstrom and Havighurst, 1971). Delinquents, rightly or wrongly, are more likely to perceive their selves as

Tracy *Age 18* **On Sex Roles**

Me: *Do you think there are some real differences in the roles men and women play? During adolescence. For example do you think there are differences in interests and in personality that are related to the person's sex?*
Tracy: *Well I think men are more aggressive than women, because 1. of their size, and 2. because of their history of superiority, you know. All through history we don't have famous women artists, and you don't have famous women composers. That's happened in the last century that* *women have started to stand up, you know, and speak up for themselves. Cause women have talent too. But I think that they have, as far as the physical side is concerned, they don't have as much talent as men. Men can run faster and they're stronger. Things like that.*

bad, lazy, ignorant, and stupid. In short, their opinions of themselves tend to conform to those of the "generalized other" in society. This observation has led to the hypothesis (not without additional corroborating evidence; see Chapter 11) that negative self-concept may be causally related to delinquency. Conversely, positive self-concept may act as insulation against the appearance of delinquent behavior.

Factors Affecting Self-Concept

It is true that everything that adolescents do, all the reactions that they observe in others relative to their own behavior, and all the reinforcement or lack of it that results from their behavior, is instrumental in determining the type of self that they will develop. However, there are a number of specific factors that seem to be closely related to the type of self-concepts that they are most likely to develop.

Sex A topic of considerable current interest and controversy concerns the existence, usefulness, pervasiveness, and questionable equity of the roles that men and women exhibit in their behavior and attitudes. Various women's liberation groups and other observers have had no difficulty in identifying the many ways in which men and women are expected to behave differently, and indeed *do* behave differently. It is not the purpose of this section to examine the controversy that surrounds these observations, but merely to examine some of the manifestations and causes of sex-role differences. There is little doubt that they can be very powerful forces in determining adolescents' self-concepts.

Lynn (1974) notes that the development of sex-role differences seems to involve the interaction of three separate forces: biological, family based, and cultural. Biological forces would be manifested in innate predispositions for the sexes to behave, think, or feel differently. Admittedly, there is little research that clearly demonstrates causal links between biological factors and male or female behavior (Maccoby, 1972), save, of course, with respect to actual sexual behavior where the specific roles played by men and women are usually different given their different anatomical structures. This observation does not imply, however, that their attitudes toward sexual behavior

Donalda *Age 14* **On Sports**

Me: *What turns you on? What do you get excited about?*
Donalda: *Nothing.*
Me: *Is there anything you look forward to? Anything you get excited about when you anticipate doing it?*
Donalda: *Yeah. Hockey. I like hockey.*
Me: *Do you go to many games?*
Donalda: *Mostly I watch it on TV. And football. I really like football cause like last year when we played a lot and I was the champ.*
. . . 8 minutes later . . .

Me: *What's the most fun? If you had a choice of doing anything you want this afternoon, what would you do?*
Donalda: *I'd go and do a couple of sports, and after that just . . . go swimming after we had a couple hours of sports.*
Me: *Is that what you do mostly in your spare time—sports?*
Donalda: *Yeah.*

must also be different for biological reasons. There is some evidence, however, that the greater male aggressiveness that has repeatedly been noted in research is perhaps due to biological factors. The line of reasoning, as presented by Lynn (1974) is as follows: evidence of a biological influence for any specific sex difference would be provided by the observation that 1. the difference is manifested at a very young age prior to the time that other forces would have been particularly effective in fostering it; 2. the difference is characteristic of most cultures and therefore not due solely to cultural factors; 3. the difference is also evident in other primates; and 4. the difference is corroborated by research employing sex hormones (p. 143). These four criteria appear to have been met with respect to aggression. It has been observed that males are more aggressive than females at a very early age (Bandura and Walters, 1959); males tend to be more aggressive than females in most cultures (Mitchell *et al.*, 1967); nonhuman primates exhibit the same sex differences with respect to aggression (Mitchell *et al.*, 1967); and the injection of male hormones in pregnant mothers affected the subsequent aggressiveness of the female children who had been in uteri at the time (Money and Ehrhardt, 1968).

Family and cultural factors cannot be discounted, however, in attempting to explain the greater aggressiveness of boys relative to girls. Considerable research has demonstrated, for example, that parents treat male infants differently from female infants (Lewis, 1972). In general girls are treated less aggressively, are reinforced less for aggressive behavior, and are perhaps subjected to more affection and tenderness. In addition, cultural norms and models are clearly biased in favor of supporting aggression in males and acquiescence in females, as is evident from carefully watching a single evening's television offerings.

Numerous investigations of sex-role differences have been reported in psychological literature. Rosenkrantz *et al.* (1968) investigated beliefs about masculinity and femininity among a group of college men and women. They were asked to rate a number of personality traits such as "aggressive," "independent," and "tender" in terms of their masculinity or femininity and also in terms of their social desirability. They were not to rate them necessarily for any specific sex, but for the sexes in general. Two results of the study are very striking. The first is that there was overwhelming agreement among men and women concerning which traits were primarily masculine and which feminine (correlations of .96 and .95). Second, there was marked agreement that many

more masculine traits were socially desirable than feminine traits. That is, both men and women gave masculine traits higher ratings in terms of social desirability.

It is interesting, and perhaps not surprising, to note that those traits considered to be most masculine included (Rosenkrantz *et al.*, 1968): aggressive, dominant, unemotional, objective, hides emotions, logical, and active. Some of the traits assigned to femininity were: tactful, gentle, religious, interested in own appearance, strong need for security, and appreciates art and literature.

Bennett and Cohen (1959) make the point that feminine personality characteristics are acquired before masculine traits. Because much of the care of children is traditionally undertaken by women, both in the home and in the school, they believe that feminine traits are initially stronger in both sexes and that masculine traits are acquired later as boys begin to identify with their fathers, a process that continues into adolescence. Numerous studies have shown, however, that masculinity is more desirable than femininity for young girls and boys (with numerous exceptions nevertheless). It appears that more young girls want to be boys than boys want to be girls.

During adolescence there are powerful social forces that have significant effects on the nature of the developing self-concept. Social stereotypes play no small role in determining customary ways of behaving and feeling for both men and women. These stereotypes, communicated informally through peer groups, significant adults, and the mass media, dictate that "real" men should be aggressive, unemotional, and rugged; and that "real" women should be tender, emotional, and nonaggressive. There is little doubt that life may be extremely difficult for adolescents whose selves do not easily conform to these social stereotypes. Not that the social stereotypes are necessarily good or necessarily bad. They are, nevertheless, a sociocultural fact.

Expectations Social stereotypes play a considerable role in determining what adolescents' expectations will be for themselves because these are frequently a reflection of the expectations of others. Hence expectations are important in determining self-concept. In turn, self-concept is instrumental in determining the expectations that individuals have for themselves. The role of expectations in determining self is clearly illustrated by reference to sex stereotypes.

Race Palmer and Masling (1969) investigated the effects of **race** on self-concept. Specifically, they looked at the extent to which being black would be reflected in the preoccupations of black children. Their argument was that because being black is devalued by society, black adolescents would be significantly more preoccupied with skin color in an attempt to develop a positive self-concept. Groups of black and white American children were asked to describe pictures of black and white baseball players. Not surprisingly, black children spent considerably more time describing skin color than did white children.

Generalizing from this study, we can reasonably suppose that those adolescents who are in a **minority,** particularly in a socially undesirable minority, would experience more difficulty in integrating aspects of their minority into a positive self-concept. This might apply equally to the intellectually disadvantaged, racial minorities, the athletically or physically inferior, the less attractive, and so on. In other words, any adolescents who are markedly and obviously lacking in some quality that is highly valued by their society, or who are markedly different from the ideal stereotype for their age and sex in that society, will experience more difficulty in arriving at positive self-concepts.

Note, for example, that the self-concepts of Catholic children in the United States are likely to be less favorable than those of the dominant majority — protestant whites (Coopersmith, 1967; Rosenberg, 1965). Lynn (1974) identifies Catholics as a minority in America. Interestingly, however, Jewish children, also members of a minority, are more likely to have favorable self-concepts than Catholic children. This finding is most often explained in terms of the Jewish tradition of warmth and parental support.

Self-concepts of black adolescents are characterized by considerably less self-esteem than is typical of whites (Johnson, 1967; Parsons and Clark, 1966; Proshansky and Newton, 1968). Being a member of an oppressed minority, however subtle the oppression, may engender conflicts in adolescents concerning their personal identity. They learn, for example, that for social and economic reasons, many of the apparent advantages of the dominant society are beyond their grasp. But because they find themselves in that society, though perhaps on its fringe, they adopt many of its values. At the same time, however, they retain some loyalty to a culture that is in many ways antithetical to the dominant American culture. The resulting uncertainty and confusion is hardly conducive to the development of self-esteem and confidence.

It should be noted that the civil rights movement coupled with a growing awareness of cultural identity and an increasing pride in cultural origins are apparently having an effect on the black adolescent's self-concept. Baughman (1971) reports that the lower self-esteem that has been characteristic of black and Mexican-American adolescents is apparently giving way to increasingly positive self-concepts. A black adolescent who knows that "black is beautiful" is perhaps not fundamentally different from a white adolescent whose convictions concerning the attractiveness of white have required little cultural reinforcement.

A word of caution is in order at this point. In interpreting studies that compare minority groups with the dominant white protestant American majority, it is well to bear in mind that observed differences, no matter their direction, can in no way be attributed to race. There is clearly a complex of social and economic factors that collectively accounts for many of the differences evident not only between the dominant group and various minorities, but also among the minorities themselves. In addition, generalizations concerning minority groups are, in fact, not applicable to a large number of individuals within a specific minority. As has frequently been pointed out, differences within racial groups, for example, are considerably greater than differences among races. In the same way, differences within identifiable minority groups are probably greater than differences among the groups themselves, or differences between single minorities and the dominant majority.

Names and Clothes A wide variety of seemingly unimportant factors exert a subtle but powerful effect on the adolescent's developing self-concept. The individual's name is one such factor. Nicknames and strange names have been associated with maladjustment or superior adjustment. Savage and Wells (1948) identified Harvard students with highly unusual names and found a much higher proportion of failures among these students than among the remainder of Harvard students. Nicknames can have similar effects. Highly derogatory nicknames are, in effect, a reflection of others' attitudes towards an individual. Consequently, the characteristics associated with the name can become incorporated into the individual's self-concept. Persons whose friends call them "stupid" may come to believe that they probably are; and they may,

— JUST CALL ME
FINGERS.......

203

in order to gain some measure of social acceptance, exaggerate those qualities that gave rise to the appellation. Nicknames that reflect some specific weakness, abnormality, or socially undesirable quality can have a highly detrimental effect on the adolescent's self-concept. Conversely, names that reflect some achievement or some highly prized skill or quality can have a beneficial effect on self-concept. If "Fingers" is called Fingers because he has impressive control over the movements of a baseball, his reaction to the name will probably be very different than if he is called Fingers because he has bony, calloused, double-jointed, broken-nailed, scarred, crooked, blue-colored fingers.*

Clothing among adolescents is much more than a protective covering made necessary by climatic conditions, modesty, and social custom. It is, at times, an expression of peer conformity, at other times it is an expression of individuality — a definition and exposition of self. It can reveal a "self" that is concerned with its physical appearance, preoccupied with it, or unconcerned; a self that is deliberately and ruggedly nonconformist, or an approval-seeking, conformist self; a self that is strongly masculine or feminine, or a self that is unisexual; an active self, a quiet self; a happy self, a sad self.

Self-Actualization

Recall that the highest set of needs in Maslow's (1954) hierarchy of human needs (Chapter 4) is the need for self-actualization. The phrase implies that every individual has a potential self that is the best of all possible selves, and that the best and most intrinsically human thing that the individual can do is to develop that self, to make it real or actual. And again, as Erikson pointed out (Chapter 5), it is not so much a question of discovering what that self is as of determining what it can and should be. The development of self through self-actualization involves unique experiences of growth and development leading toward the development of a "better" person, given that person's complement of skills, abilities, personality characteristics, and potentialities. Self-actualization is not concerned with the satisfaction of basic needs or with achieving acceptance, status, or self-esteem. These lower-level needs, though

---

* It would be tempting here to commit the "correlational fallacy"; that is, to assume that the occasional correlation between name and self-concept is evidence of a causal relationship between the two. That conclusion is not warranted by the data.

they still exist in the person engaged in self-actualization, have become of secondary importance. Maslow (1954) lists the following as traits most descriptive of the truly self-actualizing person:

1. Realistic perception of the world;

2. Acceptance of self, others, and the world for what they are;

3. Spontaneity in behavior and inner experience;

4. Focus of interests on problems rather than self;

5. Capacity for detachment;

6. Independence in the sense of self-containment;

7. Freshness of appreciation of people and things;

8. Capacity for profound mystical experiences;

9. Identification with the human race;

10. Deep emotional relations with small circle of friends;

11. Democratic attitude and values;

12. Ability to discriminate between means and ends;

13. Philosophical rather than hostile sense of humor;

14. Creativeness; and

15. Resistance to cultural conformity.

Many of these characteristics appear to be typical of contemporary adolescents, perhaps because their concerns with lower-level needs are not as primary as they are in the younger child or as they will be when they assume complete financial, economic, and emotional independence from their families. During the hiatus represented by adolescence, they are free to indulge in preoccupations with self-enhancement and in grandiose schemes for making the world a better place. Their newly found idealism expresses itself clearly in their resistance to cultural conformity, in their commitment to the human race, and in their focus of interests on problems rather than on selfish ends.

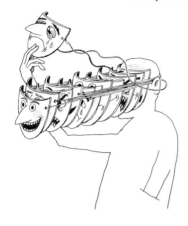

Unfortunately, admission to adult ranks sometimes results in an abrupt clash with brutal everyday reality. And the process of self-actualization is sometimes temporarily lost in the search for material comfort and emotional and financial stability.

Personality

Personality has been defined as the total conglomeration of an individual's habits, traits, beliefs, attitudes, interests, and customary ways of behaving as these are manifested in the individual's behavior. Personality and self were contrasted at the beginning of this chapter, where the point was made that personality is a person's appearance as it is viewed from the outside whereas self is the individual's own view from the inside.

The term personality derives from *persona*, a word employed to denote the masks once worn by Roman actors. By changing his *persona*, a single actor could become many different characters in short order. Goffman (1959), in his discussion of the various manifestations of human personality, makes the point that we all, in a sense, possess a variety of *personas*, a variety of masks that we present in different social situations. Thus individuals wear their sober, serious, concerned, and intelligent masks when attending business meetings with their superiors; and their debonair, devil-may-care, extroverted masks when attending a neighborhood party.

Do masks ever drop? Is it possible to ever see the real person behind these various *personas?* Is the real you your self as you know it? How closely does your self, as you know it, correspond with the self that you present to the world (or with the selves that you present)?

The study of human personality is very difficult because these questions cannot be answered easily. There is also a very real possibility that the "personality" that any individual presents to the world on a specific occasion has been chosen—perhaps unconsciously—just for that occasion and others like it. It therefore becomes relatively meaningless to speak of an individual's personality as though there were in fact a single conglomeration of traits that, taken together, provide a good description of that individual. For example, an individual who can justifiably be described as unkind, cruel, and vindictive in one situation will probably not be unkind, cruel, and vindictive in all social situations and with all people.

Table 7.1   Some of Cattell's Personality Traits*

Conservative	Experimenting	Practical	Imaginative
Emotional	Stable	Relaxed	Tense
Forthright	Shrewd	Reserved	Outgoing
Expedient	Conscientious	Shy	Venturesome
Humble	Assertive	Sober	Happy-go-lucky
Placid	Apprehensive	Trusting	Suspicious

*Cattell identified these traits using popular adjectives that could be used to describe people in meaningful ways. Note that these traits are arranged in pairs of opposites.

At best, then, when describing human personality an attempt is made to identify those characteristics that are predominant—that is, those that are manifested most regularly. Because it is impossible ever to get inside another person in order to really know what that person is like, we must content ourselves with approximate descriptions of appearance, and make inferences on the basis of the behaviors that we observe. These descriptions are clearly limited in their generality and perhaps in their validity as well.

Approaches to Personality

There are two broad approaches to the study of human personality: the **trait** and the **type** approach. One is relatively specific; the other, more global. Traits are ordinarily defined as specific characteristics of individuals that tend to be highly persistent from one situation to another. Dominance, aggression, intelligence, gregariousness, and so on may all be considered human personality traits. Types, on the other hand, are classifications of individuals according to clusters or conglomeration of traits. An individual possessing all or several of the traits mentioned above might be classified as an independent type, as opposed to a dependent type.

A classical example of a trait approach is provided by Cattell's (1946) systematic attempt to catalogue human traits. He began with a list of seventeen thousand adjectives that could be descriptive of human behavior, reduced this list by eliminating all synonyms or near-synonyms, and reduced it even further by grouping together those adjectives that seemed to be related. A portion of his final list of traits is given in Table 7.1.

One of the principal weaknesses of the trait approaches to human personality is that they typically result in a bewildering array of adjectives that do very little to simplify or clarify our understanding of either human personality or a single individual. Partly for this reason a number of psychologists have attempted to reduce traits even further by studying typical patterns of traits and assigning them labels. These labels, in fact, correspond to personality types. For example, it is common for individuals who are aggressive also to be ambitious, assertive, venturesome, and so on. All of these traits might be considered to be aspects of a general personality type that could be labeled "aggressive" or whatever label the investigator thought appropriate.

Figure 7.2 The three basic body types identified by Sheldon.

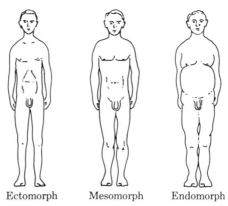

Ectomorph   Mesomorph   Endomorph

207

An early type approach to the classification of human personality characteristics was provided by the ancient Greek philosophers. They spoke
of four distinct types of human personalities, distinguishable in terms of the
"humours" in the blood and in terms of overt behavioral characteristics. Thus
sanguine individuals were optimistic and happy people who had a preponderance of blood. **Melancholic** individuals, endowed with an excessive
amount of black bile, were unhappy and depressed. Persons given to violent
displays of temper were termed **choleric;** the corresponding humour was
ordinary bile. Those with an excessive amount of phlegm were the **phlegmatic**
individuals; they were the apathetic people, not easily moved to displays of
sorrow, anger, love, or, indeed, any other strong emotion.

Although subsequent research in medicine and biology have largely discounted the validity of this typology, other more recent typologies remain
sufficiently confused and speculative that history will probably accord them
little more credence than is now accorded to these ancient Greek typologies.
Sheldon (1936), for example, attempted to arrive at a classification of personality types according to body types (see Figure 7.2). He investigated some
of the common stereotypes that exist concerning the relationship between body
size and proportion and personality; for example, that fat people are jovial,
that skinny people are more intellectual, and that well-built people (relatively)
are more athletically and socially oriented.

Sheldon began by classifying some two thousand photographs in terms of
physical appearance. He and his co-workers arrived at three broad classifications: **ectomorphs, mesomorphs, and endomorphs.** Ectomorphs are
fragile, long limbed, and frail; mesomorphs are muscular and strong and have
high specific gravities, thus tending to float more easily than ectomorphs;
endomorphs are characterized by massive viscera—that is, their stomach,
bowels, and associated organs are highly developed. Following this initial
classification, Sheldon and his associates interviewed a large number of individuals in an attempt to determine whether there would be some relationship between their body types and their personality characteristics. He
reported an overwhelming correspondence between three temperaments and
their associated traits and overt physical characteristics. The temperaments,
which are highly reflective of the specific traits, are as follows: mesomorphs
were labeled *somatotonic*, concerned with the body; endomorphs, *viscerotonic*,
concerned with digestive organs; and ectomorphs, *cerebrotonic*, concerned with

Table 7.2   Some of Sheldon's Traits Arranged According to Body Type*

Ectomorph–Primarily Cerebrotonic	Mesomorph–Primarily Somatotonic	Endomorph–Primarily Viscerotonic
Restrained in movement	Love of adventure	Relaxed in movement
Physiological overresponse	Need for exercise	Love of comfort
Love of privacy	Assertive and bold	Slow reaction
Secretiveness of feeling	Lust for power	Love of eating
Inhibited social address	Physical courage	Sociable
Hypersensitivity to pain	Psychological callousness	Tolerant
	Unrestrained voice	Complacent

*Note that, while the endomorph is more viscerotonic than cerebrotonic or somatotonic, the endomorph is more accurately a combination of all three types. This, of course, is also true for the other two body types.

the mind. Some of the personality traits associated with each of these are presented in Table 7.2.

Sheldon's findings were initially met with a great deal of interest and were accorded considerable scientific credibility. It seemed that he had provided experimental validation for long-held beliefs that appeared, at least to some degree, to coincide with casual observation. The validity of his conclusions were questioned, however, following the realization that those investigators who had originally classified individuals according to body types were the same investigators who subsequently assigned personality traits to the subjects. Lubin (1950) later reanalyzed Sheldon's data and uncovered numerous computational errors. Subsequent replications of the same investigation under more controlled conditions (Hood, 1963) revealed that relationships between body types and personality traits were so small as to be virtually insignificant.

Another typology that has received wider recognition was first introduced by Jung (1923) and by Eysenck (1947) among others. According to this typology, individuals can be characterized as being **introverted** or **extroverted.** Introverted individuals are assumed to be interested in internal events: ideas, imaginings, emotions. The introverted individual is typically withdrawn and not particularly interested in social or athletic involvement. Extroverted individuals, on the other hand, are outgoing, gregarious, interested in athletic activities, and practical rather than idealistic.

Assessing Personality

Given the inordinate interest that people have in knowing who or what they are, a large number of pseudoscientific methods of determining personality have flourished. Notable among these are **palmistry,** the analysis of lines on the palm; **phrenology,** the assessment of personality through an examination of the contours of the head; **graphology,** the analysis of handwriting; and **astrology,** the interpretation of personality according to relative positions of various astral bodies at the time of birth. Evidence supporting the usefulness of each of these approaches is tenuous at best. Proof of their validity is intuitive rather than scientific.

The two approaches to a more scientific assessment of personality that are in widest current use are the projective techniques and simple paper and

Figure 7.3 An inkblot similar to some used in the Rorschach inkblot projective personality test.

pencil tests. Interviews, questionnaires, and behavioral observation are also employed but are somewhat more difficult to validate.

Projective techniques are based on the assumption that human personality cannot easily be described accurately by the individual, but that significant aspects of personality can be revealed in situations where the individual appears to be engaged in activities not directly related to a personality test. The assumption is that basic elements of personality characteristics will be "projected" in such situations. The best known projective tests are the Rorschach inkblot test and the Thematic Apperception Test (TAT). The Rorschach requires that the subject respond to a relatively nebulous stimulus, such as might result from an uncontrolled **inkblot** (see Figure 7.3). In describing what they see in the inkblot, the individuals may reveal their major preoccupations, interests, and attitudes—in short, their personality characteristics. The TAT presents subjects with a series of photographs to which they respond. Many of these are of domestic or work scenes. Again, the assumption is that adolescents will project their interests and preoccupations into their descriptions of the photographs. A further assumption basic to the TAT is that the hero or heroine of the stories told by the adolescents are projections of the adolescents themselves.

Paper and pencil tests such as the Minnesota Multiphasic Personality Inventory (MMPI) and the California Personality Inventory (CPI) ask the subjects to provide information about themselves and their behavior in specific situations.

Adolescent Personality

During adolescence, personality is at a formative stage. Individuals are still in the process of discovering and developing who they are. They are fashioning their *persona*. These will, to a considerable extent, reflect their principal interests, attitudes, and values.

An attitude is simply a tendency to react in a predetermined way. It is, in short, a predisposition. Attitudes are either negative or positive. Positive attitudes lead to involvement; negative attitudes lead to avoidance. For example, if adolescents have positive attitudes toward school, they will want to engage in school related activities; they will be involved in their school work. Conversely, if their attitudes toward school are negative, they will tend

210

to become involved in extracurricular activities. An interest can be defined as a favorable attitude.

Interests are, to a large degree, dictated by social expectations. Thus they are related to the children's age, sex, and culture. Most young boys in contemporary Western cultures are interested in physical activity, in motor games, and in constructing things. Young girls are more interested in social activities and in role-playing games. Adolescent interests reflect the biological, physical, and social changes they are undergoing. Thus their interests tend to be more social than solitary, more serious, less active in a physical sense, more introspective, and more concerned with appearance and social acceptance.

Although it is possible to describe in some detail the typical interests of adolescents, their values, and their attitudes, it would be highly presumptuous to try to describe the typical adolescent personality. One of the errors most frequently made when discussing adolescents (or children for that matter) is to proceed as though the subject under discussion can be isolated and described in some consistent and uniform manner. Few writers would presume to describe what an adult is like because we know very well that adults differ a great deal one from the other. Yet we presume to describe what a five-year-old is like, what a seven-year-old is like, and, on occasion, what an adolescent is like. At best, all we can do with some degree of validity, is describe how typical, average, but mythical, five-, seven-, and fourteen-year-olds differ one from the other; and how, within age groups, they resemble each other.* But we cannot describe the personality of the average adolescent any more than we can describe the personality of the average thirty-year-old. There are adolescents who are aggressive and those who are docile; some who are athletic and some who are intellectual; some who are sensitive and some who are callous; some who are introverted and some who are extroverted. There is no average adolescent.

Summary

This chapter began with a marriage proposal from Mary Lou of Gustavus Adolphus College—for Sam, not me. Sam continues to consider counterpro-

---

* Gesell (see Chapter 5) did just that, but the validity and usefulness of his descriptions have been questioned.

posals. It moved, then, to a discussion of individuals as they are seen from without and as they see themselves from within. The outside view defines personality; the inward view, self. There is no guarantee that each individual has a single unique self in the same way that there is no guarantee that the personality manifested by an individual in a given situation is an accurate reflection of the real self, if there is such a thing. In the end the chapter moved toward a discussion of factors that affect the development of self and the language invented by psychologists to discuss personality. The initial issues remain unresolved. No one has yet established that a person has a single identifiable personality. At the same time, however, psychologists have not yet made it common practice to discuss an individual's *personalities* except when dealing with such individuals as Eve who apparently had three. The chapter concluded with the highly revealing statement that there is no average adolescent personality even as there is no average adult personality.

Main Points

1. Sam is considering a marriage counterproposal. Failing that, he may accept the initial proposal.

2. One way of distinguishing between self and personality is to say that the self is the inside view of individuals (individuals as they see themselves) whereas personality is the outside view (individuals as others see them).

3. It is generally believed that notions of self arise in social situations as a function of individuals' perceptions of the reaction of others to themselves and their behavior.

4. Research indicates that the expectations of others can have a profound influence not only on our concept of self, but also on our behavior. In one study the academic performance and the measured intelligence of a group of students were positively affected by teachers' expectations.

5. One of the principal developmental tasks of adolescence is that of developing a strong, integrated, positive sense of self. The biological changes that herald adolescence are intimately related to children's changing self-concept.

6. Conflict between behavior and expectations, between ideal self and observed self, or between beliefs and behavior may give rise to what Festinger labels cognitive dissonance. Cognitive dissonance is considered to be a motivating force that gives rise to behavior designed to reduce dissonance.

7. Among alternative ways of reducing dissonance are behavior change, attitude change, denial, or perceptual distortion.

8. Adolescents' self-concept is affected by their sex. Such traits as aggression, independence, unemotionality, and logic are considered to be primarily masculine; emotionality, dependence, gentleness, and an orientation toward art and literature are considered feminine.

9. Social stereotypes concerning male and female roles are to a large degree instrumental in determining both self-concept and personality.

10. Some research indicates that race and cultural background have an influence in determining self-concept.

11. Other factors subtly related to self-concept include such things as name and clothing. Clothing is sometimes a manifestation of self or of ideal self. Names appear to be related, on occasion, to the way individuals perceive themselves and, perhaps more often, to the way others perceive the individuals. This is most readily apparent with respect to nicknames.

12. Self-actualization, the process of making the self actual or real, or of developing one's potential, is the highest human need in Maslow's hierarchy. Among the characteristics of self-actualized individuals, Maslow includes: a capacity for detachment, a realistic perception of the world, creativeness, resistance to cultural conformity, and spontaneity in behavior and inner experience.

13. The term personality is derived from the word *persona*, which was employed to denote the masks once worn by Roman actors. A change of mask meant, in effect, a change of personality. In a real sense, individuals change their personalities in different social situations, or at least the external manifestations of their personalities.

14. Personality is most often described either in terms of traits or types. Traits are relatively enduring personality predispositions that tend to be

specific rather than general. Dominance, intelligence, aggression, and so on, are personality traits.

15. Personality types are defined in terms of conglomerations of related traits. The ancient Greek classification of individuals into the categories of sanguine, melancholic, choleric, or phlegmatic is an example of a type approach.

16. Sheldon's typology of human personality characteristics was based on body types. He identified three distinct body builds: the endomorph (large), the ectomorph (frail), and the mesomorph (athletic). His research indicated that each of these was characterized by different temperaments, and that some personality characteristics could therefore be deduced directly from an observation of a person's body build. Subsequent research has shown that these conclusions are largely incorrect.

17. A more currently popular type approach is that advanced by Jung and refined by Eysenck, among others. It identifies individuals on the basis of their qualities of introversion and extroversion. Introverted individuals are withdrawn and concerned with internal events; extroverted individuals are more outgoing.

18. Personality tests are frequently of the self-report paper and pencil variety or of a projective nature. Projective tests require that individuals respond to some relatively nebulous stimulus. The assumption is that subjects will unconsciously project their preoccupations and interests in responding to such stimuli and will thereby unwittingly reveal aspects of their personalities.

19. Attitudes are defined as tendencies to react in predetermined ways in specific situations. An interest is simply a positive attitude. That is, it is a tendency to react in a positive manner.

20. There is no average adolescent personality any more than there is an average adult personality. It is important to note, however, that personality is still very much at a formative stage during adolescence.

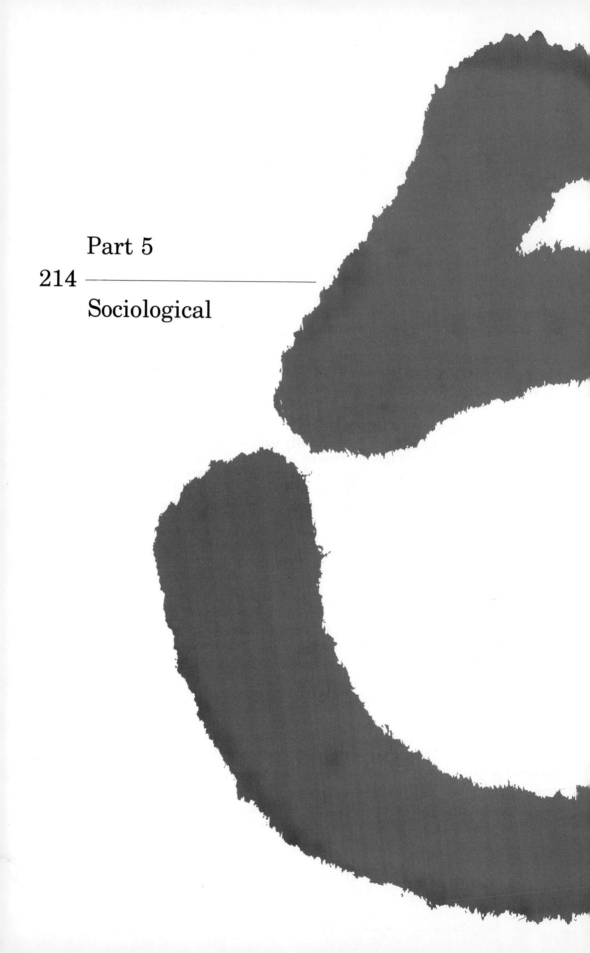

Part 5

214 ————————————

Sociological

215

Chapter 8

**Mothers and Fathers: Adolescence
and the Family**

Chapter 9

**Youth and Flouris Green:
Adolescent Peer Groups**

Chapter 10

**Visions and Teachers: Schools
and Adolescents**

Chapter 8

216

Mothers and Fathers:
Adolescence and
the Family

Shelley Drinkwater, Grade 11

217

218

Sam's father, may his soul . . . , died of an unidentified viral infection whose symptoms were hauntingly reminiscent of those that had once accompanied that great killer, the bubonic plague. I knew of this through previous conversations with Sam, but was totally unaware of several other pertinent facts revealed to me by Sam in a rare moment of nostalgia no more than two hours ago. Sam and I were huddled together in the dim glow of a single tallow candle reading this manuscript, which is now over half complete. What moved him to this nostalgia was his realization that the next chapter would deal with the adolescent and the family.

"I had a family too, once," Sam began, the candlelight reflecting softly on his pale features. Sam has not seen the sun for a long time. "My father was the most influential person in my life," he announced almost as though this were a rare and unusual state of affairs. "It is because of him that I am what I am today."

Kindly, I refrained from asking him what it was that he thinks he is today, but asked him instead how his father had influenced him. He told me.

It seems that Sam's father was employed by the Alberta Rat Patrol during Sam's most formative adolescent years. It is a fact that Alberta is probably the largest geographical land area on earth that is completely free of rats — a fact of which we Albertans are justifiably proud. Mother Nature, politics, and sheer determination all played a role in bringing about this happy state of affairs. For her part, Mother Nature provided the Rocky Mountains on our western border and the frozen desolation of arctic wastes on our northern border. Rats cross neither border, even reluctantly, because Mother Nature quite impersonally freezes those who would come from the north, and drowns, loses, or frightens to death those who would cross from the west. Our southern boundary consists of a peaceful border between the United States and Canada. For some unexplained reason, probably linked with political beliefs, visas, and customs officials, no rats enter from the south either. There remains only our eastern boundary, most geographical areas on earth being describable in relation to four orthogonal directions, or so Sam assures me. The Alberta government, in a moment of rare insight, deduced that if rats were prevented from crossing into Alberta from Saskatchewan, an area not entirely free of several varieties of rats, Alberta might well become a rat-free province. This important fact could then be announced in the various brochures that so tantalizingly beckon tourists to Our Alberta. And so the Alberta Rat Patrol was set up following an extensive program during which all rats then residing in Alberta were executed or otherwise persuaded to leave. The Rat Patrol's mission was simple. They were to patrol the Saskatchewan-Alberta border in search of rats. Those that showed any inclination to go West rather than back East were to be shot on the spot.

Sam and his father had a close relationship. During summer vacation they spent many evenings together, huddled in a Rat Patrol tent near the border, discussing the day's work. It was inevitable that the young Sam would develop a profound interest in rats. And when he discovered that laboratory rats had remained legal in the province, he quickly obtained his first breeding pair. For some reason, he kept his new acquisition from his father until the old man lay dying of the viral infection mentioned earlier.

"I did not approve of his work, but he was a good man," Sam concluded, a single tear flowing uninterruptedly down his cheek. He probably was.

Sam's family life was, as I understand it, not exceptional in other respects. He offered little toward this chapter save a number of emotional platitudes. I proceeded alone.

The Contemporary Family

A number of assumptions have traditionally been made about changing relationships between children and their immediate families as they pass through adolescence. It is widely accepted that the **family** is the most important socializing force in the life of young children, but that following early childhood other socializing agencies including the school, sometimes the church, various community organizations, and, most important, the peer group, gradually supplant the family as socializing forces. In adolescence children become even more reliant on groups of peers and less attached to their immediate families, a situation that is not viewed with alarm by objective investigators and theorists, but that does, on occasion, cause severe strife and upheaval in the families concerned.

Additional assumptions that are too little questioned concern the nature of the relationship that is believed to exist between many parents and their adolescents. Uncritical proponents of the "sturm und drang" viewpoint are not surprised to observe that adolescents become excessively moody, prone to

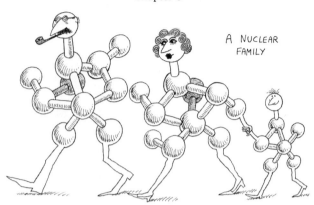

A NUCLEAR FAMILY

220

violent outbursts of temper, on occasion gregarious in the extreme, and at other times sullen and withdrawn; that they reject parental authority and struggle bitterly against restraints that are imposed on them; that they equate all forms of authority, including parental authority, with an oppressive "establishment" whose behavior is a dramatic contradiction of its expressed beliefs; that they have too little in common with their ancient parents to engage them in meaningful conversation concerning those things that are of most importance to them. That, in short, there is not simply a generation gap, but a generational abyss (Conger, 1973), the existence of which is made obvious by the violence, turmoil, and strife characteristic of contemporary parent-adolescent relationships.

These assumptions, though clearly true in some cases, have been so overstated as to become untrue in the main. They require further examination, some of which is provided in the remaining pages of this chapter.

The Family and Social Change

Although no one knows precisely what the origins of the family are, it is interesting to speculate about these origins, particularly because none of our phylogenetic predecessors appears to have developed families of the types most common at present. Early sociologists (for example, Morgan, 1894, 1896) assumed that the social organization of primitive humans was not unlike that of the monkeys and apes whose behaviors now amuse us. Morgan thought that men and women lived apart, coming together only when men were overpowered by the urge to rape the women. Engels (1902) also believed that men and women did not live together in family groups as we know them, but in communal bands where sexual activity was indiscriminate and where responsibility for child-rearing belonged to the entire group rather than to natural parents.

Whatever the true origin of the family, it is now true that most of the world's societies are characterized by one of two types of family organization, both of which revolve around a relatively permanent mother-father relationship. In the **nuclear family,** characteristic of most Western civilizations, the family unit is composed of mother, father, and immediate children. **Extended families,** which account for a greater proportion of the world's populations, are comprised of parents, immediate children, grandparents, and, on occasion, other assorted relatives.

A number of important social changes have taken place in the nuclear family unit in recent decades, many of them linked with wider social changes. Some of these have significant implications for an understanding of the contemporary family and its role in child-rearing. Chief among them has been the progressive isolation of nuclear family units one from the other. With increasing urbanization, the formerly cohesive community group of which the family was an intrinsic part is largely disappearing. Nuclear families typically live in large, impersonal bedroom communities or in equally impersonal and transient suburban communities, characterized by a high degree of isolation one from the other. Personal and lifelong friends, significant adults such as teachers or pastors, grandparents, and cousins rarely belong to the same social or geographic group. One of the obvious results of this increased isolation and of the tremendously increased mobility of family units, particularly among the middle class, is a significant reduction in security both for parents and for children. Child-rearing problems must be faced alone, or with the help of impersonal "experts" whose identities are revealed as clearly by a telephone book as they are by interviewing the parents who have consulted them. Unlike close-knit communities, contemporary urban and suburban ghettos harbor a wide range of values and life-styles, thus providing either few adult models for the developing adolescent or providing a confusing and contradictory assortment of models. Parental values are often contradicted by the values of other parents with whose children their own children associate; as a result, parents frequently receive little support in their attempts to control the behavior of their children. Schools tend to be large congregations of children from a wide geographic area and from very diverse backgrounds. In short, contemporary urban and suburban existence is characterized by impermanence and lack of close emotional ties outside the immediate family. And the fact that one in three contemporary marriages will eventually result in divorce does not add to the permanence of the family unit.

A clear implication of these social changes is that members of the family have become more dependent on each other for emotional support and perhaps more cohesive than would be the case in a rural community. The increased interdependency of family members has also been a function of family sizes becoming smaller. We can speculate that the nuclear family is becoming more cohesive as communities become less cohesive, and that one of the indirect effects of these changes will be reflected in a closer relationship between parental characteristics and child-rearing qualities on the one hand and child characteristics and adjustment on the other.

Importance of the Family

With their peculiar penchant for making the obvious even more obvious, psychologists and sociologists have long maintained that the family is of considerable importance to young children. At an early age they find themselves completely dependent on the family. Their physical needs are usually satisfied in direct interaction with members of their immediate family. In addition, the family provides them with important feelings of security and belongingness, thus satisfying their emotional needs and promoting their psychological growth. Almost as important, the family serves as the major transmitter of cultural information in the early years, a role that is later partly taken over by schools and peer groups.

But the importance of the family goes considerably beyond the mere satisfaction of needs or the imparting of cultural information. It is also instrumental in determining the types of individuals the children will eventually become—their values, ideals, personality characteristics, and so on. The quality of parent-child interaction, the emotional relationship between parents and children, parental values, the number and sex of **siblings** in the family, and the children's birth order are all important variables in determining eventual adjustment and predominant characteristics of adolescents.

Family Size

In 1790 over half of all American families had six or more children; the average number of children per family is now very close to two, with large families being much more frequent among lower-socioeconomic groups largely comprised of various ethnic minorities. Relatively few studies have examined the relationship between family size and the characteristics of adolescents.

Bossard and Sanger (1952) and Bossard and Boll (1956) did several large-scale investigations of large families. They report that these families seem to be more **authoritarian** than smaller families; and, perhaps by necessity, they are less overprotective, less overindulgent, and less intrusive. Bowerman and Kinch (1959), in an investigation of shifts from family to peer orientation during adolescence, found that changes in orientation occurred earlier and were also greater for children from large families than for those from small families. They defined large families as those with four or more children; small families were those with three or fewer children. These findings are not surprising given that there is a relationship between parental control and adolescent emancipation. This topic is examined in more detail later in this chapter.

The smallest family of interest to a child psychologist, that with only one child, has also been investigated. The results of these investigations contradict the popular belief that "only children" tend to have more difficulties adjusting to peers and to life than children with siblings, that they are indulged more highly and are therefore more dependent, that their language development is slower than that of other children, and that they do less well in school. None of these venerable beliefs appears to be true. Davis (1937), Faris (1940), McCurdy (1957), and West (1960) provide evidence of superior intellectual achievement among only children; more rapid development early in life, particularly in the area of language learning; and greater eminence among adults who were only children. In addition, there is no conclusive evidence of poorer adjustment among these children or of difficulties in interacting with peers.

The advantages enjoyed by the only child have most often been explained in terms of the quality and quantity of interaction provided by the mother—and perhaps by the father as well. Only children do not have to compete with siblings for their mothers' attention. In addition, they have nothing but adult models around them, a fact that is probably of considerable significance in explaining their earlier language acquisition. It has been known for some time, for example, that twins, triplets, and quadruplets fare less well in language development than do children who do not have a twin (Davis, 1937; Blatz, 1937). This is not particularly surprising in view of the fact that children from multiple births would enjoy less interaction with their parents and would also be in closer contact with other infant or child models.

Birth Order

The advantages enjoyed by only children are also enjoyed by those who are oldest in the family. Galton (1896) was among the first to notice that among Britain's great men of science, there were a preponderance of firstborn children. More recently *Newsweek* (1969) noted that of the seven original astronauts, five were firstborn; the remaining two were only children. Of the first twenty-three astronauts to travel space, twenty-one were either firstborn or had no siblings. Of the other two, one had an older brother who died as an infant, so that he was in fact reared as an only child. The other was thirteen years younger than his older brother.

Koch (1955) studied a large group of five- and six-year-old children and concluded that firstborn children have an advantage in several areas of development. They learn to speak at an earlier age, articulate better, show a higher degree of responsibility, and perform better on measures of intellectual performance. Numerous other studies have corroborated these findings, and have indicated advantages in other areas as well. Firstborns have a higher achievement motive (higher need to achieve) (Sampson, 1962); they do better in school (Altus, 1965, 1967); they are more curious and competitive (Altus, 1967; Brim, 1956); and they are more likely to attend college (Bayer, 1966). Schachter (1963) found a higher-than-chance proportion of firstborn men in *American Men of Science, Who's Who,* and various other similar publications.

Siblings

In families with more than one child, the sex and birth order of siblings appears to be of some importance in determining personality characteristics of adolescents, particularly with respect to the adoption of sex roles. Masculinity-femininity appear to be highly influenced by siblings. Strauss (1959) found, for example, that girls who had a number of brothers but no sisters tended to adopt an extreme sex role. Such girls were either highly feminine, behaving very much as though they believed their femininity was some remarkable attribute that would be forever worshiped by lesser males; or they were highly masculine, modeling on their brothers rather than exaggerating the differences between them. Koch (1956) reports that boys who have an older sister, in two-child families, tend to be more passive and more feminine than would otherwise be the case. Similarly, a girl who has a single older brother will tend to display masculine characteristics, being more aggressive and dominant than other girls without older brothers (Sutton-Smith, Roberts, and Rosenberg, 1964). In much the same way, girl-girl dyads tend to produce highly feminine characteristics in both girls and boy-boy dyads tend to produce highly masculine characteristics in both boys.

Changes in Adolescent-Parent Relationships

Initially the family is central in children's lives; in middle childhood, peers assume a more important role, although the family continues to be of central importance. In adolescence, however, perhaps in preparation for more independent adult roles, children almost inevitably shift their orientation from family to peers and wider society. This change in orientation, however, does not necessarily imply conflict between parents and children. In fact, conflict is relatively infrequent, contrary to popular belief. And when conflict does arise, it is frequently related to a neurotic parent's reluctance to abdicate control over a child or to sever emotional ties that have existed for more than a decade, or to a maladjusted adolescent's unwillingness to accept the responsibilities that are attendant upon adulthood. Traditional views of adolescence as an almost invariably stressful period are far from completely accurate. It is true that adolescents have to undergo major readjustments to changes of crucial importance to them. It is also true that adolescence represents a profound social change for children. But it is not true that these changes can be brought about only in direct confrontation with parents and other supposedly opposing forces.

Bowerman and Kinch (1959) conducted an extensive investigation of parent-child relationships employing a sample of 686 students in grades four to ten. Specifically they were concerned with the extent to which children identify with their peers and their family, the extent to which they associate with each, and the extent to which their values and beliefs were similar to those of family and peers. Subjects were asked a number of relevant questions: for example, which group understood them best, family or friends; which groups they most enjoyed doing things with; whether they would like to be adults similar to their parents or similar to the adults they thought their friends would be; and whose ideas were most like theirs with respect to right and wrong, with respect to activities that are enjoyable, and with respect to things that are important and those that aren't.

As expected, the investigators found a predicted shift from family to peer orientation from grades four to ten. In grade four, for example, 87.1 percent of the students were more family than peer oriented. By tenth grade, however, only 31.6 percent were primarily family oriented. The percentage of subjects who were peer oriented had changed from 5.9 to 48.1 in the same period of time. Interestingly, however, the greatest change occurred in what the investigators refer to as "association," and the least change, in "identification." That is, older adolescents tended to associate more and more with peers, but continue to identify strongly with their families. As Gold and Douvan (1969) point out, adolescents' increasing need for emotional independence has probably been exaggerated. While there is evidently some need for emotional detachment, greater attachment to peers does not imply that there will be a corresponding decline in attachment to family. In a very real sense, adolescents do not really abdicate their families as a source of emotional support, but merely extend their world to include more peers. And the fact that peers are accorded more importance does not imply that parents are accorded less importance. Bowerman and Kinch (1959) make the observation that when adolescents' adjustment to their families is good, their orientation to the family (in terms of association, identification, and similarity of values) will tend to remain high throughout adolescence. Conversely, when their adjustment to the family is poor, their orientation to peer groups will change more significantly. That is, they will become more oriented to friends and less to family.

A number of interesting studies have been conducted comparing parents' perceptions of themselves and of their adolescents with perceptions by adolescents of parents. Hess (1959–60) found that parents expected adolescents to overrate their own maturity and ability and to underrate that of the parents. Similarly, adolescents thought parents would underrate them. In fact, however, adolescents almost invariably rate parents higher than parents rate themselves. Messner (1965) found that, in general, adolescent attitudes toward parents were positive, although there were consistent differences in the ways in which fathers and mothers were perceived. Typically fathers were seen

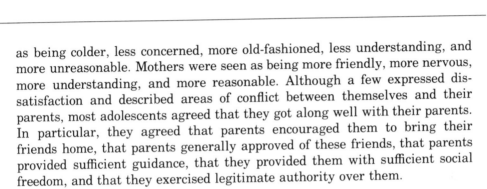

as being colder, less concerned, more old-fashioned, less understanding, and more unreasonable. Mothers were seen as being more friendly, more nervous, more understanding, and more reasonable. Although a few expressed dissatisfaction and described areas of conflict between themselves and their parents, most adolescents agreed that they got along well with their parents. In particular, they agreed that parents encouraged them to bring their friends home, that parents generally approved of these friends, that parents provided sufficient guidance, that they provided them with sufficient social freedom, and that they exercised legitimate authority over them.

Parent and Adolescent Characteristics

Because the family is one of the more pervasive influences on children, and because human characteristics are only partly determined by genetic factors, it is inevitable that the family will exercise a profound effect on children's personalities and interests as well as on their values. Numerous investigators have attempted to discover specific relationships that might exist between parental and adolescent characteristics. The area is a difficult one to research for a number of reasons. It is as difficult to ascertain precisely what the nature of the relationship between a parent and a child is as it is to determine specifically what the parent or the child's personality characteristics are. Hatfield et al., (1967), for example, observed mothers and their children in a playroom setting and found that their behaviors were so inconsistent from one time to another that it was virtually impossible to arrive at some clear notion of what the nature of the specific mother-child interaction was. The problems associated with measuring personality are legion. Some have been mentioned in the preceding chapter. A major problem is the questionable validity and the low reliability of many of the instruments that are employed. Even more basic is the problem concerning the fluctuation of personality variables over time. To say that a given person is introverted, independent, masochistic, or whatever is always at least slightly misleading unless the specific conditions under which behavioral manifestations of these characteristics have been observed are detailed.

Despite these difficulties, there are a number of apparently valid generalizations concerning the relationships between certain parental characteristics and adolescent characteristics. It should not be inferred, however, that one is a cause of the other. None of the studies provide evidence sufficient for inferring causation. At best we can simply say that there appears to be a relationship between such and such in a parent and such and such in an adolescent.

Values

There appears to be relatively high agreement between parental **values** and adolescent values, again contrary to popular beliefs concerning the generation gap. Reiss (1966) found a high correlation between parents' beliefs and the beliefs of their older adolescents. Although parents and adolescents frequently disagreed on specific values, general patterns of beliefs tended to be highly related. Liberal parents were more likely to have liberal children; conservative parents were most likely to have conservative children.

More specifically, Warriner, Foster, and Trites (1966) found that parents who did not value education highly and who had themselves dropped out of school prior to completion were more likely to have children who would also drop out of school. Those who had acquired advanced degrees were also more likely to have children who would acquire advanced degrees.

Affection and Control

Child-rearing styles are often classified as being accepting or rejecting, **authoritarian** or **democratic,** active or passive. These adjectives are simply descriptive of the amount of affection and control exercised by parents. A large number of studies bear directly on the supposed relationships between these variables and various characteristics observed in adolescents. Only a few of the more representative are mentioned here, with the caution that there is sufficient contradiction among these studies and sufficient variability among people to make excessive generalizations from any of these studies highly questionable at best.

Crandall and Preston (1961) report that excessive affection is frequently detrimental to children's adjustment. Children's reactions to smothering affection and overindulgence can take one of two forms when they leave their

parents and begin to interact with peers. They either become highly dependent, displaying no initiative, and complying docilely to the wishes of others;
or they become highly withdrawn. In either case, their adjustment to social
situations tends to be less than desirable. Affection, on the other hand, has
highly positive effects if it is supportive (accepting) but not overly possessive
(Carlson, 1963).

Douvan and Adelson (1966) studied a large number of adolescents. Their
findings corroborated those mentioned above: there is a high relationship
between parental involvement and the child's adjustment. The relationship
appears to be a curvilinear one, where too much or too little parental affection
and involvement both serve to inhibit the development of the adolescent's
sense of autonomy. Too little involvement leads to a sense of insecurity and
does not promote the sort of confidence that is necessary to produce autonomy;
too much involvement leads to an exaggerated dependency that also inter-
feres with the development of autonomy. These findings are also corroborated
by Mussen et al. (1963) who found that parental affection was of considerable
importance for the development of security, confidence, and optimal social
adjustment. Similarly, Bronfenbrenner (1961) found a high relationship between parental rejection, neglect, and companionship on the one hand, and
the development of a sense of responsibility among fifteen- and sixteen-year-
old boys. Specifically, boys who were least mature in their development of
responsibility had parents who ridiculed them, compared them unfavorably
with other adolescents, and spent little time with them.

The father appears to be of some importance for the development of the male
adolescent in particular and the female adolescent to a lesser degree. Heath
(1965) studied a group of college males and selected from these the ten men
considered to be the most mature and the most highly achieving. Eight out of
these ten considered their fathers to have been the most important influence
in their lives. Interestingly, three out of four of the least mature and most
poorly adjusted males described their mothers as dominating, aggressive, or
subject to excessive drinking and fits of depression. Related to this, Bronfenbrenner (1961) concludes that discipline and firm authority from the father
appears to be especially important for the development of a sense of responsibility in boys, but that it is negatively related to the development of responsibility in girls. This may well be due to the fact that an authoritarian but loving
father provides a clear model of responsible adult behavior for boys. Because

the girl is more likely to model after her mother, it is conceivable that an authoritarian father would develop the sort of dependence in her that might well be characteristic of her mother. Hence her development of responsibility would be negatively influenced by her father's behavior.

It is difficult to draw any sort of precise rules for the guidance of adolescents or their parents from studies such as those reviewed in this section. None of the findings are particularly surprising; there is a high correlation between parental and child values; parental child-rearing styles, particularly as they reflect affection and acceptance, are intimately related to the successful social adjustment of adolescents. Perhaps more important, parental rejection or overindulgence appear to be highly related to the eventual maladjustment of adolescents.

Rejection can take a variety of forms, many so subtle and unconscious that only a skilled observer can interpret them correctly. Ridicule, overt demeaning comparisons, and neglect are some of the obvious forms of rejection. Less obvious are those instances where one or both parents are so involved in their own lives that they are unable to relate meaningfully with their children. Rejection takes the form of an emotional neglect so subtle that perhaps both parent and child remain unaware of it. In other instances, parents find it difficult to express their emotions. This is particularly true of fathers who have been reared in a culture that does not reinforce the expression of emotion in males.

The parent-adolescent conflict that has preoccupied many observers of the contemporary scene may have some of its roots in early parent-child relationships. Some of its other roots appear to be elsewhere.

Minority Groups

Although it is impossible to give a complete account of the implications of being a minority group adolescent, there are certain apparent differences between the dominant majority and minority groups that should be mentioned. As pointed out in Chapter 7, these differences can most logically be attributed to a rather nebulous complex of socioeconomic forces rather than to racial factors, despite the fact that minority groups are most clearly identifiable in terms of ethnic origins. Most minority groups have one important thing in common: they are subject to varying amounts of prejudice and discrimination. In addition, most are characterized by inferior economic conditions, evident in the different standards of living predominant in each. Jewish minority groups form a notable exception with respect to economic conditions. The effects of these different social and economic conditions on the adolescents' developing self-concepts are discussed in Chapter 7. This section discusses briefly some of the child-rearing practices and dominant family characteristics of American blacks and Mexican-Americans (Chicanos).

Forbes (1966) notes that the Chicano family is typically a very cohesive, male-dominated, extended family. That is, the family includes a host of relatives, but the male breadwinner is clearly dominant. Interestingly, his primary motivating values center around the family rather than around himself. That is, he tends to think of himself as responsible to the family and as responsible for its welfare, spending little time in activities designed to bring comfort to himself alone. As patriarch of this extended family, the male Chicano is concerned with the manifestation of his dominance; with obtaining repeated evidence that he is "rooster in the house" (Madsen, 1964). Accordingly, Chicano women tend to behave in a subservient and acquiescent manner in relation to their men. Outside the home, the male attains stature relative to his *machismo* – his manliness – most obviously expressed in his ability to impregnate women and particularly to father sons.

Child-rearing practices among Mexican-Americans, as described by Madsen (1964), are relatively permissive and emotionally supportive. At puberty, however, the father typically becomes considerably more authoritarian, perhaps because he feels that the activities of his sons and daughters reflect directly on himself as leader of the house. Mothers, on the other hand, tend to be highly permissive with their sons and highly supportive of those activities that provide evidence that he too is becoming a man and achieving machismo. Accordingly, she is much more likely than the father to tolerate the son's staying out late.

Mexican-American adolescent peer groups are perhaps of greater importance than are peer groups to most white Americans. It is in this group that males establish their manliness, and they continually return to it with tales of their exploits so that they might receive further corroboration of their machismo. Madsen (1964) reports that even after marriage, the peer group continues to be of central importance to the Chicano male.

Unlike the Chicano family, the American black family has frequently been described as matriarchal. There are several reasons for this. For example, there are approximately three times more father-absent homes among American blacks than among American whites. In addition, the American welfare system, highly active in many minority group residential areas, tends to favor women raising children alone. Even in those families where both parents are present, Rainwater (1966) reports that the mother tends to make most of the decisions important to the household and the children. This maternal dominance is apparently reflected in adolescent black girls who, according to some research, are less likely to conform to social pressure than are either white girls or black boys (Brink and Harris, 1967).

Other research (for example, Tenhouten, 1970) has not supported the contention that mothers are more often dominant in black families than are fathers. Results appear to be equivocal at best, and child-rearing practices are difficult to describe because they vary a great deal.

Generally supported conclusions regarding the influence of the family on black adolescents concern such topics as delinquency and school achievement. It has been found, for example, that father absence is related to delinquency in boys (Anderson, 1968). (More is said about the relationship between socio-economic factors and delinquency in Chapter 11.) It has also been found that black parents generally have lower educational aspirations for their children, a finding that appears to be valid for many other minority groups as well. Not surprisingly, nationwide achievement tests administered at all grade levels in 1965 revealed significantly lower achievement scores for blacks, Puerto Ricans, Indian-Americans, Oriental-Americans, and Mexican-Americans (Coleman, 1966). Among the numerous reasons advanced for this discrepancy are: the language problems frequently characteristic of minority groups whose languages are either different or a dialectic variation of the dominant language; unequal schooling opportunity most often evident in terms of inferior facilities and teachers; and peer and parental values that do not emphasize educational achievement.

In discussing minority groups, there is a temptation to attempt to identify similarities and differences among these and dominant groups and to deal with them as though present conditions are an accurate reflection of the way things will be. It should be clear, however, that because present conditions

are dramatically different from those that obtained only generations ago, they may be even more different in the very near future.

The Generation Gap

Davis (1960) describes adolescence as a developmental phase when social maturity lags far behind physical and mental maturity. At the termination of the adolescent period, physical development is almost at its peak both in terms of size and strength and in terms of sexual development. Similarly, intellectual potential, as reflected in such mental capabilities as are involved in solving problems, playing chess, or mastering advanced mathematical and algebraic theories, is as fully developed as it will ever be. Social maturity, however, defined in terms of sociological position, is still some distance from being fully realized. A person's sociological position is defined primarily in terms of occupation, reproductive control, authority position, and cultural acquisition (Davis, 1960). Adolescents typically remain unemployed, cannot easily reproduce while conforming to social standards, remain in an inferior position with respect to decision-making within the family, and have yet to learn many of the complexities of the culture of which they are part, because advanced technological cultures cannot be transmitted as easily to adolescents as can the more primitive cultures discussed briefly in the opening chapter of this text. The conflict that sometimes exists between generations — and specifically between parents and adolescents within the family because they too are of different generations — stems in part from adolescents' social immaturity and in part from the rate of social change that tends to exaggerate the difference between successive generations. That is, not only did parents live in a generation that came before that of their children, but the changes that have intervened between these generations create an increasing disparity between parent-child values, aspirations, ideals, and beliefs. Yet parent-adolescent conflicts are not nearly as prevalent or as serious as popular literature would lead us to believe. Offer (1969) interviewed parents and adolescents in an attempt to investigate the so-called generation gap. Although both parents and adolescents admitted that there was some distance between the generations, neither group saw this as a particularly severe problem. Re-

Tracy *Age 17* **Going Out**

Me: *What are your mother's feelings about you going out? You said you don't always agree about your going out.*
Tracy: *Well, she's afraid that I'll be hurt or harmed. She says that she doesn't mind me going out. She's not afraid of what I'll do; she's afraid of what other people'll do to me.*

234 ──────────────────────────────────

lated to this, Douvan and Adelson (1966) note that the majority of adolescents believe that their parents approve of their values, although they might not necessarily approve of the younger generation's way of expressing itself. Although there is obviously a great deal of discrepancy between parents and adolescents with respect to hair styles, dress, and musical taste, there appears to be little discrepancy with respect to fundamental values (Reiss, 1966).

Sex, drugs, and activism are three additional topics of particular interest in a study of adolescence. They are also of particular interest to a number of adolescents. An examination of each of these topics, undertaken in a later section of this book, provides additional insights into possible sources of conflict between adolescents and their parents. It should be made clear, however, that these are sources of conflict only for a minority. While it may be true, for example, that most adolescents experiment with drugs and that most parents do not approve of this behavior, it is also true that drugs are not a source of conflict between most parents and their adolescents. Here, as in other instances, the most visible minority has attracted the greatest public attention. Because you and I don't read or hear very often in the public media about adolescents who pass normally and uneventfully through this developmental phase, we begin to wonder whether anyone ever does.

Some do. In fact, most do.

Summary

This chapter began with a visit with Sam who reminisced about his father. It moved then to other families, noting that there have been some changes in the family since Sam's parents were children. The importance of the family and the effects of such family variables as size, birth order, and siblings were examined. Finally the chapter stopped to look at some of the relationships between parental characteristics and behavior and the qualities typically manifested by adolescents from identifiably different families. A final word concerned the generation gap that appears to be less wide than has often been supposed.

Main Points

1. Alberta is a rat-free province. Sam's father died of a viral infection whose symptoms resembled those of bubonic plague.

2. Assumptions regarding the incompatibility of parents and adolescents and the family turmoil that ensues during adolescence are frequently inaccurate.

3. A nuclear family is one comprised of children and immediate parents. Extended families, typical of many of the world's societies, though not of Western societies, include parents, children, grandparents, uncles, aunts, and assorted relatives.

4. With increasing urbanization, nuclear families have become more isolated from close extrafamilial relationships. The implications of this are yet unclear.

5. The importance of the family is not limited to providing for children's emotional and physical needs, but includes as well the transmission of significant cultural knowledge.

6. Families have been decreasing in average size for a number of decades. Many Western societies are at or close to zero population growth.

7. Contrary to folklore, only children are not at any disadvantage in terms of social, emotional, and intellectual development. Indeed, they appear to be at an advantage.

8. Firstborn children enjoy many of the same advantages that are characteristic of only children. Specifically, their language development, scholastic achievement, independence, and likelihood of future eminence are all superior to that of children with siblings who are close in age. These findings are most often explained in terms of the closer parent-child interaction with respect to only children or to firstborn children.

9. Sibling position appears to have some effect on masculinity and femininity. A girl with an older brother tends to be more masculine; a boy with an older sister tends to be more feminine.

(aboriginal art)

236

10. There is a shift from family to peer orientation beginning in middle childhood but becoming more pronounced in adolescence. This shift does not necessarily imply parent-adolescent conflict.

11. There is a high agreement among parents and their adolescents with respect to basic values despite the fact that adolescents tend to behave in accordance with peer standards.

12. Child-rearing styles are intimately linked with adolescent personality characteristics and adjustment. Maladjusted adolescents most often have cold, rejecting parents, or overly protective, authoritarian parents. Too much or too little parental involvement can inhibit the adolescent's development of a sense of autonomy.

13. Adolescence can be described as the developmental period where social maturity lags far behind intellectual, physical, or sexual maturity.

14. Research that has attempted to uncover the extent to which parents and adolescents are typically in conflict has most often tended to support a moderate view. It appears that parent-adolescent conflicts are not nearly as prevalent or as serious as popular literature and media reports have led many to believe.

Shelley Drinkwater, Grade 11

* Gaudeamus igitur,
Juvenes dum sumus

> *(Let us be happy while we are young —*
> *from a student song traced to 1267)*

O youth, be glad into thy flouris green
O youth, thy flouris fadis ferly sone!

> *(from* The Reasoning Betwixt Youth
> and Age *by Robert Henryson)*

Gather ye rose-buds while ye may

> *(from* To the Virgins, to Make Much of
> Time *by Robert Herrick)*

In contemporary American societies, the greatest of all evils is surely to grow old, and the greatest good must certainly be to remain forever young. It is likely that no other people in the history of the world has had such a profound fear that they would awake one morning and find their faces wrinkled, their hair gray, their muscles atrophied and wizened. Age must be combated at all costs, for there is nothing so precious as youth.

The cult of youthfulness has become a fetish in our times. Countless millions are spent on hair tints, dyes, wigs, hair pieces, hair transplants, toupees, elevator shoes, cosmetic glasses, face lifts, silicone implantations, and wart removals; cosmetics, both surgical and chemical; powders, creams; perfumes, both odorant and deodorant; eyebrow tweezers, pluckers, combs, and brushes; lipsticks, rouges, polish; lipstick remover, polish remover, and an endless variety of instruments for the application or removal of these. Weight reducing programs, body building courses, and various esoteric exercises have become quasi-religious in nature. "Think young," we are told, and then we are exhorted to purchase any of a number of books, medications, cosmetics, shampoos, deodorants, and programs that are designed to make us think and feel young. But those of us who are not now young will never be young again given the peculiar linearity of time. We have committed the unforgivable sin; we have aged. Our punishment is inevitable. We will be ignored both by the young and by those

---

* An excerpt from Sam's essay on adolescence. Reprinted with his permission.

among the middle-aged who have not yet realized that their youth is passed.

I think it deplorable that culture does not permit middle-aged men and women to grow old gracefully, but encourages them instead to cavort about as they did when they were adolescents. Psychologists have for some time maintained that the types of relationships that are fostered in adolescent peer groups are useful in that they serve as prototypes of future adult relationships particularly in the heterosexual sphere. It is becoming increasingly true, however, that adults themselves imitate the behaviors of adolescent groups. This is most obvious with respect to such superficial things as dress and hair styles, language, and musical taste. It is becoming increasingly obvious in more subtle areas. There is a parallel, for example, between the serial polygamy of the middle-aged playboy (marriage following divorce following marriage ad nauseam) and the succession of "steady" relationships and "breakups" characteristic of many adolescents. And the structure of the adolescent peer group is highly similar to that which is now developing in small middle-class communities among the middle-aged.

Many middle-aged people repeatedly assert that they would do it differently if they had it to do all over again. In the dim past the thought remained a hopeless wish. Now many among the middle-aged think they can do it all over again. Take, for example, my obese friend John. John . . .

Succeeding sections of Sam's essay are somewhat irrelevant for our purposes and have not been included here. The cult of youth is, however, a very real phenomenon though it may not be as universal or as serious as Sam supposes. This chapter deals with the functions and structure of adolescent peer groups. Perhaps there is a parallel between these and the middle-aged peer group.

Peer Groups

Peer groups are not peculiar to adolescents; babies have them as do adults, old people, and all others in between or beyond. A group of peers is simply a group of equals — equals in one or more respects. Thus it is possible to say that there are age peers, sex peers, grade peers, age-sex peers, age-grade peers, sex-age-grade peers, intellectual peers, social peers, and a variety of other

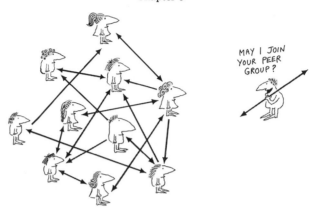

MAY I JOIN
YOUR PEER
GROUP?

242

peers. But the peers that infants have are of relatively little importance to their immediate development — parents, family, and immediate physical environment being of much greater consequence. Early in middle childhood, however, peers begin to assume more importance but are still of considerably less moment than they will be later. In their initially brief forays from their immediate family, young children encounter groups of peers with whom they interact in various ways. Piaget notes (1932) that this interaction is initially highly egocentric. While young children play together, the nature of their play is not truly social. Indeed, it has been described as parallel rather than social play. Two young children play with cars, side by side in the same sand box, but the activities of one have little effect on the other unless one violates the other's space, or unless there arises some disagreement concerning temporary ownership of the toys in question.

Later children begin to engage in a more social form of play, a form of play that requires interaction among peers, and that also requires that members understand and abide by certain rules. At this stage, children do not really understand the nature of rules and consequently change them continually to conform to their immediate desires (ages three to five approximately). By the time children have reached the age of seven or eight, they have begun to understand rules and to play in a genuinely social manner where all players rigidly adhere to the rules. It is not until the age of eleven or twelve that the true nature of rules is fully understood. At that point rules can be changed by mutual consent.

There is an interesting parallel that can be drawn between the understanding of rules as it is reflected in play behavior and the verbalized notion of rules. At the earliest stage (prior to age three) when children play as though there were no rules, they will not verbalize any notions concerning rules. At the next stage, when they begin to play with rules but change them constantly to conform to their immediate needs and wishes, they believe that rules come from God or some other Great Power and that they are therefore fixed and unchangeable. But their behavior gives the lie to this belief at every turn. In the subsequent stage (age seven to eleven), when they rigidly adhere to The Rules, never daring to change or break them, they have come to understand that rules are made by people and that they can be changed by them. At both of these stages children's behavior and their expressed beliefs are in contradiction. During the final stage children's play behavior and their understanding of rules are again in harmony. They believe that rules can be changed, that they exist as necessary, though human-made, dimensions of games, and that they can be changed when the occasion warrants it.

Children's first prolonged contact with peers generally occurs in play situations and, later, in school situations or other organized extracurricular activities. The importance of these contacts cannot be underestimated, for it is through them that children and adolescents begin to develop the skills that are essential for adaptation to the adult world—social and physical skills. It is also through contact with peers that they begin their gradual emancipation from a family dominated environment, an emancipation that ordinarily becomes final during late adolescence or early adulthood. Unlike the great eagles who, weary of feeding their young or perhaps aware of the fact that the young must also become independent if the species is to flourish, push their progeny from the nest when the little ones are too glutted and too comfortable to take that first step on their own, human parents wait patiently for their young to fly. There is but a short space between being ejected from a nest and becoming independent; there is a long span between venturing out of the home to play independently with peers and finally going out to live independently.

Family versus Peers

Most psychologists agree that it is during adolescence that peers reach their greatest importance in the socialization and emancipation process. Despite children's earlier association with peers, they have until adolescence derived most of their physical, emotional, and social satisfaction from their immediate families. With the advent of adolescence, however, biological and social drives move them away from the family and toward wider social groups. Although it has appeared reasonable to a number of writers to suppose that peers and family exert opposing forces and that adolescence must therefore usually imply a considerable amount of conflict between adolescents and their families, this point of view is not entirely accurate.

Brittain (1963) conducted a study designed to investigate the relative influence of parents and peers. Specifically, he attempted to discover to what extent adolescents would rely on parents or peers when faced with competing pressures from each of these groups. Subjects were a group of girls in grades nine to eleven. At the time of the initial test, stories were read to the subjects. In each of these stories, the principal character had to make a decision that would conform to the expressed wishes either of her parents or of her friends. Subjects were asked to make this decision. A second form of the test employed exactly the same stories and required the same decisions except that in this case choices that had previously conformed to parents or friends were reversed. For example, a choice had to be made between taking one of two courses in school. In the first form of the test, course A was recommended by parents and course B by friends. In the second form, course A was recommended by friends and course B by parents. An indication of the relative influences of parents and friends was derived by tabulating the number of shifts for each of the subjects. That is, if a subject chose course A on both forms of the test, she would be responding in terms of the course itself rather than in terms of parental or peer pressure. If, however, she chose a different course the second time, she would be responding either to peer or to family pressure depending on the specific choice made. The experimental group consisted of 280 girls. A control group (58 subjects) were administered identical forms of the test on two occasions in order to ensure that response shifts did not occur on a random basis.

Results of the experiment are striking and potentially significant. First, they do not support the contention that peers are more important than parents as an influence in decision-making. Second, they do not support the opposite contention either. In fact, it appears that the relative influences of parents and peers is highly dependent upon the content of the specific situations rather than on any general tendency to conform either to parents or to peers. Thus, in those situations where status and identity within peer groups was involved, subjects tended to conform to peers. Questions of which dress to buy, which courses to take in school (where proximity with friends would be affected), and what to wear to a party or a football game most often elicited responses conforming to the advice of peers. Such questions as how to get selected for a school honor, which of two boys to date, and which part-time job to take evoked greater agreement with parents, presumably because these activities are more closely related to adult status than to position in peer groups. It is interesting to note that more items were significantly associated with conformity to parents than with conformity to peers. This might be due to the content of

the items; however, it does indicate that the family does not become impotent in the face of increasing allegiance to peers. Also, this experimental situation may not be entirely representative of actual life, because it presents just those situations where there is a clear conflict between parental and peer pressures. It is reasonable to assume that there are many such situations in real life, and that the results of this study can probably be generalized to a great number of these situations. At the same time, it must be kept in mind that in many situations there will be no conflict between parental and peer pressures. It cannot be assumed that adolescents are in a constant state of conflict between the wishes of their parents and those of their friends. Nor can it be assumed that they have greater allegiance to their friends, and that they will therefore conform to their wishes more often than to those of their parents.

Brittain (1963, p. 390) presents four hypotheses that are supported by this investigation:

1. The responses indicate that the adolescent views parents and peers as competent to make judgments in different areas. Brittain indicates that the social orientation of the adolescent is dual, tending both toward parents and toward peers depending on the specific area in question.

2. Adolescents are concerned about not being radically different from their peers. This appears to be most obvious in such superficial but highly visible areas as dress styles.

3. Adolescents are concerned about not being separated from their friends. In the item involving choice between two courses where choice of one course would mean being isolated from friends, the opposite choice was generally made.

4. Adolescent choices tend to be made in accordance with perceived differences and similarities between the subject and friends or parents. With respect to some of the more important and basic values, adolescents perceive themselves as more like their parents and tend to rely on them for advice. In matters of taste (clothing for example) adolescents perceive themselves as more like their peers and tend to conform with them.

246 ───

Peer Group Functions

The function of the peer group in primitive societies is neither as apparent nor as crucial as it is in modern societies. Farnsworth (1967) notes that peer groups serve a useful function in simply filling the void that might otherwise exist in adolescence. Peer groups, both in and out of schools and colleges, become the major socializing agents of adolescence.

Peer groups are assumed to provide adolescents with a wide variety of experiences in interaction with people. In this way, they promote the development of essential social skills related to conversation; to judging people; to interpreting verbal and nonverbal cues concerning one's own position and power in a group; and to determining what is appropriate and inappropriate in terms of behavior, dress, and to a lesser extent, values and ideals.

A second function of the peer group is to provide an opportunity for the development of loyalties that go beyond the immediate family group. Such loyalties are important for future adjustment to the adult world where larger political and social loyalties as well as smaller community and work loyalties are of some importance.

Third, the peer group serves to provide adolescents with a considerable degree of emotional security. This is particularly important where adolescents are experiencing difficulties adjusting to parental demands and restrictions, and where they are still in the process of developing a sense of identity.

Related to this, peer groups serve a fourth function. They provide a wide number of models that will be helpful in the development of a sense of identity. The peer group also facilitates the development of identity by providing adolescents with information concerning the self. Consolidation of adolescents' self-images occurs largely within the framework of interaction with peers.

Fifth, the peer group facilitates adolescents' transition from a family to a peer orientation. It is obvious that this transition must take place if adolescents are to adjust to adult roles, because these roles seldom permit children to remain within their original nuclear family group.

A final function of the peer group, and perhaps one of the most important, is that of providing opportunities for interpersonal relationships that become prototypes for future adult relationships. At the beginning of the period of adolescence, children have just come through the long period labeled the latency stage by Freud, Erikson, and others. During this stage they have been

NICE HUH!

relatively unconcerned with members of the opposite sex; they have therefore formed few, if any, close heterosexual friendships. One of the significant things that happens in their peer group relationships during adolescence is a movement from predominantly homosexual relationships to a balance between these and heterosexual relationships. Appropriate procedures, times, and behaviors for these relationships are embodied in the informal but highly significant instruction that adolescents receive from peer groups. More is said concerning this subject in later portions of this chapter, and in Chapter 12.

Undoubtedly, the peer group serves other functions related to adolescents' emotional, psychological, and physical well-being. It is true, as well, that on occasion the peer group is implicated in adolescents' maladjustment. Adolescence can be an extremely trying time for those who do not "belong," those whose social and emotional maturity or whose personality characteristics or behavioral mannerisms make them less acceptable than others among their peers. Social isolates, of whom there are always one or two on the fringes of most large groups, are caught in a vicious circle. Not only have they not developed those characteristics or acquired the savoir faire that would make them acceptable, but they are also denied the opportunity to develop these qualities through interaction with their peers. Consequently their self-concepts suffer, they become juvenile offenders of one kind or another, they withdraw from any serious attempt to achieve acceptance among their peers, or they become pathetic hangers-on seeking solace in small gestures of acceptance and friendship, more often imagined than real.

Friends

In order to understand the world of adolescents, it is useful to consider those qualities that they prize most highly in others. An indirect indication of these is provided by the many studies of friendship patterns among groups of adolescents. A large majority of these studies make use of one of a variety of **sociometric** techniques, the most common of which provides the experimenter with information concerning patterns of likes and dislikes within specific groups. Typically questionnaires or interviews are employed in an attempt to discover the most popular, least popular, most intelligent, least intelligent, most powerful, least powerful person in a group—to name but a

few of the many characteristics that can be identified in this way. Frequently the information gathered from these sociometric techniques is interpreted in graphical or pictorial form (called a **sociogram** or sociograph). A simple sociogram is presented in Figure 9.1.

Gold and Douvan (1969), in discussing peer groups during adolescence, point out that there is an almost desperate need for friends during this period, and that the strength of this need is evident in the fierce allegiance to group norms manifested by most members of such groups. Dunphy (1963) noted that failure to conform to group norms (that is, being different from other members of the group) was one of the primary causes of exclusion from the group; and that, conversely, admission to a **clique** or **crowd** was based on conformity as well. Members who were already in specific cliques or crowds freely admitted that they would accept only people who were like them and who liked to do the same sorts of things as they did.

Who Are Friends?

In view of the strong tendency of adolescents to conform to peer standards, at least in obvious though relatively superficial areas such as dress and personal grooming, it is not surprising that the majority of studies that have examined patterns of likes and dislikes among adolescent groups have found that friendships tend to reflect the attraction of similars rather than of opposites. Gold and Douvan (1969) note that the selection of friends among adolescents is very much like the selection of mates in marriage. Both friends and eventual spouses tend to be chosen from the same socioeconomic background as the chooser; probably live in the same neighborhood; and have similar values, interests, and ideals (Hollingshead, 1949). Willerman and Swanson (1952) note these same trends among friendship patterns in college age adolescents. They found that an overwhelming number of friends were dormitory roommates, attended the same classes, or had the same major. The authors argue that physical proximity is the single most important factor in determining friendships: students with the same college major are friends not because they both have similar interests but because they are in more frequent contact because they take the same classes.

Despite the fact that similarity in social background and mere physical

Figure 9.1 A sociogram. Subjects were asked, "Who do you like the most in your class?" The more popular children are Sam, Bob, Joan, and Marie. The unpopular ones are Rose and Guy.

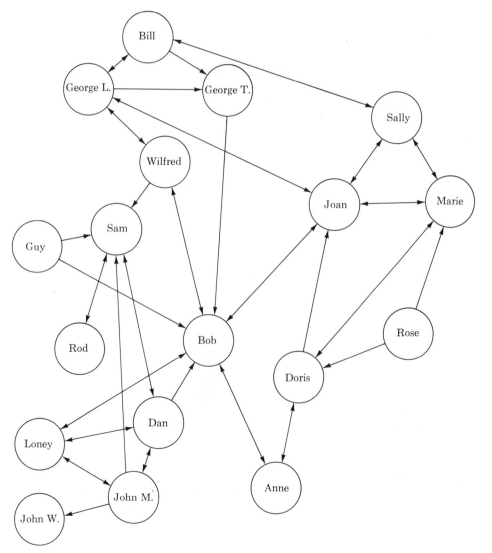

proximity are important factors in determining friendships, there are other factors of considerable importance. For example, most adolescents form very close friendships with a limited number of individuals "chosen" from among many others who might also be eligible if it were simply a matter of proximity and similarity. I say "chosen" advisedly because friendships usually simply happen; they are not deliberately planned.

In an extensive study (Project Talent) involving 1437 males and 1505 females selected from eight different high schools judged to be highly representative of the entire nation, Horowitz (1967) investigated potential sources of popularity and rejection. All subjects were asked to list three girls and three boys they would most like to be with and three girls and three boys they would least like to be with. Names were limited to those within classrooms so that indexes of popularity and unpopularity could be arrived at for each member of every classroom. Data derived from Project Talent, including a wide variety of measures, were then employed in an effort to determine which specific characteristics were most highly related to popularity or to rejection. Overall findings suggest that males consider sports to be a primary consideration in popularity; females consider leadership and scholarship necessary to being well liked. Only one of the fifteen predictors employed, impulsiveness, seemed to be related solely to rejection. In psychological literature, impulsiveness is most frequently defined as a response or behavioral style characterized by lack of reflection. Impulsive individuals typically answer questions or solve problems more rapidly than nonimpulsive (reflective) individuals; but in the process, all other relevant factors being equal, they will make more errors. It should be noted that in the Horowitz (1967) study, correlations between all of the predictors and measures of popularity or rejection were extremely low, accounting for a very small percentage of the total variation. In other words, findings indicate that there are probably many other significant factors that were not included in the study.

Cole and Hall (1970), after an extensive survey of various relevant studies, present an exhaustive list of characteristics that have been found to be associated with being liked or not being liked among adolescents. They point out that characteristics associated with not being liked are not always the opposite of those associated with being liked. Horowitz (1967) made much the same point based on his observation that some variables appear to be related both

to rejection and to popularity while others are related to only one of these or to neither.

Stability of Friendships

Among certain North American Indian tribes it was not an altogether uncommon practice for young men to seal and formalize their friendship through ritual. These young men would each slash one of their wrists and press their bleeding wounds firmly together. From that day on, when one would say to the other, "You are my brother," he would, in effect, be saying, "You have my blood. I have your blood. I would die for my brother; and I know that he would die for me." But there was no need to say all this, for it was understood. Such was the bond of friendship that bound blood brothers.

Friendships among contemporary adolescents do not appear to be as intense or as lasting as those created among Indians through their blood bonds. Yet they are intense and very real while they last. And they are very different both from the emotional ties that bind family members together and from the friendships that children form in middle childhood. Family ties are virtually irrevocable. Children have no choice about whom their parents will be; nor do parents ordinarily have much choice about whom they will have for children. And it is probably true that family relationships are premised largely on the satisfaction of initially unlearned needs, needs that give rise to a complex network of physical, social, and emotional interdependency. Gold and Douvan (1969) draw attention to the fact that family ties frequently rest on an intricate love-hate-conflict-harmony basis. In contrast, peer group friendships are freely chosen, changeable, and do not bring with them the complex of obligations that characterize family ties.

Preadolescent friendships are relatively unemotional. They are based primarily on mutuality of interest in activities and therefore exist largely in the joint activities that they permit. In these friendships, the activities involved rather than the interaction among friends is of primary importance. With the advent of adolescence, there evolve relationships that are centered around interpersonal interaction rather than around specific activities. Frequently the emotional investment is extremely intense, including feelings of love as

252 ——

well as hate, and permitting the resolution of conflicts (Gold and Douvan, 1969). Earlier friendships tend to give rise to fewer emotional interpersonal conflicts because they do not involve emotions to the same degree. Nor do they permit the resolution of such conflicts when they do arise. Friends in conflict in middle childhood simply cease to be friends. Friends in conflict during adolescence can frequently explore and resolve their conflicts as is evidenced in the numerous break-up and make-up sequences in adolescent courtship behavior.

Another highly significant difference between preadolescent and adolescent friendships concerns their stability. Horrocks and Buker (1951) and Thompson and Horrocks (1947) investigated the extent to which friendships remain stable in groups of children ranging in age from five to eighteen years. Their experimental procedure was very simple. Children were asked to name their three best friends in the classroom. Friends were to be ranked best, second best, and third best. The same question was presented again two weeks later, and friendship fluctuation scores were derived by comparing these responses with responses obtained two weeks earlier. The most obvious and clearly substantiated finding of these studies was that stability of friendships increases consistently with advancing chronological age, at least between ages five and eighteen. A second interesting finding that corroborated an earlier study (Jones, 1948) was that the friendships of boys are more stable than those of girls. That is, girls were more likely to change their minds about who their three best friends were and about which of the three was the "best" friend of all although the time span between testing was a mere two weeks. Ausubel (1954) reports a number of studies that indicate that girls' friendships are more intense and more often reciprocal than are those of boys. Gold and Douvan (1969) present the argument that the greater stability observed in male friendships may be due to the fact that their less intense friendships are subject to fewer conflicts and therefore easier to maintain.

Additional differences in friendship patterns between boys and girls have been discovered through a number of studies (reported in Ausubel, 1954). It has been found, for example, that girls are more prone than boys to form cliques (small, highly cohesive and highly exclusive groups of friends); they spend a greater amount of time with their friends than do boys; and they pay more attention to social class in their selection of friends than do boys.

Cliques and Crowds

The social structure of adolescent groups has been a subject of considerable study. Among other things, researchers have found that these groups tend to conform to social class boundaries (Coleman, 1961), are based on similarity in social skills and values (Havighurst *et al.*, 1962), and are characterized by different criteria of acceptance for boys and girls. Athletic skills are most important for boys; social skills are most important for girls (Coleman, 1961; Horowitz, 1967). Probably the most comprehensive and most often cited study of adolescent social groups is that undertaken by Dunphy (1963).

Dunphy undertook an extensive investigation and analysis of social structure among a group of 303 adolescents ranging in age from thirteen to twenty-one. Subjects were all residents of Sydney, Australia, and were approximately equally divided between the sexes. Data gathering procedures involved questionnaires, observation, tape-recorded interviews, and the analysis of adolescent diaries that were kept specifically for the project. Subjects knew they were participants in a study and agreed to cooperate with the investigator so that he was included in many of their formal and informal activities. Over a period of three years he spent a considerable amount of time "on street corners, in milkbars and homes, at parties, and on Sydney beaches."

Dunphy was particularly interested in the composition and formation of cliques and crowds among this group of adolescents. Cliques are small, highly cohesive groups of friends that combine in various ways to form larger groups referred to as crowds. Cliques and crowds appear to have been relatively easy to identify in this sample. Forty-four cliques were identified, ranging in size from three to nine members (average membership was 6.2). These cliques formed a total of twelve crowds whose memberships ranged from fifteen to thirty adolescents. Attention is drawn to the fact that there were no groups with memberships ranging between ten and fourteen. This may be because the highly cohesive interaction characteristic of the clique would be difficult if the membership were larger. Because crowds are associations of cliques, they are necessarily larger, consisting, on the average, of 3.1 cliques.

Cliques, then, represent associations of very close friends of highly similar ages, social backgrounds, tastes, and interests. Members of separate cliques that interact to form crowds are acceptable associates, also quite similar, but

not "buddies" as are members of the same clique. In order to belong to a crowd, an adolescent must first belong to a clique, but the converse is not true. It is as though the clique acts as a screening procedure for admission to crowds. Not all cliques among the groups studied were members of crowds. Five of the forty-four cliques involved were not members of any crowd. In addition, a number of individuals were members neither of cliques nor, necessarily, of crowds. More is said about these individuals later.

Dunphy notes that within specific localities crowds could easily be differentiated on the basis of age, with higher status being accorded to the older crowds. At any one time there would be a number of individuals who belonged to more than one crowd, these generally being upper-status members of a lower-aged crowd and lower-status members of an upper-aged crowd. Age appeared to be the major factor differentiating crowds one from the other. The average age differences between adjacent crowds was two years. Younger cliques were primarily male or female only. Older cliques tended to be heterosexual. Crowds were heterosexual, and girls were typically younger than boys in the same crowd (approximately ten months on the average). The general developmental pattern of clique and crowd structure is presented in Figure 9.2.

During the first stage, characteristic of early adolescence, boys and girls associate in separate cliques. This stage, reminiscent of preadolescent social structure, is marked by an absence of interaction between sexes. Initial heterosexual interaction, leading to the eventual formation of crowds, involves interaction between cliques rather than between individuals. The teasing, bantering, and apparently aimless chatter between boys and girls takes place among cliques rather than among individuals and is illustrated in Stage 2 of Figure 9.2. Transition from Stage 2 to Stage 3 occurs when some of the older, upper-status members of single sex cliques begin to interact on an individual basis, displaying the initiation of dating behavior. Gradually, (Stage 4) some of these formerly single sex cliques become heterosexual cliques associated in groups to form crowds. In late adolescence (Stage 5) the crowds begin to disintegrate as adolescents become more preoccupied with dating and courtship, subsequently forming loosely associated groups of couples rather than groups of cliques.

The fact that cliques eventually become associated in crowds does not imply that they cease to exist as functioning social structures. Dunphy points out that cliques and crowds appear to serve different functions, meeting at differ-

Figure 9.2   Dunphy's diagram of stages in peer group development during adolescence. (From "The social structure of urban adolescent peer groups" by Dexter C. Dunphy, *Sociometry*, 1963, **26,** 230–246, p. 236. Copyright 1963 by the American Sociological Association. Used by permission of the American Sociological Association and the author.)

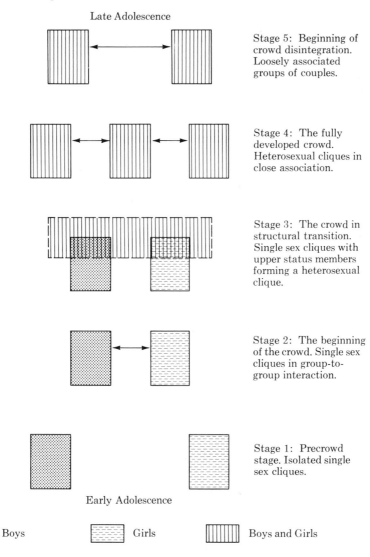

Late Adolescence

Stage 5: Beginning of crowd disintegration. Loosely associated groups of couples.

Stage 4: The fully developed crowd. Heterosexual cliques in close association.

Stage 3: The crowd in structural transition. Single sex cliques with upper status members forming a heterosexual clique.

Stage 2: The beginning of the crowd. Single sex cliques in group-to-group interaction.

Stage 1: Precrowd stage. Isolated single sex cliques.

Early Adolescence

Boys   Girls   Boys and Girls

Joe *Age 16* **On Topics of Conversation**

Me: *Do you listen to the news or read newspapers and talk with your friends about what's going on.*

Joe: *No. We don't really talk about what's going on in the news unless maybe if we have nothing else to talk about. I don't really read newspapers very often. You know, maybe once a month or so. I should really read it more often but I don't.*

Me: *Do the kids you know read newspapers?*

Joe: *Yeah. I just don't like reading.*

Me: *What do you typically talk about when you're with a bunch of your friends.*

Joe: *(pause) Well, just about anything, you know. Anything that comes up. You know, something that just happened the night before, or something. Hockey games, sports.*

Me: *Do you talk about people a lot?*

Joe: *Sometimes. If you don't like somebody, and you talk about why. Like at work, there's a lot of talking behind people's backs, so we're trying to get it out in the open, so we're trying to talk to more people. You know. There's a lot of politics.*

ent times, and functioning as cliques or as crowds depending on the membership present and on the occasion. Typically there were more crowd gatherings on weekends than during the week. The converse is true of cliques, which tended to gather during the week rather than during the weekend. The predominant activity in the clique was simply conversation. According to diary reports, for example, of sixty-nine different clique settings, conversation was the principal activity in fifty-six. This was the case in only five of twenty-five crowd settings, the remainder of these meetings being devoted to such organized social activities as parties, dancing, and so on.

Cliques and crowds appeared to have very definite boundaries; members who had been excluded from membership were generally clearly aware of their position. Dunphy arranged to have several isolates invited to a party that included two separate crowds. Clique membership was most obvious upon arrival and departure when members of individual cliques gathered together. During the course of the evening, there was little interaction among members of different crowds except in the case of those individuals who seemed to have been accorded lower-status position in the older crowd, but who still retained upper-status position in the younger crowd. These, presumably, were individuals in transition between crowds. Interaction among cliques within single groups was highly common.

The behavior of the isolates is of special interest. One made no effort to join any of the groups, remaining seated by herself throughout the evening, rarely speaking with anyone. At the end of the party she left alone. A second isolate tried desperately to interact with the leader of the older crowd, but was largely ignored. He spent most of his time on the fringe of the group clustered around this leader.

Admission to a clique appears to be largely a function of conformity to clique standards. Thus those individuals most alike in terms of values, interests, and heterosexual behavior would tend to be members of the same clique. Individuals who were obviously different were simply not admitted. Once admitted as a member of a clique, an individual could then be ostracized for one of several reasons. Dunphy reports that ostracism most often occurred for failure to conform to group authority or for failure to achieve at the same level as other clique members with respect to heterosexual activity. It is noteworthy that clique leaders not only tended to be the older members of the clique, but also tended to be those who dated more frequently, and who were

Jean *Age 18* **A Typical Weekend**

Me: *What sorts of things do you do on a typical weekend?*
Jean: *What do you mean?*
Me: *Um . . . what sorts of activities — social activities — things you do with your friends or alone.*
Jean: *Well I work. And I like sewing. I don't really go out a lot.*
Me: *So you don't go to a lot of parties and things like that?*
Jean: *No.*
Me: *Do you do drugs? Go to bars?*

Jean: *No. Sometimes to the bar. I don't believe in drugs.*
Me: *Why?*
Jean: *Because they're bad for you.*
Me: *Do a lot of your friends feel the same way as you do?*
Jean: *Yes. But there's quite a lot of drugs around.*

257

more successful in establishing relationships with members of the opposite sex. As has been noted elsewhere, sex roles and appropriate heterosexual behavior is of primary concern among adolescents.

One of the more striking findings of this study was that members of cliques tend to select clique and crowd leaders most often when asked to name their associates or friends, although it could easily be observed that these were not always the people with whom they associated most. Dunphy interprets this finding as corroboration of Freud's (1922) contention that the bond among members of groups derives from their common identification with a leader. It appears reasonable to suppose that clique leaders serve to some degree as replacements of parental models in the socialization process. Adolescent membership in cliques and crowds provides ample opportunity for progressively more adult modes of interaction with like- and opposite-sexed peers, and thus provides an essential function that could not easily be provided by the family.

Youth Culture

Much has been written in recent years concerning an adolescent culture assumed to be a reaction against prevailing cultural norms — the counterculture. The greatest amount of attention has been paid to activist, rebellious, and socially alienated youth who, by definition, do exhibit behaviors and values that typically oppose those of adult society. These groups, however, represent only a small minority of the adolescent population.

A culture may be defined as patterns of acceptable behaviors, beliefs, and values that are shared by a large and readily identifiable group of people. Adolescents have patterns of communication and behavior that not only distinguish them from adults, but that are also seen as rejections of adult culture. Evidence of this "youth culture" is most obvious in the dress, grooming, and jargon characteristic of some adolescent groups. However, present youth culture is so often adopted by adults as to no longer be a distinctive youth culture. Hair and dress styles become popular with young (and sometimes old) adults almost as soon as they are popular with adolescents, and there are relatively few adults who are not up-to-date with significant portions of adolescent slang and jargon. One no longer has to be "cool," "neat," "hip," or "out-a-sight" to know what these terms mean.

There have been attempts to differentiate youth culture from adult culture on the basis of values. However, numerous studies have shown that there is more correspondence between the values of parents and their adolescents than there is among adolescent peers (see Chapter 8). Few studies have shown that adolescence is typically a time of parent-child conflict; none have established that gaining independence requires revolt; none have demonstrated that the majority of adolescents are disaffected and disenchanted with society. If there is a youth culture in general, it is clearly not a counterculture as many have been led to believe. On the other hand, it is appropriate to consider various minorities among adolescents as representative of specific countercultures. Among these could be included some activist groups, drug-centered groups, delinquent groups, and various quasi-criminal gangs. These are discussed in Chapter 14.

Summary

This chapter began with Sam's discussion of the cult of youth and ended with a discussion of youth culture. In between it looked at the functions of peer groups, their influence relative to that of the family, the nature and stability of friendships, and the social structure of adolescent cliques and crowds.

Main Points

1. Though we are reluctant to admit it, youth, thy flouris fadis ferly sone!

2. A peer group is a group of equals. It may include age-peers, sex-peers, grade-peers, intellectual-peers, social-peers, or any combination of these.

3. The peer groups of middle childhood are typically centered around common activities. They exist for the activities that they make possible rather than for the social interaction that occurs in them.

4. Adolescent peer groups are more concerned with social interaction than with simply sharing common activities.

5. During adolescence, children gradually move from a family orientation to a peer orientation. This move does not imply conflict, although conflict sometimes accompanies it.

6. Adolescents are concerned about not being different from their peers.

7. The adolescent peer group serves an important socializing function. In particular, it is crucial in the development of notions of self.

8. Additional functions served by the peer group include: facilitating the transition from family dependency to independence; providing an opportunity for the development of loyalties that extend beyond the immediate family; serving as models for socially appropriate behavior; and fostering the development of interpersonal relationships that become prototypes of adult relationships.

9. Friendship patterns are most often studied through the use of sociograms. These are graphical representations of patterns of likes and dislikes within groups. They may be arrived at through interviews, observation, questionnaires, or combinations of these.

10. The single most important basis for choosing friends is simple proximity. Friends tend to come from the same areas, attend the same classes, belong to the same social groups, and have similar interests. It is not a fact that opposites attract, at least among humans.

11. Male adolescents consider sports skills or interest of primary importance in rating popularity. Female adolescents rate leaders and scholars as most popular.

12. Friendships become more stable with advancing age from middle childhood through adolescence. They appear to be more stable among boys than girls, but are not invested with the same emotional intensity among the former. Preadolescent friendships are relatively emotionless.

13. Dunphy's study of social structure among adolescents identified two major groupings: cliques and crowds. Each serves different functions and can be differentiated largely on the basis of size.

14. A clique is a small group of individuals with highly similar interests.

Cliques tend to be highly selective, quite exclusive, and appear to include no less than three and no more than nine members.

15. Combinations of cliques with similar backgrounds, interests, and ages are frequently associated in crowds. Members of cliques are close "buddies"; members of crowds are "acceptable associates" but not "buddies."

16. The predominant activity among cliques is conversation; crowds tend to come together for social or athletic activity.

17. Not all individuals belong to cliques; some are social isolates. In order to be a member of a crowd, it is essential to first belong to a clique, though not all cliques form part of a crowd.

18. The social structure of adolescence progresses from separate single-sex cliques to a stage where there is interaction between these cliques. Subsequently single sex cliques join to form a number of heterosexual cliques that may then begin to interact in crowds. At a later stage the crowd breaks up into groups of loosely knit couples.

19. A culture may be defined in terms of behaviors, beliefs, and values that are shared by a significant number of individuals who are readily identifiable as a group. Accordingly, cultures typically follow national or racial boundaries, although in recent times numerous subcultures have sprung up within larger cultural groups.

20. One such subculture has been identified as the youth culture. However, because there is so much variation among the behaviors, beliefs, and values of youth, it is misleading to say that there is, for example, an American youth culture.

21. If there is a youth culture, it is clearly not a counterculture, although various subcultures within the larger youth culture may be so labeled. These subcultures center around activism, drugs, delinquency, and various other forms of protest.

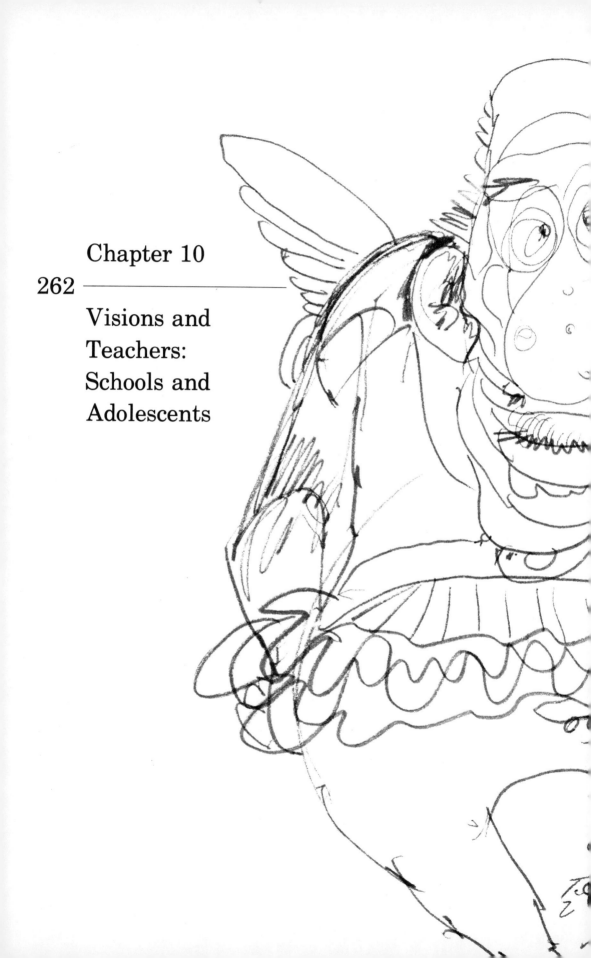

Chapter 10

Visions and
Teachers:
Schools and
Adolescents

School Enrollment

Dropping Out
Attitudes toward School
Social Class
Family Background
Achievement
Intelligence
Sex
The Remedy?

Staying In
Achievement
Adolescent Values
Cheating
School and Family

Summary

Main Points

Francie Binder, Grade 11

Forty-eight pages of Sam's essay on adolescence are devoted to a discussion of schools, with particular emphasis on the contemporary high school. Unfortunately, Sam hasn't been in a single high school since he dropped out in his final year. His "contemporary" schools are therefore something less than contemporary. Partly for this reason, and partly because his view is so highly negative, no portion of that essay was judged suitable for this chapter. It is filled with comments such as the following: "Today's schools do little to train the mind—and very little more for the body. Small wonder that society is burdened with so many small minds in overweight bodies." Or again: "Do you ever wonder why it is that some 30 percent of all high school graduates are functionally illiterate? You needn't wonder any longer."

In a moment of greater weakness, he did admit that there are a number of excellent teachers lost in the country's high schools. He paints a picture of them desperately fighting parents and administration in their quest to engender some wisdom and some vision in the hearts and minds of their students.

Sam was a high school dropout, but unlike most dropouts he eventually resumed his academic career and became a university professor. He claims that universities were more tolerant of his brilliance and creativity than high school had been. I suspect that they were simply less concerned with his eccentricities.

School Enrollment

Society's monolithic acculturation machinery is most evident in the millions of schools scattered throughout its urbs, suburbs, superurbs, and exurbs. Close to twenty million adolescents attend high schools in the United States alone; and millions more are scattered in various elementary schools, private schools, and assorted postsecondary schools and colleges. The impact of schools on contemporary society in general and on adolescents in particular cannot be overestimated.

Less than a century ago, only approximately 7 percent of all adolescents between the ages of fourteen and eighteen attended school. Now, according to the U.S. Bureau of the Census (1971a), over 94 percent of these adolescents are in high school.

A number of reasons have been advanced as explanation for this dramatic

increase in high school enrollment. Clearly, increases in the age for compulsory attendance from twelve or fourteen to sixteen or eighteen are responsible for some of the increase. In addition, significant changes in the skills and information that are required for successful adjustment to modern technological societies have made it considerably more likely that adolescents who do not complete high school will not attain the more desired positions in society. Numerous studies have shown that those without high school diplomas are significantly more likely to be among the unskilled or semi-skilled labor force, or to be simply unemployed. Indications are, too, that the high school diploma is losing some of its value as high-paying positions require more specialization, more skills, and, consequently, more formal education beyond high school. Even as money can be, and has been, devalued, so can diplomas. But the high school diploma continues to be mandatory for admission to most post high school educational facilities, and adolescents must therefore reconcile themselves to remaining in high school whether they like it or not. If they drop out, there is relatively little they can do, as has been pointed out, except nothing. And that tends to lack the excitement and involvement that most adolescents need and want.

Dropping Out

Do adolescents like school? There is no simple answer, but some 33 percent of them do drop out before they complete their twelfth grade (Schreiber, 1968; Ginzberg, 1968). Some are involuntary dropouts who are expelled from school—an infrequent but still existent practice—or who are forced to find work in order to support themselves and their families. However, the majority of dropouts chose to do so, and a number of factors appear to be associated with voluntarily leaving school in adolescence.

Attitudes toward School

A complex of related environmental factors including family, social class, race, early educational opportunity, educational motivation, and general aspirations contribute significantly to an adolescent's eventual decision to

Dominique *Age 15* **On Schools and Learning**

Dominique: *. . . It's a changing world.*
Me: *For better or for worse?*
Dominique: *Better.*
Me: *That's interesting. I think so too, but why do you think things are getting better?*
Dominique: *You can learn more things . . . and . . . get better kicks out of more things.*
Me: *Do you get a kick out of learning more things?*
Dominique: *Yes, but not in school. I learn them . . . I'd rather spend a year on the outside than in school.*

Me: *What kind of teachers did you have? How did you like school?*
Dominique: *I don't like judging every teacher. I just don't like being taught. I like learning by myself.*
Me: *Why did you get kicked out of school?*
Dominique: *Because I wouldn't listen to 'em, and because I stole all the money out of the lockers and out of the school funds.*

266

leave school prior to completion. These factors, and others, are clearly related to an adolescent's attitude toward school. It is probably this attitude that is most closely related to the decision to drop out.

Flanders *et al.* (1968) administered questionnaires to 101 sixth grade classes, 30 of which were then selected for detailed analysis concerning student attitudes toward schools. One of their most consistent and significant findings was that students' attitudes toward school became increasingly negative during the course of the school year. Almost invariably, students who were readministered questionnaires four months after the beginning of school responded less favorably toward both their teachers and their schools. It seems that much of the enthusiasm and optimism that had characterized the beginning of the school year (October testing) was no longer evident after the students had been exposed to the school for a period of time (January).

Further analysis revealed that these observed changes in attitudes were not related to average intelligence, socioeconomic status, or even to grades given by teachers. Two other factors did emerge as being significantly related to declines in positive attitudes. Students were administered tests designed to assess "externality" and "internality." These categories, described by Rotter *et al.* (1962), are manifested in the extent to which individuals assume responsibility for the outcomes of their actions (internal), and the extent to which they place responsibility on others (external). Not surprisingly, students oriented toward internal control showed significantly less decline in positive attitudes.

A second factor that appeared to be highly related to students' more negative perceptions of their schools was the extent to which they were exposed to teachers described as "high-praise" in contrast to those described as "low-praise." Other studies (for example, Sears, 1963) have corroborated these findings. Sears (1963) also found that teachers who were more prone to praise students, who listened to them attentively, and who gave other signs of personal interest in their activities were more likely to encourage expressions of creativity in students. These same teachers were also more likely to have students who got along well with their peers. Related to this, Rosenfeld and Zander (1961) found a high relationship between teacher behavior and student aspirations. Specifically, it appears that those teachers who are supportive and rewarding and who make legitimate use of power are more likely to have students with high aspiration levels. Significantly, these teachers tend to be better liked by their students.

Dissatisfaction with schools and teachers and lack of interest in school activities is a frequently cited reason for dropping out of school, particularly among boys (Combs and Cooley, 1968). Girls most often claim that they dropped out because of plans to get married. It has been suggested, however, that the reasons most often given by the dropouts themselves may not be accurate. Frequently a boy who says he has dropped out because of lack of interest or because he was failing is, in fact, failing or disinterested because he has to devote most of his out-of-school hours to earning money in order to support himself and his family (Combs and Cooley, 1968). Numerous other factors appear to be involved as well.

Social Class

Abrahamson (1952) presents the argument that American society, despite theoretical arguments to the contrary, is very much a class society. In contrast to the more rigid class or caste systems of some Asiatic countries or of European countries of a few centuries ago, American society permits movement among classes. Typically, individual aspirations are toward upward mobility. Changes in status may be brought about in a variety of ways (Abrahamson, 1952). Most obvious, and perhaps simplest, is marriage, where a lower-class individual can obtain status in a higher class simply by marrying someone from that class. Clearly there aren't enough higher-class individuals around to permit this type of movement indefinitely. Besides, research has repeatedly shown that individuals tend to marry others from their own social positions.

Such personality characteristics as charm, tact, savoir faire, and intuitive political sense can also serve to increase a person's social status, as can special talents (most obviously in the fields of entertainment or sports). Hard work and perseverance are sometimes rewarded by eventual acceptance in a higher class. Finally, and probably most important, education is a key to upward social mobility.

Ironically, it is a key that is much more readily available to those who don't

need it than to those for whom the doors were locked at birth. Abrahamson (1952) explored the contention that American schools are middle-class oriented, not only in terms of the teachers employed in them, but in terms of the allocation of rewards and punishments in the system. He found rather overwhelming support for this hypothesis. Adolescents from the higher social classes received better grades; they were accorded more favors by teachers and received significantly less than their share of the punishment; they were more accepted by their peers; they held more school offices; they participated in more extracurricular activities; and they received most of the school's prizes and awards for both athletic and academic achievements. Abrahamson argues that these discrepancies are not a function of intelligence but of social class.

Social status per se does little to explain differences in school achievement, in dropout rates, or in eventual job positions, although it is clearly related to all three. It is likely that a complex of motivational and interest factors, coupled with opportunity factors, account for many of the differences that appear to exist between lower-status and higher-status adolescents. In addition, teacher expectations may well have a negative effect on the performance of adolescents from disadvantaged backgrounds (see Rosenthal and Jacobsen, 1968a); conversely, they may have a beneficial effect on adolescents who come from supposedly advantaged home environments.

Family Background

Closely related to social status is family background. It appears that high school dropouts can sometimes be distinguished from adolescents who complete high school in terms of their family relationships. Cervantes (1965) interviewed groups of adolescents and their families matched in terms of intelligence and so on. The principal obvious difference between the two groups was that one consisted of high school dropouts and the other of high school students. He found the families of the dropouts to be significantly less accepting, less communicating, less involved in group activities, and less encouraging. Cervantes describes the family relationships of the nondropout group as constituting a *primary* group in the Freudian sense. This is essentially a group where the interactions are such that every member develops a sense of "we" with respect to the group. In these families parents were more approving, more trusting, more encouraging, less restrictive and severe, and more sharing in activities with their adolescents.

Morrow and Wilson (1961) compared the parents of bright high achievers with the parents of equally bright low achievers and found essentially the same differences as Cervantes. There appears to be little doubt that family relationships play a significant role in the school adjustment of adolescents, and specifically in their school achievement.

Achievement

One of the principal reasons given for dropping out of school is difficulty with school work, poor marks, and a consequent fear of failure. Grinder (1973) reports that most adolescents who drop out of high school are at least one year behind their age peers (80 percent of them). Of all dropouts, 50 percent are at least two years behind their peers. Among the brighter dropouts who have fallen behind their peers, the single major contributing factor appears to be a reading problem (Anduri, 1965). Other contributing factors include the individual's sex; the predominant values of the school and of the peer culture; and, to some degree, intelligence. It is notable that four times more boys drop out of school than do girls. Ringness (1967) contends that the peer norm for achievement in high school is simply to do enough to "get by." Other studies have shown that the peer culture places considerably more emphasis on athletics than it does on academic achievement, and that most adolescent boys would prefer to be known as athletes than as scholars. Interestingly, while there is some pressure on girls to do well in school, there is a corresponding pressure on them not to do too well (Coleman, 1961).

Intelligence

There is little doubt that intelligence, or the lack thereof, is highly related to school achievement and therefore, at least indirectly, to high school dropouts. McCandless (1970) reports that the correlation between intelligence and achievement ranges from .50 to .75 in a variety of studies. Intelligence,

particularly as it is reflected in verbal ability, is a good predictor of school achievement. As pointed out earlier, however, it is not as good a predictor of future success in American society as is success in school (Cohen, 1972).

At a time when the importance of self-image and self-esteem is paramount, it is not at all surprising that adolescents who are experiencing considerable difficulty in school, and who are consequently less likely to be accepted by their peers because peer groups do not easily tolerate differences (see Chapter 9), seek other areas where they can develop themselves and be accepted. Many assume, perhaps naively, that they can find rewarding work, achieve economic independence, and, in a sense, surpass their less fortunate peers who remain in school. Unfortunately, however, these are the adolescents who are most likely to become the unemployed or the lower-class workers. Indeed, it has been noted that high school dropouts frequently represent a striking example of downward social mobility, where the adolescents eventually arrive at a lower social position than that occupied by their parents.

Sex

Several reasons have been mentioned to account for the fact that considerably more boys than girls drop out of high school. Among these are the lower peer group pressure for achievement among boys (Ringness, 1967) and the greater emphasis on athletics (Coleman, 1961). Several other sex-related factors also contribute significantly. One of these is the different intelligence test profiles of girls and boys. It has frequently been noted that the profiles of various specific abilities thought to be related to intelligence are considerably more uniform in girls than in boys, despite the fact that there is no consistent difference in their overall IQ scores. Boys tend to exhibit more extremes, being outstanding in some specific areas and below average in others. Their school grades reflect these differences. Many boys do exceptionally well in one or two subjects (notably mathematics and the sciences), are mediocre in several more, and perform at a level well below the average in one or more. Girls, on the other hand, tend to do more uniformly well in most subjects. Coleman (1961) notes that girls do consistently better in high school than do boys *on the average*. Despite this, they are relatively seldom among the highest achieving students in school; nor are they among the lowest achieving. Coleman advances the contention that girls are under double constraints with respect to school achievement. On the one hand various pressures exhort them to do well in school; on the other, they are also exhorted, primarily by peer pressures, not to do overly well. Given that girls are perhaps less aggressive than boys and more acquiescent to school demands, they endeavor to do well (but not brilliantly) in all subjects whether they are interested in the subject or not. Their score distributions are therefore significantly more compressed than those of boys. That is, they exhibit considerably less variation with few very high or very low scores.

Additional reasons why more boys than girls drop out of schools include the greater aggressiveness of boys and their consequent restlessness in schools that demand conformity and compliance rather than self-assertion and aggressiveness. Moreover, there is considerably more social pressure on boys to gain independence than there is on girls. And because one of the hallmarks of independence is financial emancipation, the attraction of the job market is considerable.

The Remedy?

Few social ailments have easy cures. Most of the panaceas that have been proposed by educational reformers have had little effect on the schools, have proven not to be cure-alls, or both. Nevertheless, it is likely that school dropout rates can be reduced significantly as educators and parents become more acutely aware of the situation and take steps to rectify it.

Increasing concern with high school dropout rates in the early 1960s led to a number of changes in a few schools. Among these, open classrooms, college-style campuses that require more responsibility on the part of students both in planning their programs and in attending classes, and individualized forms of instruction have sometimes been employed. None of these innovations, however, has been particularly widespread. Nor has any concerted effort been made to modify school offerings and practices in terms of the recognized causes of school dropouts. Clearly, many of these causes are beyond the jurisdiction of the school. This is the case, for example, with respect to social class and family background. These, however, are not clearly beyond the jurisdiction of other social agencies. Factors related to differential achievement of the sexes, to school retardation due to failure in elementary school, to poor reading skills and habits, and to differential interests of boys and girls are not beyond the scope of the school.

Staying In

Although 33 percent of all high school students drop out of school prior to completion of the twelfth grade, 67 percent remain until they have earned their diplomas. Among the important changes that affect adolescents, there are a number that are directly related to their performance and to their happiness in school. These are discussed under various headings in the remaining pages of this chapter.

Achievement

There appears to be some discontinuity between performance in elementary school and performance in high school. Although some students begin to perform better after elementary school, approximately 45 percent do not perform as well (Armstrong, 1964). Popular speculation holds that this reduction in academic achievement is due largely to greater preoccupation with peer group activities or to rebelliousness, apathy, or the variety of social ills sometimes assumed to be characteristic of the adolescent period.

Finger and Silverman (1966) conducted an extensive investigation in an effort to discover some of the differences that might exist between elementary school students who continue to do well or who do better in high school and those who do less well. Specifically, they administered the Personal Values Inventory (PVI), a questionnaire designed to identify student values, to a large group of junior high school students. Among other things, these investigators discovered that while measured intelligence (IQ) is highly related to marks, it appears to be minimally related to changes that occur from elementary to high school. Changes in grades, however, were highly related to measures of persistence and to academic motivation. High achievers exhibited more "self control deliberateness" than did lower achievers. At the same time, they were less preoccupied with social activities. The academic

plans of high achievers were typically more demanding than were the academic plans of lower achievers.

In short, then, it appears that a host of personality variables including perseverance, values placed on academic achievement, and motivational variables are of considerable importance in determining the performance of high school students. Although it is clear that intellectual and verbal ability are also of considerable importance, it is likely that, given sufficient capability for adequate performance, personality variables are of even more importance in determining eventual performance.

Adolescent Values

It has often been said that adolescent values vis-à-vis the school are essentially antiintellectual. Corroborative evidence for this statement has been obtained from a variety of sources, but most notably from the research of J. S. Coleman (1961). Coleman examined the values of several hundred high school boys and girls. Among other things, he asked them how they would like to be remembered after leaving high school. Boys designated as among the leading crowds (selected more often by all other students) overwhelmingly preferred to be remembered as athletes rather than as scholars. In fact, among these leading crowds fewer people considered themselves intellectuals than was the case among people who were not in leading crowds or who were members of no crowd at all. The evidence indicates that being accepted in a crowd militates to some degree against the image of being brilliant. Hence, many of those who could be classed as the most brilliant were effectively ostracized by their peers (or chose not to belong to a group).

It is notable, as well, that although relatively few boys wanted to be remembered as scholars, even fewer girls desired the scholarly image. Of those boys identified as best scholars, less than 60 percent wished to be remembered as brilliant students. The remaining 40 percent wished to be remembered as athletes or as most popular in approximately equal proportions. Of those named as athlete-scholars—individuals who could clearly choose between either of the two images with some justification—the majority wished to be remembered as athletes rather than as scholars.

The proportions are even more striking among the girls. Of girls named as

274

best scholar, only slightly more than 40 percent wished to be remembered as having been brilliant. These data provide evidence that the image of being brilliant is less desirable for a girl than it is for a boy. Coleman notes, as well, that girls become even less desirous of being remembered as scholars as they progress through the high school years, although they continue to do better than boys on the average. Despite this, they are seldom among the brightest (best achieving) of the students; they are equally seldom among the lowest achieving. From the adolescent girl's point of view, high grades are not nearly as important in making her popular with boys as they are in making her popular with girls. Because she prizes popularity with boys, she gives leadership activities and general popularity precedence over academic achievement.

Significant portions of Coleman's study were replicated several years later employing Canadian students (Friesen, 1968). Some 10,019 students from various parts of Canada were administered questionnaires similar to those employed by Coleman, but with certain elaborations. The intent of the study was to discover whether Canadian students also wished to be remembered as athletes if boys, or as most popular if girls. In addition, Friesen attempted to discover the relative importance placed on athletics, academic achievement, and popularity in relation to acceptance at school and success in later life. His findings do, in fact, contradict those of the Coleman study.

When asked which of the three characteristics they would most like to be remembered by, the majority of students chose the category "outstanding student." The category "athletic star" was only slightly ahead of "popularity." Broken down by sex, the order was academic, athletics, and popularity for boys; academics, popularity, and athletics for girls. Recall that Coleman's findings were that athletics were most important for boys and popularity for girls, while academic achievement was rated low by both. Friesen suggests that there might have been some "semantic ambiguity" in the Coleman questionnaires where such phrases as "honor roll," "outstanding student," "brilliant student," and "high grades" were all employed to refer to the academic category. He makes no other attempt to reconcile the discrepancy between his results and those reported by Coleman. One additional possible explanation, however, is that Canadian students are different from American students in terms of school related values. Still another possible explanation

is that students in both Canada and the United States changed dramatically between 1961 and 1967.

Additional findings from the Friesen investigation are noteworthy. Subjects were asked which area of achievement was most important for being happy at school as well as which area was most important for success in later life. Being happy at school was, according to the boys, more related to academic achievement than to popularity or athletic ability, with popularity being second in importance. For girls, popularity was most important; again, athletics were least important. Both boys and girls agreed overwhelmingly that academic success was the most important factor for the future and athletics was the least important.

In interpreting and reconciling these two studies, it is important to keep in mind that the questionnaires employed were different, though similar; that the samples were different not only geographically but also in terms of size, with Friesen's sample being considerably larger; and that the studies were conducted at different times by different individuals. Contradictory studies are common in psychological or sociological research, though the differences are frequently superficial and easily accounted for. For the moment, however, no highly generalizable conclusions are warranted.

Cheating

One possible indication of the increasing importance of performing adequately in school within the constraints of the time and energy available for school activities can be derived from a study of cheating patterns among adolescents. Burton (1963) and Hartshorne and May (1928) found that girls cheat at least as frequently as boys during elementary school. Feldman and Feldman (1967) speculated that as boys enter adolescence and high school, they become more academically motivated and will therefore take greater risks to succeed. In an ingenious experiment, they tested this hypothesis.

Groups of seventh and twelfth grade students were administered a difficult objective examination (creative achievement). The next day, teachers advised the subjects that the tests had not been scored, but that the students themselves could do so from a key that was placed on the blackboard. Students

Table 10.1   Incidence of Cheating as a Function of Grade and Sex

	Seventh Graders		Twelfth Graders	
	Cheaters	Noncheaters	Cheaters	Noncheaters
Males	10	35	20	20
Females	13	23	11	22

From S. E. Feldman and M. T. Feldman, "Transition of sex differences in cheating," *Psychological Reports*, 1967, **20**, 957–958. Reprinted with permission of author and publisher.

276

were also told that they could compare grades once they had finished. Soon after subjects began marking their own examinations, which had, of course, been marked previously, the teacher was called from the classroom. Comparison of teacher and student marks revealed which students had availed themselves of the opportunity to cheat. For purposes of analysis, any student marked paper that differed by two or more marks from the teacher's scoring was considered to have been cheated on. Table 10.1 presents the obtained results. While there was an increase in the incidence of boys cheating (22.2 to 50 percent from seventh to twelfth grade), there was a negligible decline in the incidence of girls cheating.

Because cheating, by definition, involves some considerable effort on the part of the transgressors to hide their behavior, few inferences can be derived from observations of classroom behavior. Teachers are frequently unaware that students cheat, or how frequently they cheat. It is perhaps remarkable that a full 50 percent of the twelfth grade boys in the Feldman and Feldman (1967) study cheated. And perhaps, again, it is not so remarkable. After all, many adults also cheat, and society reacts inconsistently. Cheating the government is frequently seen as being laudable; cheating in business among strangers is often applauded if it is successful; but cheating friends is frequently frowned upon. Is cheating in school very different from cheating the government?

School and Family

Studies reported earlier (for example, Reiss, 1966) indicated that there is stronger correspondence between parent-adolescent values—especially in such important areas as choice of life-styles, beliefs about right and wrong, and questions of adult status and achievement—than there is among peers. When faced with conflicting pressures, peers tend to agree with parents on questions involving adult status and basic values, and with peers on questions relating to immediate acceptance in the peer group. It is not surprising, therefore, that there should be a high correlation between parental educational achievements, educational values and educational aspirations, and the actual academic achievement of their children.

Sewell and Shah (1968) report, in particular, that there is a high relation-

Tracy *Age 18* **On Cheating in School**

Me: *How about cheating in school? Is there a lot of that that goes on?*
Tracy: *Oh yeah! I did it myself once or twice and feel really bad about it because you're cheating yourself, because you can't cheat on a final examination. You can cheat on quizzes. You're the one who suffers.*
Me: *Why do students cheat?*

Tracy: *The ability to get higher marks. You know, like high marks mean a lot in school and like if you say I have a 70 average rather than a 68 it makes all the difference to someone.*
Me: *How do they cheat?*
Tracy: *Well, you look at the person who sits beside you, and you know that he's mentally superior, and you copy from his paper. Or drawing on your hand. Or on your arm. Things like that.*

277

ship between parental educational achievements and the educational aspirations of their children. And one of the factors that appears to be most instrumental in determining level of achievement in high schools is precisely adolescent academic motivation, a factor that reflects their educational aspirations (Finger and Silverman, 1966).

Sewell and Shah also found that those parents who had gone to college were more likely to have children who would also go to college. Swift (1967) found that those parents who view education as important are more likely to have adolescents who are successful in school. In short, there is little doubt that the attitudes of parents with respect to education, as well as their own educational achievements, are a significant factor in determining the adolescent's relationship to school and the probability of a successful college career.

Summary

This chapter opened with the admission that Sam's highly prejudiced views on the school would not be included. Instead it moved directly to a consideration of changes in high school enrollment. Following this the phenomenon of high school dropouts was introduced. Attitude toward school, social class, family background, intelligence, achievement, and sex were examined as possible explanations for dropping out of school. Adolescent values vis-à-vis the school, changes in student performance from elementary to high school, cheating patterns, and the influence of the family on the adolescent's adjustment to school were then discussed. It is reassuring to note that although many adolescents drop out of school prior to graduation, the majority stay in.

Main Points

1. Sam is not kindly disposed to the contemporary high school—or at least to the high schools that were contemporary when he was.

2. High school enrollments have increased dramatically in the last few decades. This is partly because many states have raised the age of compulsory attendance. It may also be due to a changing labor market with advancing

Me: *You don't know any other exotic techniques.*
Tracy: *Well I've heard of kids stealing copies of exams and selling them for five dollars each. These kids are making a big raking off these exams, cause sometimes they can sell fifty copies before they write the exam. If you don't know your material and you have to cheat, you're in a pretty sad predicament.*

technologies. The high school diploma has been devalued considerably, but continues to be mandatory for admission to a large number of postsecondary educational institutions.

3. Approximately 33 percent of all adolescents drop out of school prior to completion of twelfth grade. A number of these finish later; some adapt successfully to adult life; and others remain among the unemployed, become recipients of social aid, or become part of the labor force.

4. Evidence suggests that social class is closely related to the probability of having a successful school career. In general, adolescents from the lower classes are less likely to succeed and, consequently, considerably less likely to attend college or other postsecondary educational facilities.

5. Parents who have themselves dropped out of school prior to completion and who have a relatively low evaluation of education are more likely to have adolescents who also drop out of school.

6. One of the principal reasons given for dropping out of school is difficulty with school work. It is notable that the single most important factor is poor reading ability.

7. There is little doubt that intelligence is closely related to the dropout phenomenon. Less intelligent individuals tend to have more difficulty with school work, more likelihood of failure, and perhaps less motivation to succeed.

8. The achievement profiles of girls and boys in high school are quite different. In general, boys tend to do much better in some subjects (notably the sciences) and much poorer in others (languages). Girls, on the other hand, tend to do moderately well on all subjects, but perform brilliantly much less frequently. Their achievement profiles are considerably more compressed than those of boys.

9. Coleman advances the argument that there is pressure on girls not to do too well in school.

10. Educational authorities have not yet discovered or implemented any widespread remedy for the tragedy that is represented by school dropouts.

11. While a number of adolescents drop out of school, the large majority remain until they have graduated.

12. Approximately 45 percent of all students do not perform as well in high school as they did in elementary school. Changes in motivation and in persistence appear to account for some of this decline in achievement.

13. Adolescent values have been described as typically antiintellectual following a study showing that very few adolescents want to be remembered primarily as good scholars, particularly girls. The majority of boys would prefer to be remembered as athletes. Among girls, leadership activities and general popularity are given precedence over academic achievement. A second study did not support the first. Instead, it provided evidence that academic achievement is prized above athletics. No firm conclusions are warranted.

14. Cheating is less related to beliefs about right and wrong than it is to the probability of being caught. In one study 50 percent of the twelfth grade boys cheated when it appeared that they would not be caught.

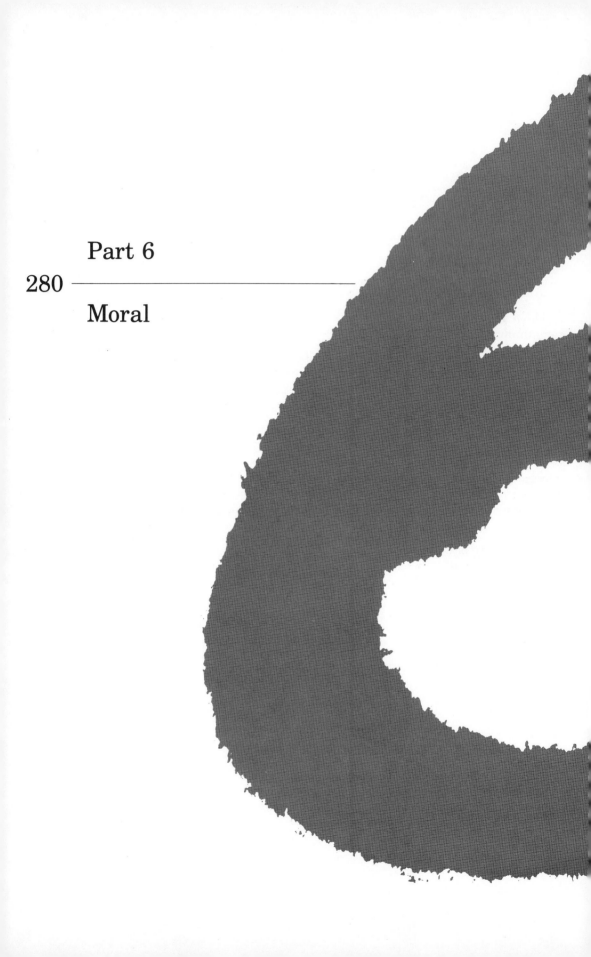

Part 6

280

Moral

Chapter 11

Population and Pollution: Morality and Delinquency

Brian Campbell, Grade 11

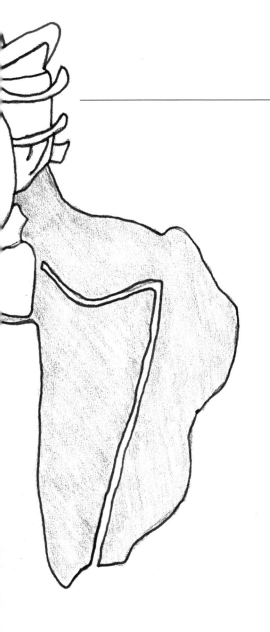

Morality

Definitions
Theories of Moral Development
Piaget
Kohlberg

Values

Delinquency

Who is Delinquent?
Related Factors
Age
Social Class
Peer Group

Father
Sex
Types of Delinquents

Summary

Main Points

Figure 11.1 Population growth for Homo sapiens on Earth. The part of the graph to the left of the axis (that is, the part that isn't shown) would be perhaps a half mile long if it reached to the time when humans first appeared.

One of the topics about which Sam feels most passionately is the present state of the world as he sees it. As Sam puts it, "Discussion of today's adolescents often centers around their sometimes vocal, sometimes physical, and sometimes passive objection to much of what they see around them." In the following, somewhat scholastic excerpt from his essay, Sam describes some of the things to which the adolescent might object.

Humans made their rather inconspicuous appearance on this planet perhaps one million years ago—a mere three billion years after the appearance of the first elementary life forms on a planet that had already been devoid of life for probably another two billion years.* Following the appearance of modern humans, it took close to a million years before the population, at least on this planet, reached one billion. The second billion required only one hundred years; the third, just thirty years. The fourth may require slightly over fifteen years. By the year 2000 there could well be six billion people on this planet, despite the fact that a number of major countries, including the United States, have now reached zero population growth. As zero population growth is ordinarily interpreted, it does not lead to the immediate cessation of world population growth. It simply indicates that every adult reproduces only one other human being; they just replace themselves. Although it appears as though two people have simply replaced themselves when they have no more than two children, these two children (and two others, to be sure) will theoretically (whatever that is) have had two children while the grandparents are still alive. Hence, where there were two people, there will now be six; or perhaps even eight if the great-grandparents are still alive at the birth of their allotted great-grand-children. It becomes clear that holding the world's population at a reasonable figure requires something less than zero population growth. The dramatic effects of the geometric growth nature of human population is represented in Figure 11.1.**

For many reasons, increasing population is the world's greatest problem.

---

*Findings recently reported by Leaky (1971) suggest that modern humans may be considerably more than a mere million years old. But in dealing with these cosmic matters, a few million years, more or less, does seem somewhat trivial.

** Perhaps because of his passionate concern about these problems, Sam has apparently abandoned his customary "overstated, essay approach" and attempts here to convince by weight of argument, documentation, and appeal to graphic representation.

Population in Billions

Earth Year (A.D.)

Although attention is often focused more dramatically on problems of starvation, energy shortages, pollution, and so on, it is rather clear that these are the result of overpopulation. At present, for example, over half of the world's population is undernourished, and this despite the fact that there are now 1.2 acres under cultivation for every man, woman, and child (Lerner, 1968). For adequate nourishment of the world's present population, not only does acreage under cultivation have to increase considerably, but alternative food sources, more efficient ways of producing food, and better means of distributing it have to be found. And the world's present population is still under four billion; what will the general food situation be when it reaches six billion? If we're not intelligent enough to predict a reasonable answer for this question now, we should not have to wait more than another twenty-five or thirty years to find out. But by then it may be too late.

Energy and pollution problems are largely a result of overpopulation as well. Not only do we continue to use irreplaceable resources at a high rate, but we also fail to replace them with anything other than garbage.

More people; more demand for resources; more production of wastes. And there are other reasons why it's not a good world. One of them has to do with humanity's relationship with itself, its world, and its god (whoever it may be, which is why the "g" is an insignificant noncapital). Humans have become increasingly materialistic, increasingly concerned with the accumulation of the fruits of an advanced industrialistic and capitalistic society. At the same time they have become less concerned about their fellow humans. Not only do people themselves depersonalize other people, but the institutions that they create also depersonalize. Political, economic, and social structures have become so complex, so large, and so unwieldly that the individual suffers from an overwhelming sense of powerlessness. And it is, to some degree, this sense of powerlessness and frustration that is manifested in the increasing degeneracy and immorality of the human race. Never in the history of the human race . . .

Sam's essay becomes less scholastic and considerably more emotional following this rather sober introduction to the world's population and pollution problems. His intention was to consider the morality of adolescents within the context of some of the contemporary world's most obvious and most pressing problems. It appeared to me, however, that his view of adolescents is perhaps biased, though highly revealing of general attitudes that have been

286

prevalent for some time. The portions of Sam's essays included in the following chapters clarify the nature of these biases. The remainder of this chapter
presents what is hopefully a more objective view of adolescent morality.

Morality

We have for some time assumed that morality is a peculiarly human
characteristic; that lower animals, preoccupied as they are with their immediate physical survival, are neither good nor evil in a moral sense. They
simply behave in accordance with their animal nature. It is interesting to
note, however, that we sometimes find it appropriate to ascribe relative
degrees of morality to those animals with which we are most familiar. Thus
we sometimes refer to a dog as being bad or another as being particularly
gentle. But here again we would not go so far as to say that the first dog has
a warped conscience and that the second has better morals. Better manners
perhaps, but never better morals.

Humans, on the other hand, are often described in terms of the elusive
qualities of goodness and evil that are reflected in their behavior and beliefs. And because we are such gregarious animals, so dependent upon interaction with other humans, the qualities of good and evil that are assumed to
be characteristic of each of us are of considerable importance not only to our
adjustment, but to the well-being of the entire race.

Morality, defined in terms of the qualities of good and evil that characterize
human behavior, is an extremely complicated topic—considerably more complicated, for example, than such other human characteristics as intelligence
and creativity. These can be measured, although imprecisely, and can be observed in most facets of a single individual's behavior. Morality, however,
cannot easily be measured. And once certain individuals have been identified,
by whatever means are at hand, as being particularly good or evil, we still
have no guarantee that their behavior will invariably reflect these qualities.
Thus it is that a nation made up of presumably "good" individuals will make
war against another nation also made up of "good" individuals, depending on
who is doing the assessing. And thus it is that devoutly moral individuals will
unblushingly steal from their government (perhaps legally but frequently
immorally as well), from an anonymous stranger, or from a large corporation.

But never from their grandmothers, for they have morals. These same individuals can preach passionately concerning the sanctity and necessity of the legislation that governs human conduct; at the same time, they are breaking such "minor" laws as they think they can get away with.

Despite these contradictions in human behavior, it is possible to discriminate among various levels of morality and to characterize people in general ways in terms of their relative goodness and evilness. In addition, it is possible to trace the development of morality in children and in adolescents and to identify some of the factors that are most closely related to the morality or immorality of adolescent behavior—a topic that is of considerable importance to an understanding of adolescence.

Definitions

Morality, as a global term, refers simply to the relative goodness of people as it is reflected in their behavior and beliefs. Kohlberg (1964) distinguishes between three aspects of morality; the first two are those to which we are most likely to react when judging the morals of an individual. There is, to begin with, the behavioral aspect of morality that is reflected in a person's ability to resist temptation. Second, there are the reactions of individuals to their own behavior, specifically to their transgression of moral rules. Thus greater morality is ordinarily associated with greater feelings of guilt following an immoral act. Individuals who feel little guilt as a result of immoral behavior are assumed to have lower morals or less strong consciences than those who feel a great deal of guilt.

A third aspect of morality, and one that is receiving considerable current attention in psychological research, concerns individuals' estimates of the morality of a given act in terms of some personal standards of good and evil by which they judge human behavior.

Related terms that are also of importance in understanding the remainder of this section are **values, conscience,** and **morals.** Values can be defined as specific beliefs concerning the relative worth of certain behaviors and attitudes. Thus individuals who place a high value on honesty believe that behaviors that reflect or promote honesty are moral whereas those that reflect dishonesty are immoral. Morals are standards of behavior premised on certain values. That is, they are standards by which individuals assess the rightness or wrongness of behavior. Conscience is defined as an integrated set of beliefs about right and wrong, an integration of morals in other words.

Although it is possible to arrive at relatively clear definitions of these related terms, it is not, in fact, possible to make direct inferences from one to another. It does not necessarily follow, for example, that an individual with a strong conscience—that is, with a well-integrated set of strong beliefs concerning what is right and wrong—will behave in a more moral manner than one with a less strong conscience. Various studies and reports indicate that the strength of conscience is not directly related to actual behavior; there is, in fact, a very low correlation between what a person believes and what that person does (Hendry, 1960; Havighurst and Taba, 1949). Kohlberg (1964) also summarizes a number of studies that indicate very low relationships between religious training and morality of behavior, a finding that may in part explain religious wars. Based on these findings, Kohlberg argues that morality is primarily a question of strength of ego rather than of superego. Recall that the superego is that level of human personality that defines the conscience. It embodies religious and social prescripts concerning right and wrong.

Theories of Moral Development

The two theories of moral development described in this section do not present alternatives one to the other, but are simply complementary. A third theory, that of Freud, has been mentioned previously and is not discussed in detail here primarily because of its generality. In essence it maintains that morality is an expression of the strength of the superego as it is expressed in behavior and belief, and that the superego is the individual's internalization of societal and religious constraints imposed on behavior. It is assumed to develop primarily through a process of identification with parents as well as from specific religious training. Other, more detailed discussions of moral development have been proposed by Piaget and Kohlberg.

Piaget In an earlier passage a discussion is presented of Piaget's investigation of rules governing children's play behavior. Through observation and interviews, Piaget discovered four stages in children's understanding of rules, progressing from an initial stage where there is no understanding of rules; to an intermediate stage where the children believe that rules are fixed, come from some external source, and are unchangeable; to a second intermediate stage where they believe that rules are made by people and can be changed by mutual consent; and finally to a stage where children understand rules fully. It is interesting to note that children's behavior does not always reflect their understanding of rules. In the first of the intermediate stages (ages three to five approximately), children believe that rules are fixed and unchangeable. Yet they change them constantly as they play. In the succeeding stage (approximately ages five to eleven or twelve) they believe that rules can be changed, but they adhere to them fanatically in their play. This rather striking contradiction between belief about rules and behavior is evident in other areas of morality as well. Hartshorne and May (1928–30), among others, have observed that there is relatively little correspondence between adolescents' beliefs about right and wrong and their behavior; for example, cheating is affected more by the probability of being caught than by the individual's beliefs concerning the morality of cheating.

Piaget's notions concerning the development of morality are derived largely from his investigations of the development of notions about rules. Morals are, in a real sense, internalizations of rules concerning behavior. Whereas games rules apply only to specific social situations, moral rules apply to larger aspects of individual behavior.

Piaget notes, in particular, that morality progresses from an initially egocentric and highly changeable set of beliefs to more socially determined beliefs, and finally to individualized convictions concerning right and wrong. In other words, right and wrong is judged initially in terms of children's immediate interests and desires. Later it is determined largely in terms of relationships in social groups and is directed toward maintaining good relationships both with peers and with parents. Finally, in adolescence, children reexamine rules of conscience and arrive at individual moral rules.

Additional experiments conducted by Piaget to investigate child morality made use of stories told to children and to which they responded. One example concerns the story of a child who accidentally breaks a large number of dishes while doing an errand for his mother. His behavior is compared to that of another child who breaks a single dish while attempting to obtain some object that has been forbidden her. At a young age children tend to assess moral culpability in terms of the seriousness of the objective results of the act rather

Table 11.1   Kohlberg's Levels and Types of Morality

Level 1   Premoral
    Type 1   Punishment and obedience orientation
    Type 2   Naive instrumental hedonism
Level 2   Morality of conventional role conformity
    Type 3   Morality of maintaining good relations, approval of others
    Type 4   Authority maintains morality
Level 3   Morality of self-accepted principles
    Type 5   Morality of contract, of individual rights, and of democratically accepted law
    Type 6   Morality of individual principles of conscience

From "Development of moral character and moral ideology," by Lawrence Kohlberg in *Review of Child Development Research, Vol. 1,* edited by Martin L. Hoffman and Lois Wladis Hoffman. Copyright © 1964 by Russell Sage Foundation. Used by permission.

290

than in terms of the intentions of the wrongdoer. Thus the child who accidentally broke a large number of dishes is clearly guilty of a greater offence than the one who broke a single dish although the circumstances under which the two transgressions occurred are clearly very different.

Following this initial stage, children's judgments of morality become more adultlike and tend to be more concerned with the motives of the transgressor than with the objective consequences of the act. It should be noted, however, that adults frequently judge moral culpability in objective terms very similar to that of young children. Thus a child who accidentally causes a great deal of damage to her parent's home is sometimes punished more severely than one who causes only minor damage regardless of the circumstances under which the acts occurred.

Kohlberg Kohlberg's theory of moral development is not essentially different from Piaget's, although it is more detailed and has involved considerably more research. The bulk of Kohlberg's analysis of moral development is based on children's responses to questions involving guilt and the moral rightness and wrongness of characters in brief stories. He identified three sequential levels of moral development, each consisting of two types of moral orientation. Although the three levels are sequential, one never entirely replaces the other so that adults are quite capable of making moral judgments not essentially different from those made by very young children. Indeed, Kohlberg found that the highest stage of moral orientation was reached by a relatively small number of adults in his sample. These three levels of moral development are depicted in Table 11.1. In brief, they indicate that children progress from an initial premoral stage in which they respond primarily to rewards and punishment; to a highly conforming, rule-bound, authority-dominated type of morality; and finally to a morality of self-accepted principles of conduct. The progression is then from hedonism, to social contract-type rules, to self-determined principles. This final stage of moral development, referred to as a stage of postconventional morality, is reached by relatively few adults. Kohlberg reports that only 10 percent of the twenty-four-year-olds in his sample were operating at this level. Another 24 percent were at a social contract stage, and the remainder still responded either in terms of hedonistic (pain-pleasure) principles or in terms of immediate authority (see Figure 11.2).

The progression of children through these levels of moral development is

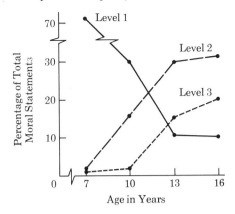

Figure 11.2 Mean percentage of moral statements of six moral types made by boys aged seven to sixteen. The chart illustrates the typical decrement from the first type of moral reasoning with advancing age and an increase to more advanced moral judgments. (From "Development of moral character and moral ideology," by Lawrence Kohlberg in *Review of Child Development Research, Vol. I,* edited by Martin L. Hoffman and Lois Wladis Hoffman. Copyright © 1964 by Russell Sage Foundation. Used by permission.)

interesting and informative. At the earliest stage, the premoral, morality is determined in terms of the immediate effect of the behavior on the children themselves. Thus those things that are viewed as bad are those most likely to bring about punishment, and explicit obedience of immediate authority becomes the measure of goodness. Similarly, those behaviors that have immediate pleasurable outcomes are better in a moral sense than those that do not have pleasurable outcomes.

At the second stage children become less egocentric and more socialized. These changes are reflected in their moral orientation as well, becoming most evident in their desire to maintain good relations not only with parents and teachers but also with peers. The criteria of good behavior are no longer limited to hedonistic concerns but now become more concerned with the effects of behavior on children's relationships with their social milieu. This second level of moral development is therefore characterized by a type of reciprocity where children willingly make sacrifices for the sake of others. This is a far cry from the moral orientation of the preceding stage where the children would go out of their way to do something for someone else only if they thought they would benefit directly from it.

At the highest level children reexamine the rules by which they have previously judged the morality of behavior. With the advent of adolescent idealism, there comes a reevaluation of good and evil, and sometimes a rejection of many rules that appear arbitrary and not in the best interests of the ideal society that the adolescent can now envision. Morality now becomes a question of individual rights, of ideals and principles, and of beliefs that have merit in and of themselves quite apart from the social approval or disapproval to which they are subject.

The great value of Kohlberg's (1969; Kohlberg and Turiel, 1971) work lies not only in the theoretical framework that has evolved from it, but also in the empirical data that he has gathered in support of this theory. The bulk of his work has involved investigations of moral development among a group of seventy-five boys between the ages of ten and seventeen; it therefore provides data of a longitudinal nature not present in most studies of moral development. It is revealing to note, then, that the theoretical position advanced is highly similar to such other positions as Piaget's. Piaget (1932) had described morality as progressing from an initial stage of **heteronomy** to a final stage of **autonomy.** By heteronomy of morality, Piaget meant moral judgment based

on outside authority — a morality of conformity. This clearly corresponds to Kohlberg's second level of moral development. The final Piagetian stage, that of autonomy, corresponds to Kohlberg's third level, that of self-accepted principles. In short, the literature on moral development, unlike that in many other areas, is in relatively high agreement concerning children's progression from a premoral to a highly conforming and finally to a relatively autonomous morality. It must be kept in mind, however, that adolescent and even adult moral judgments do not become exclusively autonomous. Although autonomous moral judgments are notably lacking among younger children, morality based on conformity, and frequently on hedonistic concerns as well, is readily apparent in adolescent and adult behavior.

Considerable research has now been conducted employing Kohlberg's theoretical model and attempting to relate it to the actual behavior of subjects. Turiel (1974), in a large-scale investigation, found that the transition between the fourth and fifth of Kohlberg's stages occurred somewhat later than had been predicted. Recall that the fourth stage is characterized by an orientation toward authority designed to maintain social order. The fifth stage shows a contractual-legalistic orientation. Turiel's subjects typically did not reach the fifth stage until late adolescence or early adulthood. The sixth stage, morality of self-determined principles of conscience, does not appear to be characteristic of the adolescent. Both Turiel and Kohlberg found that relatively few adults operated from this orientation. This observation is not a clear contradiction of Piagetian theory, despite the fact that Piagetian adolescents are presumed to be at a stage when they can reexamine their rules of moral behavior and arrive at individual principles of conscience. Formal operations, in this area as in all others, is simply a possibility given the nature of adolescent thought processes. It does not appear to be an actuality for all adolescents.

It is interesting to note that morality scores on Kohlberg-type scales are highly correlated with delinquency. Fodor (1972) found that delinquents typically exhibited lower levels of moral orientation than did comparable nondelinquent subjects. In addition, delinquents who could be convinced by the investigator to change their minds had lower scores than those who refused to alter their initial decisions. Kohlberg's interviews present the subjects with a moral dilemma where they are forced to make a choice and explain their reasons for the choice. For example, a subject is asked whether a man should steal an expensive drug in an attempt to save his wife's life. The nature of the decision is irrelevant to the subject's score; it is determined by his or her explanation for the choice.

Additional evidence of the relationship between moral orientation and adolescent behavior is provided by Haan *et al.* (1968). A sample of college students and of Peace Corps volunteers were administered the Kohlberg Moral Judgment Scale, and their scores were related to various other measures. Among other things, the investigators found that those subjects who scored highest in terms of moral orientation were considerably more active politically and socially. In addition, their views were less similar to those of their parents, despite the fact that they tended to have relatively liberal parents. Not surprisingly, they experienced more conflict in the home than did subjects whose moral orientations were still primarily authority oriented.

Values

Values, the beliefs that individuals hold concerning the worth of specific behaviors and attitudes, are intimately linked with morality. They are, in effect, the bases upon which moral judgments are frequently made. An examination of adolescent moral values is therefore of considerable importance in this text.

It is generally agreed that morality is the product of a process of socialization, that the combined influences of all the socializing agents at work in children's environments have an effect on their ultimate understanding of right and wrong and, consequently, on their behavior. The relationship between behavior and beliefs, however, is not as direct as most grandmothers would suppose—a fact that has been mentioned previously and that is discussed in more detail below.

Parents appear to be of considerable importance in determining adolescent values. A large number of studies (for example, Reiss, 1966) have demonstrated a high correlation between basic parental values and the values of their adolescents. Parents who value education tend to have children who also value education and who are least likely to drop out of school prior to graduation; parents who are liberal tend to have children who are liberal; parents who are highly critical of social systems tend to have children who are highly critical.

A second important factor in the determination of values is attendance at college. Webster, Freedman, and Heist (1962) found significant changes in adolescent values as a function of college attendance. Not surprisingly, these changes were in the direction of increased liberalism in social, religious, and political values.

The adolescent's sex also appears to be an important factor in the determination of values. Probably largely for cultural reasons boys are significantly more prone to antisocial, amoral, and deviant behavior; this finding has been corroborated repeatedly in studies of juvenile delinquency and is documented in some detail in a later section of this chapter. Wright and Cox (1967) also found that girls tend to be considerably more severe in their judgments of right and wrong than are boys.

Religious training may also be of some significance in the determination of adolescent values. Strunk (1958) found, for example, that there is a high correlation between self-concept and religiosity (belief in the principles of an established religion; attendance at church; and so on). In the samples studied, those individuals who scored highest on measures of religiosity tended to have better self-concepts as measured through self-report techniques. Wright and Cox (1967) also found a high correlation between religious beliefs and moral judgment among a group of adolescents. Those characterized by higher religious beliefs tended to present stricter religious judgments.

Finally, peers probably exert considerable influence on the establishment of adolescent values, notwithstanding the fact that there is greater resemblance between adolescent-parent values than there is between adolescent-peer values. As was indicated previously, parental values tend to be adopted in those areas where the parent is seen as the greatest expert; that is, in those areas where questions of adult status and conduct in adult life are concerned.

In more immediate areas affecting adolescent acceptance and status among peers, adolescents are more likely to adopt the values of their immediate peer groups. It should also be noted, as Dunphy's (1963) work illustrated, that adolescent peer groups tend to be comprised of individuals with similar values. The function of the peer groups is perhaps not so much to foster the development of values as to reinforce those that already exist. It is revealing to note, as well, that the agreement between parent and adolescent values is frequently contradicted in the behavior of adolescents. Remmers and Radler (1957) presented questionnaires to samples of adolescents and discovered that

although adolescents tend to accept adult values verbally, they frequently behave in accordance with their peers even when that behavior is a denial of the values they accept. Thus, although only 11 percent of the adolescents in the sample were in favor of drinking, some 37 percent admitted that they drank on occasion.

Delinquency

It seems appropriate to consider **delinquency** in the same chapter as morality because in a very real sense delinquency is both a rejection of morality and an expression of amorality (or perhaps simply of immorality). Recall the Fodor (1972) study that indicated that delinquents typically score lower on Kohlberg's measure of moral orientation.

Delinquency, as it is discussed in this chapter, includes those behaviors that represent transgressions of established laws and social conventions, some of which are serious enough to lead to the institutionalization of the adolescent in question. The problem of juvenile delinquency is neither as serious nor as widespread as much research and writing have indicated. On the other hand, where it does occur, it is frequently considerably more complex and much less amenable to treatment than is sometimes naively suggested by other research and writing.

Who Is Delinquent?

Delinquency is, in fact, a legal rather than a scientific category. It is defined by the courts, by police records, sometimes by school records, and frequently in the records of the various institutions where juvenile offenders are sent for "treatment." Significantly, adults guilty of the transgressions for which adolescents merit the label delinquent are themselves not termed delinquent, but simply criminal. Hence, in order to be a delinquent, it is also usually necessary to be a juvenile. And that too is a legal rather than a scientific category, variable both across international and across state or provincial boundaries.

In one sense almost all adolescents are delinquents. Short and Nye (1957–

58) studied delinquents by employing self-report techniques rather than the usual practice of going directly to police or institutional records. Among a number of striking findings was the rather unsurprising discovery that well over 80 percent of all subjects in the sample had at one time or another been guilty of breaking various laws pertaining to drinking, driving, loitering, littering, petty theft, and so on. By the same token, it is highly likely that almost all adults are criminals in fact if not in name.

The legal category, juvenile delinquent, is defined in a highly arbitrary and highly variable manner. An adolescent does not officially become a delinquent until he or she has been apprehended by law enforcement officers, the nature of the transgression has been recorded, and the matter has been placed before the appropriate jurisdictional bodies. Hence membership in this category depends not only on the adolescent's behavior, but also on the law enforcers, and on the nature of the laws that exist at the time. The frequency of delinquency is therefore difficult to assess. The picture provided by self-report techniques such as that employed by Short and Nye (1957–58) presents a very different picture from that provided by more traditional techniques.

Related Factors

Although the nature of delinquency can be described satisfactorily given that the phenomenon exists as a legal-social definition, its causes cannot readily be determined. Most of the studies that have investigated the possible roots of delinquent behavior have been of a correlational nature. That is, they have shown the presence or absence of correlation between incidence of delinquency and a variety of factors including home background, age, sex, peer influences, and so on. Recall, however, that one cannot logically infer causation from a correlational study. At best, it is possible to say with some degree of confidence that certain variables appear to be related to delinquency in adolescents; one cannot say that they *cause* delinquency. A number of these factors are examined below.

Age Ball, Ross, and Simpson (1964), making use of police and court records in a study involving some twenty-five thousand boys and girls between the ages of six and seventeen in Kentucky, found that approximately 2 percent of the boys and .5 percent of the girls were involved in delinquent behavior.

The incidence of delinquent behavior doubled in boys between the ages of eleven and twelve, and tripled between the ages of twelve and seventeen. Seven percent of the seventeen-year-olds were classified as delinquents. The picture for girls was dramatically different with almost no change in the incidence of delinquency between the ages of six and seventeen.

The relationship of delinquency to age has been made apparent in a number of other studies. Beller (1949) presented subjects with a number of stories involving some delinquent act. In one such story, for example, a boy who boarded a bus is prevented from immediately paying his fare by the pressure of the crowd. He then decides that he will not pay the fare, because it is highly unlikely that anyone will notice. Subjects were asked two questions. "What would you do?" and "Would it be right for you to do what he did?" The first question is designed to discover the subject's willingness to engage in a delinquent act. The second is meant to discover the subject's understanding of right and wrong. Beller found that the behavior of adolescents becomes progressively less moral with increasing age between the ages of nine and fifteen, but that their understanding of right and wrong as revealed by their responses to the second type of question increases significantly. Here, again, is additional evidence that knowledge of right and wrong is not necessarily a strong deterrent to delinquent behavior.

Social Class Returning to the original question of "Who is delinquent?", no simple answer can be provided. It has long been accepted, for example, that the delinquent is primarily from the lower socioeconomic classes. And, in fact, most research in the area of juvenile delinquency seems to support this contention. Investigators have repeatedly found that institutions that house delinquents contain an inordinate number of individuals from the lower classes. This in itself, however, does not provide adequate evidence for the contention that lower-class adolescents are more likely to be delinquent. The observed imbalance may, to some extent, be a function of predetermined social biases that affect not only law enforcement officers, but the judicial system as well. It is no secret that affluent middle-class parents are considerably more successful at extricating their errant adolescents from the clutches of the law. In many cases, these adolescents are released with scarcely a blemish on their records.

It is also true that law enforcement officers in the course of apprehending juvenile lawbreakers (or suspects) are frequently called upon to make immediate judgments concerning the seriousness of the offence, the probable guilt of the adolescents before them, their character, the probability that they will again engage in the behavior in question, and so on. Hence the fact that there are more lower-class boys classed as delinquents may well reflect prosecution and corrective agency prejudices rather than actual differences in lower- and middle-class adolescent behavior. These agencies may be guilty of perpetuating a self-fulfilling prophecy of which they are an integral part. An officer believes that there are more "real" delinquents among the poor and makes more arrests among them, thus, in a sense, providing psychologists with evidence that he or she was in fact right to begin with.

The relationship between social class and delinquency is, therefore, by no means clear. It appears probable that there is a higher incidence of delinquency among lower classes, but at the same time that there is considerably more unapprehended or unprosecuted delinquency among middle classes than official records would indicate.

Miller (1958) interviewed a number of delinquent boys and arrived at the conclusion that delinquency among lower classes is not, as has sometimes been supposed, a rebellion against middle-class values. He maintains, instead, that it is an expression of conformity to lower-class values, values that are concerned with such immediate intangibles as trouble, fate, smartness, toughness, and excitement. Related to this, Scarpitti (1965) found that delinquents tended to be negatively predisposed to middle-class values. They were primarily lower-class boys who were acutely conscious of the limited opportunities that life provided for them relative to that provided for middle-class adolescents. In addition, delinquents were characterized by inadequate socialization and by poor images of themselves.

Peer Group The effect of the peer group on delinquent behavior has also been investigated, most notably in studies of juvenile gangs (for example, Bloch and Niederhoffer, 1958; Cartwright *et al.*, 1975). Not unlike other adolescent peer groups, the delinquent gang serves to reinforce the dominant values of its members. Buehler, Patterson, and Furniss (1966) maintain that the delinquent gang not only reinforces its members for their behavior but serves as well to provide acceptable models of delinquent behavior. Because correctional institutions are comprised primarily of delinquent peer groups,

it is not particularly surprising that they have been notoriously ineffective in providing deterrents to delinquent behavior. In fact, slightly more than 60 percent of all admissions to juvenile correctional institutions are readmissions (Stuart, 1969). The same observation could be substantiated with respect to adult correctional institutions.

Father A number of studies suggest that the father is more crucial than the mother in affecting delinquency, particularly in boys (Glueck and Glueck, 1959; McCord *et al.*, 1963; Schaefer, 1965). Among the most relevant findings are: fathers of delinquent boys are, on the average, more authoritarian, more rigid, more prone to alcoholism, and more likely to have engaged in deviant behavior; and delinquent boys more often perceive their fathers as cold and rejecting, as well as overly controlling. Other research (Herzog and Sudia, 1970) has found a high relationship between delinquency and father absence. It is not clear whether this is due to the absence of a male model, to aggressive protest against feminine domination, or simply to inadequate supervision. It is likely that these and other related factors are involved.

Delinquency among girls also appears to be affected by the father, although there is considerably less research on this topic. Friedman (1969) suggests that a girl's need for a father is almost as strong and important as is a boy's and that delinquency characteristic of girls in father-absent homes may be an expression of sexual acting-out as retaliation against a mother who deprecates the absent father. Alternately, delinquency among girls whose fathers are present in the home may sometimes be explained in terms of the father's concern and fear regarding his adolescent daughter's sexuality and her subsequent rebellion in the face of his overly strict control.

Sex It has already been mentioned that there have traditionally been more male than female delinquents. This observation is most often explained in terms of the male's greater aggressiveness and lesser acquiescence. Patterns of delinquency are, in fact, markedly different for boys and girls. Delinquency among males typically takes some aggressive form (breaking and entering, theft, vandalism, and so on). The majority of female delinquents are apprehended for engaging in sexually promiscuous behavior or in such nonaggressive activities as shoplifting. It should be noted that male adolescents are not arrested or classified as delinquent for sexual behaviors of the kind that mark girls as delinquent.

Donalda *Age 14* **On Home**

Me: *Why did you do the B and E?*
Donalda: *Well I was on the run and we needed supplies and stuff.*
Me: *You were on the run. Had you run away from home?*
Donalda: *Yeah.*
Me: *Where were you going?*
Donalda: *Nowhere really.*
Me: *Can you tell me why you ran away from home.*
Donalda: *Things weren't going good at home.*

Me: *Was it mostly your parents? Or your brothers and sisters . . .*
Donalda: *Well, I'm always left out. If there's something that comes up and stuff; it's always the other kids.*

300

In interpreting research concerning factors related to delinquency, it is important to keep in mind that these factors have not been shown to be causally related; also, very seldom will there be only one clearly identifiable factor in each individual case. There is, in fact, a complex of related social and psychological forces that impinge on the potential delinquent. Frequently, lower social class, broken homes, and delinquent peer models are all closely associated. It is unlikely that delinquency will ever be clearly understood within the context of research that pays attention only to isolated factors.

Types of Delinquents

A considerable portion of the research on juvenile delinquency has made no distinction between various types of delinquents, most often simply classifying adolescents as delinquent or nondelinquent. Obviously, however, there are major qualitative differences among individuals classed as delinquents. Elkind (1967), who strongly maintains that delinquency is not solely a lower-class phenomenon, attributes delinquency, particularly among middle-class adolescents, to the child's reaction to "parental exploitation." This exploitation is assumed to take various forms, the most notable of which include the parents' attempts to bolster their own egos frequently by demanding and expecting outstanding achievement from their children; parental use of children as a form of "slave labor"; and the use of children's transgressions as an opportunity for parents to proclaim their "moral rectitude."

Elkind identifies three groups of delinquents. Among the smallest group numerically are those who suffer from various emotional disturbances most often manifested in incomplete and inadequate socialization. A larger group includes those individuals who engage in delinquent behavior and are apprehended only once. Among these would be included those guilty of participating in unlawful pranks who are basically nondelinquent and who will not likely repeat the offence.

The third group consists of hard-core repeated offenders. These, Elkind maintains, are almost always in open conflict with their parents who have violated the implicit social contract that governs parent-child relationships. This contract states, in effect, that the parent will look after the child's emotional and physical needs. In return, the child is expected to abide by the norms

Darcy *Age 14* **On Running Away**

Me: *Do you care that you're in here? Does it make you angry, or sad, or sorry?*
Darcy: *No. Like from here, you can run anytime if you don't like it.*
Me: *But you know that you'll likely get caught and brought back.*
Darcy: *Yeah.*
Me: *Have you run from here?*
Darcy: *From this unit? Three times.*
Me: *And you got caught?*

Darcy: *I got lost in the hospital. Like I went downtown for some tests and blood samples and stuff. And I went to the bathroom and used the other door to get out.*
Me: *And you got lost.*
Darcy: *Yeah, I got lost in the hospital and couldn't find a way out. I ran from there three times and the last time I went to the hospital they wouldn't let me go to the bathroom.*

of middle-class society. In most families the contract is broken only temporarily, though perhaps relatively frequently, particularly in adolescence. In the homes of juvenile delinquents, the contract is often broken for a prolonged period of time particularly with respect to providing for the child's emotional well-being.

Elkind draws a parallel between a work situation where the employer has broken a contract, and the home where parents have violated their social contract. Workers have a number of alternatives: they can quit, go on strike, sabotage the plant, or submit docilely to their employer's wishes. Similarly, children can leave home, can refuse to behave according to accepted family norms, can become delinquent, or can submit to parental wishes.

Jenkins and Boyer (1967) present alternative classifications of delinquents. There is, to begin with, "socialized cooperative delinquents." They are characterized by normal personalities and by strong allegiance to peer groups. In other terminology, socialized cooperative delinquents are the gang members. A second group includes "unsocialized runaway delinquents." Their personalities are the most poorly organized, this being reflected not only in their inability to get along with parents, but also in their inability to get along with peers.

A third group of delinquents are labeled the "unsocialized aggressive." These are delinquents whose personalities are better organized than those of the unsocialized runaway delinquent, but not as well integrated as those of the socialized cooperative delinquent. These are the "lone wolves" whose family relationships are characterized by combinations of overprotectiveness and rejection. They are frequently protected from outside authority but are seldom left with the feeling that they are a well-loved, integral member of the family.

The importance of these classifications is not that they provide an accurate description of delinquent adolescents. They might. But then there are other classifications possible as well and their value probably lies as much in the alterations they cause in the thinking of professionals and laypersons alike as in their validity and immediate practical usefulness. They serve to highlight what should have been obvious: namely, that it is misleading and inaccurate to label adolescents as delinquent or nondelinquent. Among allegedly delinquent adolescents there are a wide variety of adolescents whose moral development and whose adherence to morals in at least some ways resembles that of those adolescents who are fortunate enough to remain within the category of nondelinquents. It is unfortunate that treatments are often based on identifying labels rather than on the specific individual involved.

Summary

Sam opened this chapter with a rather horrifying description of the world's population growth coupled with increasingly drastic shortages of food, energy, and shelter. Is overpopulation less moral than birth control? From the introduction, the chapter moved to a discussion of morality and the theories that have been advanced to explain its development and its characteristics at different ages. Delinquency was discussed as an example of amorality. Care was taken to point out that statistics concerning juvenile delinquency tend to be misleading because of the arbitrariness not only of laws but also of their enforcement.

Main Points

1. According to Sam, all of the world's major problems can be reduced to a single problem — overpopulation.

2. Morality may be defined in terms of the qualities of good and evil that characterize human behavior. It is difficult to identify and perhaps even more difficult to measure.

3. Kohlberg speaks of three different aspects of morality: the ability to resist temptation; the amount of guilt that accompanies moral transgression; and the standards by which individuals judge right and wrong.

4. Values may be defined as beliefs concerning the relative worth of certain behaviors, or of certain abstractions (such as truth, goodness, honesty).

5. Morals are the standards by which behavior is judged to be good or evil.

6. Conscience refers to individuals' interpretations of their beliefs about right and wrong.

7. Freud defined conscience in terms of the superego—the embodiment of societal and religious constraints on behavior, acquired through a process of socialization.

8. Piaget investigated morality by reference to children's acquisition of an understanding of rules. He maintains that children progress from an initial premoral stage to a stage where morality is defined by outside authority (heteronomy). The final stage is one of moral autonomy where morality is defined in terms of the individual's personal estimate of right and wrong.

9. Among the most intensive and extensive investigations of morality are those conducted by Kohlberg. Most of his research has involved a single group of male subjects who are interviewed at various times between the ages of five and seventeen.

10. Kohlberg describes three progressive levels of moral development. The first is labeled premoral and is characterized by an authority-oriented definition of good and evil as well as by the belief that behaviors that lead to immediately pleasurable outcomes are good whereas those that lead to less pleasant outcomes are bad.

11. The second level of moral development is a period of conformity to family and peer standards, motivated in part by a desire to maintain good social relations.

12. At the highest level of moral development, children reexamine the rules that have previously governed their behavior and, theoretically, arrive at a set of self-accepted principles of moral conduct.

13. Delinquency, a rejection of conventional morality and an expression of immorality or amorality, is not solely an adolescent phenomenon. However, those behaviors that frequently lead to the label delinquent among children and adolescents sometimes lead to the label criminal among adults.

14. Delinquency is a legal rather than a social category. That is, it is defined not only in terms of laws (which are variable from country to country and even within countries) but also in terms of enforcement and recording practices. Officially, individuals are not delinquent until they have been apprehended by law enforcement officers and until their transgressions have been placed before the appropriate jurisdictional bodies.

15. The frequency of delinquency is difficult to assess. It is more common among boys than girls and among lower- than upper-class adolescents. This, however, may in part be a function of different law enforcement practices for middle-class adolescents whose parents frequently succeed in rescuing them before they are officially classified as delinquents.

16. Age, peer groups, sex, social class, and home characteristics appear to be related to the incidence of delinquency.

17. Various classifications of delinquents have been offered. Their major contribution is that they recognize qualitative differences among so-called delinquents. In short, they are an admission that some delinquents are more delinquent than others.

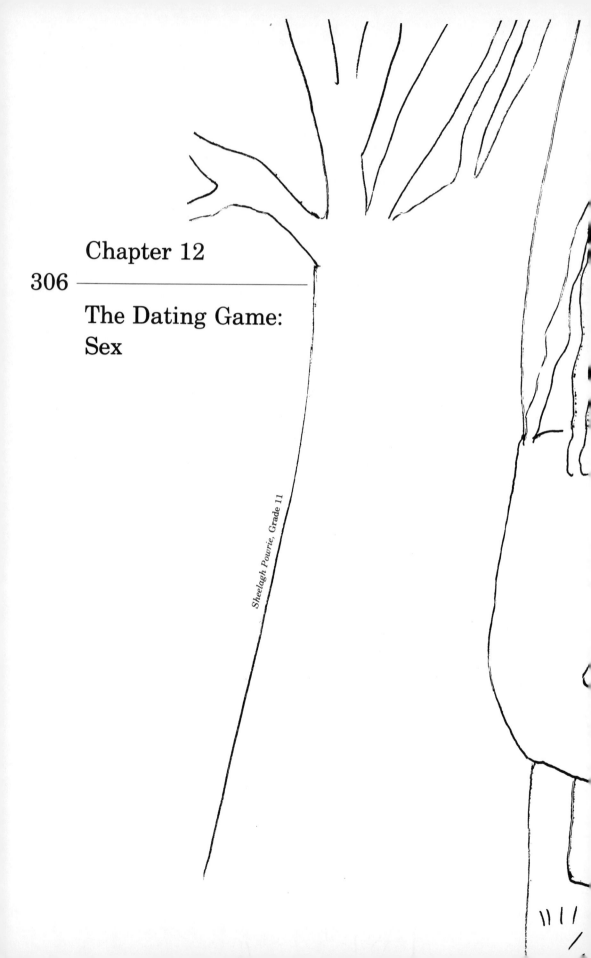

Chapter 12

The Dating Game:
Sex

Sheelagh Pourie, Grade 11

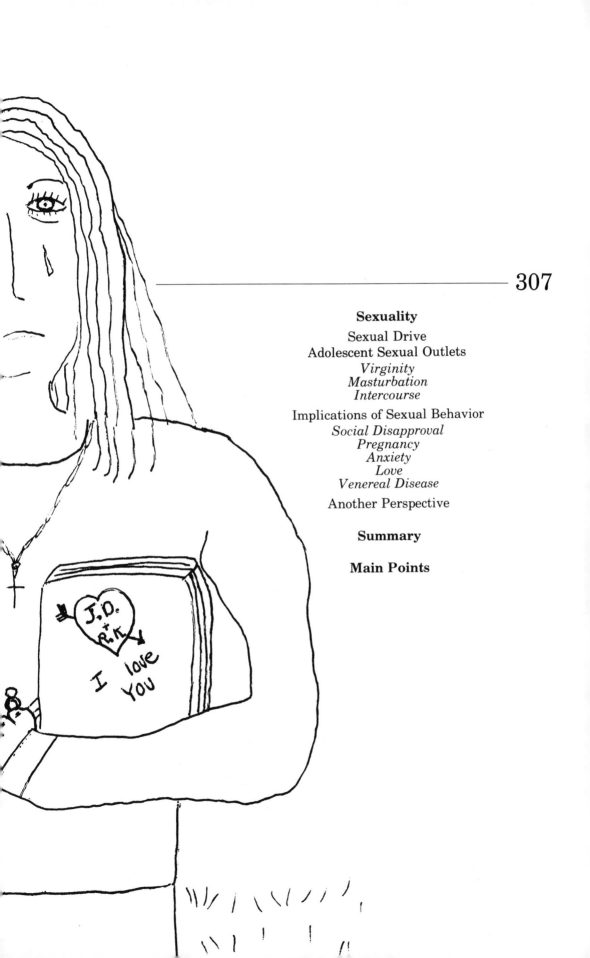

Sexuality

Sexual Drive
Adolescent Sexual Outlets
Virginity
Masturbation
Intercourse

Implications of Sexual Behavior
Social Disapproval
Pregnancy
Anxiety
Love
Venereal Disease

Another Perspective

Summary

Main Points

* [*F*]*oot in my oral aperture. Again.*

I knew I was blushing. I was always blushing in those days. In fact I spent most of the school day sitting at my desk blushing — and with my legs crossed, knowing that even then everybody must have been aware of my perpetual condition, a condition of which I myself was most painfully aware.

I had a bad case of acne as well. I once counted seventy-eight pimples between my jawline and an imaginary line from the tops of my ears through my eyebrows. There was little recognition for those sorts of records.

I was sixteen years old that summer. Probably the only sixteen-year-old virgin in town. And it wasn't because I didn't know the rules. Of course there were girls who would do IT. At least that's what the rumor said. But these girls always went out with guys from the college. It had got to the point where most of the girls in twelfth grade wouldn't go out with guys unless they were already in college. In any case there were different rules for those sorts of girls, and I didn't know them as well as I knew the rules for the younger girls that we used to go to dances with. It was terribly important for a guy to know these rules well. I did.

If you were sitting beside a girl, like in a car, with a lot of other people around, you could maybe hold her hand. Certainly, it was expected that you would try to hold her hand, but it wasn't always certain that she would let you. If she did, you would squeeze it, and rub it, until both your hands got all sweaty and sticky. You always held the girl's hand while sitting next to her, talking with other people or laughing at what they said. If you turned toward her and tried to look into her eyes in one of those personal, meaningful ways, she would most likely take her hand away to fix her hair, and then she would lay it down where it would be difficult to get at in an unobtrusive way. One always had to be very unobtrusive.

If you were alone with a girl — say your own date for one of the big dances where people were expected to bring their own date, you could go a little further. It always started out with kissing on the lips with both the guy and the girl holding their hands very still on the other person's back. If you moved your hands around too much initially, the girl would usually find something terribly important to talk about, making it awkward to kiss.

It was sort of accepted that you didn't try to kiss a girl until she had closed

---

* Taken from the thirteenth chapter of Sam's unpublished autobiography. Used with his permission.

her mouth in between sentences, and had kept it closed for a decent period of time.

It usually took three or four dates before you could progress to "French" kissing. This was always a big step because it meant that if a guy persisted through several more dates, he might get even further! And if he didn't, he could always tell the guys that he had spent hours French kissing. It was important for a guy's status, and for his self-image. I'm not sure how important it was for the girl.

Ah, it was torture working through all the steps, but it was exciting. From French kissing, a guy usually went to the "quick feel." Now the quick feel takes both dexterity and a considerable amount of acting skill. Essentially it involves a brushing movement with the inside of the wrist or the outside of the hand over the girl's fully clothed breast. The best time to try this move for the first time was when the girl had heavy clothing on including, if possible, a winter overcoat. The movement had to be both fleeting and rather nonchalant, as if it were only half intended, but the girl had to be sufficiently aware of it that she would immediately interrupt the French kissing that would be going on at the same time. Only a very foolhardy individual would attempt the quick feel for the first time while not in the actual process of heated French kissing.

According to the rules, the girl would draw back at this point and begin to talk animatedly about something, but never about the present situation. If she did, it was a sure sign that she was offended, that the move had been premature, and that several dates would now be required before regaining all the ground that had been lost through this hasty and ill-advised move. If things went well, however, it might sometimes be possible to engage in one or more additional quick feels before the evening was through.

It was always important to keep in mind that on subsequent dates one could never begin exactly where one had left off. True, the entire sequence was shortened considerably in terms of time, but not in terms of moves. It was always necessary to begin with ordinary kissing with the hands held quite stationary, progress to slight movements of the hands on the back, finally an interlude of French kissing, culminating in the inevitable quick feel.

At this point, the boy had to be a good judge of female reactions in order to determine the risk involved in modifying the quick feel to a "slow feel." There were several ways of effecting this move, depending on the boy's courage and the girl's reaction. One of the braver moves was to alter the position of the hand slightly so that the feel occurred not on the wrist or on the back of the hand, but

310

on the palm of the hand. In this case the movement would have to be as rapid and unobtrusive as it had always been. Alternatively, the movement could be slowed down considerably and made more deliberate if the boy continued to use the wrist or the back of the hand. The ultimate objective, of course, was to arrive at a slow feel with the palm of the hand. On top of the overcoat to be sure. And then you could go back to the boys and proudly claim, "I felt her up all night." Only in our most private dreams did we dare imagine "going all the way." There were still a long, but exciting, number of steps before one could reach that great moment. Few ever did.

Several pages from Sam's autobiography have been deleted here. They are rather irrelevant, and, I'm sure, of little interest to you. In them Sam describes in graphic detail the remaining rules. Finally he returns to a consideration of his present "foot in my **oral aperture**" situation.

I had been going out with Jennie Roberts as often as I could all that spring, and had finally worked my way into a relatively reliable mixture of the quick and slow feel—a sort of in-between feel sometimes lasting four or five seconds using the flat of my palm. I had not yet attempted to close my hand on her overcoat.

That night my condition was worse than it had ever been. I had been refraining from you-know-what because of the possibility that it was affecting me. Jennie and I were sitting in the front seat of my dad's old Chev. We had gotten through the straight kissing, the French kissing, and one or two quick feels. Then I lost control. I swear I don't know what came over me. I just reached inside that heavy green tweed overcoat and closed my hand on that tiny forbidden breast. And its owner screamed, "I'm not that kind of girl, Sam Bellott. You'd better find yourself somebody else," and ran out of the car, back into the dance hall.

I stood around with the guys in the stag line for a while. They kept ribbing me about not dancing with Jennie. I said I had a sore foot, although my foot wasn't nearly as sore as some of the rest of me. Finally, I gathered my failing courage and went up to her. I figured I hadn't violated the rules so badly that she wouldn't dance with me. Surely I, Sam Bellott, despite the fact that I had a bad case of acne, was a pretty desirable sort of fellow to go around with since I had quit spending all my time with the rats in the laboratory at school.

---

* Sam has since returned to his rats.

"Dance?" I croaked. My voice always broke at the most awkward moments.
"No thank you, Mr. Bellott." The answer was quite definite. It left little room for argument.

I don't think you can imagine the agony that I lived through as I walked thirty or so feet to the outside door, and on to the car, down the road to the bluff overlooking the ravine where Old Man Watts had jumped to meet his Maker. We called it Lovers' Point.

I stood there, unloved on Lovers' Point, thinking most seriously about jumping, wondering whether my Maker would rise to meet me before I reached the bottom. I figured that's the least He could do after what had happened to me that night.

But I didn't have enough confidence in Him. I was scared. Too scared.
Besides, after Jennie, there was Kris. And then Vicki.
Now Vicki, that's another story altogether. Let me tell you about Vicki . . .

Because it is unlikely that you would be interested in the remainder of this section of Sam's autobiography it is not included. The short section included here is presented for several reasons. It is, to begin with, a poignant introduction to a subject of deep concern to most adolescents. At the same time it is a relatively accurate portrayal of the way things were at some time, in some places, for some people. You are the only judge of how accurately it reflects the way things were in your time for you.

Sexuality

Most adolescents become more or less passionately interested in sex after the developmental period that Freud labeled latent. Sex, as it is discussed in esoteric academic writings, is three things. It is, to begin with, simply a category, often dichotomous, into which most living plants and animals conveniently fall. There is on the one hand, the female; on the other, the male. And, at least in the case of humans, obvious biological differences make the categorization relatively easy.

Sex is also a psychoanalytic term that, in Freud's writings, refers to such diverse activities as thumbsucking, smoking, masturbation, fantasies, re-

pressions, fixations, regressions, and, indeed, to all of life. For Freud, sexual urges were the basic explanatory concepts for all of behavior.

In addition to being a category and a psychoanalytic term, sex also denotes a specific activity involving physical union usually between a mature male and female, but also sometimes among males, among females, or among combinations of these. Its essential biological function is procreation, especially when two different sexes are involved; but, largely because of the pleasures often associated with it, it serves important motivational and reinforcing functions as well.

Sexual Drive

The sexual drive in humans is related to hormonal changes that occur in early adolescence. These were discussed in Chapter 2. Among the psychological effects of these hormonal changes is the urge to achieve sexual release — an urge that seemingly becomes more forceful throughout the adolescent years.

Considerable ink has been devoted to the differences between male and female sex drives. It was long believed that males are more easily aroused than are females, and that they therefore spend a greater amount of time in states of actual or incipient sexual arousal. In fact, however, there is little evidence to support this. Fundamental biological differences between males and females, particularly with respect to hormones, cannot easily be linked to measures of sexual arousal or sexual drive; these variables are confounded by social and cultural factors. Traditional, stereotyped views have tended to dismiss the existence of the sexual drive in females or to underestimate its strength and its importance. It was long thought, for example, that women did not, should not, and indeed could not enjoy sex — that **orgasm** was an experience reserved for men alone. In these stereotypes the male was always viewed as the aggressor; the female was viewed as passive, reluctantly acquiescent, and motivated by duty but never by desire.

The twentieth century has, to some extent, succeeded in liberating woman from her Victorian shackles, although the liberation is still far from complete. Research on the physiology and psychology of sex (Kinsey *et al.*, 1953; and Masters and Johnson, 1966, for example) has shown conclusively that the orgasm is not solely a male prerogative — a fact that many grandmothers had secretly known for some time.

The sexual revolution of this age is reflected not only in attitude changes concerning accepted sexual roles, but also in the behavior of adolescents and adults. It is apparent that contemporary sexual behavior is less subject to the conventional moral and social constraints of a few generations ago (Smigel and Seiden, 1968). And, as shown in subsequent sections of this chapter, available evidence tends to corroborate this view. Among the significant factors in the sexual revolution is The Pill. Fear of pregnancy is no longer a common deterrent to premarital sexual intercourse; for the sexually oriented, this age has almost become a paradise. In other ways, it is still something less than a paradise.

Although it is now known that women are capable of enjoying orgasm and that they are motivated by sexual drives, it is still not certain that these drives are as strong and as immediately insistent as they are in men. Ehrmann (1959) believes that man is erotic; woman, romantic. Sexual arousal may be brought about in a male by any of a variety of specific stimuli that have direct or indirect sexual connotations. The sight of a nude female or portions thereof, the often innocent but titillating movements and gestures of a naive adolescent girl, photographs, illustrations, and a host of situations and events can all serve to bring about rapid sexual arousal in the male. The female, on the other hand, is less often aroused by looking at nude males, or by a variety of other stimuli that may have direct sexual connotations. Words, music, expressions of affection and love are more likely to arouse her. It should be noted, however, that although the female responds sexually to fewer stimuli, and is frequently slower to become aroused, there is no real evidence that her arousal is any less intense, though it may be considerably more generalized. Nor is there any evidence that the orgasm enjoyed by women is any less intense or any less pleasurable than that enjoyed by men. Recent writings suggest that it may, in fact, be more intense. Furthermore, women are capable of considerably more orgasms in a given period of time than are men. The sexual revolution is perhaps merely at its beginning.

Adolescent Sexual Outlets

Contemporary Western social mores dictate that sexual intercourse is not acceptable outside of marriage. Although a significant number of individuals within these societies openly violate these mores, it remains true that society

Tracy *Age 17* **On Virginity**

Tracy has expressed a rather strong conviction that girls should be virgins when they marry, and that it is not "ok" for boys to "fool around" any more than it is for girls to do so. Like many others, she rejects the double standard; but unlike many, she doesn't say, "What's good for you is good for me." Instead, she seems to be saying, "What's good for me should be good for you." And there is a difference between the two. I have just asked her whether she does, in fact, mean that boys should be virgins when they marry.	**Tracy:** *Well. Hum ... Now it's coming back on me. Maybe not virgins. Well, like you can take two points of view. One's the physical part of it. If you really love somebody, it shouldn't matter. That's one part of it. And another part of it ... boys seem to have a type of thing where they brag to each other on how far they got with each individual person and how many ... well what they call a "score." And I don't know ... I think in a way they're people.*

314

does not ordinarily provide adolescents with opportunities to openly and unashamedly express their sexuality. And although the guilt that adolescents feel after engaging in sexual intercourse may be minimal or even nonexistent, they must still pursue their activities in relative secrecy. What, in fact, do adolescents do?

Virginity A number of adolescents do very little; they remain virgins until they marry. Some may remain virgins for even longer than that. Contrary to popular belief, **virginity** is not solely characteristic of girls. A large-scale study (*Involvement in Developmental Psychology,* 1971) recently found that 20 percent of the males in a college sample had not engaged in premarital sexual intercourse. Surprisingly, the same study found that only 22 percent of the females had not engaged in premarital sexual intercourse. These, however, were primarily college students.* Percentages of virgins tend to be considerably higher among high school students. Until the 1960s, it was commonly accepted that approximately 75 percent of all girls remained virgins until marriage (Bell, 1966). Subsequent studies (Reiss, 1966; Kaats and Davis, 1970) found that with the advent of The Pill, this percentage dropped significantly in the 1960s to between 45 and 60 percent.

Masturbation The most common sexual outlet for both males and females is self-stimulation of the genitals, a practice that is nearly universal among adolescent boys, though less frequent among girls. Virtually all males have reached orgasm prior to marriage, the majority through masturbation (Kinsey *et al.,* 1948, 1953). Although Kinsey found that only 30 percent of the females in his samples had reached orgasm, it is possible that a larger percentage than this had masturbated. Gagnon and Simon (1969) report that 95 percent of college men have masturbated compared with approximately 66 percent of college women.

It was long thought that masturbation could lead to mental deficiencies, acne, and various debilitating illnesses. Masters and Johnson (1966) report that even some doctors ask them whether it has deleterious medical effects.

---

* As was noted in Chapter 1, this study suffered from at least two limitations. Not only were the subjects restricted to those who subscribed to the magazine *Psychology Today,* but they were further limited to those who *chose* to return the questionnaire. The problem of having to rely on the honesty of the participants is a further limitation of most similar studies.

Boys have exactly the same emotions as girls, except they're physically different. They should have some kind of bad feelings about it too. When they lose their virginity, there has to be some type of emotion attached to it. It's not just "hurrah," you know. Cause . . . I don't know how boys feel about it.

There is no evidence whatsoever that masturbation, as it is ordinarily practiced, has any detrimental effects on health. Its most pronounced negative effect is related solely to the anxiety and guilt that adolescents might feel as a consequence. The anxiety, unfortunately, is often due to adolescent fears that masturbation might have undesirable consequences. Shipman (1968) reports that 20 percent of all boys are frightened on the occasion of their first ejaculation—an event that occurs slightly more often through masturbation than through a nocturnal emission (commonly called a wet dream). Of all the boys in his sample, including those who were indifferent or pleased at the event, only 6 percent felt that they had been adequately prepared. An amazing 90 percent claimed that they had received no prior information about the event from their parents; and many attempted to hide soiled sheets and clothing so that they would not be discovered.

Despite this, masturbation is extremely common among adolescent boys, reaching its peak between the ages of sixteen and seventeen; and it occasionally occurs in groups. During this period boys average 3.4 orgasms per week primarily through masturbation (Kinsey *et al.*, 1953). As was mentioned earlier, masturbation is less frequent among girls. Nor is the female sexual peak, defined in terms of orgasms, reached in adolescence as it is for males. Evidence suggests that it occurs between the ages of thirty-five and forty when women average 1.8 orgasms per week (Kinsey *et al.*, 1953). Kinsey reports that 10 percent of all women never reach orgasm. The CRM study (*Involvement in Developmental Psychology*, 1971) corroborated these findings. Among their sample, 20 percent of all women never or rarely reached orgasm.

Intercourse Another sexual outlet for adolescents is, of course, sexual intercourse. This is an activity not entirely sanctioned by society prior to marriage, but one that is not treated as harshly now as was once the case. The CRM study (*Involvement in Developmental Psychology*, 1971) reports that 80 percent of all college men have engaged in sexual intercourse at least once; 78 percent of all college women have done likewise. Other interesting findings from this survey were that women tended to have significantly fewer one night affairs, that their first sexual experience was most often with a steady boyfriend rather than with a casual acquaintance, and that it never occurred with a prostitute. Almost as many women engaged in extramarital sex as did men—36 percent compared with 40 percent. It does appear, however, that

Dan *Age 14* **On Sexual Permissiveness**

Me: . . . *but getting back to what you said about girls being more promiscuous — being easier. Is this true?*
Dan: *Yeah. Like I know a lot of girls that, like, instead of guys picking up girls, girls picking up guys.*
Me: *How common is it for a girl to be a virgin . . .*
Dan: *You may think like I'm bragging but I don't think I know one girl that is.*
Me: *At what age do you think they stop being virgins?*
Dan: *After about thirteen.*

316

---

sexual relations are not as casual and matter-of-fact among women as they are among men. Women are more likely to engage in sexual activities with men for whom they have considerable affection. Consequently they tend to have fewer partners over a given period of time. However, given the rapidly changing nature of contemporary sexual beliefs and behavior, it is hazardous in the extreme to make statements such as these expecting that they will continue to be true. They well might not.

Smigel and Seiden (1968) compared reported sexual behavior of the 1920s with that reported at various times between 1920 and 1960. They found that there had, in fact, been a sexual revolution in the direction of greater permissiveness; however, this revolution, particularly in recent years, is not nearly as dramatic as that which has apparently taken place with respect to the "double standard." In essence, this double standard maintained that while it was permissible for men to engage in premarital sexual intercourse, it was not equally permissible for women to do so. Following analyses of a wide variety of data collected from different samples concerning attitudes toward the acceptability of sexual intercourse for men and for women, the authors concluded that there is a trend toward "a single standard of permissiveness with affection." In other words, contemporary adolescents are more likely than their parents to view premarital sexual relations as being acceptable for *both* men and women providing there is affection between them.

Similar findings are reported by Collins (1974) for a group of Australian adolescents who were asked to report on their typical behavior when on their first date, on subsequent dates, when going steady, and when engaged to be married. Several of their findings are particularly noteworthy. First, as expected, there is a sharp increase in intimacy, both for boys and for girls, with increasing seriousness of the relationship. Thus, while **kissing** is expected and frequently engaged in on the first or second date, heavy petting and intercourse are seldom engaged in until the couple is going steady or engaged. Considerably more boys than girls report having engaged in sexual intercourse during the first date (10 percent compared with 1.9 percent).

A second finding of considerable importance is that both boys and girls expect their peers to engage in more intimate behaviors than they actually do. For example, girls expect 66 percent of their peers to have sexual intercourse when going steady. Actual reported percentage for this category is 28. Similarly, boys expect 90.9 percent of their peers to engage in sexual intercourse

when engaged to be married; actual reported percentage is 44.5. The significance of this observed difference between actual behavior and expected behavior is that adolescents may, as a result, feel considerable pressure to conform to what they think peer norms are. The result may be a degree of intimacy not really desired by the adolescents and not justified by the affection involved. Such forced intimacy, to the extent that it does exist, may partly justify the bleak picture of matter-of-fact, uninvolved sex described by Cobliner (1974) in his examination of **pregnancy** among unmarried adolescent girls. As Cobliner describes it, intercourse is frequently viewed by these girls as the price they must pay for a boy's company. Many of these girls, who later became **pregnant,** believed that all their friends were behaving in a similar manner, and that if they refused to engage in sexual intimacies, they would not be sought out by boys.

There is obviously a contradiction between the "permissiveness with affection" standard described by Smigel and Seiden, and the indiscriminate, matter-of-fact peer standards described by Cobliner. It should be noted, however, that most of the pregnant adolescent girls interviewed by Cobliner were from subsistence homes. Available research indicates that patterns of sexual behavior and attitudes among adolescents living in poverty are typically quite different from those characteristic of America's middle class youth. Rosenberg and Bensman (1968) interviewed white Appalachians in Chicago; blacks in Washington, D.C.; and Puerto Ricans in New York. They comment (p. 73):

> For these submerged peoples, our dominant sexual ideologies have little relevance. Neither emotional and material responsibilities, nor their opposite, pure joy in unrestrained sexuality, is much in evidence. Sexual fulfillment is experienced merely as a physical release — "the friction of two membranes" — in which the female is the necessary but unequal partner. Otherwise, sexual conquest provides a trophy calculated to enhance one's prestige in peer-group competition.

Clearly not all adolescents who are members of ethnic minority groups or of poverty groups behave and believe as would be implied by this description; nor have all middle-class adolescents adopted "permissiveness with affection" standards. But perhaps this contrast serves to provide useful insights into possible class differences in sexual behavior; it may also serve to point out the

318 ──

difficulties inherent in attempting to make valid general statements concerning the "typical" adolescent's sexual attitudes and practices.

Implications of Sexual Behavior

Sexual behavior and abstinence from sexual activity both have tremendous implications for understanding adolescents. During this period of transition between childhood and adulthood, among the most significant changes that occur in their lives are those that relate to their sexual desires and abilities. Social structure and accepted mores make it difficult for adolescents to attend to these desires as openly or as frequently as they might wish. The consequences of their sexual unemployment or of their surreptitious sexual employment can take a wide variety of forms, some of which are discussed below.

Social Disapproval Most adolescents who engage in heterosexual activities prior to marriage are subjected to explicit or implicit social disapproval. The extent to which this disapproval will affect adolescents' adjustment and emotional well-being depends largely on their estimate of the worth of social approval. The situation is one that can give rise to considerable cognitive dissonance (see Chapter 7) arising from a variety of sources. If adolescents refrain from sexual activity, there may be conflict between desires and actions, and a consequent frustration that can be more or less severe. If they do engage in sexual activity, dissonance may arise from the conflict between behavior and the ideals that they set for themselves in terms of explicit or implicit expectations of society. The severity of the conflict may, in this case, be related to the particular social milieu in which they find themselves, to their relationships with parents, and perhaps to religious training as well.

Another source of dissonance concerns conflict between peer expectations and pressures and individual behavior. The eighteen-year-old boy who has not yet had sexual intercourse may find himself having to lie to his friends in order to maintain his image of manliness. Among males variety and frequency of sexual exploits have long been reinforced. This has been less common among girls, although with the advent of Liberated Women, the situation may be changing.

It should not be inferred from the preceding passages that all adolescents more or less urgently desire sexual relations with the opposite sex. A number desire relations with individuals of the same sex; still others wait quite happily, and probably with considerably less frustration than might generally be assumed, for marriage.

Pregnancy A second consequence of sexual relations may be pregnancy, a condition that affects both males and females though in quite different ways. There are no accurate figures concerning the number of adolescent girls who become pregnant because many have abortions, many get married, and still others simply have a child out of wedlock. It is probable that with the advent of The Pill, there are considerably fewer pregnant adolescents than might otherwise be the case. There are certainly fewer pregnant adults. Nevertheless, Howard (1968–69) reports that in 1966 there were seventy-two thousand unwed mothers under the age of eighteen in the United States; and, that number was increasing by approximately four thousand per year. Population growth probably accounts for most of the increase.

Approximately 50 percent of all high school marriages are due to fear of pregnancy (Burchinal, 1959; Vincent, 1966). Indeed, of all new brides, some 20 percent are pregnant when they marry. More recent studies do not show any appreciable decline in these figures, despite the wide availability of contraceptive information and material. Howard (1971) found, for example, that among very early marriages, between 50 and 85 percent of the brides were pregnant. One of the unfortunate aspects of this resolution of pregnancy is that the divorce rate for teen-age marriages is three to four times greater than that of the general population (Landis and Landis, 1963). When one considers that among the general population one in three marriages results in separation or divorce, this figure becomes rather alarming. But then other resolutions of pregnancy also have unfortunate aspects. In retrospect, prevention frequently seems considerably wiser.

Numerous theories have been advanced to explain why it is that adolescent girls become pregnant out of wedlock, but none do so adequately. The most popular Freudian explanations were based on the notion that the girl is unconsciously punishing her mother or her father. Research indicates, however, that pregnancy results not only from carelessness, unwillingness or inability to overcome the passion of the moment, or a nonchalant willingness to accept

Tracy *Age 18* **On Premarital Pregnancy**

Me: *Why do these girls get pregnant?*
Tracy: *Well it's purely biological you know. (laughter) No, I guess she never took the necessary precautions.*
Me: *But since they are available, why does a girl not take them?*
Tracy: *I think girls have the feeling that "I won't get pregnant." It's a kind of a mental set thing, "Well, I'm doing it, but I won't get pregnant."*
Me: *Precisely. The "risk-takers."*

Tracy: *Yeah, but, like that's an awful big risk to take. Like I'm to go to the university. I want to. I'll be the first in my family to go cause my parents don't come from a very rich background. Even if I never get a job, if I can just get a degree.*

320

the risks involved, but that ignorance is frequently a factor. This is apparently more often the case among lower-class adolescents who are sometimes abysmally ignorant of the most primitive of birth control methods.

Cobliner (1974) interviewed a large number of pregnant adolescent girls in an effort to discover why they had become pregnant. Most of these girls were from subsistence homes, a fact that does not detract from the usefulness of the research because the proportion of unwanted pregnancies among unmarried adolescent girls is considerable greater in poverty groups than it is among the more affluent middle class.

Cobliner found that relatively few of the pregnancies were intended (27 percent). Of these, the majority were designed either to force a marriage or to get even with a parent. Most of these girls had become pregnant accidentally, largely as a function of a willingness to take risks (43 percent). A common statement was "I didn't think it would happen to me." Of the remainder, some 10 percent had practiced birth control unsuccessfully; 17 percent had attempted to obtain birth control devices; and the remainder had been victims of misinformation, sometimes given by peers, and in several cases, given by professionals. One girl had been told by a doctor, for example, that because there had been no visible sign of menstruation, she was not ovulating and therefore could not get pregnant. Others believed that if they had intercourse infrequently or if they did not experience an orgasm, pregnancy would not result. Perhaps sex education, as it becomes more widely accepted and practiced, may serve to partially alleviate this problem.

Anxiety Still another possible outcome of sexual behavior is anxiety. The point was made earlier that a significant percentage of boys suffer anxiety as a result of their first ejaculation. Similarly, a great many suffer anxiety because of masturbation. Fewer girls are subjected to the same feelings concerning masturbation, probably because the practice is less common and less frequent among girls. However, some of them—approximately 10 percent—report experiencing considerable anxiety at the time of menarche (Shipman, 1968).

Shipman (1968) also reports that anxiety frequently follows heavy petting, particularly among boys who cite pains in their testicles for which they have no explanation. Forty-four percent of the boys in the sample and 38 percent of the girls admitted anxiety following petting. It is likely that the percentage experiencing anxiety after sexual intercourse, particularly if it has not become common practice for them, is considerably higher. Here anxiety might be related to fear of pregnancy, to social or religious values that have been contravened, to fear of disclosure, or to any of the various conflicts that might be engendered.

Love Still another consequence of adolescent sexual behavior may be infatuation or love, terms that are difficult to define in any precise manner. Most adolescents are "in love" a number of times, beginning with the secret infatuations of early adolescence, progressing through a series of "steady" relationships, finally culminating in the one "true love," marriage, and everlasting happiness. That is the great American fairy tale. True, a large number of individuals do progress through a succession of "loves" similar to that described above, marry, and live together until one or both die. Their happiness, relative to that of those who undergo different progressions, cannot really be established. Many others marry, unmarry, marry again, and so on. Indeed, in a number of American states, the divorce rate has almost caught up with the marriage rate, a fact that is due both to an increase in the number of divorces and to a relative decline in number of marriages. Other life-styles, including communal living, common-law marriages, trial marriages, contract marriages, temporary **shack-ups,** permanent shack-ups, and celibacy, present themselves as plausible alternatives.

The heterosexual relationships that develop during adolescence are of considerable importance to the teen-ager's emotional growth. As was noted earlier, these may serve as prototypes of future adult relationships. In addition, they go a long way toward establishing adolescent identity, confidence in social interaction, and ability to relate emotionally in relatively adult fashion. Sam has frequently observed, however, that adult emotional interaction is often reminiscent of adolescent interaction.

Venereal Disease The sexual behavior of adolescents can also have undesirable consequences in the form of one of a variety of venereal diseases — sometimes euphemistically called social diseases.

Venereal diseases (V.D.) are almost always transmitted through sexual intercourse. However, it should be stressed that venereal diseases are not always contracted following exposure; one of the simplest and most effective ways of ensuring that they are not is simple cleanliness. Washing the genitals thoroughly with soap and warm water following intercourse is said to be 80 to 90 percent effective in preventing gonorrhea in the uninfected partner. It was long believed, and probably rightfully so, that carriers of V.D. were seldom "good" girls, and that if men stayed away from prostitutes, they were relatively safe. Unfortunately, V.D. has become a common disease, equally rampant in the middle class as it is in lower classes.

The most common venereal disease is **gonorrhea;** the most dangerous, **syphilis.** Prior to the discovery of the effectiveness of penicillin for combatting V.D., thousands of people were ravaged by these diseases and many died. With the increasingly common use of penicillin in the 1940s, the incidence of V.D. was reduced to 3.8 cases per 100,000 in the United States (Breen, 1967). However, with increasing sexual permissiveness in the 1960s, the incidence of V.D. among adolescents had increased by 225 percent up till 1969; and the percentage continues to increase yearly. Breen (1967) reports, for example, that among a large sample of fifteen- to twenty-four-year-olds in New Jersey, a frightening 41 percent had venereal disease. Newspaper reports now indicate that following the return of American soldiers from Vietnam, venereal disease – particularly gonorrhea – has assumed epidemic proportions in many large cities rivalling the common cold as the most widespread infection in the United States. Yet it is a fact that if it were possible to control either of these diseases through the use of penicillin or of some yet undiscovered vaccine, it could be wiped out completely in two generations.

Gonorrhea, the most common venereal disease, is almost always transmitted through sexual intercourse. The gonococcus bacteria thrives in warm, moist areas of the body, but dies quickly when exposed to the outside air. Thus infections are commonly located in the urethral tract, the vagina, the anal tract, and sometimes the mouth (buccal gonorrhea). Its incubation period is ordinarily from two to four days. Initial symptoms are readily apparent in the male; these include a discharge from the penis and pain during urination. Verifying that the disease is present requires a simple laboratory examination of the discharge. Treatment involves the administration of large doses of penicillin or related drugs. Usually a single dose of penicillin is sufficient to completely kill the organism, so that cure is effected within a day or two.

Symptoms in the female are more subtle and often go unnoticed until the girl in question is informed by her boyfriend or by a public health agency

that she has been in contact with a carrier. If undetected in its early stages, later symptoms include vaginal discharge, pain when urinating, and stomach cramps. Treatment is the same as it is for males. Unfortunately, however, because the girl is frequently unaware that she has gonorrhea until some time has elapsed, there is always a very real possibility that she will pass it on to someone else, and that he will then pass it on again. Obviously the treatment is always some distance behind the spread of gonorrhea; otherwise it would, in fact, be eradicated.

Syphilis is, fortunately, less common than gonorrhea. Unlike gonorrhea, its symptoms often go undetected for a long period of time, because they are neither particularly obvious, nor painful in either the male or the female. An examination of a blood sample is ordinarily required to determine its presence (a Wassermann test, for example). Once it has been detected, it can be treated very effectively with penicillin and related drugs.

Initial symptoms of syphilis, which is also transmitted primarily through sexual intercourse, include the appearance of a painless **chancre** (sore, usually brown in color) on a sex organ. This chancre appears between ten and ninety days following exposure to the disease. After a short while it simply disappears and the individual, feeling no discomfort, assumes that it was nothing serious. Second-stage symptoms, which appear from one to six months later, might consist of one or more of the following: temporary spots of baldness, fevers, headaches, small sores in the moist areas of the body, loss of weight, and various aches and pains. At this stage the disease may be communicated through bodily contact other than sexual intercourse. Kissing or simply holding hands may be sufficient. If it remains untreated, second-stage symptoms of syphilis will eventually disappear—perhaps after a single year; perhaps after five. It now enters a latent or dormant stage that may last an indefinite number of years. In the end, however, it may reappear causing, among other things, mental deterioration, blindness, cardiovascular problems, and even death.

Routine medical practice has now made it unlikely that anyone will remain infected with syphilis long enough to suffer these dire consequences. Obtaining a marriage licence, for example, requires that the parties concerned undergo Wassermann tests, or other tests, to detect the possible presence of syphilis. Similarly, all individuals treated for gonorrhea are also checked for syphilis.

324

Another Perspective

It would be misleading to treat sex and its manifestations during adolescence only in a clinical and academic manner. Sex is much more than orgasms and their frequency, masturbation and its prevalence, virginity, intercourse, unwanted pregnancies, love, social disapproval, and the possibility of venereal disease. It is, in addition, one of the principal preoccupations of many individuals, an intensely unique and personal area, a source of incredible frustration for some, and a source of great joy for others.

Summary

This chapter began with a slightly risqué but generously edited extract from Sam's autobiography. It moved then, to sexuality, considering the importance of the adolescent's newfound sexual powers, possible sex differences in arousal and desire, and the frustrations occasionally experienced in attempting to deal with sexuality. Virginity, masturbation, and intercourse were examined, along with some of their possible implications.

Main Points

1. Sam blushed frequently when he was an adolescent, a phenomenon that has not entirely disappeared.

2. The sexual drive in humans is related to hormonal change.

3. There is evidence of an ongoing revolution in sexual behavior and beliefs, with a movement toward greater permissiveness and a lowering of the "double standard."

4. Sexual intercourse is less frequent among girls than boys prior to marriage, although it has increased in frequency since the 1960s. This is partly due to the advent of The Pill.

5. Masturbation is an almost universal practice among boys and a somewhat less frequent practice among girls. A number of misconceptions still exist concerning its possible effects. In fact, its only adverse consequences appear to be related to the anxiety and guilt that is sometimes associated with the act.

6. Open expression of sexual desires among adolescents is often met with considerable social disapproval.

7. A majority of all high school marriages appear to be related to the bride's pregnancy.

8. The divorce rate for teen-age marriages is approximately three times that of the general population.

9. Gonorrhea and syphilis are among the most common of the venereal diseases, with the former assuming near-epidemic proportions in some areas.

10. Gonorrhea is easily detected and cured in the male. It is less easily detected in the female, but equally easily cured.

11. Syphilis is less easily detected than gonorrhea, although it too can be cured relatively easily through penicillin and related drugs. If left untreated it can cause blindness, mental deterioration, cardiovascular problems, and eventually death.

Chapter 13

Peace? Love? Drugs

Francie Binder, Grade 11

328

*I saunter casually into the street. An observer. Inconspicuous; probing but nonchalant; every sense alert. I have come alone to sense and feel the Greenwich Villages, the Left Banks, the Haight-Ashburys, the Gastowns of the modern world laid before me on a single short street hemmed in by its boutiques and eateries. Obscure names vying with each other for the attention of the Street's children. Here and there in its recessed doorways, the debris of the Flower crop: children and adults; all adolescents; garbed in the violent colors of their passive rebellion. Beads and leather; shells from the seas and shiny studs from the factories. Smells of incense and marijuana mingling uncertainly with the scent of bodies washed and unwashed too.

An obtrusive pimple on the face of the establishment. And I, one of the establishment, my jeans too new; too crisp. My beads, my sandals, my shirt blatantly shouting to the world "Why Not?"; all out of synchrony with my head, for it cannot bring itself to say more than simply "Why?" Like a missionary, I have an overwhelming urge to tell them "Why Not?"

I move into a dappling sunlight. My head pointed securely at some vague and distant place beyond the end of the street. My feet move with my head as if it is there that I must go. But my eyes look around. The terror of the small deer that found itself surrounded by humans on the fifteenth fairway of the Spyglass Golf Course last week. Nowhere to run, for to run would be to betray fear.

And so I walk by the soft-eyed girl. Playing clumsily on her battered guitar. Her symbol of belonging. Her voice off-key; the melody lost painfully among sounds foreign to its nature. Unconsciously I finger my beads; my symbol of belonging. Too late I realize my fingers move in fashion identical to that of bereaved or frightened nuns and monks. "Peace," the girl smiles. "Love Jesus," she adds. Not imploring. Just telling.

A boy approaches me. I smile. Uncertainly perhaps, but smiling is the custom among our species. "A nickel bag?" he asks. "I need some bread, man," he explains. I know. But I had not foreseen. I hesitate, generations of "straights," of clear-conscienced, law-abiding impulses asserting themselves in the face of my momentary impulse. The boy's friend misreads my lack of immediate response. "Narc," he says simply. They leave.

The Street has seen me. I have been approached, tested. And I have failed.

---

* From Sam Bellott's unpublished autobiography. Used with permission.

Dan *Age 14* **On the Validity of Questionnaires**

Dan: *They lie because when they get this questionnaire in the mail, like have you ever done drugs? When was the last time you did drugs? For instance, the cops could have sent it out. Like you say a lot of the girls are supposed to be virgins. Like they won't admit that, a lot of them.*

329

Quickly I turn. Three steps and I am beyond the street. There is a park there. An empty park. A neutral zone. The grass is real and green. I move to the people beyond, for they too are real and green. I bump into a hurrying lady. Gently. "Watch where you're going," she snaps.

"Peace," I answer. And I throw a quiet "love" toward her disappearing back.

Drugs

Drugs are a fact of contemporary American life. Indeed the variety of drugs currently available for nonmedical use makes it likely that no society in history has ever been as drug oriented as this one: headache tablets, sleeping pills, coffee, cigarettes, alcohol, some twenty-five thousand varieties of amphetamines, marijuana, morphine and its derivatives, LSD, THC, STP, cocaine and mescaline, to name but a few of the more common. Some are more harmful than others; some are more socially accepted despite the fact that they are not necessarily the most harmless.

Adolescent Use

Humans have been familiar with drugs for centuries, despite the fact that they were not always aware of the chemical components of those substances that they chose to eat, smoke, drink, stuff in nostrils, chew or otherwise apply to their persons. Jalkanen (1973) reports, for example, that opium was known to the Sumerians in 5000 B.C. Cocaine, mescaline, and marijuana, in one form or another, were all discovered many centuries before they made an appearance on the American scene. In fact, the **chemical drugs** (uppers and downers, LSD, and so on) appear to be the only recently discovered drugs.

Historically, drug abuse has been a lower-class phenomenon, relegated largely to the ghettoes of major American centers. Originally most of the addicts in the United States were Oriental or Caucasian. This group gradually came to include an ever-increasing number of blacks and Puerto Ricans (Jalkanen, 1973). With the introduction of marijuana in the 1930s, the discovery of the hallucinogenic properties of LSD in 1943, and the rise of self-appointed missionaries of the drug cult, the affluent middle class entered the

Donalda *Age 14* **On Not Doing Drugs**

Me: *Are you into drugs at all?*
Donalda: *No.*
Me: *What are your feelings about drugs?*
Donalda: *I just don't want to touch the stuff cause I was told what would happen to your head if you did.*
Me: *Unh-unh.*
Donalda: *It would just blow your head and you'd be like a vegetable.*
Me: *I see. You've never done grass or anything like that or have you tried?*
Donalda: *I've tried.*

Me: *Have you tried other stuff, other than grass?*
Donalda: *No.*
Me: *Are there a lot of kids like you who don't do anything—any drugs?*
Donalda: *No.*
Me: *Is there a lot of pressure on you? Like when you're at parties or hanging around shopping centers.*
Donalda: *Yeah. Like they're always saying you're scared and it won't hurt you.*

330

drug scene en masse. Jalkanen (1973) estimates that some twenty-six million Americans use drugs inappropriately at the present time. The estimate may, in fact, be conservative for there is no way of reliably ascertaining the extent of drug use. Typically, estimates have been based on questionnaires given to selected groups. However, because admitting to the use of drugs is equal to an admission of a crime (or even of a felony in some states), it is probable that most investigations of drug use provide underestimates of actual usage. It is notable that Weil, Zinberg, and Nelson (1968) report extreme difficulty in locating "marijuana naive" students in Boston.

Most reported investigations of the extent of drug use in high schools and colleges do, however, provide more conservative estimates. Wozny (1971), in a large-scale investigation of personality variables associated with drug use, found that 21 percent of a freshman university sample had tried marijuana at least once; another 18 percent would try it "under the right circumstances"; 61 percent insisted that they would not try it under any circumstance. Goldstein (1966) reports that approximately 15 percent of all high school students will have tried marijuana prior to leaving school. A more recent survey reported in *Newsweek* (January 25, 1971, p. 52) indicated that 42 percent of a college sample had tried marijuana, 14 percent had tried LSD, and an impressive 75 percent had used alcohol in various forms—50 percent within the previous thirty days. All accounts indicate that drugs are not replacing alcohol but merely supplementing it.*

Reasons for Use

There are perhaps as many reasons for drug use as there are effects of drugs. Clearly, for example, amphetamines have an effect essentially opposite to that of grass or sedatives, and the reasons for taking either would necessarily be different once the user is familiar with these effects. Initial experimentation with drugs, however, does not presuppose any direct knowledge of their effects on the individual. Hence the motives for initial use are frequently quite

---

* An overwhelming majority of eleventh and twelfth grade adolescents that I interviewed claimed *not* to use drugs, although most had tried marijuana once or twice. Interestingly, many believe that the incidence of use is considerably higher than their combined self-reports would indicate. In contrast, almost all drank alcohol and went to bars quite frequently.

different from those of the habitual user. Among the many explanations offered for drug use by adolescents, the following appear to be the most common.

Loken (1973) advances a theory of drug use based on Keniston's (1965) notions regarding the search for "sentience" of alienated youth. Essentially, adolescents are alienated when they do not adjust to the norms, expectations, and values of society. It is as though they were, in a sense, placed on the out-side of this society—hence alienated. The **alienation** may be a matter of choice, compulsion, or both. Their search for "sentience" takes the form of a passive desire for stimulation and experience. Because contemporary children are reared in a world filled with toys, sights, and sounds that provide intensive stimulation without requiring activity, they become easily bored in adoles-cence. Bored, alienated, and lacking sufficient energy (or imagination) to create for themselves the exciting world that they left as children, they search for stimulation—for sentience—that will not require much activity on their part. In Loken's (1973, p. 30) words, "'popping a pill' or 'taking a fix' can recreate the multi-dimensional world of stereophonic technicolor which is reminiscent of his youth."

Bender (1963) attributes drug use to the rebelliousness of adolescents. The use of drugs provides adolescents with a potentially pleasant experience that is also an expression of defiance not only with respect to parents and teachers, but also with respect to society to the extent that its norms and values are expressed in its laws.

Other explanations, most of them simpler and perhaps more accurate for the majority of adolescents, have also been advanced. Many adolescents take drugs simply for the experience involved. Drug use is, in this case, a form of experimentation sanctioned by the peer group if not by all of society. Clearly, peer group pressure also serves as a motivating factor. Given the adolescent need to be accepted by peers and the peer group's tendency to include within its cliques only those individuals who conform to group standards, many adolescents who would otherwise rely on the advice of their parents, teachers, and others, find themselves in situations where saying "no" is considerably more difficult than bravely saying "yes." Still others, though probably a minority, experiment with drugs in an effort to solve personal problems. Depression, inhibition, and lack of confidence can all, to some degree, be temporarily alleviated through the appropriate drugs.

One final explanation for the use of drugs is premised on the notion that all individuals possess transcendental urges—desires to go beyond temporal existence as we know it. Timothy Leary, self-proclaimed prophet of an LSD-centered drug cult, was to some degree responsible for the relatively wide-spread use of hallucinogenic drugs among adolescent subcultures. Part of the mystique surrounding the use of these drugs was that they could expose adolescents to experiences that they would never otherwise encounter—that drugs could transport them out of their limited consciousness, allowing them to transcend mere physical existence. Thus the drugs came to be known as "mind-expanding" or "consciousness-expanding" and were considered to have potentially unlimited powers, though these powers were not always completely known.

It is obvious that the motivation for drug use varies from individual to individual and from situation to situation. It is also true that the users do not always know why they take drugs. Indeed, as Mitchell (1971) points out, the reasons why adolescents first take drugs and the reasons why they continue to do so are often very different. Initially the motivation may be nothing more complex or dangerous than the simple desire to experiment with some potentially new experience. The same adolescents, however, may continue to take the drug in question because of its effects on behavior and feelings, eventually developing a psychological if not a physiological dependence on the drug. At that point they are no longer taking the drug simply to experiment.

The dangers of drug use, so frequently exaggerated both by concerned and sometimes misinformed parents and by legislation that has made few distinctions among drugs or made such arbitrary distinctions that their credibility has been severely weakened, can perhaps best be understood through an examination of the various drugs most often used. These dangers, although they have in fact been exaggerated in many cases, have often been under-estimated by the users themselves. Users too could profit from a more thorough understanding of the implications of drug abuse. This applies most notably to the naive high school or elementary school students who obtain drugs in an illicit market, never knowing for certain what it is that they are buying— a fact that compounds the dangers of drugs.

Types of Drugs

The drugs most frequently abused by adolescents include alcohol, tobacco, tranquilizers, marijuana, stimulants, barbiturates, LSD, opiates, and glue.

Of these, marijuana and LSD have received the greatest amount of public attention and are discussed in greatest detail below. Various classifications of drugs have been offered. These are almost always based on effects rather than on composition. Thus there are **narcotics,** which are addictive drugs that produce sensations of well-being; **sedatives** such as tranquilizers and barbiturates; **stimulants** such as the amphetamines; and **hallucinogenic drugs,** the most widely known of which is LSD. **Marijuana** is also sometimes classed as a hallucinogenic drug although its effects in moderate doses are seldom of the kind produced by LSD or **mescaline.**

In ordinary speech it has become common to classify drugs as "hard" or "soft," the distinction between the two simply being that hard drugs are physiologically addictive and therefore result in withdrawal symptoms of varying severity when their use is discontinued. Soft drugs, on the other hand, are assumed not to be physiologically addictive although these may, for some individuals, be psychologically addictive. This means that although the body does not react adversely when their use is discontinued, individuals may experience considerable difficulty in adjusting to life as it appears to them without the mediation of drugs. A third category of drugs is described by the terms hallucinogenic, psychometic, psychedelic, or psychoactive. These too are allegedly nonaddictive drugs, but their effects on perceptual, cognitive, and affective functioning is usually much more severe and much less predictable than those of the soft drugs.

Marijuana Marijuana is derived from a variety of the hemp plant (*Cannabis sativa*) that appears in both male and female forms. It grows well in a great variety of temperate climates and may be grown indoors as well as outdoors. A mature plant may reach heights up to sixteen feet, although the indoor variety is usually harvested before it has reached that height. The plant itself has long been used in making rope, fiber, and paper; its seeds, though most often in sterilized form, are frequently found in birdfood.

Although marijuana is legally defined as all parts of this hemp plant except the stalk and seeds, the active ingredient is found in the flowering top of the female plant and in odd numbered leaves on both male and female plants. Consequently, when adolescents buy a "lid" of marijuana, they often buy a limited amount of the active ingredient (**tetrahydrocannibinol** – THC). The active ingredient itself consists of over forty distinct molecules, only a handful of which have been synthesized. Its chemical properties remain obscure, as do the reasons for its effects.

A number of different drugs may be derived from the hemp plant, although the active ingredient is the same in each. Essentially the difference between these substances lies in the concentration of THC present. Thus "grass," the street name for the form of marijuana most commonly used by adolescents, is in fact a mixture of all parts of the marijuana plant, often including roots, and also often including other substances, not the least common of which is ordinary lawn grass. In this form the marijuana plant is simply crushed, dried, and smoked in a cigarette — called a joint, a reefer, or a stick — or in a pipe.

Hash, or hashish, also a product of the hemp plant, consists of dried and pressed leaves and flowering stems. This product, commonly called hash, contains approximately 40 percent resin. It is in the resin that THC is found. Even stronger products may be derived by scraping the resin directly off the plant's leaves and drying it. These forms of marijuana, called "charas," are relatively uncommon.

A large percentage of the marijuana products sold in the United States and Canada are grown in Mexico. A smaller amount is grown domestically in gardens and on farms. No reliable estimates exist concerning the amount that is grown in homes and apartments, but the practice is not altogether uncommon.

Although marijuana is ordinarily smoked and inhaled, it may also be eaten or drunk. Subjective reports of its effects vary, although the following observations appear to be generally true — with numerous individual exceptions. Its effects appear to be relatively rapid, sometimes beginning as soon as three or four minutes following inhalation. The experience, euphemistically described as a "high," may last only a short time, depending on the amount smoked, the concentration of THC present, the individual's mood and personality predispositions, and the accuracy with which feelings are interpreted and reported. According to Goode (1969) the primary effect is a pleasant emotional state resulting more from "experience enhancement" than from the drug itself. That is, marijuana is reported to sometimes enhance pleasures derived from such other activities as listening to music, making love, eating, conversing, or simply sensing. On occasion users report no significant changes in themselves following use of the drug. This may be a function of the individual, of the absence of active ingredient in the drug, or of both.

Dominique *Age 15* **On the Effects of Too Much Dope**

Dominique: *Well that's what happened. We were on the run from here last week. We went and got some dope and did some and did too much.*
Me: *What happens when you do too much?*
Dominique: *Either . . . black out and it wears off in a couple days or you go to the hospital and get your stomach pumped or else you go seven feet under. Or intra-venous . . . I don't know.*
Me: *Do you think it affects you. I don't mean when you do it, but later on if you have done a lot.*

Dominique: *Well . . . I've been on it four years now and it hasn't affected me.*

335

Physical reactions to marijuana include increased heart rate and blood pressure, pupil dilation, a lowering of body temperature, and a subsequent tendency to rest or sleep. In addition motor coordination and reflexive activity are frequently impaired, much as is the case for alcohol; and such activities as driving are rendered considerably more dangerous.

Less positive reactions to marijuana have also been reported, including panic, severe depression, suicidal tendencies, and perceptual distortion. Some evidence suggests that if taken in sufficiently high doses and in suffi-ciently pure forms, marijuana may have the same hallucinogenic effects as LSD or mescaline (Gershon and Angrist, 1967).

Marijuana is not believed to be physiologically addictive, and there is as yet no evidence that it impairs physical health. Indeed, proponents of mari-juana usage claim that all evidence suggests that it is harmless, particularly in contrast to such socially accepted drugs as alcohol and nicotine. It is perhaps unfortunate that law enforcement agencies often include marijuana with all other known narcotic agents and treat offenders in much the same way re-gardless of the drug involved. Given this fact, it is little wonder that the credibility of the adult world, when it speaks to the adolescent about drugs, is suspect, to say the least.

LSD D-lysergic acid diethylamide tartrate, commonly known as **LSD,** is the most powerful semi-synthetic hallucinogenic drug known. It was dis-covered by Dr. Albert Hofmann in Switzerland in 1938, but its properties were unknown until he accidentally ingested a small quantity of it in 1943. Subsequently, it became widely believed that LSD produced a temporary psychotic-like state in the individual and that it could therefore be used to study psychoses—particularly schizophrenia. It wasn't until Leary and Alpert lost their positions at Harvard for allegedly involving large numbers of students in "acid" trips that the drug became widely known in the United States.

LSD is derived from the ergot, a fungus that grows on rye and other grains in the form of what is commonly called rust. Ergot derivatives have a number of medical uses (as do most narcotics, incidentally) and are often prescribed by physicians to stimulate contraction of the uterus and prevent bleeding following childbirth. Related derivatives can also be used to bring about abortions.

In a pure form, LSD is a tasteless, odorless, white powder or liquid. A dose

of a mere fifty to one hundred micrograms—a speck—is sufficient for a "trip" lasting the better part of a twenty-four-hour day. It can easily be concealed on a stick of gum, a sugar cube, or almost any other substance; it is therefore extremely difficult to detect. In addition it can be manufactured simply in a clandestine laboratory at very little cost. Street prices vary considerably, averaging between five and ten dollars per trip.

Like marijuana, LSD is considered to be nonaddictive, but its effects are considerably less predictable and far more dangerous. No statistics are available concerning the number of adolescents who are presently in mental institutions following what are euphemistically called "bad trips," but the number appears to be significant.

The predominant characteristic of an LSD experience is heightened sensory experience with frequent perceptual distortion (Ebin, 1961). For some individuals, this experience is described as intensely satisfying, rewarding, and revealing; for others it is the complete opposite. A number of studies have attempted to identify personality variables that could be used to predict the nature of the LSD trip, but none of these has arrived at any conclusive results. Although it is frequently argued that a "bad trip" is a function of the individual's mental set prior to taking LSD, it cannot be shown that this is always the case. In addition, when LSD is purchased on the street there is no guarantee of its purity, nor even of the dosage. Numerous acid trips have, in fact, proved suicidal. Evidence also suggests that LSD may be instrumental in chromosomal damage that would be reflected in abnormalities among offspring—abnormalities that might not be very different from those encountered with thalidomide (Alexander, 1967). In addition, Louria (1966) indicates that serious mental disturbance can result even after the effects of the drug have worn off. One of the often noted characteristics of an LSD trip has been the subsequent recurrence of sensations experienced while under the drug's influence. Hallucinations, feelings of acute pain, depression, suicidal tendencies, and paranoia are but a few of the possibilities of a bad trip; and any of these may recur for periods of up to three months following the initial experience.

It is difficult to describe a "good trip" given its highly subjective nature and its variability from individual to individual. In general, it involves distortions of reality: colors, sounds, tastes, smells are all subject to uncontrollable changes. Individuals frequently become intensely interested in some insignificant detail of the environment, appearing almost as if in a trance. At times they may experience feelings of invulnerability and of superhuman powers—feelings that are sometimes translated into bizarre and potentially suicidal behaviors. They may attempt to jump from a window, swim an ocean, or stop a bus thinking that none of these are beyond their powers. Presumably during a "good trip" individuals experience these feelings without attempting to verify them.

Subjective accounts of the effects of LSD (Ebin, 1961) suggest that various more-or-less profound insights may sometimes result. It is not altogether uncommon for LSD users to emerge with new perceptions of the existing social order and with new ideas and motivations for establishing alternative lifestyles. Smith and Sternfield (1970) report that spiritual or mystical experiences frequently accompany the LSD experience. Skeptics who maintain that these experiences may be more imagined than real have perhaps not realized that the reality of a mystical experience resides primarily in the individual's belief that it has in fact occurred. Hence it is possible to say that LSD may be instrumental in effecting very profound changes in the lives of some of its users. Unfortunately, the direction of these changes can not always be predicted. Although it is true that thousands of people have experimented with LSD with no apparent ill effects, the possibility of serious psychological or physical injury is real.

Mescaline Mescaline, also an hallucinogenic drug, has effects relatively similar to those of LSD. It was originally derived from the buttons of the peyote cactus, but has now been synthesized in the laboratory where it is produced as a white powder. It can be dissolved and injected directly into the bloodstream like heroin; or it can be taken orally, most frequently in the form of a capsule or mixed into a fruit juice. By all reports, it is relatively uncommon on high school campuses.

Opium and Derivatives Heroin, morphine, and codeine are all derived from juices at the base of the **opium** poppy. They are all classified as "hard" drugs, and each results in physiological addiction, the severity of which usually depends on the dosages taken and the length of time during which the individual has been addicted.

Morphine and codeine have important medical uses. Morphine is used primarily as an analgesic to relieve pain; codeine has proven effective as a cough suppressant and also as a pain reliever. Although morphine is difficult for the adolescent to obtain, the same is not true of codeine, which is present in numerous cough syrups, tablets, and pain killers. It is not an uncommon practice for the user to combine a codeine cough syrup with alcohol or some other beverage in order to obtain a high.

The primary effect of these narcotics is a feeling of euphoria that occurs almost immediately, particularly when the drug is injected, and that may last for a period of up to four hours. There is little evidence that they result in the perceptual distortions characteristic of hallucinogenic drugs or that they have the same sorts of recurring effects. Their dangers result more from the physiological addiction that may result – that inevitably results with prolonged use – and with the difficulty of obtaining them. The human body quickly builds up tolerance to these drugs so that progressively larger doses are required to obtain the same effect. Because the drugs are themselves extremely expensive, maintaining a habit requires not only that individuals have ready access to a "pusher," but also that they have ready access to a considerable amount of money. This is the principal reason why addicts are so often involved in criminal activity. It isn't that the drugs themselves lead them to asocial behavior, but simply that there frequently appears to be no other alternative if they are to maintain their habit.

Heroin is probably the most prevalent and the most dangerous of these drugs. Interestingly, it was introduced into the United States as a substitute for opium under the mistaken belief that it was nonaddictive and that it could be employed to relieve withdrawal symptoms among those addicted to opium. Much the same thing is now happening with methadone as a legal substitute for heroin.

Heroin is considerably more powerful than other narcotics and produces an almost immediate feeling of intense well-being when main-lined (injected directly into the veins). Grinder (1973) describes the process of addiction as follows. After the first injection, users ordinarily experience no withdrawal symptoms. Following three injections, they begin to feel withdrawal pains some twelve to eighteen hours after each injection. Pains become more severe after five or six injections, and they are likely to be physiologically dependent on the drug after ten injections. Withdrawal pains at this stage are very acute and frightening, and may, in some cases, result in the addict's death.

These symptoms reach their peak within thirty-six to seventy-two hours, their intensity then reducing over the next five to ten days. Insomnia, aches, and nervousness may persist for considerably longer.

Cocaine Cocaine is not classified as a hard drug because it is not physiologically addictive. It has been described as the queen of drugs, being among the most expensive (ten to fifteen thousand dollars an ounce). Hence it has not been prevalent among adolescents. It is ordinarily sniffed, swallowed, or injected and is alleged to result in a euphoric "high." Long-term usage of cocaine has on occasion resulted in convulsions or in depressed mental states.

Inhalants Glue and other similar toxic substances are used more frequently in the younger grades beginning, sometimes, in elementary school. Plastic cement is readily available and most commonly used although a wide variety of other substances, including paint, nail polish, lighter fluid, and various cleaning fluids have similar effects. Young users typically place the substance they are using into a plastic bag, put the bag up to their face, and inhale deeply. For the novice, two or three deep breaths are usually sufficient to produce an intoxicated state; with continued use, however, tolerance develops and inhalation of more fumes is required to produce the same effect. The user's typical reaction is one of excitement and exhilaration. This may be accompanied by a variety of behavioral and physiological symptoms including loss of coordination, slurred speech, double vision, and sometimes hallucinations. Numerous chronic glue users (dope users because plastic cement is also called dope) are admitted to hospitals every year. Although the evidence is inconclusive, it suggests that continued use of glue may lead to permanent brain damage as well as to other physical and psychological disturbances. Because these toxic **inhalants** are so readily available and relatively inexpensive, their use is extremely difficult to control. There is little doubt, however, that their effects can be considerably more serious than those of marijuana.

Barbiturates Barbiturates, of which there are several thousand different varieties, are readily available as prescription drugs. These, along with milder sedatives (tranquilizers) are frequently called "downers" because their primary effect is relaxation and drowsiness. Again, it is difficult to

Kris *Age 16* **On Drinking**

Me: *What sorts of things do you typically do? When you go out?*
Kris: *Go to the bar.*
Me: *At sixteen . . .*
Kris: *Well . . .*
Me: *Do you borrow a false ID to go in?*
Kris: *Sometimes.*
Me: *I understand that if you go to the _____ you don't need it.*
Kris: *I've only been there once. Usually we go to the _____. We just go to have a good time.*

Me: *What is a good time?*

Kris: *Well. Like last weekend my sister's friend invited me to this beer keg party. There were about twenty-five people there. I had a really good time. Like I didn't know a lot of people there. They were my sister's friends, and I got talking to some of them, and I had a really good time. I really get off on talking to people. Like I like to get into people's minds.*

340

ascertain the extent of their use by adolescents. Smart (1970) reports that close to 10 percent of the ninth grade students in a sample comprising 6,447 students had used barbiturates during the last six months. An approximately equal number had sniffed glue. These figures are not appreciably different from those pertaining to the incidence of marijuana use at that grade. By twelfth grade, however, use of both barbiturates and glue had declined.

Barbiturates are physiologically addictive and, if taken over a long period of time, may lead to very severe withdrawal symptoms. Taken in combination with alcohol, they can be very dangerous or even fatal.

Amphetamines Sometimes called "uppers" because their effect is quite opposed to that of the barbiturates, **amphetamines** are not thought to be physiologically addictive. Some of their common trade names are benzedrine, dexedrine, and methadrine (speed). Amphetamines have been widely used in weight reducing programs because they curb appetite; they have also been used to combat fatigue. They appear to be used with about the same frequency as glue and barbiturates (Smart, 1970).

Methadrine (speed) is frequently injected intravenously (main-lined). Its immediate effect has been compared to a sexual orgasm (Cox and Smart, 1970). Following the initial "rush," the individual continues to function at an increased metabolic level—hence the origin of the street name for the drug. Users sometimes inject methadrine as many as eight or more times per day in order to maintain a peak state. It is not uncommon for users to go without sleeping or eating for several days. Eventually they succumb to fatigue and may sleep continuously for one or two days, at the end of which time they will be rather hungry. Extremely depressed states are common following temporary withdrawal of use and are frequently combatted by beginning another series of injections.*

Alcohol Although marijuana, barbiturates, sedatives, stimulants, and other drugs are currently receiving the greatest amount of attention, **alcohol**

---

* It is significant to note that a large proportion of the delinquents I interviewed use speed rather than other drugs. One of these adolescents did, in fact, describe its effects as comparable to an orgasm.

is used more extensively and more frequently by adolescents. Suchman (1968), for example, reports a survey involving six hundred West Coast university students where the incidence of frequent alcohol use was slightly more than three times greater than the incidence of frequent marijuana use, and around forty times greater than the use of LSD. The use of alcohol does not appear to have declined in the last several decades (Straus and Bacon, 1953) despite a dramatic increase in the use of other drugs.

The reasons that adolescents drink alcohol are probably not very different from the reasons for which they take other drugs. Research suggests that use of alcohol is frequently an expression of rebellion against authoritative parents or an expression of hostility toward social authority (Alexander, 1967). Adolescents whose parents drink are also more likely to drink. Probability of drinking appears to be directly related to the relationship between adolescents and their parents as well. Alexander (1967) found that adolescent boys whose fathers were abstinent were more likely to drink if they were not emotionally close to their father, but relatively unlikely to drink if they were close to him.

Alcohol is a central nervous system depressant. Its primary effect is the suppression of inhibition. Frequently, therefore, it causes individuals to behave as though they had taken a stimulant. Excessive use may also lead to impairment of higher brain functions manifested in lowered concentration, poorer judgment, and reduced self-control. Behavioral symptoms of varying degrees of alcoholic intoxication include impaired muscular control, coordination, and balance; this is frequently evident in the individual's staggering gait; thick and uncertain speech; visual impairment; significantly longer reaction times; faintness; nausea; blackouts; amnesia; and, if taken in sufficiently large doses, paralysis of heart and lung muscles sometimes leading to death (Harger, 1964).

Alcohol is addictive, although physiological addiction does not ordinarily result until the individual has consumed excessive amounts over a relatively long period of time. One of its major physiological effects is cirrhosis of the liver, which has the dubious distinction of being among the top ten causes of death in the United States. In addition, it is implicated in between 50 and 70 percent of all highway accident deaths, a relatively large number of which involve adolescents (Fort, 1968).

Table 13.1   Drug Related Words and Expressions

Amphetamines. Bennies, happy pills, dexies, meth, speed, hearts, jolly beans, uppers, wake ups.
Barbiturates. Goof balls, barbs, reds, yellow jackets, blue heavens, purple hearts.
Brick. A kilogram of marijuana.
Cap. A capsule of powdered drugs.
Cocaine. Coke, gold dust, flake, speedball (with heroin).
Downer. A depressant such as a barbiturate.
Fix. A drug injection, usually heroin. Also called a "hit."
Flip Out. A bad trip.
Freak. One who uses amphetamines.
Hallucinogenic. Psychoactive, psychometric, psychedelic. LSD, for example.
Head. One who uses marijuana.

342

Tobacco The use of tobacco in cigarettes, pipes, cigars, snuff, and chewing tobacco has been highly prevalent both among adults and adolescents for many years. Recent evidence linking the use of tobacco with a variety of diseases does not appear to have significantly affected sales in the tobacco industry. Nor have increased prices and warning labels required by law on all packages of cigarettes. Yet tobacco-linked deaths now exceed traffic accident deaths. Many of these result from lung cancer and coronary heart disease. In addition, cigarette smoking has been linked with chronic bronchitis; emphysema; pneumonia; cirrhosis of the liver; and cancer of such tissues as the tongue, lips, esophagus, and mouth.

There is some disagreement concerning the degree to which individuals can become addicted to nicotine, the active ingredient in tobacco. Studies have shown that injecting nicotine directly into the bloodstream is more pleasurable for some smokers than inhaling tobacco smoke (Lawton, 1963). It appears, however, that physiological addiction to nicotine is not nearly as strong as it is to alcohol or other addictive drugs. On the other hand, habituation, characterized by an overwhelming desire to continue smoking, appears to play a significant role in the smoker's inability or reluctance to stop smoking.

The effects of smoking are not as clear as the effects of most other drugs. It does not produce a high as marijuana or heroin might; it does not intoxicate as glue and alcohol do. It has been suggested that it helps relieve tension, is conducive to relaxation, and satisfies certain oral cravings a la Freud. It has also been associated with masculine and feminine images, perhaps partly as a result of widespread advertising campaigns. Hence adolescent smokers may use tobacco in order to enhance their status and their self-image. At the same time, smoking may represent a rebellion against parental or school authority, although Lawton (1963) maintains that the number of adolescents who smoke despite parental prohibitions is so small as to invalidate this contention.

The Remedy

Drug abuse is a major social problem not restricted to adolescents but pervading all age groups. It has by now become apparent that drugs can neither be legislated out of existence, nor can users be compelled to cease

Heroin. Horse, H, junk, skag, smack, snow, joy powder, hard stuff, shit. An addict is said to have a monkey.
Inebriated (as from alcohol). Plastered, drunk, high, loaded, pissed, zonko.
Lid. An ounce of marijuana.
LSD. Acid, cubes, sugar cubes, trip, big D.
Main-line. To inject drugs intravenously.
Marijuana. Dawamesc, hashish, bhang, grass, ganja, charas, muta, grefa, muggles, pot, reefer, gauge, stick, tea, joint, roach, Acapulco Gold, number, smoke.
Mescaline. Mesc, cactus, payola.
Morphine. Morf, Miss Emma, M, Dreamer, white stuff.

employing drugs as a consequence of the harshness of the law. Indeed, in many ways drug laws are reminiscent of laws that once governed the treatment of the mentally ill (Szasz, 1970). Those who are in abject need of medical and psychological help are too frequently treated in the same manner as those who prey on the addicted through illegal drug markets.

At the high school level, and perhaps at all levels of society, probably the best approach to the drug problem is through education. It is likely that factual information concerning drugs and their effects is significantly more effective than moralistic preachings or fear campaigns based on exaggerations of these effects. Similarly, attempts to appeal to adolescents by reference to the illegal nature of drug abuse and the legal consequences of being apprehended is not likely to be effective as long as the law is too insensitive to discriminate among various types of drugs and their abusers.

Jargon

The drug culture is characterized by a plethora of slang, code names, and abbreviations for various drugs and the people involved with drugs. Table 13.1 summarizes some of the more common of these.

Summary

This chapter opened in the street and moved quickly to a consideration of drug use in general society and among adolescents. Detailed descriptions were provided of the various drugs most commonly employed and of their effects, including a discussion of alcohol and tobacco. In the end the chapter looked briefly at some of the jargon of the drug world.

Main Points

1. Sam is straight.

2. Drugs are widely prevalent in American adult society. They are also prevalent among adolescents.

Narc. A narcotics agent. Presumed straight.

Nickle or Dime Bag. A five or ten dollar bag of marijuana.

Pusher. One who sells drugs. Also called a dealer.

Score. Buy drugs as in "I scored a lid."

Stoned. High on drugs—usually marijuana. Also turned on, high, ripped, zonked.

Straight. Not using drugs.

Toke Up. Smoke marijuana. Also "do" as in "we did a number." Also called a "hit" as in "hit up."

Tracks. Marks left from hypodermic needle as a result of repeated intravenous injections.

Trip. What happens after taking an hallucinogenic drug.

Upper. A stimulant such as amphetamine.

344

3. Among the reasons for adolescent drug use are the search for new sensations (search for sentience), rebellion, experimentation, peer pressure, the solution of personal problems, and the urge to transcend the present limits of physical existence.

4. Marijuana is one of the most widely used drugs among adolescents. Estimates of its use vary, but it is likely that the majority of high school students have tried it at least once prior to leaving school.

5. The active ingredient in marijuana, THC, is derived from the hemp plant, *Cannabis sativa*. It is ordinarily smoked, although it may be also eaten or drunk. Its primary effects are a form of intoxication accompanied by mildly euphoric sensations.

6. Hash or hashish is simply a form of marijuana containing more of the active ingredient. It is made primarily from the leaves and from the flowering tops of the female plant.

7. Marijuana and hashish are not believed to be physiologically addictive, and hence are classified as "soft" drugs (or as hallucinogenic drugs). They may be psychologically addictive for some individuals.

8. LSD (d-lysergic acid diethylamide tartrate) is the most powerful hallucinogenic drug known. It is derived from the ergot, a fungus that grows on rye grains, and is usually made in clandestine laboratories.

9. LSD and other hallucinogenic drugs such as mescaline produce distortions in individuals' perceptions of themselves and the world. The results of each are highly unpredictable and have frequently led to psychotic breakdowns or suicidal acts. These effects frequently recur periodically for indefinite periods of time after the initial effects of the drug have disappeared.

10. There is evidence of possible brain lesions and chromosomal aberrations following the use of LSD.

11. Opium and its derivatives (morphine, heroine, and codeine) are produced from the milky extract of the opium poppy. These drugs are physiologically addictive, hence "hard" drugs. They tend to produce euphoric states in the individual. Taken in excessive doses, they can result in death. After heavy

use, or sometimes after relatively infrequent use, severe withdrawal pains are experienced when they are discontinued.

12. Cocaine is not physiologically addictive. Nor is glue. However, both can be psychologically addictive.

13. Glue appears to have very deleterious effects on the central nervous system after prolonged use. It produces a euphoric state of short duration. The body quickly habituates to it so that greater amounts are subsequently required to obtain the same high.

14. Barbiturates, also called "downers," and sedatives have a tranquilizing effect on the nervous system. They are frequently employed to come down from a bad LSD trip. They tend to produce a mild feeling of well-being and to repress anxiety.

15. Amphetamines are stimulants, in contrast to barbiturates. Hence they are called "uppers." They are frequently used to combat fatigue. Methadrine (speed) is an amphetamine.

16. Alcohol appears to be more frequently employed among adolescents than marijuana and other drugs that are currently receiving a great deal of attention. Its potential dangers in terms of illness, socially nonproductive or unhappy lives, and death are not inconsequential.

17. Tobacco, which may be habituating rather than addictive, is widely used by adolescents despite numerous campaigns to reduce its use following evidence that it is implicated in a variety of potentially fatal diseases.

Chapter 14

Shelley Drinkwater Grade 11

To the Nows of All Tomorrows

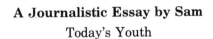

── 347

A Journalistic Essay by Sam

Today's Youth

Activism

Sources of Frustration

Rebellious and Nonrebellious Groups

Inactives
Conventionalists
Individualists
Activists
Dissenters
Alienated Adolescents
Constructivists

Tomorrow

Summary

Main Points

A Journalistic Essay by Sam*

Lefrancois has, in several of his published works, been guilty of gross, and I suspect deliberate, misrepresentation of the facts as they apply in my case. I refer, of course, to page 43 of Of Children *(Lefrancois, 1973) where Lefrancois describes himself as the "sole acquaintance of a mad psychologist—not angry, but insane (although both varieties are quite common)." I do not object to part of this categorization because I am quite aware of my "insanity" as the term is currently used by witch doctors and various other charlatans with more esoteric and more academically acceptable titles. And I am by no means ashamed of that peculiar condition that has moved me to renounce my affiliations with official academic institutions and to move, along with my rats and other necessities of scientific research, into the long-abandoned coal mines below this city. I am quite comfortable here. And quite happy.*

What I do object to, and most strenuously, is Lefrancois' totally unfounded and unjustifiable claim that he is my sole acquaintance, and that I leave my home only to search for various succulent victuals among the disposal bins of some of the large hotels situated above me. I would not deny, of course, that on many occasions I do leave these quarters for precisely those reasons. But even more important, I often leave here on warm summer evenings to watch television through the west window of the small house on the corner by the Fifth Street Bridge, to pick up discarded newspapers behind the Journal *office, or to visit with my friends. Lefrancois is definitely not my only acquaintance. I also have friends.*

One of these is John, a rather obese individual much given to weight reducing programs, chocolate ice cream, deep fried shrimp, Polish sausage, and beer. He is married and the father of two children. These children are adolescents; and it is largely because of them, as well as because of the fact that I am a voracious reader of discarded newspapers, that I know as much as I do about adolescence. And that is perhaps more than Lefrancois himself knows, because he is too close to the subject. He has lost the objectivity that is essential in scientific study and reporting.

Because I like the chocolate cakes that he still brings me from time to time and because Samuel also likes them, I have written this essay on contemporary

---

* Written by Sam Bellott especially for this text. Reproduced with his permission.

adolescence. I sincerely hope it will enlighten you as much as I'm sure it will enlighten him.

Today's Youth

Is today's youth much different from yesterday's? Did the ancient Romans not complain bitterly that youth had become lazy, self-indulgent, boisterous, and rebellious? Have youth not always been disenchanted with their world and their alleged place in it? And have they not always been in conflict with their parents and with other establishment authorities?

The questions, and their implied answers, are irrelevant. Not only is it a fact that today's youth is largely disenchanted and rebellious, but the significance of this state is incredibly greater today than it has ever been in the past. This is partly because of the communications media that have acted to solidify and to isolate youth; it is also partly because there are so many more of them today. That adolescents should, many centuries ago in Rome, refuse to obey their parents and make public disgraces of themselves while under the influence of excessive quantities of wine is little consolation to today's television-watching parents whose children have just been busted for illegal possession of drugs.

It is an obvious fact that today's parents are one generation too old. Thirty years from now, parents will probably still be one generation too old. The social and physical world is changing so rapidly that it is becoming increasingly difficult to keep abreast of it. The values, interests, modes of speech, and dress of today's youth are foreign to today's parents, even as these same values and interests will be foreign to tomorrow's parents. Ironically, tomorrow's parents are today's children.

Like Lefrancois, I was born in an isolated portion of Northern Canada. I saw my first indoor toilet at the age of nine and could never quite adjust to its function. Around twelve I saw my first plane close-up, and when I was fifteen it became possible to flick a switch in order to light up the interior of our small house. My adolescence was filled with the excitement of obtaining our first motor car, retiring the horses, and converting from wood to oil furnaces. Eventually I became interested in girls, an interest that, I am happy to say, I have since had the good sense to overcome. In between these momentous events, I had little time to engage in conflicts of will with my parents and teachers. I was not aware

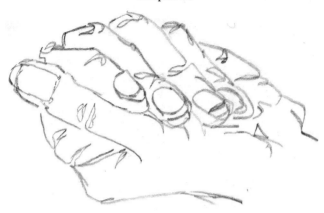

350

of the generation gap, of the beat movement, and of drugs; and I had only fleeting and temporary acquaintances with alcohol, sex, and other conventional adolescent sports.

Today's children are born in a world that is rapidly becoming steel, plastic, and concrete from ocean to ocean. Tomorrow's children may well be born in a world that is rapidly becoming steel, plastic, and concrete from continent to continent.

Yesterday's children were born in a community made up of old people, middle-aged people, children, and others in between. Today's children are born into a world made up of young–middle-aged people and children. The old people have not disappeared; society has simply moved them to "comfortable" homes with other old people. Young couples have not disappeared; they are essential to the eventual existence of middle-aged couples and old people. They have simply moved from the schools and universities to their apartment ghettos.

Yesterday's children went to school with their friends, neighbors, cousins, brothers, and sisters. Their parents knew their teachers; their teachers knew their clergymen; their clergymen knew their doctors; their doctors knew their dentists; and their dentists knew their parents. Home was small and warm. Today's children go to school with strangers. They see some of their relatives, including grandparents, once or twice a year. Their parents don't know their teachers; their teachers don't know their clergymen. Perhaps they don't know any clergymen. Their doctors and their dentists are strangers. Home is large and cold.

Yesterday's children breathed good air and ate good food. Chickens, fish, and pheasants were good then. Today's children eat mercury, breathe heavy air, and thrive on cereal. There are rumors that beer may cause cancer of the lower bowels and of the rectum; butter and other cholesterol rich foods may lead to cardiovascular problems; there are indescribable waste products in commercially sold hamburgers and frankfurters; preservatives in many foods are unhealthy; and a steak that tastes particularly good and is extraordinarily tender has probably been treated with monosodium glutamate, which is very bad for the stomach.

Young children can have ulcers as well as adults.

Sam's essay eventually became a long, rambling dissertation on a variety of adolescent related topics. Portions of it have been included in various parts of this text. At times they serve as good illustrations of textual material; on occasion they are examples of some of the myths and prejudices that continue to abound in writings concerning adolescents. The introduction to Sam's essay is a case in point. Note, for example, his statement that "Today's youth is largely disenchanted and rebellious." It is given as a factual statement and would, in fact, be accepted as such by a large number of readers who have little reason to think otherwise. The media and popular psychological literature have for some time propagated the same image. And, though to a lesser extent, less popular literature (textbooks and esoteric academic journals) has also fostered the notion that adolescents are largely unhappy with their world and with adults who are assumed to have created this world and who are also blamed for not taking steps to correct the ills that surround them.

In corroboration of Sam's prejudices, writers have variously labeled adolescents as "belligerently nonadult" (Keniston, 1963); "the pleasure-seeking now-generation" (Heath, 1970); as moved by "social idealism," "abstract altruism," and "contempt of hypocrisy" (Hadden, 1969). These descriptions are accurate only for specific minorities. If this were not the case, it is likely that far more than 2 percent of boys and .5 percent of girls would be classed as delinquents before they reached adulthood; schools would be totally unmanageable; and parents would take steps to ensure that they raised no adolescents. Children, perhaps, but never adolescents.

Adolescents who go happily through pubescence, do reasonably well in school, adjust to family and community, and move quietly into adulthood are not considered newsworthy. Those who drop out of school, sell marijuana to make ends meet, and organize an underground newspaper advocating the overthrow of conventional public school systems and the removal of all penalties for crimes without victims may well succeed in attaining headline status. The fact that there are a thousand individuals in the first group for every one in the second group appears to be largely irrelevant for news media; consequently those of us who gather our facts *and* our opinions from the publicly spoken or printed word are misled, even as Sam has been misled.

The second part of Sam's essay leads us down a path often taken by the older, established generation. In an emotional burst of nostalgia, we are informed that conditions were much better when we were children and adolescents than they are for today's generation of young people; that communities were closer knit and more personal; and even that the food and the air were better. And this may well be true, of course, even as it may be true that succeeding generations will be subjected to even more impersonal and more polluted worlds than now exist.

But the argument does not go far enough, for it is possible to base more than one point on it. The first, one that Sam makes at least by implication, is that it is more difficult to become a well-adjusted individual in a cold and impersonal world than it was (or would be) in a warmer, more personal one. But the separation of contemporary society into age-segregated layers and the consequent isolation of the nuclear family from lasting friendships and from the immediate influence of relatives and of pastors, doctors, and other professional people who are "real" friends of the entire family may, at least theoretically, have a beneficial effect on the family.

When there is no cohesive neighborhood in which to leave one's children no grandparents to call upon in time of emergency, no aunts and uncles with whom to leave the little ones overnight, then the family itself must become more cohesive and more intensely independent. That is, the family must become more independent from the community, but more emotionally interdependent within itself. Consequently, emotional ties between parents and children, as well as between siblings, may become stronger; and because the relationship between parents and children is of paramount importance in determining adjustment, particularly during adolescence (see Chapter 8), the effects of those changes described by Sam may not be nearly as deleterious as could be expected.

Popular writing that has dealt with the topic of adolescence has frequently been guilty of the type of faulty inference that is evident in Sam's essay. Prejudices fostered by media reports coupled with the greater interest accorded research dealing with deviant, rebellious, nonconformist behavior have done much to ensure that adolescence is viewed in these terms rather than in terms of a normal, healthy, and relatively uneventful transition between childhood and adulthood. In addition, among the earliest theories in adolescent psychology were those based on the "sturm und drang" (storm and stress) concept made popular by G. Stanley Hall. The storm and stress hypothesis is still frequently considered valid in relation to the contemporary adolescent. My own opinion is that it is not only invalid, but largely misleading. Furthermore, it is highly unlikely that it was valid at the time that it was first advanced. Although it is true that there have always been dissatisfied and

READ ALL ABOUT IT !!!
98 PER CENT OF BOY,
AND 99·5 PERCENT OF
GIRL TEENAGERS
LEAD **NORMAL,
HEALTHY** LIVES !!

353

rebellious groups in society, it is also true that these groups have been considerably more visible than their more satisfied counterparts. It is likely that with the new media, their visibility has increased much more dramatically than their numbers.

Despite all this, it would be a mistake to assume that the highly visible minority is unimportant. True, it is unimportant if one is attempting to arrive at a clear picture of what adolescence is generally like. But it is not at all unimportant in understanding adolescence; the drives, the needs, and the frustrations that motivate the visible minority also, at least to some extent, affect the majority. In some cases, they are less severe; in others, adolescents themselves are better able to cope with them and arrive at alternative ways of satisfying their needs and overcoming their frustrations.

In short, then, the evidence presented in this text does not support the contention that adolescence is necessarily, or even usually, a period characterized by parent-child conflict, by rebelliousness, by delinquency, or by other forms of strife. The presentation of evidence continues in this chapter with a brief consideration of adolescent activism.

Activism

The point has repeatedly been made throughout this book that the majority of adolescents progress relatively happily and "normally" toward adulthood; that parent-child struggles, rebelliousness, turmoil, and conflict that have often been assumed to be descriptive of adolescence have been exaggerated and are much less descriptive of the majority than of selected minorities. It is nevertheless true that a significant number of adolescents do not adjust well to the frustrations and demands to which they are exposed. These individuals do not quietly assume their expected places in society; they remain at some place on the outside. In short, these are the adolescents about whom so much has been said and written. Some are active; some passive. Some are extremely verbal in their denunciation of adult norms; others seek quietly to establish their own adult society. This section examines some of the causes of **activism** and some of their manifestations. Bear in mind, however, that we are not dealing here with all adolescents, but only with various adolescent subgroups.

Figure 14.1 Classification of youth in terms of sociopolitical involvement and political orientation vis-à-vis the status quo. Based on theoretical and empirical information provided by Block *et al.* (1973).

354

Sources of Frustration

There are sources of frustration for all individuals. Children who are unable to obtain some desired object may be no less frustrated than adults who fail to be promoted when they desperately want to be. Adolescence, too, has its own particular sources of frustration. Knowledge of these is helpful in understanding why it is that some adolescents become alienated, and why some choose to rebel in one of a variety of ways.

A principal source of frustration for adolescents is the distance that they perceive between the state of the world as they think it should and could be, and the world as it seems to be. Instances of waste, pollution, injustice, and the demotion of basic values are seen by adolescents not as accidental, but as caused by the stupidity, greed, and selfishness of the adult world. Because they have not yet been granted status in this world, they can assume little blame for it; but they can be profoundly distressed because of it.

Additional sources of frustration include sexual and economic unemployment. Social norms make it difficult to find acceptable outlets for sexual drives, and the educational requirements for many forms of economic employment make it necessary to remain in school long after sexual and physical maturity is reached. Ambiguity concerning present social role also compounds the frustration. They are neither children, nor adults, being treated now as one, and then as the other. Their country expects that they will rise up in her defense should they be called; but that same country forbids them to enter those establishments where alcoholic beverages are sold. Indeed, it prevents them from expressing their opinions in the polling booth, but demands that they adhere to the laws and regulations of society as though they were adults. And although age of franchise and legal drinking age have recently been lowered in many areas, they continue to be arbitrary and sometimes contradictory.

Adolescent frustration may also be linked to what political scientists call "the revolution of rising expectations" (Loken, 1973). Whenever oppressed people become aware that they are in fact oppressed, the glimpse that they get of better conditions serves as a motive for revolt. The theory maintains, essentially, that the oppressed are not initially dissatisfied with their oppression, but become dissatisfied as they begin to receive the fruits of more advanced cultures. It is this small taste of the great American apple that gives rise to the revolution. Similarly, it can be argued that adolescents who now become

Status Quo

Conventionalists

Individualists

Political Orientation

Inactives

Uninvolved — Constructivists → — Involved

Alienated

Activists

Dissenters

Rejection of
Status Quo Values

Sociopolitical Involvement

more aware of the privilege and powers that are synonymous with adulthood are motivated to achieve these for themselves. However, expressions of adolescent dissatisfaction with their roles and privileges seldom take the form of a direct attempt to achieve the way of life characteristic of adults. More often they rebel, quietly or actively, against the values and standards that characterize adult society.

Rebellious and Nonrebellious Groups

For purposes of this discussion, rebellious adolescents are not viewed solely as adolescents who actively protest, but includes as well those who protest in other ways. Clearly, there is a distinction to be made between hippies who live quietly on their vegetable-producing commune, smoking marijuana, and loving, and adolescents who join the Symbionese Liberation Army. Although both are probably dissatisfied with the status quo, they express their dissatisfaction in very different ways. In addition, there are a great many adolescents who do not protest—a number that appears to be clearly in the majority (Block *et al.*, 1973).

Various attempts have been made to classify different types of adolescent protestors and activists. Given rapidly changing social conditions, however, most of these classifications have been valid only for a short period of time. A recent classification that may have longer viability has been proposed by Block *et al.* (1973). It is summarized in Figure 14.1.

Block *et al.* (1973) describe adolescents in terms of two dimensions: involvement as it is reflected in the individual's active participation in social or political activities; and political orientation describable in terms of the adolescent's rejection of or adherence to the status quo. At the extremes of each of these two dimensions, it is possible to identify four distinct adolescent groups. Several other categorizations are possible, as is shown in Figure 14.1. Some of the descriptions of these categories are based on Block *et al.* (1973; 1969); others are derived from Haan *et al.* (1968) as well as from other research.

Inactives Inactives, apparently a large majority particularly in the 1970s relative to the 1960s, are politically apathetic. These are youth who are not politically or socially involved and who adhere passively to the status quo

Jean *Age 18* **On Helping the World**

Me: *Would you classify yourself as being idealistic, or materialistic, or as not really caring?*
Jean: *I don't really know what those two words mean.*
Me: *(I go into a lengthy and learned discussion of idealism and materialism.)*

Jean: *I'm interested in the world, but I don't really know what I can do to help.*
Me: *Unh-unh.*
Jean: *What's wrong with the world? What needs to be helped?*
Jean: *Well . . . the Irish. The war . . . war . . . I . . . hum . . . don't really know.*

without any semblance of passionate conviction to it. Haan *et al.* (1968) describe inactives as conformity oriented.

Conventionalists A second group of adolescents, the **conventionalists,** are only moderately involved in sociopolitical activity, but are manifestly committed to the status quo. Block *et al.* (1969) describe these individuals as the sorority and fraternity members — status conscious, conformist individuals whose concerns are primarily to adjust to the established social order and to reap its benefits.

Individualists Block identifies a third group, **individualists,** who are highly involved in social and political activity, but who, unlike the stereotype of the activist adolescent, are committed to the status quo rather than to its overthrow. Individualists tend to avail themselves only of legal forms of protest and are avowedly and passionately conservative in their political orientation.

Activists Activists are those individuals who are not only deeply involved in social and political activity, but who explicitly reject many of the values inherent in the status quo. These are the protesters, agitators, and demonstrators whose activities drew so much attention in the 1960s. Block *et al.* (1969) describe these adolescents as "intellectually gifted, academically superior and politically radical young people from advantaged homes." That activists are clearly in the minority becomes evident when one considers that even during the height of student protest and activism during the 1960s, seldom more than 15 percent of the student body, and usually considerably fewer than that, would actively involve themselves (Trent and Craise, 1967; Trent and Medsker, 1967). Nor can all students who actively join protest groups and activities be considered activists as defined by Block *et al.* (1973), because not all are committed to actual social or political change. Flacks (1967) believes that a great many students protest because of the sheer romanticism of fighting for causes and ideals, regardless of the cause. Others protest as an expression of moral purity that involves more a rejection of the established order rather than a commitment to new ideals. Still others protest in response to their own personal frustrations.

Dissenters Dissenters might be described as professional agitators. These are the adolescents who are committed to a rejection of status quo values, but who do not involve themselves directly in social or political efforts designed to overthrow the status quo.

Alienated Adolescents Another group comprises those individuals who are not involved in political or social activity, but who reject status quo values. They differ from dissenters and activists only in terms of actual active involvement. In a sense, they can be described as the passive protesters.

A great deal has been written about alienation and alienated youth. Research indicates that these are primarily the egocentric, aesthetically oriented adolescents (Block *et al.*, 1973). Their primary active concerns are with the gratification of their wishes and with the immediate enjoyment of life. They are the individuals of which Friedenberg (1969) speaks when he refers to a type of passive protest concerned not so much with the overthrow of established middle-class systems as with the establishment of alternative life-styles. The hippie movement appears to have been one expression of alienation.

Gold (1969) identifies three different meanings for the term alienation: not influenced by, not able to influence, and estranged from one's self. With respect to the established social order, it is apparent that many adolescents choose not to be influenced by it, feel powerless to influence it, and are, in fact, actively seeking some rapprochement with their selves. The recent rise in the popularity of Eastern religious movements and of various sensitivity and encounter movements, and the desire of many adolescents to return to more primitive, frequently communal, types of existence may be expressions of alienation. Loken (1973, p. 29) contends that the use of drugs is also related to alienation in that it provides a "nonactivist"—hence alienated—method of altering one's experience.

Constructivists A final group in the Block *et al.* (1973) classification includes those adolescents who are socially involved, but who are not protesters —the **constructivists.** Nor are they staunchly committed to the status quo as are individualists. These are the adolescents who are most likely to volunteer for social services. They are committed to activity, but not to political causes.

Tomorrow

The discussion presented here of student activism is deliberately briefer than the amount of information available would warrant; this is for two reasons. In the first place much of the "information" is highly emotional and prejudicial, having appeared in countless newspaper reports and popular writings and being geared toward the exposition of what has often been viewed by authors as a potentially devastating social uprising among adolescents. Second, the nature of student activism and protest and the prevalence and variety of adolescent subcultures have changed so dramatically in a single decade, and continue to change so rapidly, that anything written about present forms of rebellion, alienation, protest, and apathy could well be completely invalid by the time this book appears in your hands. Consider, for example, the antics of college and high school students in the late forties and fifties: the goldfish eating, phone-booth stuffing era. These now appear to have been harmless pranks, but were at the time viewed with some alarm. More than one grandmother shook her head and mumbled, "What are young people coming to nowadays?"

The sixties saw a tremendous upsurge of active rebellion and revolt throughout America, both in high schools and on university campuses. And more than one social scientist predicted that the seventies would usher in major upheavals in the structure of universities and colleges because an increasingly powerful student body would simply not tolerate conditions as they were then presumed to exist. It became of considerable importance for dedicated social scientists to do everything in their power to understand student activism, for it was a daily fact of life; and it promised to become considerably more serious if something were not done.

But the seventies failed to bring with them any significant increase in student activism. Indeed, it now appears that there is less activism than there ever was. Observers of the contemporary adolescent scene are now becoming concerned that youth is too complacent; that concern has been replaced by apathy; that students have given up on the possibility of effecting changes within the system and have, instead, either tacitly agreed to comply with it or have simply dropped out. These observers now point to hippie groups as prime examples of apathetic alienation. Hippie concerns with immediate sensual gratification, with love and peace, and the concomitant passive rejec-

tion of war, materialism, and contemporary social and sexual values are viewed as behaviors that are essentially nonconstructive. The pendulum has swung some distance. Adolescents are no longer criticized and even feared for being destructive; they are criticized, and perhaps still feared, simply for being nonconstructive.

Perhaps it is now accurate to say that except for small, sometimes highly active minority groups, adolescent protest and rebellion have taken a highly passive form at least with respect to established society. Adolescents appear to be exploring alternative life-styles without directly attempting to destroy those presently accepted. But perhaps these will serve as models that might, in time, come to replace traditional life-styles. Perhaps we will know better in 1984, because then, today's adolescents will be that day's adults. What will today's infants be doing then?

Summary

This chapter opened with a journalistic essay by Sam, a long, rambling dissertation on the alleged ills and problems of adolescence and a nostalgic comparison of present conditions with those that Sam thinks existed at the time he was an adolescent. It moved then to a consideration of activism, noting that its extent and seriousness among adolescents appear to have diminished significantly since the 1960s. Sources of adolescent frustration and some possible causes of activism were examined, and a classification of adolescents in terms of political orientation and sociopolitical involvement was presented. Within this framework, the chapter looked at inactives, the politically apathetic majority; conventionalists who are status quo oriented and politically uninvolved; constructivists, who are socially involved but who do little protesting; individualists who are intensely active but equally intensely committed to the status quo; activists who are also intensely active, but who are committed to ideals and principles that run counter to status quo values; dissenters who are, in a sense, professional agitators whose involvement in social and political activity is less intense than their commitment to a rejection of status quo values; and alienated adolescents who also reject status quo values, but who are not actively involved in attempts to replace these values. What will tomorrow's adolescents be like?

Main Points

1. Sam's most passionate beliefs about adolescents have been derived more from nostalgic reminiscence contrasted with popular media reports than from the shimmering psychologies of his contemporaries.

2. Adolescent activism, characteristic of an important minority of adolescents, may stem in part from the various sources of frustration to which adolescents are exposed.

3. Block *et al.* (1973) classify adolescents in terms of their involvement in social and political activities and in terms of their political orientation. This classification gives rise to a number of apparently distinct labels that are useful in considering activism.

4. Inactives are those adolescents who are satisfied with the status quo, and who are not socially and politically involved. They are the politically apathetic majority.

5. Conventionalists are committed to the status quo and are therefore not apathetic in the sense that inactives are apathetic.

6. Individualists are also committed to the status quo, but their commitment is translated into sociopolitical activity that may be as visible and as intense as that characteristic of activists. They are the radical conservatives.

7. Activists are committed both to a rejection of status quo values and to activities designed to promote this rejection.

8. Dissenters are not very active politically despite their professed rejection of the status quo. They are the professional protesters.

9. Alienated youth are characterized by lack of social involvement despite their rejection of established values. They are the passive objectors whose life-styles frequently represent the nature of their objections.

10. Constructivists are socially involved adolescents who are neither protesters nor passionately committed to the status quo.

Epilogue

THERE IS NO SAM, dear reader. He is my invention.

I am sorry that you have been misled into believing that Sam Bellott is as real a person as you or I. I assure you that I have, in fact, invented him although I haven't yet had the heart to tell him so. Full of contradictions and opinions as he is, he is still a lovable person, and I am not unkind enough to disappoint him by informing him that he is nothing more than a character in a book.

I know that the more intelligent among you will by now have reread the opening pages of this text and concluded that this is a disclaimer intended for the local city police and other authorities who might be moved to action by a student group somewhere in Kansas or Saskatchewan. You no doubt think that Sam and I have agreed to protect his residence, his rats, and his life-style by denying their existence. Not so. I wrote this entire text alone. There is not, and never was, a Sam Bellott as he is described in these pages.

THERE IS NO LEFRANCOIS, dear reader.

For some time Lefrancois has been behaving as though he had invented me, or at least those aspects of me that you read about in some of his books. And as my would-be creator he has, as I pointed out to you recently, taken certain liberties with my life and behavior that I, myself, would not have dared take.

The fact is that I have invented him. But he, of course, is completely unaware of that fact. Kurt Vonnegut, who believed that he had invented Kilgore Trout, was at some pains to reveal to Trout that he was an invention. Vonnegut took admirable risks in doing so and was in the process attacked by a rather vicious dog who had been invented in some earlier draft of a book, and who took it upon himself to reappear just at that point when Vonnegut himself had first made his entrance. The irony of the situation is not so much that Vonnegut was attacked by a dog that he thought he had created, but that Trout later undertook to write a book that Vonnegut might otherwise have written. And there is some doubt yet as to whether or not Vonnegut is aware of the fact that Trout has written this book.

I have invented Lefrancois. You and I are probably the only people who know this. And it is perhaps just as well. Otherwise, like Kilgore Trout, he might attempt to write an entire book, and undertaking that, would do little for the enlightenment of the people or the amazement of the scholars.

It is difficult to deny the existence of something that has already been invented. Isn't it?

Sam Bellott

Glossary

Accommodation   Involves the modification of an activity or an ability that the child already has, to conform to environmental demands. Piaget's description of development holds that assimilation and accommodation are the means by which individuals interact with their world and adapt to it. (*See* Assimilation)

Acne   An epidermic condition characterized by the appearance of pimples. Relatively common during adolescence, hence the expression "think young: wear plastic pimples."

Activism   A general term employed to describe protest and other forms of social, political, or economic rebellion.

Activists   A term employed to describe individuals who are not only deeply involved in social and political activity, but whose expressed aims are to overthrow or supplant established social and political systems.

Adaptation   Changes in an organism in response to the environment. Such changes are assumed to facilitate interaction with that environment. Adaptation plays a central role in Piaget's theory. (*See* Assimilation, Accommodation)

Ad Nauseam   Until you become sick or someone else does.

Adolescence   A general term signifying the developmental period that begins with pubescence and terminates with adulthood. Generally begins around the ages of eleven or twelve and terminates around the ages of nineteen or twenty. (*See* Puberty, Pubescence)

Adolescent   One who is in the developmental period labeled adolescence. An individual undergoing major biological changes leading to sexual maturity. An individual in the transitional phase between childhood and adulthood. Also frequently employed as an adjective to describe relatively immature attitudes and ways of behaving.

Adolescent Psychology   That branch of psychology concerned with the developmental period labeled adolescence. (*See* Adolescence) A study of the changes that occur between childhood and adulthood, and of the forces that account for these changes. A study of the interests, attitudes, behaviors, and other characteristics of individuals during adolescence.

Affective   (*See* Emotion)

Alcohol (Ethyl)   A central nervous system depressant whose primary effect is suppression of inhibition.

Alienation   An adjective employed in existential philosophy and psychology to describe individuals' feelings of separation from people and things that are important to them.

Alpha Waves   Electroencephalographic brain wave recordings typical of individuals in states of rest.

Amphetamines   Chemical drugs sometimes called "uppers" as opposed to barbiturates and sedatives, which are known as "downers." The most commonly employed amphetamine is probably "speed" (Methadrine), which is injected directly into the blood stream (main-lined).

Anal Stage   The second of Freud's psychosexual stages of development, beginning at approximately eight months and lasting until around eighteen months. It is characterized by the child's preoccupation with physical anal activities.

365

Androgen   Male sexual hormone.

Anthropologist   Social scientist concerned with the study of the human race. Anthropology contributes an historical, cultural, and evolutionary dimension to the study of humans. (*See* Psychologist, Sociologist)

A Posteriori   After the fact.

Arousal   Both a physiological and a psychological concept. Physiologically, it means changes in heart rate, respiration, electrical activity in the cortex, and in the skin's conductivity to electricity. Psychologically, arousal refers to degree of alertness, awareness, vigilance, or wakefulness. Arousal in a living human can range from low (coma or sleep) to high (panic, high anxiety).

Assimilation   The act of incorporating objects or aspects of objects to previously learned activities. To assimilate is in a sense to ingest or to employ something that is previously learned; more simply, the exercising of previously learned responses. (*See* Accommodation)

Astrology   The art of analyzing human personality, predicting the future, explaining the past, and answering various other important questions based on the positions of astral bodies at the time and place of the individual's birth in relation to the present position of those astral bodies.

Attitudes   Customary ways of reacting emotionally to events, objects, or situations.

Authoritarian   An adjective descriptive of people who consistently exhibit their need to establish authority.

Autonomy   Generally considered the final stage in moral development. It is characterized by the emergence of individual principles of conscience.

Average American   A nonexistent, psychological, sociological, cultural, historical invention.

Axillary Hair   Armpit hair.

Barbiturates   A group of sedating drugs, chemical in nature, more powerful than sedatives, and addictive if taken frequently enough and in sufficient doses.

Behavioristic Theory   A general term for those theories of learning concerned primarily with the observable components of behavior (stimuli and responses). Such theories are labeled S-R learning theories and are exemplified in classical and operant conditioning theories.

Beta Waves Relatively irregular and rapid brain waves that are characteristic of increasing arousal. May be employed as a physiological index of arousal. (*See* Arousal)

Breasts The front portion of the trunk, usually more developed in mature female humans than in males. (*See* Trunk)

Chancre A sore.

Chauvinistic Aggressively and excessively patriotic (jingoistic). (*See* Pig)

Chemical Drugs A colloquial expression for those drugs that are manufactured in laboratories rather than cultivated or found in natural states. Barbiturates and sedatives as prescription drugs, for example, are chemical drugs, as opposed to marijuana and peyote, which are natural drugs.

Child Young, human. From age two to adolescence.

Choleric A temperament characterized by ancient Greek philosophers as prone to anger.

Chromosome A microscopic body in the nucleus of all human and plant cells, containing the genes – the carriers of heredity. Each mature human sex cell (sperm or ovum) contains twenty-three chromosomes, each containing countless numbers of genes. (*See* Genes)

Circumcision Surgical removal of the foreskin on the penis. Ordinarily done during the neonatal period among a large number of societies including Western societies. Frequently employed as a puberty rite among the "primitive" tribes.

Classical Conditioning Also called learning through stimulus substitution, because it involves the repeated pairing of two stimuli so that a previously neutral (conditioned) stimulus eventually comes to elicit the same response (conditioned response) that was previously evoked by the first stimulus (unconditioned) stimulus. This type of conditioning was first described by Pavlov.

Clique A small (three to nine members), highly cohesive group of friends. (*See* Crowd)

Cocaine A very expensive drug that produces a euphoric high. Ordinarily taken by sniffing or inhaling.

Cognitive Pertaining to the intellectual functioning of humans. Related to such activities as are involved in perception, problem solving, information processing, understanding, and logical thought processes.

Cognitive Dissonance A state of conflict between beliefs and behavior, or between expectations and behavior. The term also refers to a motivational position premised on the assumption that the conflict arising from cognitive dissonance results in behavior designed to reduce the dissonance.

Cognitivism Those theories of learning that are concerned primarily with perception, problem solving, information processing, and understanding.

Combinatorial Analysis A logical thought process characteristic of children in formal operations (or at least possible at that developmental level) that is characterized by the children's systematic examination of all possible relevant combinations.

Compensation A logical rule that recognizes that in certain situations one type of physical change may be compensated for by an opposing change – hence, nullified. For example, in conservation of mass problems, increases in length or height are frequently compensated for by decrements in width or thickness.

Concrete Operations   The third of Piaget's four major stages, lasting from seven or eight to approximately eleven or twelve, and characterized primarily by children's ability to deal with concrete problems and objects, or objects and problems easily imagined in a concrete sense.

Conditioned Response (CR)   A response that is elicited by a conditioned stimulus. In some obvious way the conditioned response resembles its corresponding unconditioned response. The two are not identical, however.

Conditioned Stimulus (CS)   A stimulus that does not elicit any response or elicits a global orienting response initially; but as a result of being paired with an unconditioned stimulus, it acquires the capability of eliciting that same response.

367

Conditioning   A term employed to describe a simple type of learning. (*See* Classical Conditioning, Operant Conditioning)

Conscience   The organized totality of religious or social prescripts and values that govern individual behavior.

Conservation   A Piagetian term for the realization that certain quantitative attributes of objects remain unchanged unless something is added to or taken away from them. Such characteristics of objects as mass, number, area, volume, and so on are capable of being conserved.

Constructivists   A classification of adolescents described by Block as including those individuals who are socially involved but who are not protesters (activists). They are individuals who are involved in what would be considered to be constructive activities.

Continuous Culture   A culture that does not clearly mark the passage from one period of life to another. Contemporary Western societies are frequently described as being continuous, although there is some disagreement on this point. (*See* Discontinuous Culture)

Continuous Schedule   That type of reinforcement schedule where every correct response is followed by a reinforcer.

Control Group   Consists of subjects who are not experimented with, but who are used for comparisons with the experimental group to ascertain whether the subjects were affected by the experimental procedure. (*See* Experimental Group)

Conventionalists   A term employed to describe adolescents who are involved in social and political activity, but who are committed to the status quo rather than to rebellion as it is ordinarily understood.

Convergent Thinking   A term employed by Guilford to describe the type of thinking that results in a unique, correct solution for a problem. It is assumed that most conventional tests of intelligence measure convergent thinking abilities rather than divergent thinking abilities. (*See* Divergent Thinking)

Correlation   A statistical term that describes the relationship between variables. If two variables are highly correlated positively, as one increases so does the other. A negative correlation indicates that as one variable increases the other decreases. Intelligence and achievement are positively correlated; stupidity and achievement are negatively correlated. Correlation does not imply causation.

Creative An adjective that may be used to describe people, products, or a process. The term creativity generally refers to the capacity of individuals to produce novel or original answers or products.

Cretinism Extremely subnormal mental development, where the individual is usually deformed; that is, a cretin is a deformed idiot.

Critical Period Hypothesis The belief that there are certain periods in development during which exposure to appropriate experiences or stimuli will bring about specific learning much more easily than is the case at other times.

Cross-Sectional Study An investigatory technique that involves observing and comparing different subjects at different age levels. A cross-sectional study would compare fourteen- and sixteen-year-olds by observing both groups of adolescents at the same time, one group consisting of sixteen-year-olds and the other of fourteen-year-olds. A longitudinal study would require that the same adolescents be examined at the age of fourteen, fifteen, and perhaps again at the age of sixteen. (*See* Longitudinal Study)

Crowd When referring to adolescents, a group of fifteen to thirty individuals. Crowds are, in effect, combinations of cliques that are relatively similar in their interests and behaviors. Their primary functions are social.

Culture The sum total of mores, traditions, beliefs, values, customary ways of behaving, and explicit and implicit rules that characterize a group of people. Alternately, a culture may be viewed as that group of people that is characterized by similar mores, traditions, beliefs, and so on.

Defense Mechanism A relatively irrational and sometimes unhealthy method employed by persons to compensate for their inability to satisfy their basic desires and to overcome the anxiety accompanying this inability. (*See* Displacement, Reaction Formation, Intellectualization, Projection, Denial, Repression)

Delinquency A legal category defined in terms of transgression of laws, and apprehension. It is generally assumed that in order to be a delinquent, an individual must be a juvenile (adults are classed as criminals), must transgress some laws, and must be apprehended by law enforcement officers.

Democratic An adjective descriptive of individuals who do not display a strong need to establish authority in an autocratic sense, but who frequently defer to the wishes and opinions of others.

Denial A Freudian defense mechanism that involves distorting perceptions of the world. Denial is illustrated by the sour grapes phenomenon, where the fox distorted its perception of the grapes when it discovered that it could not reach them.

Deoxyribonucleic Acid (DNA) A substance assumed to be the basis of all life, consisting of four chemical bases arranged in an extremely large number of combinations. The two strands of the DNA molecule that comprise genes are arranged in the form of a double spiral (helix). These double strands are capable of replicating themselves as well as crossing over from one strand to the spiral of the other and forming new combinations of their genetic material. The nucleus of all cells contains DNA molecules.

Dependent Variable The variable that may or may not be affected by

368

manipulations of the independent variable in an experimental situation. (*See* Variable, Independent Variable)

Development The total process whereby individuals adapt to their environment. Development includes growth, maturation, and learning.

Developmental Psychology That aspect of psychology concerned with the development of individuals from birth to maturity, and sometimes on to death.

Developmental Tasks Capabilities that must be acquired, or skills that must be mastered in the process of growing up. Havighurst's theory of development is based on the notion that at every level in development there are a series of developmental tasks that must be mastered by children.

Discontinuous Culture Culture that clearly marks passage from one period of life to another. "Primitive" cultures are typically described as being discontinuous as they are characterized by rites de passage during adolescence. (*See* Continuous Culture)

Displacement A Freudian defense mechanism referring to the appearance of previously suppressed behavior in a somewhat more acceptable form. For example, individuals who have tendencies toward violence against people may displace this tendency in aggression against animals.

Dissenters An adjective employed to describe what have been called "professional agitators." These are adolescents who are passionately committed to a rejection of the status quo, but who are not themselves involved in a social or political activity designed to achieve these things.

Divergent Thinking An expression employed by Guilford to describe the type of thinking that results in the production of several different solutions for one problem. Divergent thinking is assumed to be closely related to creative behavior, and the term is often used interchangeably with the term creativity. (*See* Convergent Thinking)

Double-Blind Procedure An experimental technique where neither the investigator nor the subjects are aware of the expected outcomes of the experiment. A double-blind procedure generally requires that the experimenter not know which of the subjects are in fact experimental subjects, and which are control subjects.

Drugs Chemical substances that have physiological effects on living organisms.

Early Maturers Adolescents who begin pubescence earlier than is average for their sex.

Ectomorph One of Sheldon's somatotype classifications; ectomorphs are frail, cerebrotonic individuals who are seen to be restrained in movement, concerned with privacy, sensitive, and socially inhibited. (*See* Endomorph, Mezomorph)

Ego One aspect of basic personality structure, according to Freud. It is the rational reality-oriented level of human personality, which develops as the child becomes aware of what the environment makes possible and impossible, and therefore serves as a damper to the id. The id tends toward immediate gratification of impulses as they are felt, whereas the ego imposes restrictions that are based on environmental reality. (*See* Id, Superego)

Electra Complex A Freudian stage occurring around the age of four or five years, when a girl's awareness of her genital area leads her to desire her father and become jealous of her mother. (*See* Oedipus Complex)

Eliciting Effect   That type of imitative behavior where the observer does not copy the models' responses but simply behaves in a related manner. (*See* Modeling Effect, Inhibitory/Disinhibitory Effect)

Emotion   Refers to feeling, or affection aspects of human behavior and includes such human feelings as fear, rage, love, or desire.

Endomorph   One of Sheldon's somatotype classifications; endomorphs are viscerotonic and are believed to love comfort, be relaxed and slow in movement, be social, and love eating. (*See* Ectomorph, Mezomorph)

Eros   A Greek word meaning love, employed by Freud to describe what he also called the life instinct — the human urge for survival. Eros is sometimes used in contrast to Thanatos. (*See* Thanatos)

Estrogen   A female sexual hormone, although it is produced in small quantities by males as well.

Eugenics   A form of genetic engineering that selects specific individuals for reproduction. The term as applied to humans raises a number of serious moral and ethical questions. It is widely accepted and practiced with animals, however.

Evolution   The lengthy process whereby life forms — through natural selection and diversification brought about by environmental pressures — live, die, or change. Evolutionary processes are assumed to be responsible for the present variety and distribution of life forms on this planet.

Expectations   Anticipated behavior. Teacher expectations have been found, in some research, to be important in that they affect the behavior of some students. Other research has not supported this finding.

Experiment   A procedure for scientific investigation requiring the manipulation of some aspect of the environment to determine what the effects of this manipulation will be.

Experimental Group   A group of subjects who undergo experimental manipulation. The group to which something is done in order to observe its effects. (*See* Control Group)

Extended Family   A large family group consisting of parents, children, and occasionally uncles, aunts, cousins, and so on. (*See* Nuclear Family)

Extinction   The cessation of a response as a function of the withdrawal of reinforcement.

Extroverted   A term describing individuals whose personalities are characterized by sociability and preoccupation with external rather than internal events. (*See* Introverted)

Family   A social unit consisting of one or more persons, generally charged with the production and rearing of children. (*See* Nuclear Family, Extended Family)

Femininity   A complex of biological, physical, and personality variables traditionally associated with the female sex. (*See* Masculinity)

Fixation   A Freudian term describing the inability (or unwillingness) of a particular individual to progress normally through the psychosexual stages

370

of development. Such individuals become fixated at fixed stages. (*See* Regression)

Fixed Schedule A type of intermittent schedule of reinforcement when the reinforcement occurs at a fixed interval of time, in the case of an interval schedule; or after a specific number of trials, in the case of a ratio schedule (*See* Variable Schedule)

Flouris Green Green flowers.

Formal Operations The last of Piaget's major stages. It begins around the age of eleven or twelve and lasts until about fourteen or fifteen. It is characterized by the child's increasing ability to use logical thought processes.

Fraternal Twins Twins whose genetic origins are two different eggs. Such twins are as genetically dissimilar as average siblings. (*See* Identical Twins)

Functional Invariant A Piagetian term describing those aspects of human interaction with the environment that are unchanging as the individual develops. The functional invariants of adaptation are assimilation and accommodation, because the process of assimilating and accommodating remain constant as the child grows. (*See* Functioning)

Functioning A Piagetian term describing the processes by which organisms adapt to their environment. These processes are assimilation and accommodation. (*See* Assimilation, Accommodation)

Generalizability The extent to which a conclusion, principle, law, or rule that appears to be applicable in a specific situation will also be found to be applicable to different situations. One of the frequent criticisms of research in the social sciences is that conclusions are not always highly generalizable.

Generation Gap The cliché assumed to be descriptive of the value, interest, and attitude differences between a parent generation and its adolescents.

Genes The carriers of heredity. Each of the twenty-three chromosomes contributed by the sperm cell and the ovum at conception is believed to contain between forty and sixty thousand genes.

Genital Stage The last of Freud's stages of psychosexual development, beginning around the age of eleven and lasting until around eighteen. It is characterized by involvement with normal adult modes of sexual gratification.

Gonorrhea An extremely common venereal disease, achieving epidemic proportions in many parts of the world. Its initial symptoms, particularly in the male, are easily detected; and it can be treated effectively with penicillin.

Graphology The art of analyzing predominant personality characteristics of individuals by examining their customary handwriting.

Growth Ordinarily refers to such physical changes as increasing height or weight.

Hallucinogenic Drugs Drugs that have the effect of distorting perceptual functioning. Marijuana and LSD are hallucinogenic drugs.

Hedonistic Principle The belief that humans are motivated to avoid pain and obtain pleasure.

Hero or Heroine The most common figure in your daydreams.

Heteronomy An early stage in moral development during which individuals

371

respond to situations primarily in terms of the effects on themselves. (*See* Autonomy)

Hormone A substance secreted by certain glands that has the effect of stimulating activity in various organs of the body.

Hypothesis A prediction of the outcome of an event or a situation, or a possible explanation for some phenomenon.

Hypothetico- Deductive A type of thinking process involving the deduction of possible states of affairs from hypothetical states of affairs.

Id One aspect of human personality structure according to Freudian theory. The id is defined as all the instinctual urges of humans; it is the level of personality that contains human motives; in short, it is Eros and Thanatos. A newborn child's personality, according to Freud, is all id. (*See* Thanatos, Eros, Ego, Superego)

Identical Twins Twins whose genetic origin is a single egg. Such twins are genetically identical. (*See* Fraternal Twins)

Identification A general term referring to the process of assuming the goals, ambitions, mannerisms, and so on, of another person – of identifying with that person. (*See* Imitation)

Identity A rule specifying that certain activities leave objects or situations unchanged. (*See* Reversibility)

Imitation A relatively specific term that refers to the copying behavior of an organism. To imitate a person's behavior is simply to employ that person's behavior as a pattern. Bandura and Walters describe three different effects of imitation. (*See* Modeling Effect, Inhibitory/Disinhibitory Effect, Eliciting Effect)

Impotence One or more of: the inability to achieve and/or maintain an erection; the inability to ejaculate semen (reach an orgasm) during sexual intercourse; premature ejaculation.

Inactivist A term employed to describe adolescents who are politically and socially apathetic – that is, who are uninvolved in social or political activity.

Incest Sexual intercourse of related individuals. Ordinarily forbidden by law or by social custom. Among "advanced" societies, incest law is ordinarily justified in terms of possible genetic complications resulting from the attempt by closely related individuals to have children. Laws that prohibit marriage between "in-laws" are not justified in the same manner.

Independent Variable The variable in an experiment that can be manipulated to observe its effects on other variables. (*See* Variable, Dependent Variable)

Individualists A term employed to describe those individuals who are intensely involved in social and political activity, but who are not involved in protest as are activists. Individualists tend to be committed to the status quo rather than to its overthrow.

Infancy A developmental period that begins a few weeks after birth and lasts until approximately two years of age.

Inhalants Collective term for glue and other similar toxic substances that are frequently inhaled in order to bring about a state of euphoria. Commonly used inhalants include paint, nail polish, lighter fluid, and various cleaning fluids.

Inhibitory/Disinhibitory Effect That type of imitative behavior that results either in the suppression (inhibition) or appearance (disinhibition) of previously acquired deviant behavior. (*See* Modeling Effect, Eliciting Effect)

Inkblot An impolite, amorphous stain sometimes left by a pen on paper and other objects. More frequent when using quill pens than when using contemporary pens.

Instinct Complex, species specific, relatively unmodifiable behavior patterns such as migration in birds, hibernation in some mammals, and leadership behavior in fish.

Instrumental Conditioning A type of learning that is sometimes differentiated from operant conditioning but that may also be considered a part of operant conditioning. It refers specifically to those situations in which a response is instrumental in bringing about reinforcement. (*See* Operant Conditioning)

373

Intellectualization A Freudian defense mechanism whereby individuals emphasize the intellectual or rational content of their behavior in order to exclude the emotional connotations of that behavior. Intellectualization is sometimes referred to as rationalization.

Intelligence A property measured by intelligence tests. Seems to refer primarily to the capacity of individuals to adjust to their environments.

Intelligence Quotient (IQ) An index of an individual's measured intelligence. IQ scores on most intelligence tests average 100.

Intercourse Mutual dealings. Communication.

Intermittent Reinforcement A schedule of reinforcement that does not present a reinforcer for all correct responses. (*See* Interval Schedule, Ratio Schedule)

Interval Schedule An intermittent schedule of reinforcement that is based on the passage of time. (*See* Fixed Schedule, Random Schedule)

Introverted An adjective describing individuals who are withdrawn and concerned with internal rather than external events. (*See* Extroverted)

Intuitive Thinking One of the substages of preoperational thought, beginning around age four and lasting until around age seven or eight. Intuitive thought is marked by the ability to solve many problems intuitively and by the inability to respond correctly in face of misleading perceptual features of problems.

Kissing Usually the act of placing one's lips upon the lips or some other portion of another human's (or other animal's) anatomy. Sometimes may involve noses.

Language Complex arrangement of arbitrary sounds that have accepted referents and therefore can be used for communication among humans.

Late Maturers Individuals who undergo physical changes leading to sexual maturity at a later age than is normal (average) for their sex.

Latency Stage (Latency) The fourth of Freud's stages of psychosexual development, characterized by the development of the superego (conscience) and by loss of interest in sexual gratification. This stage is assumed to last from the age of six to eleven years.

Learning   Includes all changes in behavior that are due to experience. Does not include temporary changes brought about by drugs or fatigue, or changes in behavior simply resulting from maturation or growth. (*See* Maturation, Growth, Development)

Libido   A general Freudian term denoting sexual urges. The libido is assumed to be the source of energy for sexual urges. Freud considers these urges the most important forces in human motivation.

Longitudinal Study   A research technique that involves observing the same subjects over a long period of time. (*See* Cross-Sectional Study)

LSD (D-Lysergic Acid Diethylamide Tartrate)   A particularly powerful hallucinogenic drug; an inexpensive, easily made, synthetic chemical that sometimes can have profound influences on human perception. In everyday parlance it is often referred to as "acid."

Machiavellian   Unprincipled, crafty, shrewd, perfidious, dedicated to one's own ends. Dangerous in a rather awesome way. A worthy opponent for a team made up of Superman, Superwoman, the Green Hornet, and various other Heroes.

Marijuana   A highly common, mildly hallucinogenic drug derived from a variety of the hemp plant. The active ingredient in marijuana is tetrahydrocannabinol. (*See* Tetrahydrocannabinol)

Masculinity   A complex of biological, physical, and personality variables that are traditionally associated with the male sex. There is some disagreement concerning the extent to which masculinity and femininity are determined by genetic or cultural forces. (*See* Femininity)

Masochists   Those who derive pleasure from having injury inflicted upon themselves.

Masturbation   Self-stimulation of genital areas, frequently resulting in orgasm.

Maturation   A developmental process defined by changes that are relatively independent of a child's environment. While the nature and timing of maturational changes are assumed to result from genetic predispositions, their manifestation is at least partly a function of the environment. Many of the changes associated with pubescence are assumed to be related to maturation.

Maturational Theory   A theory of adolescent development that is based largely on the belief that the various capabilities and personality characteristics of adolescence result from genetically predetermined forces — hence maturation. Well-known examples of maturational theory are those of Gesell and Hall.

Maze-Bright   An adjective describing those rats able to learn to run through mazes very easily. A maze-bright rat is the counterpart of an intelligent person. (*See* Maze-Dull)

Maze-Dull   An adjective describing those rats who have a great deal of difficulty in learning how to run a maze. The maze-dull rat is the counterpart of the stupid person. (*See* Maze-Bright)

374

Meiosis The division of a single sex cell into two separate cells, each consisting of twenty-three chromosomes rather than twenty-three pairs of chromosomes. Meiosis therefore results in cells that are different, whereas mitosis results in identical cells. (*See* Mitosis)

Melancholic A temperament characterized by early Greek philosophers as sad and depressed.

Menarche A girl's first menstrual period. An event that occurs during pubescence.

Mescaline A relatively powerful hallucinogenic drug, originally derived from the buttons of the peyote cactus, but now available as a laboratory product.

Mezomorph One of Sheldon's somatotype classifications; a mezomorph is an athletically built individual who is assumed to love adventure, exercise, and activities that demand boldness and courage. (*See* Endomorph, Ectomorph)

375

Minority Groups Clearly identifiable groups who are not members of the dominant majority within a country or within a large social structure. Minority groups are frequently subject to varying amounts of prejudice and discrimination. They are frequently identified in socioeconomic terms.

Mitosis The division of a single somatic (body) cell into two identical cells. Occurs in body cells as opposed to sex cells. (*See* Meiosis)

Modeling Effect That type of imitative behavior that involves learning of a novel response. (*See* Inhibitory/Disinhibitory Effect, Eliciting Effect)

Models Those human males or females whose physical attributes are sufficiently attractive by cultural norms to serve as ideals. In cultures such as ours that are highly tolerant of incompetence, models are frequently used to sell or inspire.

Morality Refers to the ethical aspects of human behavior. Morality is intimately bound to the development of an awareness of acceptable and unacceptable behaviors. It is therefore linked to what is often called conscience. (*See* Conscience)

Morphogenesis Literally, changes or growth in form. Gesell believed that morphogenesis, determined by maturational forces, accounted for developmental changes in adolescence as well as in earlier childhood.

Motivation That which instigates, maintains, and directs behavior. Theories of motivation attempt to explain why humans behave as they do.

Narcotics Addictive drugs that generally produce sensations of well-being. Among the better known of the narcotics is heroin.

Nature/Nurture Controversy A very old psychological argument concerning whether genetics (nature) or environment (nurture) is more responsible for determining development.

Need A lack or deficit in the human organism that gives rise to behavior. Needs may be unlearned (for example, the need for food) or learned (the need for money).

Need for Achievement The urge that some individuals have to reach some standard of excellence. An indicator of motivation. Aggressive and ambitious people possess a higher need for achievement than more passive, less ambitious people.

Negative Identity   A term attributed to Erikson, descriptive of the assumption of a social role that runs counter to accepted roles in the individual's society. Juvenile delinquents are frequently characterized by negative identities.

Neo-Behavioristic   A term employed to describe learning theories that are concerned with events that intervene (mediate) between stimuli and responses.

Neonate   A newborn infant. The neonatal period terminates when birth weight is regained. Lasts approximately two weeks.

Nervous System   In humans, the total arrangement of nerve cells. The nervous system includes the brain, the spinal cord, all sensory pathways, and all sensory receptor cells such as those found in the eye and ear.

Nocturnal Emission   Spontaneous ejaculation of semen by mature male during sleep. Common among males who have no other sexual outlet.

No-No   A taboo.

Norm   An average, or a standard way of behaving. Cultural norms, for example, refer to the behavior that is expected of individuals who are members of that culture.

Nuclear Family   A family consisting of a mother, a father, and their immediate offspring. (*See* Extended Family)

Object Concept   Piaget's expression for children's understanding that the world is composed of objects that continue to exist quite apart from their perception of them.

Objective   Refers to research, theory, or experimental methods dealing with observable events. The assumption is that objective observations are not affected by the observer. (*See* Subjective, Projective)

Observational Learning   A term employed synonymously with the expression "learning through imitation." (*See* Imitation)

Oedipus Complex   A Freudian concept denoting the developmental stage (around four years) when a boy's increasing awareness of the sexual meaning of his genitals leads him to desire his mother and envy his father. (*See* Electra Complex)

Ontogenetic Development   The development of a single individual within a species. For example, the development of a child from birth to maturity is an example of ontogenetic development. (*See* Phylogenetic Development)

Operant   The label employed by Skinner to describe a response not elicited by any known or obvious stimulus. Most significant human behaviors appear to be operant. Such behaviors as writing a letter or going for a walk are operants, if no known specific stimulus elicits them.

Operant Conditioning   A type of learning involving an increase in the probability of a response occurring as a result of reinforcement. Much of the experimental work of B. F. Skinner investigates the principles of operant conditioning.

Opium   A narcotic drug derived from the juices at the base of the opium poppy. Ordinarily taken by injecting directly into the blood stream, or by

376

smoking. Heroin, morphine, and codeine are all narcotics derived from the same poppy.

Oral Aperture Mouth. Buccal cavity.

Oral Stage The first stage of psychosexual development, lasting from birth to approximately eight months of age. The oral stage is characterized by children's preoccupation with the immediate gratification of their desires. This they accomplish primarily through the oral regions, by sucking, biting, swallowing, playing with the lips, and so on.

Orgasm Paroxysm of emotion. Sometimes employed to describe the moment of sexual release.

Ovum (Ova) The sex cell produced by a matured female approximately once every twenty-eight days. When mature, consists of twenty-three chromosomes as opposed to all other human body cells (somatoplasm), which consist of 23 pairs of chromosomes. It is often referred to as an egg cell. (*See* Sperm Cell)

377

Palmistry The devious art of discovering an individual's past, present, or future from the configuration of lines, crevices, or other features of his or her open palm.

Peer Group A group of equals. Peer groups may be social groups, age groups, intellectual groups, or work groups. When the term is applied to adolescents, it typically refers to age and grade peers.

Penis External male sex organ serving several functions not the least important of which are procreation and elimination of liquid wastes.

Perception The translation of physical energies (stimuli; sensation) into neurological impulses that can be interpreted by the individual.

Personality The unique combination of characteristics, traits, habits, interests, values, and so on that distinguish one individual from another. The term personality is often distinguished from the term *self*. The self is individuals as they perceive themselves; personality is individuals as they are perceived by others.

Phallic Stage The third stage of psychosexual development. It begins at the age of eighteen months and lasts to approximately the age of six years. During this stage children become concerned with their genitals and may show evidence of the much discussed complexes labeled Oedipus and Electra. (*See* Oedipus Complex, Electra Complex)

Phlegmatic A temperment characterized by Greek philosophers as lethargic.

Phrenology The art of assessing human personality characteristics by examining the shape and size of individuals' heads along with any abnormal protuberances on their heads.

Phylogenetic Development The development of an entire species. The study of biological adaptation in an historical sense is the study of phylogenetic development. (*See* Ontogenetic Development)

Pig A four-footed, long-snouted animal, the more patriotic of which have recently been identified as being chauvinistic. (*See* Chauvinistic, Snout)

Placeboes Harmless, nonmedicinal pills. Sometimes given to a control group particularly in medical research. Subjects are duped into thinking that they have received actual medication.

Polygamy A marital state where a husband will have several wives. A similar state, polyandry, involves one woman having several husbands.

Pregnancy A condition that occurs in women, but never in men. It involves being pregnant. (*See* Pregnant)

Pregnant An adjective describing a woman who has had an ovum (egg cell) fertilized, and who, nature and others willing, will eventually give birth to a human child.

Preoperational The second of Piaget's four major stages, lasting from about two to seven or eight years. Consists of two substages: intuitive thinking and preconceptual thinking. (*See* Intuitive Thinking)

Primitive Societies A term employed by "advanced" societies to describe other societies not characterized by as advanced a degree of technological, social, and material sophistication.

Projection A Freudian defense mechanism whereby individuals attribute anxieties that are really their own to someone else. For example, individuals who are afraid of the dark and assume that everyone else is also afraid of the dark are said to be projecting.

Projective A method of investigation or observation in which subjects are encouraged to respond in their own way to relatively nebulous stimuli, and where the investigator then interprets the subjects' responses. The assumption is that subjects will project their true feelings, thoughts, or beliefs. (*See* Objective, Subjective)

Proposition A term that grandmothers consider to imply impure intentions. In psychological jargon it refers to a statement that can be either true or false. Hence, propositional thought deals with statements rather than with concrete objects or events.

Psychoanalytic Relating to the elaborate psychological system developed by Freud.

Psychologist An individual who is concerned with the study of human behavior and that of other animals as well, or with the application of knowledge concerning human behavior.

Psychopath An individual suffering from a character disorder characterized by absence of feelings of guilt concerning transgressions of social or moral rules. Such an individual will engage in deviant behavior and feel no guilt whatsoever.

Psychosexual Development A Freudian term describing child development as a series of stages that are sexually based. (*See* Oral Stage, Anal Stage, Phallic Stage, Latency Stage, Genital Stage)

Puberty Sexual maturity following pubescence. (*See* Pubescence)

Pubescence Changes that occur in late childhood or early adolescence, preceding sexual maturity. In boys these changes include enlargement of the testes, growth of axillary hair, changes in the voice, and the ability to ejaculate semen. In the girl, pubescence is characterized by rapid physical growth, occurrence of the first menstrual period (menarche), a slight lowering of the voice, and enlargement and development of the breasts.

Pubic Pertaining to the genital area. Sometimes called crotch.

Race A concept about which there has been considerable disagreement in professional literature. Race ordinarily refers to significant groups of individuals whose genetic pools are different from those of other groups of individuals. Obvious differences among these groups would involve such superficial attributes as hair color, skin color, facial characteristics, etc. While some writers identify several dozen races, others reduce the number to three or four. Still others maintain there are no pure genetic pools remaining, and that the concept of race is archaic and not particularly useful.

Random Schedule (*See* Variable Schedule)

Rat A small animal with a long tail and a peculiar sense of humor.

Ratio Schedule An intermittent schedule of reinforcement that is based on a proportion of correct responses. (*See* Fixed Schedule, Random Schedule)

379

Reaction Formation A Freudian defense mechanism whereby individuals behave in a manner opposite to their inclinations. Reaction formation is illustrated by the individual who deeply desires a Cadillac, can't afford one, and convinces himself and his neighbors that he much prefers to drive a Volkswagen in any case.

Recidivism A term employed to describe the "repeated offender" phenomenon. It has been discovered, for example, that the recidivism rate in contemporary prisons and detention centers is high. What this means is that a large proportion of those who are presently incarcerated have been incarcerated previously.

Reflex An unlearned stimulus response connection. Flinching or withdrawing as a result of pain is an example of a reflex.

Regression A Freudian term describing reversion to an earlier stage of psychosexual development. Individuals at the genital stage of development, for example, may regress to the oral stage and show evidence of their regression through such activities as smoking. (*See* Genital Stage, Oral Stage, Fixation)

Reinforcement The effect of a reinforcer. Specifically, to increase the probability of a response occurring.

Reinforcement Schedule The manner and order in which reinforcement is presented to an organism as it learns. (*See* Random Schedule, Fixed Schedule, Continuous Schedule)

Reliability Accuracy in a numerical measurement sense. A test is reliable to the extent that it measures accurately whatever it does measure.

Repression A Freudian defense mechanism where unpleasant (traumatic) experiences are unconsciously "forgotten." That is, they are stored deep in the subconscious mind where, according to Freud, they affect behavior although the individual is no longer conscious of them because they are inaccessible to waking memory.

Respondent A term employed by Skinner in contrast to the term operant (also synonymous with elicited response). A respondent is a response elicited by a known specific stimulus. Unconditioned responses of the type referred to in classical conditioning are examples of respondents.

Response Any organic, muscular, glandular, or psychic reaction resulting from stimulation.

Reversibility The logical property manifested in the ability to reverse or undo activity in either an empirical or a conceptual sense. An idea is said to be reversible when children can "unthink it" and when they realize that certain logical consequences follow from so doing.

Rites de Passage Ceremonial rites frequently specific to an entire culture or tribe, employed to mark the passage from one developmental or cultural stage to another. A distinction is frequently made between rites de passage and initiation rites, the latter referring specifically to ceremonial rites that are employed as an initiation into adulthood. Hence the term initiation rite is frequently used interchangeably with the term puberty rite.

Sadist One who derives pleasure from inflicting injury on others.

Salivation A flow of saliva; a restrained form of drooling.

380

Sample A group of individuals or observations investigated. A sample is assumed to be representative of a larger group of individuals or observations (populations). It is therefore assumed in scientific investigations that results derived from a study of a sample are also valid for the population from which the sample has been drawn.

Sanguine The temperament characterized by ancient Greek philosophers as optimistic and happy.

Schemes (also Schema or Schemata) A label employed by Piaget to describe a unit in cognitive structure. A scheme is, in one sense, an activity together with its structural connotations. In another sense, a scheme may be thought of as an idea or a concept. It usually labels a specific activity; a looking scheme, a grasping scheme, or a sucking scheme.

Scrotum A saclike appendage in the human male containing the testes. Being somewhat external to the body, it serves the remarkably useful function of keeping the sperm cells slightly below body temperature, thereby increasing their viability.

Sedatives Drugs that have a depressant effect on the nervous system. Tranquilizers and barbiturates are among the more common examples of sedatives.

Self-Actualization The process of becoming the fullest expression of one's self, developing one's potential, achieving an awareness of one's identity, fulfilling one's self. Self-actualization is central to humanistic psychology.

Self-Concept The attitudes or opinions that an individual has of him- or herself. Appears to be very closely related to psychological adjustment.

Self-Identification A relatively nebulous term referring to the notion that individuals must discover who they are. This, according to many theorists, is one of the major tasks of adolescents. Perhaps the problem is not so much one of discovering who one is as a problem of discovering who one can be, and therefore, who one will choose to be.

Semen Substance produced by mature male and released during ejaculation. Contains sperm cells.

Sensorimotor The first stage of development in Piaget's classification. It lasts from birth to approximately age two. Children understand this world primarily through their activities toward it and sensations of it.

Shack-Up Colloquial expression for living together as husband and wife, or in various other combinations, without being legally married. Does not occur solely in shacks.

Siblings   Offspring whose parents are the same. Siblings are simply brothers and sisters.

Skinner Box   Refers to the experimental apparatus employed by Skinner in much of his research with rats and pigeons. It is a cagelike structure, equipped to allow the animal to make a response and the experimenter to reinforce or punish it for the response.

Snout   A nose, usually on a nonhuman animal.

Social Learning   The acquiring of patterns of behavior that conform to social expectations. Learning what is acceptable and what is not acceptable in a given culture.

Sociogram   A pictorial or graphic representation of the social structure of a group. Frequently depicts patterns of likes and dislikes within a group.

Sociologist   Social scientist concerned with the study of human behavior dynamics. One of the more obvious distinctions between psychologists and sociologists is that the former study individuals whereas the latter study groups.

Sociometry   A measurement procedure employed extensively in socio-logical studies. It attempts to determine patterns of likes, dislikes, power, leadership behavior, etc. in a group.

Sperm Cell   The sex cell produced by a mature male. Like egg cells (ova), sperm cells consist of twenty-three chromosomes rather than twenty-three pairs of chromosomes.

Stimulants   Drugs that have a stimulating effect on the nervous system. Amphetamines (for example, speed) are stimulants.

Stimulus (Stimuli)   Any change in the physical environment capable of exciting a sense organ. Sometimes defined as an environmental or internal condition that leads to behavior.

Structure   A phrase employed by Piaget to describe the organization of an individual's capabilities, whether they be motor or cognitive. Structures are assumed to result from interacting with the world through assimilation and accommodation. (*See* Assimilation, Accommodation, Schemes)

Sturm und Drang   A German expression sometimes used as a description of adolescence. Literally means storm and stress. It is descriptive of the turbulence, turmoil, and frustrated idealism that is sometimes assumed to be characteristic of adolescents.

Subjective   In contrast to the adjective, objective, refers to observations, theories, and experimental methods where the subjects are at least partly responsible for reporting and sometimes for interpreting aspects of their own behavior. (*See* Objective, Projective)

Superego   The level of personality that, according to Freud, defines the moral or ethnical aspects of human behavior. Like the ego, it is frequently in conflict with the id. It is assumed to develop largely as a function of the resolution of Oedipus or Electra Complexes. (*See* Id, Ego)

Syphilis   A debilitating venereal disease whose early symptoms often go unnoticed. Can be treated readily with penicillin and related drugs.

Taboo A no-no. (*See* No-No)

Testes Organs in the human male where sperm cells are formed and mature.

Tetrahydrocannabinol (THC) The active ingredient in marijuana and similar substances (hashish).

Thanatos A Greek word meaning death employed by Freud to describe what he called the death wish or death instinct. It is used in contrast with the word Eros and does not play a significant role in Freud's theory. (*See* Eros)

Theory Logically consistent system of rules and principles advanced to account for observed phenomena.

Toadstool Solid waste cunningly distributed by a froglike animal. Alternately, a small three-legged seat upon which these froglike animals sit. Toadstools, of either variety, will usually be found to be poisonous, should one be so foolish as to try and eat them.

382

Trait A specific quality of an individual that is consistent from one situation to another. (*See* Type)

Transductive Reasoning The type of semilogical reasoning that proceeds from particular to particular rather than from particular to general or from general to particular. One example of transductive reasoning is the following: Cows give milk. Goats give milk. Therefore goats are cows.

Trauma Literally means injury. As used by Freud, refers to intense anxiety resulting from highly unpleasant experiences – hence, nervous injury.

Trial-and-Error An explanation for learning based on the idea that when placed in a problem situation individuals will emit a number of responses, but will eventually learn the correct one as a result of reinforcement. Trial-and-error explanations for learning are sometimes contrasted with insight explanations.

Trunk The anterior end of an elephant. Sometimes a rectangular box in which grandmothers keep precious belongings not including pearls of wisdom. Also sometimes a portion of the body found between the neck and the waist.

Type A broad classification of individuals characterized by similar combinations of traits. Such a broad classification as introversion-extroversion is an example of a type. More specific qualities such as aggressiveness, ambition, and generosity describe traits rather than types. (*See* Trait)

Unconditioned Response A response elicited by an unconditioned stimulus.

Unconditioned Stimulus A stimulus that elicits a response prior to learning. All stimuli capable of eliciting reflexive behaviors are examples of unconditioned stimuli. For example, food is an unconditioned stimulus for the response of salivation.

Uterus (Uteri) Womb.

Validity Accuracy. Truthfulness. A test is valid to the extent that it measures what it claims to measure. (*See* Reliability)

Values Judgments or beliefs relating to the desirability of certain behaviors or goals.

Variable A property, measurement, or characteristic that is susceptible to variation. In psychological experimentation such qualities of human beings as intelligence and creativity are referred to as variables. (*See* Independent Variable, Dependent Variable)

Variable Schedule Also called random schedule. A type of intermittent schedule of reinforcement. It may be either of the interval or ratio variety, as is characterized by the presentation of rewards at random intervals or on random trials. Although both fixed and random schedules may be based on the same intervals or on the same ratios, one can predict when reward will occur under a fixed schedule whereas it is impossible to do so under a random schedule.

Virginity State of sexual innocence.

Zygote A fertilized egg cell (ovum). A zygote is formed from the union of a sperm cell and an egg cell; it contains forty-six chromosomes (full complement).

383

Bibliography

Abrahamson, S. "Our status system and scholastic rewards." *The Journal of Educational Sociology,* 1952, 25, 441–450.

Ahlstrom, W. M., and Havighurst, R. J. *400 Losers.* San Francisco: Jossey-Bass, 1971.

Alexander, C. N., Jr. "Alcohol and adolescent rebellion." *Social Forces,* 1967, 45, 542–550.

Alexander, G. "LSD: Injections early in pregnancy produce abnormalities in offspring of rats." *Science,* 1967, 157, 459–460.

Aller, M. "The definition of alcoholism and the estimation of its prevalence." In D. P. Pittman and C. R. Snyder (eds.), *Society, Culture, and Drinking Patterns.* New York: John Wiley & Sons, 1962.

Altus, W. D. "Birth order and academic primogeniture." *Journal of Personality and Social Psychology,* 1965, 2, 872–876.

Altus, W. D. "Birth order and its sequelae." *International Journal of Psychiatry,* 1967, 3, 23–32.

Ames, R. "Physical maturing among boys as related to adult social behavior: A longitudinal study." *California Journal of Educational Research,* 1957, 8, 69–75.

Anderson, R. E. "Where's Dad? Paternal deprivation and delinquency." *Archives of General Psychiatry,* 1968, 18, 641–649.

Anduri, C. E. "Identifying potential dropouts." *California Education,* 1965, 3, 31.

Angrist, S. S. "The study of sex roles." *Journal of Social Issues,* 1969, 25, 215–232.

Armstrong, C. M. *Patterns of Achievement in Selected New York State Schools.* Albany: New York State Education Department, 1964.

Ausubel, D. P. *Educational Psychology: A Cognitive View.* New York: Holt, Rinehart & Winston, 1968.

Ausubel, D. P. *The Psychology of Meaningful Verbal Learning.* New York: Gruen and Stratton, 1963.

Ausubel, D. P. *Theory and Problems of Adolescent Development.* New York: Gruen and Stratton, 1954.

Ball, J. C.; Ross, A.; and Simpson, A. "Incidents and estimated prevalence of recorded delinquency in a metropolitan area." *American Sociological Review*, 1964, 29, 90–93.

Bandura, A. *Principles of Behavior Modification.* New York: Holt, Rinehart & Winston, 1969.

Bandura, A., and Walters, R. H. *Adolescent Aggression: A Study of the Influence of Child Training Practices and Family Interrelationships.* New York: Ronald Press, 1959.

Bandura, A., and Walters, R. H. *Social Learning and Personality Development.* New York: Holt, Rinehart & Winston, 1963.

Barber, T. X., and Silver, M. J. "Fact, fiction, and the experimentor bias effect." *Psychological Bulletin Monographs Supplement*, 1969, 70, 1–29 (a).

Barber, T. X., and Silver, M. J. "Pitfalls in data analysis and interpretation: A reply to Rosenthal." *Psychological Bulletin Monographs Supplement*, 1969, 70, 48–62 (b).

Baughman, E. E. *Black Americans: A Psychological Analysis.* New York: Academic Press, 1971.

Bayer, A. E. "Birth order and college attendance." *Journal of Marriage and the Family*, 1966, 28, 480–484.

Bayley, N. "On the growth of intelligence." *American Psychologist*, 1955, 10, 805–818.

Bell, R. R. *Premarital Sex in a Changing Society.* Englewood Cliffs, N.J.: Prentice-Hall, 1966.

Beller, E. K. "Two attitude components in younger boys." *Journal of Social Psychology*, 1949, 29, 137–151.

Bender, L. "Drug addiction in adolescents." *Comprehensive Psychiatry*, 1963, 4, 181–194.

Bennett, E. M., and Cohen, L. R. "Men and women: Personality patterns and conquests." *Genetic Psychology Monographs*, 1959, 50, 122–123.

Berlyne, D. E. "Curiosity and exploration." *Science*, 1966, 153, 25–33.

Bernard, L. L. *Instinct: A Study in Social Psychology.* New York: Holt, Rinehart & Winston, 1924.

Blackwood, B. *Both Sides of the Buka Pessits: An Ethnographic Study of Social, Sexual, and Economic Questions in the Northwestern Solomon Islands.* London: Oxford University Press, 1935.

Blatz, W. E. *Collected Studies on the Dionne Quintuplets.* Toronto: University of Toronto Press, 1937.

Bloch, H. A., and Niederhoffer, A. *The Gang: A Study in Adolescent Behavior.* New York: Philosophical Library, 1958.

Block, J. H.; Haan, N.; and Smith, M. B. "Activism and apathy in contemporary adolescence." In J. F. Adams (ed.), *Understanding Adolescence: Current Developments in Adolescent Psychology.* Boston: Allyn & Bacon, 1973 (pp. 302–338).

Block, J. H.; Haan, N.; and Smith, M. B. "Socialization correlates of student activism." *The Journal of Social Issues*, 1969, 25, 143–178.

Bloom, B. S. *Stability and Change in Human Characteristics.* New York: John Wiley & Sons, 1964.

Boring, E. G. "Intelligence as the tests test it." *New Republic,* 1923, 35, 35–37.

Bossard, J. H., and Boll, E. S. *The Large Family System.* Philadelphia: University of Pennsylvania Press, 1956.

Bossard, J. H., and Sanger, W. P. "The large family system—a research report." *American Sociological Review,* 1952, 17, 3–9.

Bowerman, C. E., and Kinch, J. W. "Changes in family and peer orientation of children between the fourth and tenth grades." *Social Forces,* 1959, 37, 206–211.

Bradway, K. P., and Thompson, C. W. "Intelligence at adulthood: A twenty-five-year follow-up." *General Educational Psychology,* 1962, 53, 1–14.

Breen, J. L. "Venereal Disease." *Journal of Newark City Hospital,* 1967, 4, 25–37.

Brehm, J. W., and Cohen, A. R. *Explorations in Cognitive Dissonance.* New York: John Wiley & Sons, 1962.

Brill, A. A. (ed.). *The Basic Writing of Sigmund Freud.* New York: Random House, 1938.

Brim, O. G., Jr. "Family structure and sex role learning by children: A further analysis of Alan Koch's data." *Sociometry,* 1956, 21, 1–16.

Brink, W., and Harris, L. *Black and White.* New York: Simon and Schuster, 1967.

Brittain, C. V. "Adolescent choices and parent-peer cross-pressures." *American Sociological Review,* June 1963, 385–391.

Bronfenbrenner, U. "Some familiar antecedents of responsibility and leadership in adolescents." In L. Petrullo and B. Bass (eds.), *Leadership and Interpersonal Behavior.* New York: Holt, Rinehart & Winston, 1961.

Brown, F. A. "Living clocks." *Science,* 1959, 130, 1535–1544.

Brown, J. A. C. *Freud and the Post-Freudians.* Middlesex, England: Penguin Books, 1961.

Bruner, J. S. *Contemporary Approaches to Cognition.* Cambridge, Mass.: Harvard University Press, 1957, 41–69 (a).

Bruner, J. S. "On perceptual readiness." *Psychological Review,* 1957, 64, 123–152 (b).

Bruner, J. S. *Processes of Cognitive Growth: Infancy.* Worcester, Mass.: Clark University Press, 1968.

Buehler, R. E.; Patterson, G. R.; and Furniss, J. "The reinforcement of behavior in institutional settings." *Behavior Research and Therapy,* 1966, 4, 157–167.

Burchinal, L. "Comparison of factors related to adjustment and pregnancy-provoked and nonpregnancy-provoked youthful marriages." *Midwest Sociologist,* 1959, 21, 92–96.

Burton, R. V. "Generality of honesty reconsidered." *Psychological Review,* 1963, 70, 481–499.

386

Cameron, P. "Confirmation of the Freudian psycho-sexual stages utilizing sexual symbolism." *Psychological Reports,* 1967, 21, 33–39.

Carlson, R. "Identification and personality structure in preadolescence." *Journal of Abnormal and Social Psychology,* 1963, 67, 567–573.

Cartwright, D. S.; Tomson, B.; and Schwarts, H. *Gang Delinquency.* Monterey, Calif.: Brooks/Cole, 1975.

Cattell, R. B. *Description and Measurement of Personality.* New York: Harcourt, Brace and World, 1946.

Cervantes, L. F. "Family background, primary relationships, and the high school dropout." *Journal of Marriage and the Family,* 1965, 27, 218–223.

Clifford, E. "Body satisfaction in adolescence." *Perceptual and Motor Skills,* 1971, 33, 119–125.

Cobliner, W. G. "Pregnancy in the single, adolescent girl: The role of cognitive functions." *Journal of Youth and Adolescence,* 1974, 3, 17–29.

Cohen, D. K. "Does IQ matter?" *Current,* 1972, 141, 19–30.

Cohen, Y. A. *The Transition from Childhood to Adolescence.* Chicago: Aldine Publishing, 1964.

Cole, L., and Hall, I. N. *Psychology of Adolescence.* 7th ed. New York: Holt, Rinehart & Winston, 1970.

Coleman, J. S. *The Adolescent Society.* New York: Free Press of Glencoe, 1961.

Coleman, J. S. *Youth: Transition to Adulthood.* Chicago: University of Chicago Press, 1974.

Coleman, J. S. et al. *Equality of Educational Opportunity.* Washington, D.C.: U.S. Government Printing Office, 1966.

Collard, E. D. *Achievement motive in a four-year-old child and its relationship to achievement expectancies of the mother.* Unpublished doctoral dissertation, University of Michigan, 1964.

Collins, J. K. "Adolescent dating intimacy: Norms and peer expectations." *Journal of Youth and Adolescence,* 1974, 3, 317–328.

Combs, J., and Cooley, W. W. "Dropouts: In high school and after school." *American Educational Research Journal,* 1968, 5, 343–364.

Conger, J. J. *Adolescence and Youth: Psychological Development in a Changing World.* New York: Harper and Row, 1973.

Coopersmith, S. *The Antecedents of Self-Esteem.* San Francisco: W. H. Freeman, 1967.

Cox, C., and Smart, R. G. "The extent and nature of speed use in North America." *Canadian Medical Association Journal,* 1970, 102, 724–729.

Crandall, V. J., and Preston, A. "Verbally expressed needs and overt maternal behaviors." *Child Development,* 1961, 32, 261–270.

Cratty, B. J. *Perceptual and Motor Development in Infants and Children.* New York: Macmillan, 1970.

Cropley, A. J. "Creativity: a new kind of intellect?" *Australian Journal of Education,* 1967, 11, 120–125.

Cropley, A. J. *Originality, intelligence and personality.* Unpublished doctoral dissertation, University of Alberta, Edmonton, Alberta, 1965.

Culwick, A. T., and Culwick, G. J. *Ubena of the Rivers.* London: Alan and Onwan, 1935.

Davis, E. A. *The Development of Linguistic Skills in Twins, Single Twins with Siblings, and Only Children from Age Five to Ten Years.* Minneapolis: University of Minnesota Press, Institute of Child Welfare Series, #14, 1937.

Davis, K. "Adolescence and the social structure." In J. Seidman (ed.), *The Adolescent.* New York: Holt, Rinehart & Winston, 1960.

Deevey, E. S., Jr. "The human population." *Scientific American,* 1960, 203, 194–205.

Dellas, M., and Gaier, E. L. "Identification of creativity: The individual." *Psychological Bulletin,* 1970, 73, 55–73.

Douglas, J. W. B., and Ross, J. N. "Age of puberty related to educational ability, attainment, and school leaving age." *Journal of Child Psychology and Psychiatry,* 1964, 5, 185–196.

Douvan, E., and Adelson, J. *The Adolescent Experience.* New York: John Wiley & Sons, 1966.

Dunphy, D. C. "The social structure of urban adolescent peer groups." *Sociometry,* 1963, 26, 230–246.

Ebin, D. (ed.). *The Drug Experience: First Person Accounts of Addicts, Writers, Scientists, and Others.* New York: Orion Press, 1961.

Eggan, Fred. *Social Organization of the Western Pueblos.* Chicago: University of Chicago Press, 1950.

Ehrmann, W. W. *Premarital Dating Behavior.* New York: Holt, Rinehart & Winston, 1959.

Eiseley, Loren. *The Immense Journey.* New York: Random House, 1957.

Elkind, D. "Middle class delinquency." *Mental Hygiene,* January 1967, 80–84.

Engels, F. *The Origin of the Family, Private Property, and the State.* Chicago: Kerr, 1902.

Erikson, E. H. *Identity: Youth and Crisis.* New York: W. W. Norton, 1968.

Erikson, E. H. "The roots of virtue." In J. Huxley (ed.), *The Humanist Frame.* New York: Harper and Row, 1961 (pp. 145–166).

Erikson, E. H. *Identity and the Life Cycle: Selected papers.* From *Psychological Issue Monograph Series,* 1. New York: International University Press, 1959.

Erikson, E. H. "The problems of ego identity." *Journal of the American Psychoanalytic Association,* 1956, 4, 56–121.

Erikson, E. H. *Juvenile Delinquency.* Paper read at the staff training institute, University of Pittsburgh, 1954. (Reported in Maier, 1965.)

Erikson, E. H. *Childhood and Society.* New York: W. W. Norton, 1950.

Eysenck, H. J. *Dimensions of Personality.* London: Routledge and Kegan Paul, 1947.

Faris, R. E. "Sociological causes of genius." *The American Sociological Review,* 1940, 5, 689–699.

Farnsworth, D. L. "Are our present adolescents a new breed?" *New England Association Review,* 1967, 15, 4–10.

Faust, M. S. "Developmental maturity as a determinant in prestige of adolescent girls." *Child Development,* 1960, 31, 173–184.

Feldman, S. E., and Feldman, M. T. "Transition of sex differences in cheating." *Psychological Reports,* 1967, 20, 957–958.

Festinger, L. *A Theory of Cognitive Dissonance.* Stanford, Calif.: Stanford University Press, 1957.

Festinger, L., and Carlsmith, J. N. "Cognitive consequences of forced compliance." *Journal of Abnormal and Social Psychology,* 1959, 58, 203–210.

Finger, J. A., Jr., and Silverman, M. "Changes in academic performance in the junior high school." *Personnel Guidance Journal,* 1966, 45, 157–164.

Flacks, R. "The liberated generation: An exploration of the roots of student protest." *Journal of Social Issues,* 1967, 22, 52–75.

Flanders, N. A.; Morrison, B. N.; and Brode, E. L. "Changes in people's attitudes during the school year." *Journal of Educational Psychology,* 1968, 59, 334–338.

Flavell, J. H. *The Developmental Psychology of Jean Piaget.* New York: D. Van Nostrand, 1963.

Fodor, E. M. "Delinquency and susceptibility to social influence among adolescents as a function of level moral development." *Journal of Social Psychology,* 1972, 86, 257–260.

Forbes, J. D. *Mexican-Americans: A Handbook for Educators.* Berkeley, Calif.: Far West Laboratory for Educational Research and Development, 1966.

Fort, J. *Youth: How to produce dropins rather than dropouts.* Research Resume #38. Burlingame, Calif.: Proceedings of the 20th Annual State Conference on Educational Research, 1968.

Fowler, H. *Curiosity and Exploratory Behavior.* New York: Macmillan, 1965.

Frazier, A., and Lisonbee, L. K. "Adolescent concerns with physique." *School Review,* 1950, 58, 397–405.

French, J. D. "The reticular formation." *Scientific American,* May 1957.

Freud, A. "Adolescence." *Psychoanalytic Study of the Child,* 1958, 13, 255–278.

Freud, A. *The Ego and the Mechanism of Defense.* C. Baines (trans.). New York: International Press, 1946.

Freud, S. *Group Psychology and the Analysis of the Ego.* New York: Liveright, 1922.

Freud, S. *The Interpretation of Dreams.* New York: Random House, 1950.

Friedenberg, E. Z. "Current patterns of the generational conflict." *Journal of Social Issues,* 1969, 25, 21–38.

Friedenberg, E. Z. *The Vanishing Adolescent.* Boston: Beacon Press, 1960.

Friedman, A. S. "The family and the female delinquent: An overview." In O. Pollak and A. S. Friedman (eds.) *Family Dynamics and Female Sexual*

Delinquency. Palo Alto, Calif.: Science and Behavior Books, 1969 (pp. 113–126).

Friesen, D. "Academic-athletic-popularity syndrome in the Canadian high school society (1967)." *Adolescence,* 1968, 3, 39–52.

Frisch, R. E., and Revelle, R. "Height, and weight at menarche and a hypothesis of critical body weights and adolescent events." *Science,* 1970, 169, 397–398.

Gagne, R. M. *The Conditions of Learning.* 1st ed. New York: Holt, Rinehart & Winston, 1965.

Gagne, R. M. *The Conditions of Learning.* 2nd ed. New York: Holt, Rinehart & Winston, 1970.

Gagnon, J. H., and Simon, W. "They're going to learn in the street anyway." *Psychology Today,* 1969, 3, 46–47; 71.

Gallagher, J. J. *Analysis of Research on the Education of Gifted Children.* State of Illinois: Office of the Superintendent of Public Instruction, 1960.

Galton, F. *Hereditary Genius: An Inquiry into its Laws and Consequences.* London: Macmillan, 1896.

Garai, J. E., and Scheinfeld, A. "Sex differences in mental and behavioral traits." *Genetic Psychology Monographs,* 1968, 77, 169–299.

Gershon, S., and Angrist, B. "Drug induced psychoses: II." *Hospital Practice,* 1967, 2, 50–53.

Gesell, A. L. "The ontogeny of infant behavior." In L. Carmichael (ed.), *Manual of Child Psychology.* New York: John Wiley & Sons, 1946.

Gesell, A. L. *Wolf Child and Human Child.* New York: Harper, 1940.

Gesell, A. L.; Ilg, F. L.; and Ames, L. B. *Youth: the Years from Ten to Sixteen.* New York: Harper, 1956.

Getzels, J. W., and Jackson, P. W. *Creativity and Intelligence.* New York: John Wiley & Sons, 1962.

Ginzberg, E. "Jobs, dropouts, and automation." In D. Schreiber (ed.), *Profile of the School Dropout.* New York: Vintage Books, 1968 (pp. 125–135).

Glueck, S., and Glueck, E. *Predicting Delinquency and Crime.* Cambridge, Mass.: Harvard University Press, 1959.

Goffman, E. *The Presentation of Self in Everyday Life.* New York: Doubleday, 1959.

Gold, M. "Juvenile delinquency as a symptom of alienation." *Journal of Social Issues,* 1969, 25, 125–135.

Gold, M., and Douvan, Elizabeth. *Adolescent Development: Readings in Research and Theory.* Boston: Allyn & Bacon, 1969.

Goldstein, R. *1 in 7: Drugs on Campus.* New York: Walter, 1966.

Goode, E. (ed.). *Marijuana.* New York: Walter, 1969.

Gordon, Chard. "Social characteristics of early adolescence." In J. Kagan and R. Coles (eds.), *12–16: Early Adolescence.* New York: W. W. Norton, 1972 (pp. 25–54).

Green, R. S. "Age-intelligence relationship between ages 16–64: A rising trend." *Developmental Psychology,* 1969, 1, 618–627.

Grinder, R. E. *Adolescence.* New York: John Wiley & Sons, 1973.

Guilford, J. P. "Creativity." *American Psychologist,* 1950, 5, 444–454.

Guilford, J. P. *The Nature of Human Intelligence.* New York: McGraw-Hill, 1967.

Guilford, J. P. "Factors that aid and hinder creativity." *Teacher's College Record,* 1962, 63, 380–392.

Guilford, J. P. "Three faces of intellect." *American Psychologist,* 1959, 14, 469–479.

Gurvitz, M. S. "On the decline of performance on intelligence tests with age." *American Psychologist,* 1951, 6, 295.

Guthrie, E. R. *The Psychology of Learning.* Rev. ed. New York: Harper and Row, 1952.

Haan, N.; Smith, M. B.; and Block, J. "Moral reasoning of young adults: Political-social behavior, family background, and personality correlates." *Journal of Personality and Social Psychology,* 1968, 10, 183–201.

Hadden, J. K. "The private generation." *Psychology Today,* 1969, 3 (5), 32–35.

Hall, G. S. *Adolescence.* New York: Appleton, 1904.

Hall, G. S. *Adolescence, Two.* New York: Appleton, 1905.

Harger, R. N. "The sojourn of alcohol in the body." In R. G. McCarthy (ed.), *Alcohol Education for Classroom and Community.* New York: McGraw-Hill, 1964.

Hartshorne, H., and May, M. A. *Studies in Deceit.* New York: Macmillan, 1928.

Hartshorne, H., and May, M. A. *Studies in the Nature of Character: Volume 1, Studies in Deceit; Volume 2, Studies in Self-Control; Volume 3, Studies in the Organization of Character.* New York: Macmillan, 1928–1930.

Hatfield, J. S.; Ferguson, L. R.; and Alpert, R. "Mother-child interaction and the socialization process." *Child Development,* 1967, 38, 365–414.

Havighurst, R. J. *Developmental Tasks and Education.* New York: Longman, Green, 1951.

Havighurst, R. J.; Bowman, P. H.; Liddle, G. P.; Matthews, C. B.; and Pierce, J. D. *Growing Up in River City.* New York: John Wiley & Sons, 1962.

Havighurst, R. J., and Taba, H. *Adolescent Character and Personality.* New York: John Wiley & Sons, 1949.

Heath, D. H. *Explorations of Maturity.* New York: Appleton-Century-Crofts, 1965.

Heath, D. H. "Student alienation and school." *School Review,* 1970, 78 (4), 515–528.

Hebb, D. O. *A Textbook of Psychology.* 2nd ed. Philadelphia: W. B. Saunders, 1966.

Hebb, D. O. "Drive and the CNS (Conceptual Nervous System)." *Psychological Review,* 1955, 62, 243–354.

Hebb, D. O. *The Organization of Behavior.* New York: John Wiley & Sons, 1949.

Hendry, L. S. *Cognitive processes in a moral conflict situation.* Unpublished doctoral dissertation, Yale University, 1960.

Heron, W. "The pathology of boredom." *Scientific American,* January 1957.

Herzog, E., and Sudia, C. *Boys in Fatherless Homes.* Washington, D.C.: U.S. Department of Health, Education and Welfare, 1970.

Hess, R. D. "Parents and teenagers: Differing perspectives." *Child Studies,* 1959–1960, 37, 21–23.

Hess, R. D., and Goldblatt, Irene. "The status of adolescence in American society: A problem in social identity." *Child Development,* 1957, 28, 459–468.

Hoffman, L. W. "Early childhood experiences and women's achievement motives." *Journal of Social Issues,* 1972, 28, 129–155.

Holbrook, S. H. *Dreamers of the American Dream.* Garden City, N.Y.: Doubleday, 1957.

Holland, J. L. "Creative and academic performance among talented adolescents." *Journal of Educational Psychology,* 1961, 52, 136–147.

Hollingshead, A. B. *Elmtown's Youth.* New York: John Wiley & Sons, 1949.

Hood, A. D. "A study of the relationship between physique and personality variables measured by the MMPI." *Journal of Personality,* 1963, 31, 97–107.

Horner, M. "Woman's will to fail." *Psychology Today,* 1969, 3, 36–38.

Horney, K. "Finding the real self." *American Journal of Psychoanalysis,* 1949, 9, 3–7.

Horowitz, H. "Prediction of adolescent popularity and rejection from achievement and interest tests." *Journal of Educational Psychology,* 1967, 58, 170–174.

Horrocks, J. E., and Buker, M. E. "A study of the friendship fluctuations of pre-adolescents." *Journal of Genetic Psychology,* 1951, 78, 131–144.

Howard, M. "How to look and outreach for the younger father." *American Journal of Orthopsychiatry,* 1971, 41, 294–295.

Howard, M. "School continues for pregnant teenagers." *American Education,* 1968–69, 5, 5–7.

Hunt, J. McV. *Intelligence and Experience.* New York: Ronald Press, 1961.

Hurlock. E. "The adolescent reformer." *Adolescence,* 1968, 3, 273–306.

Inhelder, B., and Piaget, J. *The Growth of Logical Thinking from Childhood to Adolescence.* New York: Basic Books, 1958.

Involvement in Developmental Psychology. Delmar, Calif.: C.R.M. Books, 1971.

Jalkanen, A. W. "Drug use and the adolescent." In. J. F. Adams (ed.), *Understanding Adolescence: Current Developments in Adolescent Psychology.* 2nd ed. Boston: Allyn & Bacon, 1973 (pp. 375–403).

Jenkins, R. L., and Boyer, A. "Types of delinquent behavior, and background factors." *International Journal of Social Psychiatry,* 1967, 14, 65–76.

Jensen, A. R. *Genetics and Education.* New York: Harper and Row, 1972.

Jensen, A. R. "Social class, race, and genetics: Implications for education." *American Educational Research Journal,* 1968, 5, 1–42.

Jersild, A. T. *The Psychology of Adolescence.* 2nd ed. New York: Macmillan, 1963.

Johnson, C. S. *Growing Up in the Black Belt.* Washington, D.C.: American Council on Education, 1941; New York: Schocken, 1967.

392

Jones, H. E. "Adolescence in our society." In anniversary papers of the Community Service Society of New York, *The Family in a Democratic Society.* New York: Columbia University Press, 1949 (pp. 70–82).

Jones, H. E. "The environment and mental development." In L. Carmichael (ed.), *Manual of Child Psychology.* 2nd ed. New York: John Wiley & Sons, 1954, (pp. 631–696).

Jones, M. C. "Psychological correlates of somatic development." *Child Development,* 1965, 36, 899–911.

Jones, M. C. "The later careers of boys who are early- or late-maturing." *Child Development,* 1957, 28, 113–128.

Jones, M. C. "Adolescent friendships." *American Psychologist,* 1948, 3, 352.

Jones, M. C. "A laboratory study of fear: The case of Peter." *Pedagogical Seminary and Journal of Genetic Psychology,* 1924, 31, 308–315.

Jones, M. C., and Mussen, P. H. "Self conceptions, motivations, and interpersonal attitudes of early- and late-maturing girls." *Child Development,* 1958, 29, 491–501.

Jung, C. G. *Psychological Types.* New York: Harcourt, Brace, and World, 1923.

Jung, C. G. "The Stages of Life." In the *Structure and Dynamics of the Psyche.* New York: Pantheon, 1960.

Kaats, G. R., and Davis, K. E. "The dynamics of sexual behavior of college students." *Journal of Marriage and the Family,* 1970, 32, 330–339.

Kangas, J., and Bradway, K. P. "Intelligence at middle age: A 38-year follow-up." *Developmental Psychology,* 1971, 5, 333–337.

Katz, J. *No Time for Youth: Growth and Constraint in College Students.* San Francisco: Jossey-Bass, 1968.

Keniston, K. "American students and the political revival." *American Scholar,* 1963, 32, 40–60.

Keniston, K. *The Uncommitted: Alienated Youth in American Society.* New York: Harcourt, Brace, and World, 1965.

Kinsey, A. C.; Pomeroy, W. D.; and Martin, C. E. *Sexual Behavior in the Human Male.* Philadelphia: W. B. Saunders, 1948.

Kinsey, A. C.; Pomeroy, W. D.; Martin, C. E.; and Gebhard, P. H. *Sexual Behavior in the Human Female.* Philadelphia: W. B. Saunders, 1953.

Koch, H. L. "Sissiness and tom-boyishness in relation to sibling characteristics." *Journal of Genetic Psychology,* 1956, 88, 231–244.

Koch, H. L. "Some personality correlates of sex, sibling position, and sex of siblings among 5- and 6-year-old children." *Genetic Psychology Monographs,* 1955, 52, 3–50.

Kohlberg, L. "Stage and sequence: the cognitive-developmental approach to socialization." In D. Gosslin (ed.), *Handbook of Socialization Theory and Research.* Chicago: Rand McNally, 1969.

Kohlberg, L. "A cognitive developmental analysis of children's sex role concept and attitudes." In E. E. Maccoby (ed.), *The Development of Sex Differences.* Stanford, Calif.: Stanford University Press, 1966 (pp. 82–173).

Kohlberg, L. "Development of moral character and moral ideology." In M. L.

Hoffman and L. W. Hoffman (eds.), *Review of Child Development Research,* Volume 1. New York: Russell Sage Foundation, 1964 (pp. 383–432).

Kohlberg, L., and Turiel, E. *Research and Moral Development: A Cognitive Developmental Approach.* New York: John Wiley & Sons, 1971.

Landauer, T. K., and Whiting, J. W. M. "Infantile Stimulation and Adult Stature of Human Males." *American Anthropologist,* 1964, 66, 1007–1028.

Landis, J. T., and Landis, M. G. *Building a Successful Marriage.* Englewood Cliffs, N.J.: Prentice-Hall, 1963.

Lawton, M. P. "The psychology of adolescent anti-smoking education." *The Journal of School Health,* 1963, 33, 1–8.

Leaky, L. S. *Adam or Ape: A Source Book of Discovery About Early Man.* New York: Schenkman, 1971.

Lee, E. S. "Negro intelligence and selective migration: A Philadelphia test of the Klineberg hypothesis." *American Sociological Review,* 1951, 16, 227–233.

Lefrancois, G. R. *Psychology for Teaching: A Bear Usually Faces the Front.* 2nd ed. Belmont, Calif.: Wadsworth, 1975.

Lefrancois, G. R. *Of Children: An Introduction to Child Development.* Belmont, Calif.: Wadsworth, 1973.

Lefrancois, G. R. *Psychological Theories and Human Learning: Kongor's Report.* Monterey, Calif.: Brooks/Cole, 1972.

Lerner, I. M. *Heredity, Evolution, and Society.* San Francisco: W. H. Freeman, 1968.

Lewis, M. "Parents and children: Sex role development." *School Review,* 1972, 80.

Loken, J. O. *Student Alienation and Dissent.* Scarborough, Ontario: Prentice-Hall, 1973.

Louria, D. *Nightmare Drugs.* New York: Pocket Books, 1966.

Lowie, R. H. *An Introduction to Cultural Anthropology.* New York: Farrar and Rinehart, 1941.

Lubin, A. "A note on Sheldon's table of correlations between temperamental trades." *British Journal of Psychology,* 1950, 3, 186–189.

Luckey, E. B., and Nass, G. D. The comparison of sexual attitudes and behavior in an international sample. *Journal of Marriage and the Family,* 1969, 31, 364–378.

Lynn, D. B. *The Father: His Role in Child Development.* Monterey, Calif.: Brooks/Cole, 1974.

MacArthur, R. S. *Differential Ability Patterns: Inuit, Nsenga, Canadian Whites.* Paper presented at second meeting of International Association for Cross-Cultural Psychology, Kingston, Ontario, Canada, August 1974.

MacArthur, R. S. "Some ability patterns: Central Eskimos and Nsenga Africans." *International Journal of Psychology,* 1973, 8, 239–247.

Maccoby, E. E. "The meaning of being female." (A review of J. N. Bardwick, *Psychology of Women: A Study of Biocultural Conflicts.* New York: Harper and Row, 1971.) *Contemporary Psychology,* 1972, 17, 369–372.

Maccoby, E. E. "Woman's intellect." In S. M. Farber and R. H. L. Wilson (eds.), *Man and Civilization: The Potential of Woman*. New York: McGraw-Hill, 1963.

Maccoby, E. E., and Jacklin, C. N. *The Psychology of Sex Differences.* Stanford, Calif.: Stanford University Press, 1974.

Maccoby, E. E., and Rau, L. *Differential Cognitive Abilities.* Cooperative research project, number 1040, Owen House, Stanford University, Stanford, Calif., 1962.

Madsen, W. *The Mexican-American of South Texas.* New York: Holt, Rinehart & Winston, 1964.

Maier, H. W. *Three Theories of Child Development.* New York: Harper and Row, 1965.

Maslow, A. H. *Motivation and Personality.* New York: Harper and Row, 1954.

Masters, W. H., and Johnson, V. E. "A defense of love and morality." *McCalls,* November 1966, 102–103; 173.

McCandless, B. R. *Adolescents: Behavior and Development.* Hinsdale, Ill.: Breighton Press, 1970.

McCord, J.; McCord, W.; and Howard, A. "Family interaction as antecedent to the direction of male aggressiveness." *Journal of Abnormal and Social Psychology,* 1963, 66, 239–242.

McCurdy, H. G. "The childhood pattern of genius." *Journal of the Elisha Mitchell Scientific Society,* 1957, 73, 448–462.

McDougall, W. *An Introduction to Social Psychology.* London: Methuen, 1908.

Mead, G. H. *Mind, Self, and Society.* Chicago: University of Chicago Press, 1934.

Mead, M. *Sex and Temperament in Three Primitive Societies.* New York: New American Library, 1935.

Mednick, S. A. "The associative basis of the creative process." *Psychological Review,* 1962, 69, 220–232.

Melton, A. W. *Categories of Human Learning.* New York: Academic Press, 1964.

Menninger, R. "What troubles our troubled youth?" *Mental Hygiene,* 1968, 52, 323–329.

Messner, W. W. "Parental interaction of the adolescent boy." *Journal of Genetic Psychology,* 1965, 107, 225–232.

Miller, W. B. "Lower class culture as a generating milieu of gang delinquency." *Journal of Social Issues,* 1958, 14, 5–19.

Mitchell, G. D.; Arling, G. L.; and Moller, G. W. "Long term effects of maternal punishment on the behavior of monkeys." *Psychonomic Science,* 1967, 209–210.

Mitchell, J. J. *Adolescence: Some Critical Issues.* Toronto: Holt, Rinehart & Winston, 1971.

Money, J., and Ehrhardt, A. A. "Prenatal hormonal exposure: Possible effects on behavior in man." In R. P. Michael (ed.), *Endocrinology and Human Behaviour.* London: Oxford University Press, 1968 (pp. 32–48).

Morgan, C. L. *Habit and Instinct.* London: Arnold, 1896.

Morgan, C. L. *Introduction to Comparative Psychology.* London: Scott, 1894.

Morrow, W. R., and Wilson, R. C. "Family relations of bright, high-achieving and under-achieving high school boys." *Child Development,* 1961, 32, 501–510.

Mouly, G. J. *Psychology for Effective Teaching.* 2nd ed. New York: Holt, Rinehart & Winston, 1968.

Munsinger, H. *Fundamentals of Child Development.* New York: Holt, Rinehart & Winston, 1971.

Murray, H. A. *Explorations and Personality.* New York: Oxford University Press, 1938.

Mussen, P. H., and Jones, M. C. "Some conceptions, motivations, and interpersonal attitudes of late- and early-maturing boys." *Child Development,* 1957, 28, 242–256.

Mussen, P. H.; Young, H.; Gaddini, R.; and Morante, L. "The influence of father-son relationships on adolescent personality and attitudes." *Journal of Child Psychology and Psychiatry,* 1963, 4, 3–16.

Muuss, R. E. "Adolescent development and the secular trend." *Adolescence,* 1970, 5 (19) 267–284.

Newman, H. H.; Freeman, F. N.; and Holzinger, K. J. *Twins: A Study of Heredity and Environment.* Chicago: University of Chicago Press, 1937.

Newsweek, "Drugs on Campus." January 25, 1971, 52.

Newsweek, January 6, 1969, 37.

Noyes, P. B. *My Father's House: An Oneida Boyhood.* New York: Farrar & Rinehart, 1937.

Offer, D. *The Psychological World of the Teenager: A Study of Normal Adolescent Boys.* New York: Basic Books, 1969.

Osgood, C. E. *A Behavioristic Analysis of Perception and Language as Cognitive Phenomenon in Contemporary Approaches to Cognition.* Cambridge, Mass.: Harvard University Press, 1957.

Palmer, R. H., and Masling, J. "Vocabulary for skin color in Negro and white children." *Developmental Psychology,* 1969, 1, 396–401.

Parsons, T., and Clark, K. B. (eds.), *The Negro American.* Boston: Houghton Mifflin, 1966.

Piaget, J. *The Origins of Intellect.* San Francisco: W. H. Freeman, 1969.

Piaget, J. *The Origins of Intelligence in Children.* New York: International University Press, 1952.

Piaget, J. *The Moral Judgment of the Child.* London: Kegan Paul, 1932.

Piaget, J., and Inhelder, B. *Le Developpement des quantites chez L'enfant.* Neuchatel: Delachaux et Niestle, 1941.

Poppleton, P. K. "Puberty, family size and the educational progress of girls." *British Journal of Educational Psychology,* 1968, 38, 286–292.

Poppleton, P. K., and Brown, P. E. "The secular trend in puberty: Has stability been achieved?" *The British Journal of Educational Psychology,* 1966, 36, 97–101.

Proshansky, H., and Newton, P. "The nature and meaning of Negro self-identity." In M. Deutsch, I. Katz, and A. R. Jensen (eds.), *Social Class, Race,* *and Psychological Development.* New York: Holt, Rinehart & Winston, 1968 (pp. 178–218).

Rainwater, L. "Crucible of identity: The Negro lower-class family." *Daedalus,* 1966, 95, 172–216.

Raths, L. E., and Burrell, A. P. *Understanding the Problem Child.* West Orange, N.J.: Economics Press, 1963.

Reiss, I. L. *The Social Context of Premarital Sexual Permissiveness.* New York: Holt, Rinehart & Winston, 1966.

Remmers, H. H., and Radler, D. H. *The American Teenager.* New York: Bobbs-Merrill, 1957.

Ringness, T. A. "Identification patterns, motivation, and school achievement of bright, junior high school boys." *Journal of Educational Psychology,* 1967, 58, 93–102.

Rogers, Dorothy. *The Psychology of Adolescence.* 2nd ed. New York: Appleton-Century-Crofts, 1972.

Roscoe, J. *The Northern Bantu.* Cambridge, England: Cambridge University Press, 1915.

Rosenberg, B., and Bensman, J. "Sexual patterns in three ethnic subcultures of an American underclass." *Annals of the American Academy of Political and Social Sciences,* 1968, 376, 61–75.

Rosenberg, M. *Society and the Adolescent Self-Image.* Princeton, N.J.: Princeton University Press, 1965.

Rosenfeld, H., and Zander, A. "The influence of teachers on aspirations of students." *Journal of Educational Psychology,* 1961, 52, 1–11.

Rosenkrantz, P.; Vogel, S.; Bee, H.; Broverman, I.; and Broverman, D. M. "Sex role stereotypes and self-concepts in college students." *Journal of Consulting and Clinical Psychology,* 1968, 32, 287–295.

Rosenthal, R. "Experimenter expectancy and the reassuring nature of the null hypothesis decision procedure." *Psychological Bulletin Monograph Supplement,* 1969, 70, 30–47.

Rosenthal, R., and Fode, K. L. "The effect of experimenter bias on the performance of the albino rat." *Behavioral Science,* 1963, 8, 183–189.

Rosenthal, R., and Jacobsen, L. *Pygmalion in the Classroom: Teacher Expectations and Pupil's Intellectual Development.* New York: Holt, Rinehart & Winston, 1968 (a).

Rosenthal, R., and Jacobsen, L. "Teacher expectations for the disadvantaged." *Scientific American,* April 1968 (b).

Rosenzweig, S. "Available methods for studying personality." *Journal of Psychology,* 1949, 28, 345–368.

Rotter, J. B.; Seeman, M.; and Liversant, S. "Internal versus external controls of reinforcement: A major variable in behavior theory." In N. F. Washburne (ed.), *Decisions, Values, and Groups.* Volume 2. London: Pergamon, 1962.

Sampson, E. E. "Birth order, need achievement, and conformity." *Journal of Abnormal and Social Psychology,* 1962, 64, 155–159.

397

Savage, B. N., and Wells, F. L. "A note on singularity in given names." *Journal of Social Psychology,* 1948, 27, 271–272.

Scarpitti, F. R. "Delinquent and nondelinquent perceptions of self, values, and opportunity." *Mental Hygiene,* July 1965, 399–404.

Schachter, S. "Birth order, eminence, and higher education." *American Sociological Review,* 1963, 28, 757–768.

Schaefer, E. S. "Children's reports of parental behavior: An inventory." *Child Development,* 1965, 36, 413–424.

Schreiber, D. (ed.) *Profile of the School Dropout.* New York: Vintage Books, 1968.

Sears, P. S. *The Effect of Classroom Conditions on the Strength of Achievement Motive and Work Output on Elementary School Children.* U.S. Department of Health, Education and Welfare, Office of Education, Cooperative Research Project #873. Stanford, Calif.: Stanford University, 1963.

Sewell, W. H., and Shah, V. P. "Parents' education and children's educational aspirations and achievements." *American Sociological Review,* 1968, 33, 191–209.

Sheldon, W. H. *The Varieties of Temperament: A Psychology of Constitutional Differences.* New York: Harper and Row, 1936.

Shipman, G. "The psychodynamics of sex education." *Family Coordinator,* 1968, 17, 3–12.

Shirley, M. N. "The first two years; a study of 25 babies, Volume One: Postural and Locomotor Development." *Institute of Child Welfare, Monograph, Series No. 6.* Minneapolis: University of Minnesota Press, 1933.

Short, J. F., Jr., and Nye, F. I. "Reported behavior as a deviant behavior." *Social Problems,* 5, 1957–1958, 207–213.

Skinner, B. F. *Cumulative Record.* Rev. ed. New York: Appleton-Century-Crofts, 1961.

Skinner, B. F. *Science and Human Behavior.* New York: Macmillan, 1953.

Skinner, B. F. "How to teach animals." *Scientific American,* December 1951, 185, 26–29.

Skinner, B. F. *The Behavior of Organisms: An Experimental Analysis.* New York: Appleton-Century-Crofts, 1938.

Smart, M. S., and Smart, R. C. *Children: Development and Relationships.* New York: Macmillan, 1967.

Smart, R. G. "Some current studies of psycho-active and other psychogenic drug use." *Canadian Journal of Behavior Science,* 1970, 2, 232–245.

Smigel, E. O., and Seiden, R. "The decline and fall of the double standard." *Annals of the American Academy of Political and Social Sciences,* 1968, 376, 6–17.

Smith, B. E., and Sternfield, J. "The hippie communal movement: Effects on childbirth and development." *American Journal of Ortho-psychiatry,* 1970, 40, 527–530.

Straus, R., and Bacon, S. D. *Drinking in College.* New Haven, Conn.: Yale University Press, 1953.

Strauss, B. V. "The dynamics of ordinal position." *Quarterly Journal of Child Behavior,* 1959, 3, 133–145.

Stroud, J. B., and Maul, R. "The influence of age on learning and retention of poetry." *A Journal of Genetic Psychology,* 1933, 42, 242–250.

Strunk, O., Jr. "Note on self reports and religiosity." *Psychological Reports,* 1958, 4, 29.

Stuart, R. B. "Critical reappraisal and reformulation of selected 'mental health' programs." In L. A. Hamerlynck, P. O. Davidson, and L. E. Acker (eds.), *Behavior Modification and Mental Health Services.* Calgary, Alberta: University of Calgary Press, 1969, (pp. 5–100).

Suchman, E. A. "The 'hang loose' ethic and the spirit of drug use." *Journal of Health and Social Behavior,* 1968, 9, 146–155.

Super, D. E. *The Psychology of Careers.* New York: Harper and Row, 1957.

399

Sutton-Smith, B.; Roberts, J. W.; and Rosenberg, B. G. "Sibling associations and role involvement." *Merrill-Palmer Quarterly,* 1964, 10, 25–38.

Swift, D. F. "Family environment and 11-plus success: Some basic predictions." *British Journal of Educational Psychology,* 1967, 37, 10–21.

Szasz, P. S. *The Manufacture of Madness: A Comparative Study of the Inquisition and the Mental Health Movement.* New York: Harper and Row, 1970.

Tanner, J. M. *Growth at Adolescence.* Springfield, Ill.: Charles C Thomas, 1955.

Tanner, J. M. *Growth at Adolescence.* 2nd ed. Oxford: Blackwell Scientific Publications, 1962.

Tanner, J. M. "Sequence, tempo, and individual variation in growth and development of boys and girls ages 12 to 16." In J. Kagan, and R. Coles (eds.), *12–16: Early Adolescence.* New York: W. W. Norton, 1972 (pp. 1–24).

Tenhouten, W. D. "The black family: Myth and reality." *Psychiatry,* 1970, 33, 145–173.

Terman, L. M., and Merrill, M. A. *Stanford-Binet Intelligence Scale.* Boston: Houghton-Mifflin, 1960.

Terman, L. M., and Oden, M. H. *The Gifted Child Grows Up: 25 Years' Follow-up of a Superior Group.* Stanford, Calif.: Stanford University Press, 1947.

Terman, L. M., and Tyler, L. E. "Psychological sex differences." In L. Carmichael (ed.), *Manual of Child Psychology.* 2nd ed. New York: John Wiley & Sons, 1954.

Thomas, W. L. *Primitive Behavior.* New York: McGraw-Hill, 1937.

Thompson, C. G., and Horrocks, J. E. "A study of the friendship fluctuations of urban boys and girls." *Journal of Genetic Psychology,* 1947, 70, 53–63.

Thorndike, E. L. "Reward and punishment in animal learning." *Comparative Psychology Monographs,* 1932, 8, No. 39.

Thorndike, E. L. *The Psychology of Wants, Interests, and Attitudes.* New York: Appleton-Century-Crofts, 1935.

Thorpe, W. H. *Learning and Instinct in Animals.* 2nd ed. London: Methuen, 1963.

Torrance, E. P. *Guiding Creative Talent.* Englewood Cliffs, N.J.: Prentice-Hall, 1962.

Torrance, E. P. *Torrance's Tests of Creative Thinking. Norms Technical Manual.* Princeton, N.J.: Personnel Press, 1966.

Trent, J. W., and Craise, J. L. "Commitment and conformity in the American college." *Journal of Social Issues,* 1967, 22, 34–51.

Trent, J. W., and Medsker, L. L. *Beyond High School: A Study of 10,000 High School Graduates.* Berkeley, Calif.: Center for Research and Development in Higher Education, University of California, 1967.

Turiel, E. "Conflict in transition in adolescent moral development." *Child Development,* 1974, 45, 14–29.

U.S. Bureau of the Census. "Current population reports, Series P-23, No. 34." *Characteristics of American Youth: 1970.* Washington, D.C.: U.S. Government Printing Office, 1971(a).

U.S. Bureau of the Census. "Current Population Reports, Series P-25, No. 470." *Projections of the Population of the United States, by Age and Sex; 1970–2020.* Washington, D.C.: U.S. Government Printing Office, 1971(b).

U.S. Bureau of the Census. "U.S. Census of population: 1960." *General Population Characteristics, U.S. Summary.* Final Report PC (1)–(1b). Washington, D.C.: U.S. Government Printing Office, 1961.

Veroff, J. "Social comparison and development of achievement motivation." In C. P. Smith (ed.), *Achievement-Related Motives in Children.* New York: Russell Sage, 1969.

Vincent, C. E. "Teenage unwed mothers in American society." *Journal of Social Issues,* 1966, 22, 22–23.

Wagner, G. *The Bantu of North Kavirondo.* Volume One. London: Oxford University Press, 1949.

Wallach, M. A., and Kogan, N. *Modes of Thinking in Young Children: A Study of the Creativity-Intelligence Distinction.* New York: Holt, Rinehart & Winston, 1965.

Warriner, C. C.; Foster, D. A.; and Trites, D. K. "Failure to complete as a family characteristic: A college sample." *Journal of Educational Research,* 1966, 59, 466–468.

Watson, J. B. *Behaviorism.* 2nd ed. Chicago: University of Chicago Press, 1930.

Watson, J. B. *Behavior: An Introduction to Comparative Psychology.* New York: Holt, Rinehart & Winston, 1914.

Watson, J. B. "Psychology as the behaviorist views it." *Psychological Review,* 1913, 20, 157–158.

Webster, H. *Primitive Secret Societies.* New York: Macmillan, 1932.

Webster, H.; Freedman, M. G.; and Heist, P. "Personality changes in college students." In N. Sanford (ed.), *The American College.* New York: John Wiley & Sons, 1962.

Wechsler, B. *The Measurement and Appraisal of Adult Intelligence.* 4th ed. Baltimore: Williams and Wilkins, 1958.

Weil, A. T.; Zinberg, N. E.; and Nelson, J. M. "Clinical and psychological effects of marijuana in man." *Science,* 1968, 162, 1234–1242.

West, S. "Sibling configurations of scientists." *American Journal of Sociology,* 1960, 66, 268–274.

Willerman, B., and Swanson, L. "Ecological determinants of different amounts of sociometric choices within college dormitories." *Sociometry,* 1952, 15, 326–329.

Wingfield, A. H. *Twins and Orphans: the Inheritance of Intelligence.* London: Dent, 1928.

Wozny, J. R. *Psychological and sociological correlates of use and nonuse of marijuana.* Unpublished master's thesis, University of Alberta, Edmonton, Alberta, 1971.

Wright, D., and Cox, E. "A study of the relationship between moral judgment and religious belief in a sample of English adolescents." *General Social Psychology,* 1967, 72, 135–144.

Yamamoto, K. *Experimental Scoring Manual for Minnesota Tests of Creative Thinking and Writing.* Kent, Ohio: Bureau of Educational Research, Kent State University, May 1964.

Index

403